Lecture Notes in Computer Science

Commenced Publication in 1973
Founding and Former Series Editors:
Gerhard Goos, Juris Hartmanis, and Jan van Leeuwen

George Danezis   David Martin (Eds.)

Privacy Enhancing Technologies

5th International Workshop, PET 2005
Cavtat, Croatia, May 30-June 1, 2005
Revised Selected Papers

 Springer

Volume Editors

George Danezis
Katholieke Universiteit Leuven
Dept. Elektrotechniek-ESAT/COSOC
Kasteelpark Arenberg 10, 3001 Leuven-Heverlee, Belgium
E-mail: George.Danezis@esat.kuleuven.be

David Martin
University of Massachusetts
Computer Science Department
One University Ave. Lowell, MA 01854, USA
E-mail: dm@cs.uml.edu

Library of Congress Control Number: 2006926828

CR Subject Classification (1998): E.3, C.2, D.4.6, K.6.5, K.4, H.3, H.4

LNCS Sublibrary: SL 4 – Security and Cryptology

ISSN   0302-9743
ISBN-10   3-540-34745-3 Springer Berlin Heidelberg New York
ISBN-13   978-3-540-34745-3 Springer Berlin Heidelberg New York

Springer is a part of Springer Science+Business Media

springer.com

© Springer-Verlag Berlin Heidelberg 2006
Printed in Germany

Typesetting: Camera-ready by author, data conversion by Scientific Publishing Services, Chennai, India
Printed on acid-free paper   SPIN: 11767831   06/3142   5 4 3 2 1 0

Preface

PET 2005 held in Cavtat (Croatia) from May 30 to June 1, 2005, was the 5th Workshop on Privacy-Enhancing Technologies, which is now established as a yearly event. The workshop received 74 full paper submissions out of which 17 papers were ultimately selected to be presented. The selection process relied on over 200 reviews from the Program Committee, Program Chairs and additional reviewers, at least three per paper. A further 2-week long e-mail discussion led to consensus on the papers accepted–with the ultimate responsibility for the program resting on the Program Co-chairs. The number of accepted papers and final program format was to ensure that PET retains its character as a workshop, with ample time for discussion, two panel discussions, and space for the fermentation of new ideas and collaborations.

The Program Chairs would first like to thank the PET 2005 Program Committee for the high-quality reviews and discussion that led to the program:

- Martin Abadi, University of California at Santa Cruz, USA
- Alessandro Acquisti, Heinz School, Carnegie Mellon University, USA
- Caspar Bowden, Microsoft EMEA, UK
- Jean Camp, Indiana University at Bloomington, USA
- Richard Clayton, University of Cambridge, UK
- Lorrie Cranor, School of Computer Science, Carnegie Mellon University, USA
- Roger Dingledine, The Free Haven Project, USA
- Hannes Federrath, University of Regensburg, Germany
- Ian Goldberg, Zero Knowledge Systems, Canada
- Philippe Golle, Palo Alto Research Center, USA
- Marit Hansen, Independent Centre for Privacy Protection Schleswig-Holstein, Germany
- Markus Jakobsson, Indiana University at Bloomington, USA
- Dogan Kesdogan, Rheinisch-Westfaelische Technische Hochschule Aachen, Germany
- Brian Levine, University of Massachusetts at Amherst, USA
- Andreas Pfitzmann, Dresden University of Technology, Germany
- Matthias Schunter, IBM Zurich Research Lab, Switzerland
- Andrei Serjantov, The Free Haven Project, UK
- Paul Syverson, Naval Research Lab, USA
- Latanya Sweeney, Carnegie Mellon University, USA
- Matthew Wright, University of Texas at Arlington, USA

Additional reviewers included George Bissias, Rainer Böhme, Katrin Borcea, John Burgess, Jong Youl Choi, Sebastian Clauss, Elke Franz, Stephan Gross, Markus Hansen, Tom Heydt-Benjamin, Guenter Karjoth, Stefan Köpsell, Thomas Kriegelstein, Tobias Kölsch, Marc Liberatore, Katja Liesebach, Christian Maier, N. Boris Margolin, Martin Meints, Steven J. Murdoch,

Thomas Nowey, Lexi Pimenidis, Klaus Ploessl, Clay Shields, Adam Shostack, Sandra Steinbrecher, Alex Tsow, Madhu Venkateshaiah, Xiaofeng Wang, Rolf Wendolsky, and Andreas Westfeld. Their help was very much appreciated.

As is usual, final proceedings were produced only after authors had the chance to discuss their work with community members during the workshop. The final papers are now published as volume 3856 in Springer's *Lecture Notes in Computer Science.*

We are grateful to Damir Gojmerac, who originally invited PET 2005 to be held in Croatia when he was with the Financial Agency of Croatia (FINA). And we especially thank Tomislav Vintar, Slađana Miočić, and Ivor Županić for their faithful perseverance in realizing the complex logistics of the PET 2005 workshop.

Financial support for PET 2005 was generously provided by Microsoft Corporation and FINA. This funding was instrumental in making the workshop accessible to students and others who applied for travel and registration stipends. PET 2005 also benefited from synergy with the Privacy Technology Executive Briefing both in terms of overlapping attendance and organizational load sharing.

We are particularly indebted to Caspar Bowden and JC Cannon at Microsoft for the continuing support of the workshop and for funding the Award for Outstanding Research in Privacy-Enhancing Technologies. We also thank Andrei Serjantov for facilitating the process of selecting a winner for this 2005 PET award. Finally, we give our sincere thanks to Mike Gurski for his vision and his efforts in facilitating both PET 2005 and the Privacy Technology Executive Briefing immediately following it.

May 2005   George Danezis and David Martin
                                                            Program Chairs
                                                                 PET 2005

Table of Contents

Privacy Vulnerabilities in Encrypted HTTP Streams*

George Dean Bissias, Marc Liberatore, David Jensen, and Brian Neil Levine

University of Massachusetts, Amherst, MA 01003, USA
{gbiss, liberato, jensen, brian}@cs.umass.edu

Abstract. Encrypting traffic does not prevent an attacker from performing some types of traffic analysis. We present a straightforward traffic analysis attack against encrypted HTTP streams that is surprisingly
effective in identifying the source of the traffic. An attacker starts by
creating a profile of the statistical characteristics of web requests from
interesting sites, including distributions of packet sizes and inter-arrival
times. Later, candidate encrypted streams are compared against these
profiles. In our evaluations using real traffic, we find that many web sites
are subject to this attack. With a training period of 24 hours and a 1
hour delay afterwards, the attack achieves only 23% accuracy. However,
an attacker can easily pre-determine which of trained sites are easily
identifiable. Accordingly, against 25 such sites, the attack achieves 40%
accuracy; with three guesses, the attack achieves 100% accuracy for our
data. Longer delays after training decrease accuracy, but not substantially. We also propose some countermeasures and improvements to our
current method. Previous work analyzed SSL traffic to a proxy, taking
advantage of a known flaw in SSL that reveals the length of each web object. In contrast, we exploit the statistical characteristics of web streams
that are encrypted as a single flow, which is the case with WEP/WPA,
IPsec, and SSH tunnels.

1 Introduction

The problem of keeping Internet communication private is remarkably hard. One
method of protecting the privacy of a network connection is to use an encrypted
link to a proxy or server. Encrypted links are possible at the link layer using
WEP/WPA to a wireless base station, at the network layer using IPSec ESP
mode to a VPN concentrator, or at the transport layer using an SSH tunnel to
an anonymizing proxy. In all cases, the identity of the final destination is kept
confidential from an eavesdropper by encrypting IP packet headers.

Maintaining user privacy is not such a simple matter. In this paper, we show
that an encrypted connection is not sufficient for removing traffic patterns that
often reveal the web site that a user is visiting. Specifically, we examine the

---

* This paper was supported in part by National Science Foundation awards CNS-
0133055, ANI-0325868, and EIA-0080199.

G. Danezis and D. Martin (Eds.): PET 2005, LNCS 3856, pp. 1–11, 2006.

success rate of traffic analysis attacks used by an eavesdropper that test against learned profiles of web site traffic inter-arrival times and packet sizes.

We examine real traces of encrypted, proxied HTTP traffic, and our attacks attempt to discern the responder to each web request. The method of our attack is straightforward. In advance, the attacker gathers a *profile* of specific websites according to some criteria, which may be their popularity or level of interest to the attacker. The profile is composed of two features from the encrypted HTTP response stream: the packet size and inter-arrival time distributions. The attacker then monitors the traffic of a wireless link or a wired link to which he has access. When a burst of traffic occurs, the attacker tests the trace against a library of profiled web sites looking for a good match.

We tested our method by taking traces for three months of hourly retrievals of 100 popular web sites. Our evaluations show that many web sites are subject to this attack. With a training period of 24 hours and a 1 hour delay afterwards, the attack achieves only 23% accuracy. However, an attacker can easily pre-determine which of trained sites are easily identifiable. Accordingly, against 25 such sites, the attack achieves 40% accuracy; with three guesses, the attack achieves 100% accuracy for our data. Longer delays after training decrease accuracy, but not substantially. Note that with random guessing, this attack can expect to be correct only $1/n$th of the time among n profiles, and k/nth of the time with k guesses. While previous work exists on similar attacks, ours is the first to consider an encrypted web connection that does not reveal individual web objects, which is the realistic case for WEP/WPA, VPNs, and SSH tunnels.

The remainder of this paper is organized as follows. Section 2 describes recent related work. In Section 3 we present our data collection methodology, and in Section 4 we describe how we identify encrypted traffic. Section 5 is a summary of our future research goals, and Section 6 concludes.

2   Related Work

There is a large body of work on the topic of general traffic analysis and information hiding. We do not provide an extensive overview here; consult Raymond [1] for an informal overview. Instead, we present an overview of recent developments in theoretical and experimental traffic analysis and countermeasures. We include work that examines HTTP and secure HTTP and the vulnerabilities and exposures inherent in those protocols.

Hintz [?] describes a fingerprinting attack similar to ours. It is limited in several ways. First, it considers only the total amount of data sent over each SSL-encrypted connection. When the client is using more sophisticated tunneling software that re-uses connections (as we assume in this paper), this attack would degrade. Additionally, Hintz's work is a very preliminary proof-of-concept and does not provide a significant evaluation.

Sun, et al. [2] investigate the use of statistical techniques to identify encrypted web traffic. They assume an SSL encrypted link between a browser

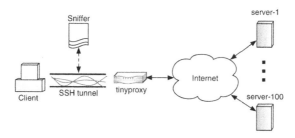

Fig. 1. Measurement setup

and an anonymizing proxy, and focus on attacking this first and weakest link. They make the strong simplifying assumption that web objects can be differentiated by examining the TCP connections between the browser and the proxy. This assumption is not valid for WEP/WPA links, VPN connections, and SSH tunnels, and in the presence of widely-available, unencrypted, pipelined HTTP connections. They use the patterns of object sizes to classify web sites and their technique cannot function without these object sizes. Privacy-aware users are likely to know that SSL/TLS alone is not sufficient to hide traffic patterns, as is mentioned in the protocol specifications [3, 4].

Fu, et al. have produced at least two related papers. In the first [5], they describe the use of active probes to determine traffic payload rate and the use of statistical pattern recognition to evaluate traffic analysis attacks and corresponding countermeasures. This differs from our work in at least two key areas. First, they determine payload rate, a much simpler problem than the more exact classification we are attempting. Second, they require the ability to inject packets into the network, in the form of active pings. This active measurement is required during both the "off-line" data collection and training and "on-line" classification. In contrast, our technique only performs active measurements during the training phase, and is entirely passive during the classification phase.

In their second paper [6], they examine link padding as a means of defeating traffic analysis attacks. In particular, the authors establish a formal theoretical framework for link padding systems and derive closed-form formulas for estimation of detection rates. Additionally, they compare two methods of introducing padding, and conclude that variable intervals between padding are superior to constant. This result may prove useful in defending against our technique; we intend to investigate this technique in the future.

3 Data Collection

To begin our study, we collected data from January 01, 2004 until March 31, 2004. In this section, we describe the procedure we used to collect our data. We used the results of a prior user study by Wright, et al. [7] to determine the sites most visited by users of the computers in our department. The study tracked

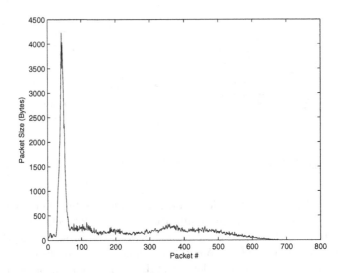

Fig. 2. A sample size profile for `www.amazon.com`

the web traffic of 24 volunteers for 214 days. We examined the proxy logs from Wright's study and used the 100 most-visited sites for experiments in our study.

To retrieve a baseline version of each site, we scripted an instance of Mozilla Firefox 1.0 to retrieve a site's main page and all graphics or other objects. Fig. 1 illustrates our measurement setup. We configured Firefox to connect through an instance of tinyproxy 1.6.3 bound on a local port via an SSH tunnel (OpenSSH 3.5p1 with compression and encryption enabled). All processes involved in the collection were running on the same machine. Our script retrieved the main page of each of the 100 sites every hour. We used tcpdump 3.7.2 to sniff and record the encrypted traffic over the SSH tunnel.

For each HTTP trace, we recorded two features: the inter-arrival time of each packet and the size of each packet. Each is a chronological data sequence that we call a *time trace* and *size trace*, respectively. No other features are available to an attacker; we did not perform any cryptanalysis.

For each day over a three month period, we collected inter-arrival and size traces once per hour, for a total of over 200,000 distinct data points.

4   Identifying Encrypted Traffic

The main goal of our study is to answer the following question: does a trace of web traffic, sent through an encrypted tunnel to a proxy, leak sufficient information to allow us to determine the site being accessed? As this section details, we have found that many popular web sites are reasonably identifiable even with relatively old training data (see Figure 4), and that some are extremely distinctive.

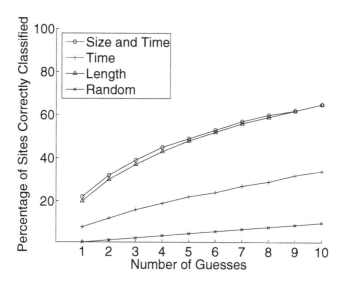

Fig. 3. Accuracy per number of guesses with a one hour gap and different classification methods. In all figures, the gap refers to the time between a 24 hour training period and a single test.

4.1   Performing the Attack

For our study, our attacker model is as follows. A client desiring privacy is connected to a server over an encrypted link. This link could be a VPN, an SSH tunnel, or a WEP-enabled access point. Before the attack, the attacker sets up a link with similar network characteristics and gathers packet traces. We believe this to be a reasonable assumption — the attacker could gather traces from the same ISP, or at the site of the victim's accesses, such as an Internet café. From these sets of packet traces, the attacker constructs a set of *profiles*, as described below. Then, the attacker monitors the encrypted link and attempts to match the profile of activity detected on the link with the set of known profiles, returning a ranked list of matching candidates. We assume that think times dominate network delay and that the attacker can easily distinguish separate sets of requests to a server.

Since we contacted each site many times over the course of months during our data collection, our data set is comprised of numerous traces from every site. For each site, there is an associated set of packet traces. We restrict our attention to two particular characteristics of each such packet trace: the inter-arrival time and the packet size. We organize our data as a set of tuples: (N, D, I, S), where N is a unique identifier for each site, D is the timestamp of the particular collection, and I and S represent inter-arrival time and packet size traces, respectively.

We define an *inter-arrival time trace*, I, as the sequence of n inter-arrival times, $\{t_1, t_2, \ldots, t_n\}$, between packets for a given trace. To construct a *time profile*, we coalesce a set of inter-arrival times, each corresponding to the same

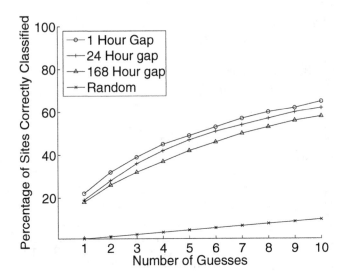

Fig. 4. Accuracy per number of guesses. The random line is the result of choosing site labels uniformly at random. In this and all following figures, we are using the combination of both the size and time profiles.

site, N, but a different time, D, into a single, new inter-arrival time trace. We take the arithmetic mean of each t_i in the set for each $1 < i < n$, and use this as the new t_i in the time profile. A corresponding trace and profile exist for packet sizes, which we denote as the *size trace* and *size profile*, respectively. Figure 2 shows, as an example, a profile of www.amazon.com.

To compare an individual trace to a profile, we use the *cross correlation* of the two sequences of values. In general, the cross correlation, r, between two sequences of real numbers $\{x_1, x_2, \ldots, x_n\}$ and $\{y_1, y_2, \ldots, y_n\}$ is defined as:

$$r = \frac{\sum\limits_{i=1}^{n} [(x_i - \bar{x})(y_i - \bar{y})]}{\sqrt{\sum\limits_{i=1}^{n}(x_i - \bar{x})} \sqrt{\sum\limits_{i=1}^{n}(y_i - \bar{y})}} \tag{1}$$

where $\bar{x}$ and $\bar{y}$ are the means of the corresponding series. Intuitively, the cross correlation estimates the degree to which two series are correlated. It is a summary statistic indicating whether the individual numbers in two sequences have similar magnitude. We call the cross correlation of a trace and a profile, the *similarity* of the trace to the profile. When attempting to classify an unknown data set, we compute its similarity to each of the profiles we have previously created. A sequence of guesses is returned, each corresponding to a particular site and ordered by the magnitude of the similarity.

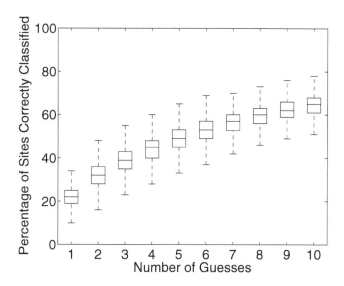

Fig. 5. Accuracy per number of guesses with a one hour gap

To evaluate our classifier, we built profiles from each contiguous 24 hour span of traces of each site. Some sites were missing data, but no 24 hour training period contained more than one missing trace. When a trace was missing from the training data, we omitted it from the profile. We then tested the performance of the classifier (as described above) on single traces from some time in the future. We call the amount of time between the last trace in the profile until the tested trace the *gap*. We evaluated the classifer with gaps of one hour, 24 hours, and 168 hours (one week). We constructed the two profile types for each training set, and we analyzed three methods of classifying data for the attacker:

– Size profile only;
– Time profile only;
– Size and time profile: the product of the size and time profile similarities.

We found the third method, shown in Figure 3, to be most effective overall, and utilized that method in all further results presented here. As shown in Figure 4, accuracy decreases as the gap between training and testing grows, but the trend remains consistent. The implications for the attacker are clear: training immediately before the attack is best, but even old data allows for some identification.

4.2 Predicting Identifiability

Some sites may be more identifiable than others. There is an obvious way to evaluate identifiability based on our classification methodology. By examining the *rank* of the correct site in the list our classifier returns, we have a metric describing how identifiable a site is. We show in Figure 6 this metric for each of the 100 sites and various gap sizes. As one would expect, smaller gap sizes result

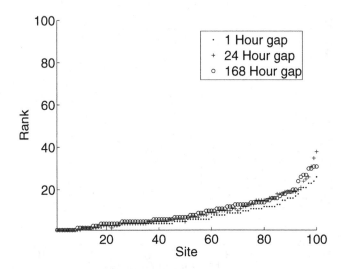

Fig. 6. Per-site rank in the ordered list of guesses

in high identifiability. Some sites are surprisingly and consistently identifiable, while others are quite difficult to differentiate. This trend is shown more explicitly in Figure 7. The accuracy of the most identifiable sites is much higher. In Figure 8, we show the accuracy for the top 25 sites. Accuracy with one guess is 40%, and increases to above 70% with two guesses.

This is of profound importance to the attacker, as she is able to tell *a priori* which sites will have such identifiability by examining the ranking data for that site. In general, an attacker would like to know which sites are most recognizable, and a defender would like to know how to make a site less distinguishable. We believe that a metric such as this ranking metric can guide both attackers and defenders in determining the relative identifiability of sites. However, further study is needed to discover the specific sources of identifiability.

5   Future Work

We intend to extend this work in a variety of ways. What follows is a short list of the improvements and extensions we are currently considering.

We expect the time profile to be highly dependent on the specific path between the server and client. However, we believe that packet sizes are not strongly dependent on that path, as the Internet has a fairly standard MTU size of 1500 bytes. Thus, it may be possible to train a size profile from one location on the Internet, and test against that profile elsewhere. Further experiments are needed to confirm this conjecture.

It is unclear what affect the specific web browser has on the profile. There are only a handful of web browsers currently in wide use, and they tend to use

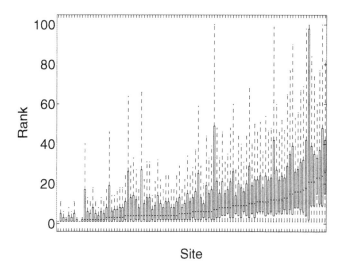

Fig. 7. Per-site rank in the ordered list of guesses with a one hour gap

one of several rendering engines: Microsoft Corporation's Internet Explorer, the Mozilla Foundation's Gecko (used in all recent versions of Netscape, AOL, and Firefox browsers), and the KDE project's khtml (used in Apple's Safari browser). A separate profile may be needed for each of these engines, or it may be the case that they perform server requests in the same order.

Examining more sites would help show the robustness of this attack. An argument can be made that there are billions of web pages and it may be impossible to distinguish among all of them. But for a targeted attack, an attacker might only need to be able to identify a few hundred or thousand with a low false positive rate. Similarly, it would be of great value for a site operator to know what characteristics of their site or network account for identifiability, and if it is possible to obfuscate these characteristics.

The technique we used for identification is not particularly insightful, and yet we are able to achieve an 20% accuracy rate with a single guess, and over 40% if we limit ourselves to a small set of possible sites and a single guess. Multiple guesses on this small set quickly drive our accuracy toward 100%. A more sophisticated approach, such as density estimation of a profile, would likely yield better results that are more robust to small fluctuations in network conditions or site changes. A more careful characterization of the identifiable characteristics of the traffic would likely also lead to a higher identification rate. Similarly, examining actual user behavior may yield further insights: users typically navigate from page to page, and we may be able to leverage some form of Bayesian inference to improve our results. It would also be enlightening to attempt to discern how much of each portion of delay, packet fragmentation, or packet size is due to server or browser configuration and network path effects.

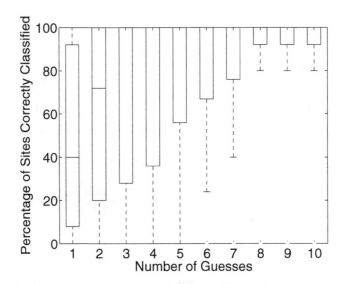

Fig. 8. Accuracy per number of guesses for the 25 most identifiable sites with a one hour gap

Also interesting would be an examination of how multiple proxies, each on separate networks on the Internet, affect our attack. Some of our previous results suggest the attack will work. Wright, et al. [8] examined a traffic analysis attack to link a single network flow routed through multiple anonymizing proxies, where the measurements are taken simultaneously at different points in the stream. In contrast, our attack creates a profile that remains effective over a long period of time (i.e., on the order of days) but has no intermediate proxies to add new statistical characteristics to the stream. We believe it would be possible, under some circumstances, to compose the two attacks if mixing is not performed by the intermediate proxies. Experiments are needed to confirm this conjecture.

Finally, an exploration of defenses is needed. The effects of delay or link padding and other traffic shaping must be quantified to help future designers of privacy-preserving protocols in avoiding this type of attack.

6   Conclusion

We have presented a straightforward, real-world, successful attack against supposedly private HTTP transactions. This attack is based upon forming profiles of possible sites being visited, and matching traffic against these profiles. It requires some preliminary work on the part of the attacker, but thereafter yields surprisingly effective and results. We have also shown a simple way of determining in advance the efficacy of the attack. Finally, we have pointed out interesting ways in which this attack could be extended, and possible methods of defense.

References

1. Raymond, J.F.: Traffic Analysis: Protocols, Attacks, Design Issues and Open Problems. In: Proceedings of the International Workshop on Design Issues in Anonymity and Unobservability. Volume 2009. (2001) 10–29
2. Sun, Q., Simon, D.R., Wang, Y.M., Russell, W., Padmanabhan, V., Qiu, L.: Statistical identification of encrypted web browsing traffic. In: Proceedings of the IEEE Security and Privacy Conference. (2003)
3. Dierks, T., Allen, C.: RFC 2246: The TLS protocol version 1 (1999)
4. Freier, A.O., Karlton, P., Kocher, P.C.: Secure Socket Layer. IETF Draft. (1996) http://home.netscape.com/eng/ssl3.
5. Fu, X., Graham, B., Bettati, R., Zhao, W.: Active Traffic Analysis Attacks and Countermeasures. In: Proceedings of the 2003 International Conference on Computer Networks and Mobile Computing. (2003) 31–39
6. Fu, X., Graham, B., Bettati, R., Zhao, W.: Analytical and Empirical Analysis of Countermeasures to Traffic Analysis Attacks. In: Proceedings of the 2003 International Conference on Parallel Processing. (2003) 483–492
7. Wright, M., Adler, M., Levine, B.N., Shields, C.: Defending Anonymous Communication Against Passive Logging Attacks. In: Proceedings of the IEEE Symposium on Security and Privacy (Oakland). (2003) 28–41
8. Levine, B.N., Reiter, M., Wang, C., Wright, M.: Stopping Timing Attacks in Low-Latency Mix-Based Systems. In: Proceedings of Financial Cryptography (FC). (2004)

An Analysis of Parallel Mixing with Attacker-Controlled Inputs

Nikita Borisov

UC Berkeley

Abstract. Parallel mixing [7] is a technique for optimizing the latency of a synchronous re-encryption mix network. We analyze the anonymity of this technique when an adversary can learn the output positions of some of the inputs to the mix network. Using probabilistic modeling, we show that parallel mixing falls short of achieving optimal anonymity in this case. In particular, when the number of unknown inputs is small, there are significant anonymity losses in the expected case. This remains true even if all the mixes in the network are honest, and becomes worse as the number of mixes increases. We also consider repeatedly applying parallel mixing to the same set of inputs. We show that an attacker who knows some input–output relationships will learn new information with each mixing and can eventually link previously unknown inputs and outputs.

1 Introduction

Re-encryption mixes [6, 10, 9, 8] are a kind of mix network [1], where each mix server re-encrypts each input ciphertext, producing an equivalent encryption of the plaintext that is unlinkable to the original. Such mix networks avoid the requirement of key agreement with the mix servers prior to sending a message, as the re-encryption operation can happen without knowing the decryption key; they have applications in electronic elections, but they could also be used in place of regular mix networks. Synchronous mix networks require that each mix server permute the entire set of inputs in sequence; in contrast, asynchronous mix networks pass different inputs to different servers freely. Synchronous mix networks avoid some of the attacks on asynchronous networks [12], but do so at the cost of performance, as each server must re-encrypt the entire set of inputs and the others must wait and be idle while it does so.

Parallel mixing [7] is a technique to speed up synchronous re-encryption mix networks while attempting to preserve their anonymity guarantees. It divides the input into batches, with each server mixing the inputs in its own batch and then passing it to other servers. The scheme parallelizes the mixing workload among all servers, increasing the per-server computation cost but dramatically lowering thetotal mixing time. Parallel mixing can be made secure even if all

G. Danezis and D. Martin (Eds.): PET 2005, LNCS 3856, pp. 12–25, 2006.

but one of the mixes are compromised, matching the security of conventional synchronous mix networks.

However, the design of parallel mixing is such that not all possible permutations of the mixed inputs are generated; therefore, when some relationships between inputs and outputs are known to the attacker, parallel mixing leaks information about the other inputs. This may happen either because the attacker controls some of the inputs and can therefore track the outputs, or when the attacker learns which inputs correspond to outputs through other means. For example, attacks such as traffic analysis or intersection attacks can help the attacker identify some of the input–output correspondences. In this paper, we set out to investigate exactly how much information is revealed by parallel mixing in this case.

We use both the anonymity metric from [7], as well as the common entropy-based metric [11, 4] to quantify anonymity. We develop two approaches to measure anonymity of parallel mixing: a probabilistic simulation, computing exact distributions of the metric, and a sampling technique that approximates the distributions, which is useful for larger mix network sizes. We find that parallel mixing falls significantly short of achieving the same anonymity levels as conventional mixing in the expected case, and in some cases, such as with few unknown inputs and many parallel mixes, reveals a lot of information about the correspondence of inputs to outputs.

We further show how an attacker can use this information when the same set of inputs are mixed repeatedly using parallel mixing. (Such a situation might occur if parallel mixing is used to provide privacy for long-term communication.) Each instance of parallel mixing is essentially an independent observation, and the attacker can combine the information from all observations to accurately pinpoint which input corresponds to which output after a small number of rounds. This attack re-introduces the anonymity degradation properties of asynchronous mix networks [12] into parallel mixing, and is effective even when *none* of the mix servers are compromised.

The anonymity shortfall we describe may not apply to the electronic election application of parallel mixing. In particular, many elections can ensure that most inputs are not controlled by the attacker and that the same inputs are not mixed multiple times. However, the speed improvements of parallel mixing may make them attractive for other applications, such as anonymous email or web surfing, where our assumptions are valid and the problems we describe are practical. Our hope is to caution against the use of parallel mixing in such applications, unless one can ensure that the attacks we describe do not apply.

The following section provides some background on parallel mixing. Section 3 analyzes the anonymity of parallel mixing when some inputs are known to the attacker. Section 4 describes how this information can be used to discover which input corresponds to which output after several repeated rounds of mixing. Finally, Section 5 concludes and discusses some future research directions.

2   Background

2.1   Parallel Mixing

The parallel mixing technique described by Golle and Juels relies on breaking the inputs into batches and then successively passing the input batches between servers for re-encryption. We proceed to give an overview of their technique; please refer to [7] for more details. (For clarity, we will use the same terminology as Golle and Juels wherever possible.) Consider a network of M re-encryption mixes operating on n inputs. We will assign inputs to individual *slots*, and each mixing round will move the input ciphertexts between slots. For symmetry, we require that $M^2 | n$. Parallel mixing is parameterized by a threshold $M' < M$, which is the maximum number of compromised mix servers.

The first step is to assign the input ciphertexts randomly to slots. The random permutation is defined from a public, ideal source of randomness (in practice, it would be computed jointly by all the servers). The slots are then partitioned into batches, $S(1), \ldots, S(M)$ of equal size, with each batch assigned to an individual mix server. Then the batches undergo $M' + 1$ mixing steps and M' rotation steps. In a mixing step, each mix permutes the inputs among the slots in the batch assigned to it. A rotation step involves passing batches between servers in succession, so server i passes its batch to server $i + 1 \pmod{M}$.

After this, a distribution step follows. In this step, the inputs in each batch are redistributed so that an equal number ends up in each resulting batch. I.e. for each original batch S_i and new batch S'_j, $|S_i \cap S'_j| = n/M^2$. After distributing the inputs in this way, there are another $M' + 1$ mixing steps, with M' rotation steps in between.

If we label the input batches as $B(1), \ldots, B(M)$ and the output batches as $C(1), \ldots, C(M)$, then the first step ensures that each ciphertext is assigned to a random batch $B(j)$. Then the batch $B(j)$ is mixed by $M' + 1$ servers, at least one of which must be honest. Therefore, before the distribution, the slot that an input i occupies within a batch j is chosen uniformly at random, and is unknown to the corrupt mixes. Then in the distribution step, i is assigned to an effectively random output batch $C(j')$. Finally, the next $M' + 1$ mixing steps ensure that the output batch $C(j')$ is once again mixed by at least one honest server, and hence the position of the input within the batch is unknown.

Following this process, each input ciphertext is equally likely to end up in each of the output slots. Golle and Juels show that if no more than M' servers are compromised, and no input–output relationships are known, the attackers cannot learn any information about the correspondence of the mix inputs and outputs.

Therefore, we discount mix corruption attacks and in fact we will assume that all the mixes are honest for the remainder of this paper. Instead, our focus will be on situations where the attacker learns some input–output relations, either through submitting rogue inputs to the mix or by other means. In this case, Golle and Juels suggest that the anonymity is statistically close to optimal. We will proceed to quantify the difference between parallel mixing and an optimal mix and examine the consequences of such a difference.

2.2 Anonymity

To perform a meaningful analysis, we need to have some measure of anonymity. Golle and Juels define an anonymity measure of a network as

$$Anon = \left(\min_{k,j} Pr(i_k \to o_j) \right)^{-1}$$

where i_k are input positions of the parallel mix and o_j are output positions. Since we are concerned with the anonymity achieved when an attacker knows some of the input output relations, the minimum should be taken over those inputs and outputs that the attacker does not know. The intuition for this measure is that when $Anon = n$, the worst-case probability of a true input–output relationship being guessed is $1/n$, or equivalent to a uniform mixing among n input–output pairs. Thus, with n unknown input–output relationships, we would like $Anon$ to be as close to n as possible.

In addition to this measure, we will use an entropy-based metric, proposed in [11, 4] and used to analyze many anonymous systems [2, 5, 3]. The metric involves computing a probability distribution X of inputs corresponding to a particular output (or vice versa), and computing the entropy of this distribution using the formula $H(X) = \sum_i -p_i \log_2 p_i$, where $p_i = Pr[t \to i]$, the probability that a target input t gets mapped to output slot i during mixing. (We will consider the problem of linking a given input to its corresponding output; the converse problem is analogous due to symmetry inherent in the mixing process.) The intuitive interpretation is that the metric represents the number of bits of uncertainty that an attacker has about the relationship between inputs and outputs. The entropy measure is also useful for certain kinds of information-theoretic analysis, which we will explore below.

The two anonymity measures are also connected by the relation:

$$H(X) \geq \log_2 Anon$$

3 Anonymity Analysis

We first motivate our analysis by a simple example. Consider a parallel mix network with $M = 3$ and $n = 9$. Initially, the 9 inputs are permuted and assigned into 3 batches of size 3. Then each batch is permuted, the inputs are redistributed into new batches, and these batches are permuted again before being output. Since we are assuming that all mixes are honest, we can assume that each batch will undergo a perfectly random permutation and therefore we can ignore the order of the inputs in each input batch, as well as the order of outputs in each output batch. Therefore, we can simplify the problem to considering which input batches the inputs get assigned to by the initial permutation (which an attacker can observe), and which output batches each input gets distributed to (which the attacker cannot see).

Suppose now that the attacker knows the input–output relations for all but 2 of the inputs. How much anonymity will parallel mixing provide the other 2?

Consider the initial permutation; with probability 3/4, the two inputs will be assigned to different batches. Therefore, some batch B will contain the unknown input i_1 as well as two attacker-known inputs a_2, a_3. After the distribution step, the inputs in batch B will be distributed among the 3 output batches. The key point here is that each output batch will have exactly *one* input from B. Therefore, if the attacker can observe the position of the outputs a_2 and a_3, he can learn which output batch C contains i_1.

The other unknown input i_2, which we assumed was in some other input batch, will be assigned to some output batch by the distribution process. With probability 2/3, it will be a batch $C' \neq C$. In that case, the other two inputs in C will be attacker-known inputs a_4, a_5. This will allow the attacker to immediately identify i_1 as the member of C and therefore determine which output it corresponds to. Combining the two probabilities, we see that in $3/4 * 2/3 = 1/2$ the cases, the parallel mixing provides *no* anonymity to the two inputs. (In the other half of the cases, the attacker does not learn anything about I_1 and I_2.)

The foregoing is an extreme example, but it helps illustrate the kind of potential problems introduced by parallel mixing. In essence, although parallel mixing can assign any input slot to any other output slot, it generates only a subset of the permutations on all inputs. Therefore, knowing the relationship between some of the inputs and their permuted positions allows an attacker to deduce information about the other inputs. We now proceed to formally analyze the extent of such information for larger mix sizes and more unknown inputs.

3.1   Previous Results

Golle and Juels show how an attacker that knows some input–output relations can use this information to estimate probabilities of unknown inputs and outputs being linked through the mix. Consider $A(I)$ be the set of inputs known to the attacker, and $A(O)$ be the set of the corresponding outputs. Let $\alpha(j) = |B(j) \cap A(I)|$ be the number of slots in input batch j occupied by known inputs and $\gamma(j') = |C(j') \cap A(O)|$ be the number of slots in output batch j' occupied by known outputs. Also, let $\delta(j, j') = |B(j) \cap A(I) \cap C(j')|$ be the number of inputs in input batch j known to the attacker that are mapped to output batch j'. Then [7, Theorem 4.2] states:

Theorem 1. *Let $s_0 \in B(j)$ and $s_1 \in C(j')$ with $s_0 \notin A(I)$ and $s_1 \notin A(O)$. Then:*

$$Pr(s_0 \to s_1) = \frac{n/M^2 - \delta(j, j')}{(n/M - \alpha(j))(n/M - \gamma(j')}$$

Theorem 1 shows that $Pr(s_0 \to s_1)$ is only dependent on $\alpha(j)$, $\delta(j, j')$, and $\gamma(j')$. Golle and Juels approximate $\alpha(j), \gamma(j')$ by Poisson random variables, with mean of $|A(I)|/M$ and standard deviation $\sqrt{|A(I)|/M}$, and $\delta(j, j')$ by a random variable with mean $|A(I)|/M^2$ and standard deviation of $\sqrt{|A(I)|/M^2}$. When each of the variables is equal to their mean, Theorem 1 shows that the anonymity is optimal: $Pr(s_i \to s_j) = \frac{1}{N - |A(I)|}$. However, variations in the values of $\alpha(j), \delta(j, j')$, and $\gamma(j)$ are going to cause the anonymity to be lower. For example, Figure 1 plots $Pr(s_0 \rightarrow s_1)^{-1}$ when $\alpha(j), \delta(j, j')$ and $\gamma(j')$ are each one standard deviation away from the mean, when 1000 inputs are distributed among 5 or 10 mixes. There is a significant distance from optimal anonymity shown in this graph, which becomes larger as the number of mixes increase.

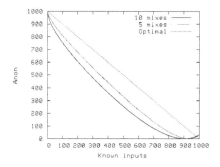
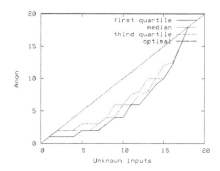

Fig. 1. Anonymity achieved at one standard deviation from the mean with 1000 inputs and 5 or 10 mix servers

Fig. 2. Anonymity of 3 mixes with 18 inputs

The Poisson model is only an approximation and does not accurately estimate how likely this scenario is, since the random variables are not in fact independent. In the rest of this section, we will use simulations to measure the possible values of $\alpha(j), \delta(j, j')$, and $\gamma(j')$ and the corresponding anonymity.

3.2   Simulation Results

We have built a probabilistic simulation of parallel mixing. At a high level, the simulation consists of taking inputs $i_1, \ldots, i_n$ and assigning them to input slots. Then we non-deterministically simulate each of the steps in parallel mixing; we compute each possible resulting assignment of inputs to slots and record the probability of arriving at each assignment. Let I denote an ordering of the inputs after the initial permutation, and O denote their ordering after all the steps of parallel mixing. Our simulation allows us to compute $Pr[I \rightarrow O]$ for all pairs I and O.

Starting with some subset of attacker-known inputs, and input and output orderings I and O we can compute the anonymity measure $Anon(I, O)$ as follows: first, we determine the positions of the attacker inputs in I and O and use that to compute $\alpha(j), \gamma(j, j')$, and $\delta(j')$ for all j, j'. Then we apply Theorem 1 to compute $Pr[s_0 \rightarrow s_1]$ for all s_0, s_1 and take $Anon(I, O) = \min_{s_0, s_1} Pr[s_0 \rightarrow s_1]^{-1}$. Using the results from our probabilistic simulation, we can then compute the expected anonymity by $\sum_{I,O} Pr[I \rightarrow O] Anon(I, O)$. We can also use them to compute the median or other measures on the distribution of anonymity.

Simulating all the permutations of inputs becomes impractical very quickly. Fortunately, for the purposes of computing the $Anon$ metric, we can make a few simplifying assumptions. First, since we are assuming at most M' mixes are corrupt, we can model the mixing and rotation steps by a uniformly random permutation of each individual batch. Second, an initial distribution with a different ordering of batches, or a different order of inputs within a batch, produces an identical distribution of outputs. Similarly, the order of inputs in the output batch does not affect the variables α, γ, δ, hence we can stop the simulation after the distribution step. Finally, we can treat all unknown inputs as identical, and all known inputs within a given mix as identical, greatly reducing the space of possible permutations.

With these simplifications, we are able to model mix networks of moderate sizes. Figure 2 shows the median as well as the first and third quartile values for the *Anon* metric calculated on a mix network with 3 mixes and 18 inputs. Even with only one known input, the *Anon* metric falls short of optimal, and in almost all the cases, the median value of the metric is significantly below the maximum. For example, with 9 unknown inputs, the median value for *Anon* is 4 meaning that in over half the cases, there exist s_0 and s_1 such that $Pr[s_0 \rightarrow s_1] \geq \frac{1}{4}$, instead of the $\frac{1}{9}$ we would hope for with an optimal system.

3.3 Sampling Based Results

The probabilistic simulation methodology does not to scale to mix networks of large sizes. In this case, we use sampling to get an estimate of what kind of anonymity to expect in such networks. Instead of simulating all possible permutations of inputs, we instead compute the results of a mix network using random permutations and apply the anonymity metric to that. We repeat this multiple times to obtain sampling of the distribution of the *Anon* metric. The estimate is inexact and will not capture the tail of the distribution (even with the smaller network sizes, we observed events of probability $< 1\%$). However, it is representative of what users of the mix network should expect to see in practice.

Figure 3 shows the cumulative distribution function of the *Anon* function on a mix network with 1008 inputs, 900 of which are unknown. The CDF was estimated using 1000 samples; the figure demonstrates the effect of different

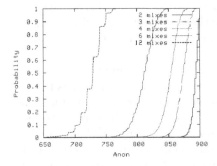

Fig. 3. Sampled anonymity CDF with 1008 inputs, 900 unknown, and 2–12 servers

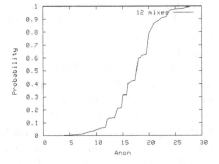

Fig. 4. Sampled anonymity CDF with 1008 inputs, 100 unknown, and 12 servers

numbers of mix servers on the anonymity of the network. Unsurprisingly, the anonymity degrades with a larger number of servers. With more mix servers, the permutations that are generated are more restricted, as the distribution step forces the inputs to be directed to one of a larger number of batches. However, what is perhaps surprising is the amount of anonymity loss. With 12 servers, the median value of *Anon* is nearly one fifth lower than optimal.

The difference is even more dramatic when the attacker knows more input–output relationships. Figure 4 shows the CDF corresponding to a network with 12 servers and 1008 inputs, 100 of which are unknown. The median value for *Anon* is only 18, and the largest we observed after 1000 trials was only 30. This figure shows that introducing parallelism into a mix system where one can expect an attacker to know a large fraction of the input–output relationships greatly reduces the anonymity provided by this system.

3.4   Entropy Metric

We can use the same techniques to compute the entropy-based anonymity metric. Both probabilistic simulations and sampling let us calculate $Pr[s_0 \rightarrow s_1]$ for each s_0, s_1. Therefore, given an input t, we can compute the probability $Pr[t \rightarrow s_1]$ for each slot s_1 and take the entropy of the resulting distribution.

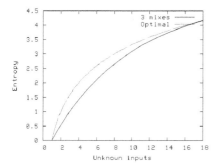
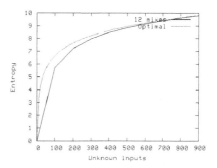

Fig. 5. Expected entropy with 3 mixes, 18 inputs

Fig. 6. Sampled expected entropy with 12 mixes, 1008 inputs

Figure 5 shows the expected entropy for a 3 mix network with 18 inputs. Note that the entropy will be larger than $\log_2 Anon$ for two reasons: the entropy metric takes into account the entire probability distribution, rather than the highest value, and the expectation is taken over a particular input, rather than the worst-case input for a given mix, as is the case with *Anon*. Therefore, the metric is more "forgiving" than *Anon*; however, there is still a significant difference between the optimal anonymity and what is achieved by parallel mixing, especially when most inputs are known to the attacker.

Figure 6 shows the expected entropy obtained by sampling a 12 mix network with 1008 inputs. Once again, the difference from optimal entropy is more significant when more of the inputs are known to the attacker. These results suggest that parallel mixing should not be used in situations where an attacker might be expected to learn many input–output correspondences, either through controlling the inputs themselves or through some outside source of information.

4   Multi-round Anonymity

In the previous section, we showed how parallel mixing fails to achieve optimal anonymity. However, in most cases, the attacker gains only a statistical advantage over the optimum, but is unable to directly link an input with an output. In this section, we show how the attacker can use this statistical advantage over repeated rounds of mixing to reveal previously unknown correspondence between inputs and outputs. Such repeated mixing may occur when parallel mixing is used to protect long-term communication, such as a regular email correspondence or a set of long-lived TCP connections.

4.1   Repeated Mixings

To begin, consider the input to the parallel mix consisting of a set of unknown inputs, $G(I)$ and a set of attacker-known inputs $A(I)$. And let's imagine the attacker wants to determine which output $i_0 \in G(I)$ corresponds to. The attacker can observe the initial permutation to find out which slot i_0 is assigned to, as well where the other inputs in $G(I)$ and $A(I)$ are assigned, and then observe the positions of $A(I)$ in the output. Let us call this entire observation $\mathcal{O}_1$. Now consider a particular output o_k; let $s_0 \in B(j)$ be the slot assigned to I_0 and $s_1 \in C(j')$ be the slot of o_k. The attacker can compute $\alpha(j), \delta(j,j')$, and $\gamma(j')$ and then derive $Pr(s_0 \to s_1)$ using Theorem 1. We can write that $Pr[i_0 \to o_k|\mathcal{O}_1] = Pr(s_0 \to s_1)$. The attacker can compute this value for each k efficiently, since all that's necessary is $\alpha(j), \delta(j,j')$, and $\gamma(j')$ for each pair j, j'.

Now suppose that the same set of inputs is sent to the mix a second time, with a different initial permutation and a different mixing process. Consider the observations he makes in this round represented by $\mathcal{O}_2$. Then, once again, the attacker can compute $Pr[i_0 \to o_k|\mathcal{O}_2]$. $\mathcal{O}_1$ and $\mathcal{O}_2$ are *independent* observations, meaning that:

$$Pr[\mathcal{O}_1 \wedge \mathcal{O}_2|i_0 \to o_k] = Pr[\mathcal{O}_1|i_0 \to o_k] \cdot Pr[\mathcal{O}_2|i_0 \to o_k]$$

Using this fact, we can show that:

$$Pr[i_0 \to o_k|\mathcal{O}_1 \wedge \mathcal{O}_2] = \frac{Pr[i_0 \to o_k|\mathcal{O}_1] \cdot Pr[i_0 \to o_k|\mathcal{O}_2]}{\sum_{j=1}^{|G(I)|} Pr[i_0 \to o_j|\mathcal{O}_1] Pr[i_0 \to o_j|\mathcal{O}_2]} \quad (1)$$

(See Theorem 2 in Appendix A for details.) Now, in the optimal anonymity case, $Pr[i_0 \to o_j|\mathcal{O}_l] = \frac{1}{|G(I)|}$ for each $l = 1,2$, $j = 1,\ldots,n$. In this case, $Pr[i_0 \to o_j|\mathcal{O}_1 \wedge \mathcal{O}_2] = \frac{1}{|G(I)|}$, i.e. the attacker learns no new information from repeated mixes. However, as we saw in the last section, we expect the anonymity to fall somewhat short of optimal with parallel mixing, in which case the attacker will be able to amplify the anonymity loss with repeated observations.

For example, consider the case where $|G(I)| = 2$, $Pr[i_0 \rightarrow o_1|\mathcal{O}_l] = 0.6$, and $Pr[i_0 \rightarrow o_2|\mathcal{O}_l] = 0.4$, for $l = 1, 2$. Then $Pr[i_0 \rightarrow o_1|\mathcal{O}_1 \wedge \mathcal{O}_2] \approx 0.69$. Therefore, given 2 observations, the attacker has more confidence that $i_0 \rightarrow o_1$ than from each individual observation.

We can extend (1) to a set of observations $\mathcal{O}_1, \ldots, \mathcal{O}_n$:

$$Pr\left[i_0 \rightarrow o_k \left| \bigwedge_{l=1}^{n} \mathcal{O}_l \right.\right] = \frac{\prod_{l=1}^{n} Pr[i_0 \rightarrow o_k|\mathcal{O}_l]}{\sum_{j=1}^{|G(I)|} \prod_{l=1}^{n} Pr[i_0 \rightarrow o_j|\mathcal{O}_l]} \tag{2}$$

If there is, as we showed in the last section, a bias in the probability distributions based on each observation towards the true o_k, this bias will be amplified with multiple observations and eventually reveal the true correspondence with a high confidence.

4.2   Simulations

We can measure the success of this attack by using simulations. The simulation set up is similar to that of Section 3.3. We simulate a mixing of a set of inputs and record an observation $\mathcal{O}_1$. Then, for a particular input i_0, we compute the probability distribution $Pr[i_0 \rightarrow o_k|\mathcal{O}_1]$ for each k. Then we perform another trial to obtain another probability distribution. After a number of trials, we apply (2) to compute the probability $Pr[i_0 \rightarrow o_k|\bigwedge \mathcal{O}_l]$ for each k.

Figure 7 shows the success of this attack for a mix network with 12 mixes and 1008 inputs total, with varying numbers of them being unknown. We plot the probability P_{right} that is assigned to the true output corresponding to i_0, and P_{wrong}, which is the highest probability assigned to each incorrect guess. Initially, there is insufficient information to identify the correct correspondence; however, after a sufficient number of rounds, P_{right} invariably tends to 1 and P_{wrong} to 0. For 100 unknown inputs, fewer than 10 rounds are required to identify the correct output. The attack remains effective even with larger numbers of unknown inputs: with 500 unknown inputs, fewer than 100 rounds successfully identify the correct link. However, as the number of unknown inputs increases, the success of the attack diminishes; with 900 unknown inputs, the most likely guess for the link is incorrect even after 700 rounds of mixing.

We can use information theory to predict how quickly this attack succeeds. Section 3.4 shows how to compute the expected entropy metric applied to parallel mixing. The expected entropy is also known as *conditional entropy*, or $H(X|O)$, where X is a random variable modeling input–output correspondences, and O is modeling observations. The conditional entropy is closely related to the mutual information between X and O:

$$I(X;O) = H(X) - H(X|O)$$

If we consider parallel mixing as a noisy communication channel, $I(X;O)$ shows how many bits of information are revealed with each mixing. Therefore, to

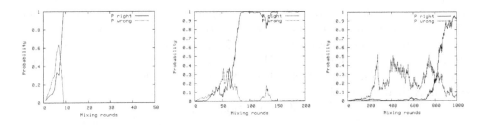

Fig. 7. Success of repeated mixing attack with 100, 500, and 900 unknown inputs

identify a particular output among $n - |A(I)|$ unknown ones, we will need at least $\log_2(n - |A(I)|)/I(X;O)$ rounds of mixing.

With $n - |A(I)|$ unknown inputs, $H(X) = \log_2(n - |A(I)|)$. We can therefore calculate the number of rounds required to reveal the input–output correspondence based on the data in Figure 6. For 100 unknown inputs, we expect to need about 7 rounds of mixing. With 500 unknown inputs, the expected number of rounds is 91, and with 900, it is as high as 880. Therefore, we can see that with 900 unknown inputs, the attack is unlikely to succeed unless very many rounds of mixing are performed, while with smaller numbers of unknown inputs, the attack can be quite effective.

Information theory offers only a lower bound on the number of rounds needed, and potentially more rounds will be required. However, the data in Figure 7 show that the lower bound comes close to being tight.

5   Conclusions and Future Work

We have presented an analysis of parallel mixing and how well it performs when the attacker can learn the relationship between some inputs and outputs. We showed that in such cases, there is a significant difference between the anonymity provided by parallel mixing and the optimal anonymity achieved by conventional mixes. In addition, we demonstrated how this difference may be exploited to reveal the secret mapping of inputs to outputs when the same inputs are mixed repeatedly by way of parallel mixing.

Note that our attacks apply even when *all* the mix servers are honest. Further, they do not require that the attackers control any of the inputs, but rather only that they know some of the input–output correspondences. Such information may be revealed through other attacks, such as traffic analysis or intersection attacks. Hence a completely passive adversary may be able to compromise the security of parallel mixing. Therefore, we strongly caution against using parallel mixing in situations when attackers may learn some input–output correspondences and/or when the same inputs are mixed multiple times.

For a more complete understanding of parallel mixing, it would be useful to analyze directly the success of combining intersection attacks or traffic analysis with our techniques for exploiting the information revealed by parallel mixing.

Such an analysis would show whether such attacks are practical in a given setting, and thus whether parallel mixing is appropriate. Unfortunately, our current simulation techniques face a state explosion problem preventing such analysis.

An important question is whether parallel mixing can be extended to correct the problems we present while maintaining some of the performance advantage. For example, it can be shown that adding another distribution and a rotation/mixing step to parallel mixing will cause it to generate all permutations of the inputs, albeit with a non-uniform distribution. Once again, our current analysis methods can only analyze this extension for very small network sizes and cannot predict its resilience against our attacks.

Our analysis in Section 4.2 touches upon a connection between conditional entropy, mutual information, and the performance of multi-round attacks. Our information-theoretic model may apply to other anonymity systems; perhaps the conditional entropy metric can be used to derive useful bounds on the success of multi-round attacks, such as a generalization of the predecessor attack [12].

Acknowledgments

We would like to thank Marco Barreno, Rob Johnson, Umesh Shankar, and Naveen Sastry for initial discussions aboutu parallel mixing that motivated this paper, David Molnar for his thoughts on efficient enumeration, and the anonymous reviewers for their insightful comments.

References

1. David Chaum. Untraceable electronic mail, return addresses, and digital pseudonyms. *Communications of the ACM*, 4(2), February 1981.
2. George Danezis. Mix-networks with restricted routes. In Roger Dingledine, editor, *Proceedings of the Privacy Enhancing Technologies (PET) Workshop*. Springer-Verlag, LNCS 2760, March 2003.
3. Claudia Diaz, Len Sassaman, and Evelyne Dewitte. Comparison between two practical mix designs. In *9th European Symposium on Research in Computer Security*, September 2004.
4. Claudia Diaz, Stefaan Seys, Joris Claessens, and Bart Preneel. Towards measuring anonymity. In Roger Dingledine and Paul Syverson, editors, *Proceedings of Privacy Enhancing Technologies (PET) Workshop*. Springer-Verlag, LNCS 2482, April 2002.
5. Roger Dingledine, Vitaly Shmatikov, and Paul Syverson. Synchronous batching: From cascades to free routes. In *Proceedings of the Privacy Enhancing Technologies (PET) Workshop*, Toronto, Canada, May 2004.
6. Jun Furukawa and Kazue Sako. An efficient scheme for proving a shuffle. In *CRYPTO*, pages 368–387, 2001.
7. Philip Golle and Ari Juels. Parallel mixing. In *ACM Conference on Communications and Computer Security*, October 2004.
8. Philippe Golle and Dan Boneh. Almost entirely correct mixing with applications to voting. In *ACM Conference on Communications and Computer Security*, pages 68–77, 2002.

9. Markus Jakobsson, Ari Juels, and Ron Rivest. Making mix nets robust for electronic voting by randomized partial checking. In *USENIX Security Symposium*, pages 339–353, 2002.
10. C. Andrew Neff. A verifiable secret shuffle and its applications to e-voting. In *ACM Conference on Communications and Computer Security*, pages 116–125, 2001.
11. Andrei Serjantov and George Danezis. Towards an information theoretic metric for anonymity. In Roger Dingledine and Paul Syverson, editors, *Proceedings of Privacy Enhancing Technologies (PET) Workshop*, San Diego, CA, April 2002. Springer-Verlag, LNCS 2482.
12. Matthew Wright, Micah Adler, Brian Neil Levine, and Clay Shields. An analysis of the degradation of anonymous protocols. In *Proceedings of the Network and Distributed Security Symposium (NDSS)*. IEEE, February 2002.

A   Conditional Probabilities

Theorem 2. *Given some set of inputs* $I = \{1, \ldots, n\}$ *and some set of observations* $\mathcal{O}$, *let* $\mathcal{O}_1, \mathcal{O}_2 \in \mathcal{O}$ *be two* independent *observations on some input* i_0. *Then:*

$$Pr[i_0 = k | \mathcal{O}_1 \wedge \mathcal{O}_2] = \frac{Pr[i_0 = k | \mathcal{O}_1] Pr[i_0 = k | \mathcal{O}_2]}{\sum_{j=1}^{n} Pr[i_0 = j | \mathcal{O}_1] Pr[i_0 = j | \mathcal{O}_2]}$$

Proof. The independence assumption can be formalized as:

$$Pr[\mathcal{O}_1 \wedge \mathcal{O}_2 | i_0 = k] = Pr[\mathcal{O}_1 | i_0 = k] Pr[\mathcal{O}_2 | i_0 = k]$$

Then on one hand:

$$Pr[\mathcal{O}_1 \wedge \mathcal{O}_2 | i_0 = k] = \frac{Pr[\mathcal{O}_1 \wedge \mathcal{O}_2 \wedge i_0 = k]}{Pr[i_0 = k]}$$

On the other hand,

$$Pr[\mathcal{O}_1 \wedge \mathcal{O}_2 | i_0 = k] = Pr[\mathcal{O}_1 | i_0 = k] Pr[\mathcal{O}_2 | i_0 = k]$$
$$= \frac{Pr[\mathcal{O}_1 \wedge i_0 = k]}{Pr[i_0 = k]} \frac{Pr[\mathcal{O}_2 \wedge i_0 = k]}{Pr[i_0 = k]}$$

Therefore,

$$\frac{Pr[\mathcal{O}_1 \wedge \mathcal{O}_2 \wedge i_0 = k]}{Pr[i_0 = k]} = \frac{Pr[\mathcal{O}_1 \wedge i_0 = k] Pr[\mathcal{O}_2 \wedge i_0 = k]}{Pr[i_0 = k]^2}$$

$$Pr[\mathcal{O}_1 \wedge \mathcal{O}_2 \wedge i_0 = k] = \frac{Pr[\mathcal{O}_1 \wedge i_0 = k] Pr[\mathcal{O}_2 \wedge i_0 = k]}{Pr[i_0 = k]}$$

And:

$$Pr[\mathcal{O}_1 \wedge \mathcal{O}_2] = \sum_{j=1}^{n} Pr[i_0 = j \wedge \mathcal{O}_1 \wedge \mathcal{O}_2] = \sum_{j=1}^{n} \frac{Pr[\mathcal{O}_1 \wedge i_0 = j] Pr[\mathcal{O}_2 \wedge i_0 = j]}{Pr[i_0 = j]}$$

$$Pr[i_0 = k | \mathcal{O}_1 \wedge \mathcal{O}_2] =$$

$$= \frac{Pr[i_0 = k \wedge \mathcal{O}_1 \wedge \mathcal{O}_2]}{Pr[\mathcal{O}_1 \wedge \mathcal{O}_2]} = \frac{\frac{Pr[\mathcal{O}_1 \wedge i_0 = k] Pr[\mathcal{O}_2 \wedge i_0 = k]}{Pr[i_0 = k]}}{\sum_{j=1}^{n} \frac{Pr[\mathcal{O}_1 \wedge i_0 = j] Pr[\mathcal{O}_2 \wedge i_0 = j]}{Pr[i_0 = j]}}$$

$$= \frac{Pr[\mathcal{O}_1 \wedge i_0 = k] Pr[\mathcal{O}_2 \wedge i_0 = k]}{\sum_{j=1}^{n} Pr[\mathcal{O}_1 \wedge i_0 = j] Pr[\mathcal{O}_2 \wedge i_0 = j]}$$

$$\text{(because } Pr[i_0 = k] = Pr[i_0 = j] = \frac{1}{n} \text{ for all } j.)$$

$$= \frac{\frac{Pr[\mathcal{O}_1 \wedge i_0 = k]}{Pr[\mathcal{O}_1]} \frac{Pr[\mathcal{O}_2 \wedge i_0 = k]}{Pr[\mathcal{O}_2]}}{\sum_{j=1}^{n} \frac{Pr[\mathcal{O}_1 \wedge i_0 = j]}{Pr[\mathcal{O}_1]} \frac{Pr[\mathcal{O}_2 \wedge i_0 = j]}{Pr[\mathcal{O}_2]}}$$

$$= \frac{Pr[i_0 = k | \mathcal{O}_1] Pr[i_0 = k | \mathcal{O}_2]}{\sum_{j=1}^{n} Pr[i_0 = j | \mathcal{O}_1] Pr[i_0 = j | \mathcal{O}_2]}$$

Message Splitting Against the Partial Adversary

Andrei Serjantov[1] and Steven J. Murdoch[2]

[1] The Free Haven Project, UK
schnur@gmail.com
[2] University of Cambridge Computer Laboratory,
15 JJ Thomson Ave,
Cambridge, CB3 0FD, UK
http://www.cl.cam.ac.uk/users/sjm217/

Abstract. We review threat models used in the evaluation of anonymity systems' vulnerability to traffic analysis. We then suggest that, under the partial adversary model, if multiple packets have to be sent through these systems, more anonymity can be achieved if senders route the packets via different paths. This is in contrast to the normal technique of using the same path for them all. We comment on the implications of this for message-based and connection-based anonymity systems. We then proceed to examine the only remaining traffic analysis attack – one which considers the entire system as a black box. We show that it is more difficult to execute than the literature suggests, and attempt to empirically estimate the parameters of the Mixmaster and the Mixminion systems needed in order to successfully execute the attack.

1   Introduction

Traffic analysis is a procedure for inferring relationships between individuals from their communication patterns. In this paper we examine traffic analysis in the context of anonymous communication systems which are designed to hide those very relationships.

The anonymity properties provided by different anonymity systems vary. Some, e.g. DC-nets, provide sender and/or receiver untraceability by hiding the very existence of traffic between their users, even against the most powerful adversaries[1]. However, users of such systems typically incur overwhelming communication costs, so we do not consider them here.

Instead, we focus on systems that provide unlinkability, e.g. Mixminion [3] and Tor [4], which only aim to prevent an adversary from linking together the sender and receiver of messages. Recent literature contains a number of exact [5, 6] and statistical [7, 8, 9, 10] traffic analysis attacks against anonymous communication systems, all based around intersection attacks. Based on these results, it can be argued that low latency communication is impossible to perform anonymously. Although given *enough* traffic, the attacker can compromise the users' anonymity, we argue that attention should be focused on finding the cases where anonymity is provided, and ensuring that practical cases fall into this category.

---

[1] see [1] and [2, Chapter 2] for a more precise definition.

G. Danezis and D. Martin (Eds.): PET 2005, LNCS 3856, pp. 26–39, 2006.

2   Threat Models for Traffic Analysis

Message-based systems [11, 3] are believed to provide good anonymity properties against a global passive adversary, as long as the sender only transmits one message through the system [3]. This is, however, unrealistic, both in the context of email and with web browsing. Hence, we consider the case where each sender transmits at least one message and possibly many more, which introduces the potential for intersection attacks [5, 6, 7, 8, 9, 10]. Connection-based anonymity systems, such as Tor [4], are thus vulnerable, as are remailers, such as Mixmaster [11] and Mixminion [3], when large files are sent.

In this section, we also assume that each sender communicates with exactly one receiver and that no receiver is communicated to by more than one sender. Initially, we assume that all packets from a sender to a receiver are sent via the same route (i.e. via the same sequence of nodes), but by relaxing this restriction later, we show that greater anonymity can be provided. We now proceed to review some threat models which are appropriate in these settings and the attacks which are made possible.

2.1   Global Passive Adversary

The global passive adversary is perhaps the most popular threat model used to evaluate anonymity properties of anonymity systems, see for instance [2, 6, 10]. While it can be argued that this threat model is stronger than realistically needed, a system that withstands this adversary is necessarily secure against a weaker attacker. In the global passive model, the adversary logs all traffic, both to and from all mixes and all users. The attacker's goal is to link incoming connections to outgoing connections.

Perhaps the simplest traffic analysis attack is packet counting. The situation shown in Figure 1 can be considered as an example of large files being sent through Mixminion. Here, the adversary can deduce that the messages from C were sent to F. It is interesting to note that even if we remove the restriction that each user must have exactly one communication partner, the adversary can still show that at least one message is sent from C to F. However, by splitting traffic, C's anonymity can be improved, at the cost of delaying when the reassembled message will arrive. For illustration, we have used routes of length 2, but this can be extended, with the constraint that the last node of all routes must be the same, so as to allow the message to be reassembled.

If C splits his traffic over two different routes, as is shown in Figure 2, the adversary can still link C to F. However, if we now remove the restriction of one communication partner per user, then from the attacker's perspective, C may also be communicating with D and E, and it is A and B who are communicating with F. While this seems to make a difference in theory, in practice, by observing the sending patterns of C, the attacker is likely to be in a good position to deduce whether the two messages C sends are destined for the same receiver or not, hence our assumption above.

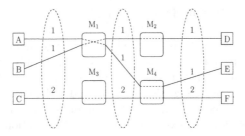

Fig. 1. Example network topology with attacker's scope of monitoring shown in dashed ellipses. From the attacker's perspective, there are two possibilities: {A–D, B–E, C–F} and {A–E, B–D, C–F}, where each user has exactly one communication partner. If this restriction is lifted, then there are two more possibilities: {A–D, B–F, C–E, C–F} and {A–F, B–D, C–E, C–F}. However, in all these cases, C must have sent at least one message to F, and so is offered no anonymity.

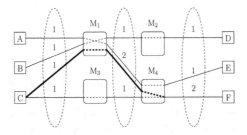

Fig. 2. Unlike Figure 1, C is provided with anonymity as there is another possibility: {A–F, B–F, C–D, C–E}. The thicker line is the new link, and we assume the attacker does not know whether there are one or two connections running over each link, only the number of packets.

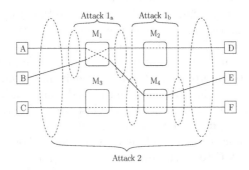

Fig. 3. Adaptive partial adversary

2.2 Adaptive Adversary

A non-global adversary can achieve the same results as a global adversary by being able to move points of monitoring, *taps*, fast enough. We call such an adversary *adaptive*. In Figure 3, Attack 1 consists of first monitoring M_1 then after establishing that the target stream, from A, goes to M_4, moving the tap there to establish the destination. This is more powerful than only monitoring inputs and outputs to the mix network, shown in Attack 2, as will be discussed further below.

In the global passive and adaptive adversary scenarios, intersection attacks are extremely difficult to defend against, so instead we consider more realistic, weaker threat models and examine how their consideration might affect the design of anonymity systems.

2.3   Partial Adversary

We have shown above that a global passive adversary can compromise anonymity through intersection attacks. As this threat model is usually considered stronger than what most realistic adversaries are capable of, this does not necessarily mean that anonymity cannot still be provided in practice. By relaxing the threat model, we can show what users can do to avoid their anonymity being compromised by a realistic adversary. In the next section we consider one particular type of partial adversary, the circumstances in which they may be encountered and how to defend against them.

The partial adversary does not monitor all links. He has a limited number of taps and may put these at some, but not all, points on the network. For example, some links may be outside his jurisdiction. Where he will place these depends on his goals. If he is interested in a particular user, he would put a tap near this user. However, if he does not know which users he is interested in or is interested in all users, he would be better advised to put the taps near as many mixes as possible, as usually there are fewer mixes than users. The key property that distinguishes the partial and the global adversary is that the partial adversary is not able to monitor all mixes or all users. Alternatively, there is at least one mix which some of the users can send traffic to, without it being observed by the attacker.

An additional restriction on the threat model would be to impose a similar restriction on the receiver side: there is at least one mix which can send messages to at least some receivers without them being observed.

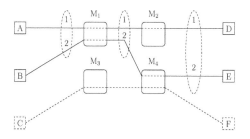

Fig. 4. Partial adversary view

As shown in Figure 4, even if an intersection attack can separate two links, if the attacker does not have a full view of all inputs and output, he cannot be sure that there is not another "2-message" connection which is unobserved. This scenario could occur if the taps are placed near M_1, D and E, but the other mixes are far away from the attacker's control.

However, if the links B to M_1 and M_4 to E both have, for example, exactly 1561 messages, then the probability of there being another connection which is unobserved, happening to have exactly the same number of packets, is low and hence the attacker can link B to E. This is, of course, a typical *traffic confirmation attack*, where the attacker confirms a previously held suspicion on sender/receiver linkage. We investigate this further in Section 3.

3 Defeating the Partial Adversary

Our method of defending against the packet-counting attack presented in the previous section is based on sending the packets via different routes through the network. First, we present the intuition, and then a concrete scheme together with an evaluation of anonymity. Finally, we note that not only does this scheme protect against the packet counting attack, but also makes various flow correlation [10] and timing attacks [12] harder.

Our definition of the attacker ensures that they will not be monitoring all the mixes to which messages will arrive from users. If the users find out which of the mixes these are, they can simply send all their traffic through them. However, this is unlikely to be the case. Hence, if a sender forwards all his traffic to a receiver via the same sequence of mixes (chosen at random), there is some probability that the traffic from him to the first mix will not be observed and hence he will remain undetected. This probability is $1 - a/n$ where a is the number of entry mixes monitored by the attacker and n is the total number of mixes. However, with probability a/n, the sender's traffic is observed, allowing the attacker to mount a simple traffic confirmation packet-counting attack and compromise the anonymity of the sender. For an exposition of this and related issues see [13, 14].

Our aim here is to present a scheme which significantly increases the probability of a sender not being traced by the attacker. To see why sending the traffic via different routes (and, crucially, via many different first nodes) helps, consider the following example.

In Figure 5, B has chosen a first mix which is being monitored. Since he is sending more data than A, and the output is monitored, the adversary knows that B is communicating with E. Of course, if B chose M_3 then he would be protected, but rather than relying on chance, if he splits the data between M_1 and M_3, as shown in Figure 6, the attacker only observes B sending one packet. Thus, the attacker cannot deduce that deduce that B really sent 2 packets and hence must have communicated with E.

Of course, not everything is as simple as might seem from the trivial examples above, but the intuition is clear – we want a scheme which hides, from a partial adversary, the number of messages sent. Several questions arise. Firstly, how

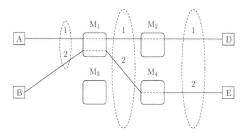

Fig. 5. Here, if B chooses M_1 rather than M_3 as his entry node, the attacker can establish that B communicates with E, and that A communicates with D

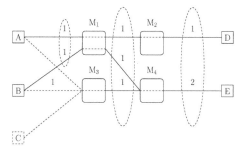

Fig. 6. By splitting the data, B hides the fact that he communicates with E, despite one of the entry nodes being monitored. The attacker is unsure whether B is communicating with E or whether A or an unmonitored C are.

should the sender choose routes for his packets, and more specifically, how many packets should he send through each of the entry nodes. Secondly, how much anonymity is really gained from this? We attempt to answer these questions in the next section.

3.1 Choosing Routes

We have made no assumptions about how the attacker monitors the messages inside the mix network, yet we want messages to be mixed to best defeat the attacker's monitoring. It is intuitively clear that after having chosen the first mix, the routes for the packets should be chosen uniformly at random, and independently from each other. The remaining problem is then how to pick the first mix on each of these routes.

Suppose the sender has s packets to send and the attacker is monitoring a out of n mixes. Sending s/n packets to each mix is not a good approach, as the attacker will observe $a \times s/n$ packets and, knowing the fraction of the mixes he is monitoring, can deduce s. A better scheme is to send c_i packets, to each mix i, where c_i is chosen from an exponential distribution. Hence, the probability of sending x packets to a particular mix is:

$$P(x) = n/se^{-n/sx}$$

Note that both the mean and the variance of this distribution is s/n. Let $\mathbf{C}$ be the set of c_i, for i in $1 \ldots n$. Call $s' = \sum_i c_i$. Now if $s' > s$, the sender can simply can add dummy packets to make up the number of packets to s'. If, however, $s < s'$, the algorithm must be rerun. Note that the probability of $\sum_i c_i \geq s = 0.5$.

Suppose the attacker observes some (s^-) messages, from which he calculates the mean and the standard deviation of the above exponential distribution in the usual fashion, call these $\hat{s_j}$. Hence the total number of messages observed by the attacker is $a\hat{s_j}$. His goal is to compute an estimate for s, the total number of messages sent. Ideally, the attacker would like to calculate the probability distribution over $\hat{s}$ and then try to mount a probabilistic version of the packet counting attack.

An easier way for him to proceed is to observe the upper and lower bounds on s, based on the his observation. The lower bound of the attacker's estimate is s^- as all the mixes the attacker was not able to observe could have received 0 packets and the upper bound is infinity. The latter is not helpful to the attacker, so we provide an alternative estimate based on a rough approximation of the 3 standard deviation event.

Based on his observations, the attacker's estimate of the total number of messages sent by the user is $n\hat{s_j}$. The attacker's estimate of the standard deviation of the exponential distribution used by the sender is also $n\hat{s_j}$. Hence, the 3 standard deviation upper bound on the number of packets sent is $n\hat{s_j} + 3\hat{s_j}\sqrt{n-a}$. Note that this estimate is based on the assumption that the numbers of packets sent to each mix were generated *independently*. Of course, they were not – if the total number of packets to be sent to the mixes was lower than the size of the actual message, the algorithm is rerun.

The attacker might try to make use of this by performing a Bayesian estimation. This requires taking a known distribution of file sizes sent through anonymous communication systems as a prior and using the observations to come up with a refined distribution. This is left for future work, mainly due to the lack of a good prior.

We have assumed that the attacker observes all the receivers, so the anonymity set of our target sender is the set of receivers who have received more than $n\hat{s_j}$ packets in the interval from when the sender sent the first message, to the attackers estimate of when all the sent messages have arrived. The length of this period varies according to the system in question; for example, in Mixminion this would be a few days after the packets were sent, as shown in Section 5.1.

However, splitting messages over several routes is not always the best option. If the sender can *a priori* determine that, even after splitting his message, the mix network will not provide him with anonymity, he should send all the messages through a single first mix. For example, this would be the case if there are no other users of the system.

This will maxmise the probability that none of his messages will pass through an observed mix. The tradeoff to be made here is beyond the scope of this paper. The route selection algorithm could also take into account the administrative domain that nodes are in, as discussed in [15], however we do not consider this option here.

We claim that we have now reduced the effectiveness of the packet counting attack. However, there are more attacks to deal with. We examine one particular attack which has recently been presented by Danezis [12, 16]. Essentially, the attacker takes a signal which represents a stream of input traffic, and a model of the mix, and convolves the two together.

The result defines the expected output. The attacker can compare this with the output traffic streams of the mix and determine which of these matches. The attack assumes that the incoming traffic is distributed according to a Poisson distribution and Danezis has shown the attack to be effective in a simulated environment under these assumptions.

Our scheme above prevents this attack being mounted on a per-mix basis: a stream of packets incoming to the first mix will scatter randomly between the outgoing links as the routes of the packet were chosen independently. Hence, rather than analysing each mix individually, the attacker has to view the entire mix network as one supermix.

Even if the attacker can see all inputs and outputs to the supermix, this is weaker than the global passive adversary threat model, as shown in Figure 7. In Attack 1, the attacker can clearly follow the data from A to D as no mixing is taking place. However in Attack 2, the supermix formed by $M_1 - M_4$ does mix the two streams.

The mix analysed in [12] is expressed via a delay characteristic. The delay characteristic is the probability distribution over the possible delays experienced by incoming messages. To mount this attack, we therefore need to know the characteristic delay function of our anonymity system abstracted as a mix.

There are two possible approaches: either to combine models of mixes into a model of a *complex mix* or to empirically measure the characteristics of the system as a whole. We present both approaches, and show that they run into difficulties. While this does not prove that such attacks are impossible to mount, they do bring into question their effectiveness in realistic environments.

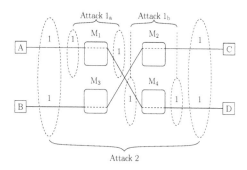

Fig. 7. Adaptive partial adversary versus supermix analysis

4 Deriving Delay Properties of "Complex Mixes"

As Serjantov et al. observed in [17], there are two main types of mix delay strategies: timed and threshold. Here we attempt to suggest characteristic delay functions for combinations of each of these types of mixes.

4.1 Timed Mixes

We assume that message arrival is uniformly distributed over the time period t, in other words, when the user sends his message, he is not aware of when the mix flushes, or he does not take that knowledge into account. In this case, the delay characteristic of a timed mix is rather simple – it is the uniform distribution between 0 and t. Note that the delay characteristic of a cascade of i timed mixes is a uniform distribution between 0 and a point in the interval between t and ti (depending on how the mixes are synchronised).

The characteristic delay function for a timed pool mix, however, depends on traffic levels which, as shown in [18], do not follow a well known probability distribution. This is because the probability of a message remaining in the mix depends on how many messages arrive at the mix during the same round.

The only easy case here is if the attacker assumes that the traffic arrives at a constant rate. In this case, the characteristic delay function is a discretized geometric distribution. If the delay is measured in rounds

$$P(\text{delay} = i) = p^{i-1}q$$

where $p = n/n + f$, n being the constant number of messages in the mix at each round and f the constant size of the pool. Of course, the above is also the probability of ti seconds delay.

The characteristic function of a cascade of m timed pool mixes is:

$$P(\text{delay} = i) = \binom{m}{i-m} p^{i-m}q^m$$

If a timed pool mix works on the basis of having a constant probability, p, of forwarding a message (a variant of the Timed Dynamic Pool Mix [11]), then its characteristic delay function is exactly the one given above. Nevertheless, these examples are slightly contrived. A more sensible mix would have a minimum pool or alter the probability of forwarding each message, based on how many messages are inside the pool [19]. From this we can safely conclude that deriving accurate characteristic delay functions for realistic timed mixes is infeasible without knowledge of the distribution of message arrivals.

4.2 Threshold Mixes

The situation is not any better with threshold mixes. Calculating the characteristic delay function for a simple threshold mix already requires assumptions on traffic and hence has the problems detailed above and in [18].

As one might expect, under the constant traffic assumption, the characteristic delay of the threshold pool mix, in rounds, is the same as that of the corresponding timed pool mix.

The characteristic delay function of a network of threshold mixes requires not only assumptions about traffic arrivals to the network, but also about the choice of routes that users take for their messages. Indeed [2, Chapter 6] suggests that calculating the delay of a mix network of threshold mixes is as hard as calculating the anonymity of it.

5   Estimating Delay Properties of Complex Mixes

One possible approach which can be used in practice is simply to sample the network under appropriate traffic conditions (i.e. those similar to the time when the target message is sent) and hence obtain the characteristic delay function. In order to test our assumptions and evaluate the consequences of our proposals, we attempted to measure the effective delay function of the Mixmaster and Mixminion "supermix" over 26 days.

The client software was run in its default configuration, except for Mixminion, where we forced the path length to 4 (by default it varies). To avoid our probe messages interfering which each other, we kept no more of our messages in the system than there are mixes. Latency data was collected by a Python [20] script and graphed in GNU R [21], based on a design described in [22]. This data is available for download[2].

We would, of course, have liked to evaluate the characteristic delay function of a more real-time anonymity system than Mixmaster or Mixminion, but the obvious candidate, Tor, optimises for efficiency and does not aim to protect itself from this attack. Hence, in order to demonstrate the difficulty of calculating the characteristic delay function, we have resorted to attempting to estimate it for the above systems.

5.1   Results

The distribution of measured latencies is shown in Figure 8, and the change of latency over time is shown in Figure 9, along with the distribution of latencies in two selected intervals. A statistical summary of the full data set, as well as the selected intervals, is shown in Table 1.

As can be seen, Mixmaster has a larger median latency than Mixminion. This is because Mixminion is currently in alpha so, by default, nodes use a 10-minute timed mix. This is more useful for testing but is belived to be less secure than the proposed final algorithm. The algorithms used by Mixminion nodes at the time of writing is shown in Table 2. Although the latency for most messages is below the 4×10 min limit expected for a path length of 4, 44% are above. Some of these are explained by the nodes using non-default mixing algorithms, but others are due to nodes which fail and later recover.

---

[2] http://www.cl.cam.ac.uk/users/sjm217/projects/anon/

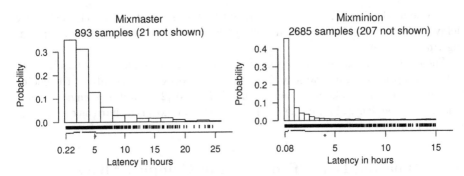

Fig. 8. Latency measurements of Mixmaster and Mixminion

Table 1. Summary of data collected

	Mixmaster latency (hours)			Mixminion latency (hours)		
	Overall	Range 1	Range 2	Overall	Range 1	Range 2
Min.	0.22	0.25	0.22	0.08	0.08	0.08
Q.1	1.49	1.54	1.30	0.36	0.36	0.34
Med.	2.70	2.91	2.60	0.55	0.51	0.51
Q.3	5.23	5.36	4.72	2.05	1.75	2.17
Max.	123.70	44.78	25.79	136.40	100.10	136.40
Mean	5.10	4.78	4.09	4.01	3.27	7.76

Table 2. Mixminion node mixing algorithms. A timed mix flushes all messages from the pool after every mix interval. A dynamic pool, as is used in Mixmaster, flushes a randomly selected set of messages after every mix interval, such that the pool size never falls below the pool minimum size, and the percentage of the pool sent out is no more than the pool rate. A binomial dynamic pool flushes a randomly chosen number of messages, based on the number that would be flushed using the dynamic pool algorithm.

Number of nodes	Mixing algorithm
25	Timed. Mix interval: 10 min (*default configuration*)
2	Timed. Mix interval: 15 min
1	Timed. Mix interval: 20 min
1	Timed. Mix interval: 30 min
1	Dynamic pool. Mix interval: 30 min, Pool Rate: 50%, Pool Minimum Size: 5
1	Binomial dynamic pool. Mix interval: 10 min, Pool Rate: 70%, Pool Minimum Size: 3
1	Binomial dynamic pool. Mix interval: 30 min, Pool Rate: 50%, Pool Minimum Size: 5

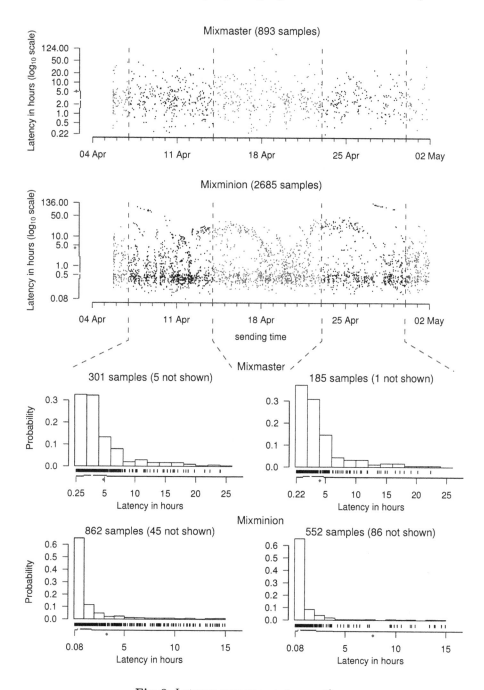

Fig. 9. Latency measurements over time

6   Conclusion

In this paper we examined the problem of sending a large message (more precisely, a sequence of many messages) through mix networks. Firstly, we presented a well-defined notion of a partial adversary threat model. We then show that in the presence of this adversary, sending packets via different routes through a mix network yields increased anonymity. To perform a packet counting attack, the attacker must now know the total number of fragments a message was split into, but by distributing the fragments over entry mixes using a non-uniform distribution, a partial adversary is uncertain as to the total. Finally, we demonstrate that intersection attacks relying on knowledge of the characteristic delay function, while powerful, are more difficult to perform on deployed mix designs than previously thought. This is due to the dependency of message latency on input traffic, which is not known and difficult to estimate. This supports previous observations on the unpredictability of traffic in anonymity systems.

Acknowledgements

We thank Roger Dingledine and the anonymous reviewers for their insightful comments, George Danezis for his honest feedback, and Len Sassaman for helpful suggestions on improving this paper.

References

1. Pfitzmann, A., Köhntopp, M.: Anonymity, unobservability, and pseudonymity: A proposal for terminology. Draft, version 0.17 (2000)
2. Serjantov, A.: On the Anonymity of Anonymity Systems. PhD thesis, University of Cambridge (2004)
3. Danezis, G., Dingledine, R., Mathewson, N.: Mixminion: Design of a Type III Anonymous Remailer Protocol. In: Proceedings of the 2003 IEEE Symposium on Security and Privacy. (2003)
4. Dingledine, R., Mathewson, N., Syverson, P.: Tor: The second-generation onion router. In: Proceedings of the 13th USENIX Security Symposium. (2004)
5. Kesdogan, D., Pimenidis, L.: The hitting set attack on anonymity protocols. In: Proceedings of 6th Information Hiding Workshop (IH 2004). LNCS, Toronto (2004)
6. Kesdogan, D., Agrawal, D., Penz, S.: Limits of anonymity in open environments. In Petitcolas, F., ed.: Proceedings of Information Hiding Workshop (IH 2002), Springer-Verlag, LNCS 2578 (2002)
7. Agrawal, D., Kesdogan, D., Penz, S.: Probabilistic Treatment of MIXes to Hamper Traffic Analysis. In: Proceedings of the 2003 IEEE Symposium on Security and Privacy. (2003)
8. Danezis, G.: Statistical disclosure attacks: Traffic confirmation in open environments. In Gritzalis, Vimercati, Samarati, Katsikas, eds.: Proceedings of Security and Privacy in the Age of Uncertainty, (SEC2003), Athens, IFIP TC11, Kluwer (2003) 421–426
9. Danezis, G., Serjantov, A.: Statistical disclosure or intersection attacks on anonymity systems. In: Proceedings of 6th Information Hiding Workshop (IH 2004). LNCS, Toronto (2004)

10. Zhu, Y., Fu, X., Graham, B., Bettati, R., Zhao, W.: On flow correlation attacks and countermeasures in mix networks. In: Proceedings of Privacy Enhancing Technologies workshop (PET 2004). LNCS (2004)
11. Möller, U., Cottrell, L., Palfrader, P., Sassaman, L.: Mixmaster Protocol – Version 2. Draft (2003)
12. Danezis, G.: The traffic analysis of continuous-time mixes. In: Proceedings of Privacy Enhancing Technologies workshop (PET 2004). LNCS (2004)
13. Syverson, P., Tsudik, G., Reed, M., Landwehr, C.: Towards an Analysis of Onion Routing Security. In Federrath, H., ed.: Proceedings of Designing Privacy Enhancing Technologies: Workshop on Design Issues in Anonymity and Unobservability, Springer-Verlag, LNCS 2009 (2000) 96–114
14. Wright, M., Adler, M., Levine, B.N., Shields, C.: An analysis of the degradation of anonymous protocols. In: Proceedings of the Network and Distributed Security Symposium – NDSS '02, IEEE (2002)
15. Feamster, N., Dingledine, R.: Location diversity in anonymity networks. In: Proceedings of the Workshop on Privacy in the Electronic Society (WPES 2004), Washington, DC, USA (2004)
16. Danezis, G.: Better Anonymous Communications. PhD thesis, University of Cambridge (2004)
17. Serjantov, A., Dingledine, R., Syverson, P.: From a trickle to a flood: Active attacks on several mix types. In Petitcolas, F., ed.: Proceedings of Information Hiding Workshop (IH 2002), Springer-Verlag, LNCS 2578 (2002)
18. Díaz, C., Sassaman, L., Dewitte, E.: Comparison between two practical mix designs. In: Proceedings of 9th European Symposium Research in Computer Security (ESORICS). LNCS, France (2004)
19. Díaz, C., Serjantov, A.: Generalising mixes. In Dingledine, R., ed.: Proceedings of Privacy Enhancing Technologies workshop (PET 2003), Springer-Verlag, LNCS 2760 (2003)
20. Python Software Foundation: Python. http://www.python.org/ (2003)
21. R Development Core Team: R: A language and environment for statistical computing. R Foundation for Statistical Computing, Vienna, Austria. (2004) ISBN 3-900051-07-0 http://www.R-project.org/.
22. Tufte, E.R.: The Visual Display of Quantitative Information. 2nd edn. Graphics Press (1992) ISBN 0-961392-10-X.

Location Privacy for Cellular Systems; Analysis and Solution

Geir M. Køien[1,2] and Vladimir A. Oleshchuk[1]

[1] Agder University College, Groosevn.36, N-4876 Grimstad, Norway
{Geir.Koien, Vladimir.Oleshchuk}@HiA.no
[2] Telenor R&D, Snarøyveien 30, N-1331 Fornebu, Norway

Abstract. Mobility is an inherent characteristic of cellular systems, and subscriber location is an essential attribute at the access link level. The system must know both user identity and location in order to forward calls/data to the user. The system is required to protect user identity and location data from eavesdropping. The system should also provide location/identity privacy with respect to the system entities. This paper presents a privacy preserving 3-way authentication and key agreement (PP3WAKA) protocol that archives this goal.

1 Introduction

1.1 Background and Motivation

A cellular system has three principal parties at the access level.

- **User Entity (UE).** The UE will normally consist of a mobile device and a tamper-resistant security module.
- **Serving Network (SN).** The physical access network provider, consisting of access points (AP) and mobility handling servers.
- **Home Server (HS).** The HS manages the UE subscription data, including subscriber services and global location handling. The HS assigns the permanent UE identity and the HS-UE security credentials.

A cellular service provider may own both HS and SN (or a set of SNs) entities. We shall consider HS and SN as independent entities since this is general case.

Location and identity privacy is emerging as an important topic for future cellular systems. The current 2G/3G cellular systems only have a rudimentary location privacy mechanism in place [1,2,3]. Home control is also a growing issue. Unfortunately, the home control requirements will often be contradictory to UE privacy requirements.

1.2 Cellular Access Security and Privacy

To understand cellular access security architectures one must understand how identity presentation, user registration and mobility is handled in cellular systems. We shall only give a brief account of cellular access security here, and refer the reader to [2,4,5,6] for a fuller account.

G. Danezis and D. Martin (Eds.): PET 2005, LNCS 3856, pp. 40–58, 2006.

The HS operator is responsible for its subscribers, and this is a concern when the subscribers roam onto foreign networks. The HS must be in control in order to protect its business and its subscribers. The user (UE) wants to have location and identity privacy, and this also applies to unwanted monitoring by the HS and SN. Cellular access services are not free. The SN therefore needs an authenticated reference to the UE in order to get the HS to accept the charging on behalf of the UE. In addition, we expect regulatory authorities to require *Lawful Interception* capabilities. This includes tracking of UE location and identity data.

A modern 3G system consists of a bewildering number of network nodes, channel types, signaling procedures etc. We shall not go into details here, but note that UE identity is presented in clear for three of the four main procedures (see Appendix A for more information on the mobility procedures).

Identity presentation for initial 3G registration is in cleartext over the radio interface every time the subscriber registers with a new SN operator and possibly also when the subscriber moves from one SN server to another. Subsequently, a temporary identity is used. This scheme allows for some protection against identity eavesdropping, but is insufficient for active attacks. See appendix B for specifics of 2G/3G subscriber identities and the identity confidentiality scheme.

1.3   Control and Privacy Issues

Privacy shortcomings of 3G. The 3GPP security architecture [2] defines the following user identity confidentiality requirements (abridged):

- **User identity confidentiality:** the property that the permanent user identity cannot be eavesdropped on the radio access link;
- **User location confidentiality:** the property that presence or arrival of a user in an area cannot be determined by eavesdropping on the radio link;
- **User untraceability:** the property that an intruder cannot deduce whether different services are delivered to the same user.

The 3GPP security architecture does not capture the case were one requires identity/location privacy from cellular system entities. This is increasingly the case, since one cannot realistically expect the SN (there may be several hundred different SNs) to adhere to the HS/UE privacy policy.

Location determination can either be done by the UE or by the SN. The SN, due to characteristics of the radio system, will always know the approximate distance between the access point (AP) and the UE. Unless the UE can verify the SN position data, the UE will have to trust the SN on this matter (or disregard location measurements altogether). The HS will never be able to independently derive or otherwise establish the UE position. It must trust the UE and/or SN in this matter. See appendix C for more on location determination.

We have established that the SN will inevitably learn the UE position. So there is no point in trying to hide the UE position from the SN. We have a corresponding situation for identity information. Due to routing issues etc, the HS must know the permanent UE identity. We have the following:

- **Eavesdropping and manipulation:** The system must ensure that the permanent UE identity under no circumstance is revealed over the A-Interface (UE-SN). An adversary may want to track a specific, but unidentified, UE and the system must protect the UE from this type of tracking.
- **UE location privacy from HS monitoring:** There may be legitimate reasons for a HS to request UE position data, but it is not evident that it is in the best interest of the UE to reveal its position to the HS.
- **UE identity privacy from SN monitoring:** The SN has a need for an authenticated UE identity, but there is no real need for the UE to know the *permanent* UE identity. Any unique identity will be sufficient provided SN gets assurance from HS that it accepts responsibility for the subscriber. To ensure untraceability, the identity must appear to be completely independent from the permanent identity or any previous (temporary) identities.

We have the following trust relationships in a cellular system.

- **HS-UE:** The UE is a subscriber with HS. The HS has security jurisdiction over the UE. We assume mutual trust.
- **HS-SN:** The HS and SN has a roaming agreement that allows HS subscribers to roam onto the SN network. Roaming agreements are normally mutual and bi-directional. We assume mutual trust.
- **UE-SN:** The UE and SN have no a priori agreements. In cellular system one will assume that the trust is transitive and that the UE and SN may therefore attain a level of mutual (indirect) trust.

The trust level between the parties should be limited to a minimum. With respect to system internal entities, we assume that the HS and SN are semi-trusted by the UE with regard to location (UE-HS) and identity (UE-SN). We assume that the derived transitive UE-SN trust relation is weaker than the direct relations. We therefore require this trust relationship to be timely and validated by the HS during security context establishment. The security context establishment should therefore be online and should explicitly include all three principals.

Home Control Issues. The AKA protocols used in 2G/3G are two-staged delegated off-line protocols (Fig.1) [3,4]. This implies that charging control is delegated to the SN. Trust can be seen as the intersection of beliefs and dependence. In the early days of mobile systems there were few and generally trustworthy operators, and one could defend believes that the roaming partner would not be deceitful. The GSM Association now has 650 2G/3G operator members serving more than 1.2 billion customers in 210 countries and territories(Dec. 2004). It is therefore clear that unqualified trust in the roaming partners cannot be justified and that the HS requirement for enhanced home control is legitimate.

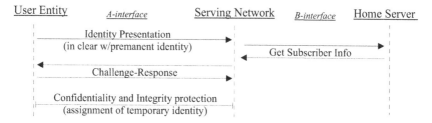

Fig. 1. Simplified initial 2G/3G registration and authentication

Exposure control dimensions. The concept of security credential exposure control is not new. Security protocols like IPsec [9] have mechanisms for controlling the temporal exposure (seconds) and the usage exposure (KBytes). For a cellular system one can envisage a spatial exposure dimension [7,8]. This may sound far fetched, but some SN operators are becoming global enterprises and with improved naming/addressing structures they may be able present a single external network-wide entry point to the HS. Unless regulatory regimes dictate it, we must assume that SN will not want to reveal network topology details (like network node locations) to its roaming partners (who likely are competitors in other markets). The HS may then be left with little control over its subscribers. Under these circumstances spatial home control is an issue.

2 Premises for an Enhanced Authentication and Key Agreement Protocol

2.1 Principals, Identities and Communication

We have three principal (UE,HS,SN) entities. We denote the respective identities $UEID$, $HSID$ and $SNID$. Communication between the parties will be over the *A-interface* and over the *B-interface*. Communication between UE and HS may logically be end-to-end, but will physically always be forwarded through the SN. The layout presented in Figure 1 is therefore still valid.

2.2 Observations and Derived Requirements

High-performance future cellular system will have high-capacity radio systems and a sophisticated radio resource scheduling mechanism in order to deliver high quality low latency IP-based services [10]. A security architecture must match these characteristics and meet the latency requirements of such a system [3]. This means that the number of round-trips must be minimized.

A 3-Way security context. We have stated that we need an online AKA protocol to allow improved Home Control. The AKA protocol for 3GPP-WLAN interworking [11, 12] achieves this by making the 3GPP AKA protocol global. However, this solution leaves the SN with little authority. We therefore insist that all parties participates actively in the AKA protocol execution.

Context Hierarchy. There is a natural hierarchy in the security contexts. The hierarchy have simultaneously both a temporal and a spatial dimension [3].

- **Long-term:** The long-term security contexts are based on roaming agreements (SN-HS) and service subscriptions (UE-HS).
- **Medium-term:** The medium-term context is established dynamically on the basis of the long-term contexts, and it includes the UE, SN and HS. The validity is restricted according to area, time and usage patterns.
- **Short-term:** The short-term contexts are derived from the medium-term context. It encompasses session key material. These contexts are short lived and will only have local validity (UE-SN).

The short-term session keys used to protect communication over the A-interface are derived from the medium-term context. Both the SN and the UE should be able to influence the key derivation. We should also be careful to not assume usage symmetry, and it is therefore sound practice to have uni-directional key sets. This will also allow for a modest measure of initiator resilience [13].

2.3   Computational Balance

The UE must be able to compute the AKA functions on-the-fly. Modern mobile devices are capable of executing all the required cryptographic functions with ease. This is true even if we assume usage of computationally expensive algorithms including Identity-Based Encryption (IBE) transformations, Diffie-Hellman (DH) exchanges and Secure Multi-party Computations (SMC).

The SN must participate actively in a privacy preserving 3-way AKA protocol. We note that the SN nodes will serve a comparatively large number of users and must be able to execute the AKA protocol on-demand. The instantaneous processing requirements may therefore be demanding, but not all sequences require real-time processing. For instance, security context renewal can be executed prior to context expiry. Pre-computation may also be possible for some operations (for instance by pre-computing DH parameters).

The HS will serve a large number of subscribers. To instantly compute context credentials may create a substantial load. AKA events are time critical, and for HS operators with distinct *busy hour* conditions it may be a problem to serve all users. The HS must therefore be dimensioned for a high instantaneous crypto-processing load. Still, with optimized crypto-primitives implemented in hardware we postulate that the capacity required need not be excessive [17].

2.4   Communication Capacity Balance

The A-interface. The radio channel is a shared physically restricted resource. There will necessarily be capacity restrictions. These restrictions will not severely affect the modest capacity requirements for signaling, but there are commonly restrictions on signaling message size during the initial phase of set-up events. This may preclude and complicate support for primitives that requires large information elements (IEs) (e.g. Diffie-Hellman based key generation). Support for data expanding ($E_K(M) \rightarrow C$, *where* $|C| \gg |M|$) primitives is also problematic.

The B-interface is a fixed network interfaces. There should be no capacity problems for the B-interface.

2.5 Environmental Aspects

Temporal aspects. The AKA protocol will be executed under real-time constraints. Processing delays are part of the induced delays, but the most important delay factor is in practice the number of round-trips required to executed the procedures [7,3]. The 3G AKA is a single pass protocol. However, one assumes that identity presentation has been executed and that the AKA (successful case) acknowledge is implicit (by virtue of a next normal signaling event). Furthermore, the 3G AKA relies on a sequence number scheme to achieve the one-pass quality. We consider use of sequence numbers to introduce unwanted complexity and potential weaknesses (ch.10 [14]), and we shall avoid it in our design.

Signaling optimization will allow us to relax the round-trip requirements. In the current 2G/3G systems one has divided the Radio Resource Management (RRM), the Mobility Management (MM) and Security procedures into separate signaling sequences. Today this is an artificial division, and we note that the triggering events for some procedures are identical [3,10]. For instance, the MM Initial Registration procedure, which includes identity presentation, is inevitably executed in conjunction with the authentication procedure. By integrating these procedures one can cut down on the total number of round-trips.

A combined MM registration and AKA procedure will require the UE to be the initiator (the registration **must** be initiated by the UE). In 2G/3G the AKA protocol is always initiated by the network, but a UE initiated scheme is beneficial since it will help facilitate improved identity privacy.

2.6 Location Privacy vs Spatial Home Control

Spatial Home Control and Validity Area. We must accept that the HS may need to know if the UE is located within some validity area (VA), but no other information should be disclosed to the HS. The get spatial home control the HS must define a VA for the roaming UEs.

The area should be sufficiently large as to be valid for normal UE mobility during the temporal validity period of the medium-term context. That is, the HS should ideally not need to require periodic VA re-verification. We assume that VA verification is done exclusively with the HS. See [7,8] for a discussion of spatial control, privacy and practical aspects of validity area definitions.

Location privacy from SN monitoring hinges on the SN not knowing the permanent UE identity. To solve this problem we propose to let the UE choose a context reference identity ($CRID$). The $CRID$ must be constructed such that there is no apparent correlation between the $UEID$ and the $CRID$. The $CRID$ will act as the common (authenticated) reference to the 3-party medium-term security context. Since we want the HS to be able to forward data to the UE, we must allow the HS to learn the $CRID$-$UEID$ association. But, importantly, the SN must not be able to learn the $UEID$-$CRID$ association or the $UEID$.

The context reference collision frequency experienced by SN and/or HS servers must very low. If we assume that there is no bias to the $CRID$ choices, we can use the approximation $p = k/m$, where p is collision probability, k the max. no. of users within the SN server area and m is the range of the $CRID$. Let us unrealistically assume that an SN can serve one billion simultaneous users ($k = 10^9$). If we conservatively require the collision to occur for at most every 100 million AKA occurrence ($p = 1/10^8$), we have that $CRID$ must have a range of $m = 10^{17}$. The $CRID$ variable must therefore have a range of ≥ 57 bits.

To protect the UE against tracking we also require the UE-SN to use a local temporary alias identity ($TAID$) for cleartext presentation. The $TAID$, which will be associated with the $CRID$, is assigned by the SN during a confidentiality protected session. The $TAID$ will be used for paging- and access request purposes. The $TAID$ should ideally be assigned for one-time use, but it may be used a limited number of times before being replaced by a new $TAID$. There should be no apparent correlation between a $CRID$ and the $TAID$, and there should be no apparent correlation between subsequent $TAID$s.

2.7 Secure Multi-party Computation (SMC)

We propose to let the SN transfer the UE location (x, y) in protected form to the HS. The HS will not be able to learn the (x, y) location, but it will be able to determine whether the UE is within the validity area (VA) by running a *point-inclusion* algorithm. SMC methods, being based on asymmetric homomorphic cryptographic primitives, will tend to require relatively large amounts of data. This may be an issue over the A-interface, but is of no concern of the B-interface.

Verification of SN observed UE position. If the UE is able to independently determine its position, the UE will indicate this to the HS. The HS may then, subsequent to normal AKA execution, request the UE to report its location. The (x', y') must be confidentiality protected against HS and SN. This procedure is executed after the AKA and is therefore not time critical. The HS verifies the UE position by computing the distance between (x, y) and (x', y'). If the distance between the UE and SN reported positions is within some limit L, the HS accepts the location. Otherwise, the *point-inclusion* algorithm must be re-run for (x', y').

2.8 Spatio-temporal Binding of the Medium-Term Security Context

The observed radio environment parameters can be used to bind the medium-term security context to an SN area. In a public cellular environment the UE will learn the SN identity, the SN area code (AC) etc. The UE can then bind $SNID$ and the AC to the context and thus create a local spatial validity to the context. When the UE move outside the area it must initiate a new AKA sequence to create a new context. The area should cover a set of access points, and should be sufficiently large to avoid causing excessively frequent AKA execution. We certainly do not want to trigger AKA events for every handover or for every (idle mode) cell relocation. The access network topology/hierarchy suggests that the spatial binding should be associated with a radio network controller area or with a network access server area. Traffic re-location/handover can be performed seamlessly within the area (radio network controller or network access server) since the security context handling is at the aggregate level. Handovers that cross area boundaries will require more preparation, but note that the UE will necessarily be able to read the broadcast channel of the target cell. Immediately after a *"prepare handover to cell xx"* command the UE initiate the AKA event. The "new AKA" may be run over the old cell control channel or over the new channel while retaining traffic on the old channel. The new context is then made available prior to traffic relocation. One may alternatively permit the old context to exist for a grace period at the new cell, and then renew the context there (this will reduce the real-time impact). Note that the SN will be able to correlate $CRID$ values during handover by correlating the channel assignments. We also propose to bind the context to a validity period. The UE has an independent clock and can include an expiry period in the context. By choosing a new $CRID$ for every AKA event, the UE will escape SN tracking (except for handover).

3   The Design of the PP3WAKA Protocol

3.1   3-Way Authentication and Key Agreement

There are few 3-way protocols described in the literature, and they do not seem to fit our environment very well. For instance, the 3-partite DH-protocol suggested by Joux [15] may be computationally feasible but will probably be too expensive in terms of communication capacity requirements (A-interface). We have therefore chosen to design our own 3-way AKA protocol to meet the specific needs of cellular access security.

3.2   The Case for Identity-Based Encryption (IBE)

The idea of IBE dates back to 1984 when Shamir [16] asked for a public key encryption scheme in which the public key is an arbitrary text string. The first acceptable solution to the IBE problem appeared in a paper by Boneh and Franklin [18]. The IBE scheme is based on three principals and four main functions. Our principals are UE, SN and HS (the Private Key Generator - PKG). The functions *Setup* and *Extract* are executed by the PKG, while *Encrypt* and *Decrypt* are executed by the UE and the SN respectively. (Please refer to [18] for a fuller account of the IBE functions.)

Our motivation for use of IBE instead of conventional asymmetrical cryptographic methods is the effortless and immediate context binding IBE will permit us to create. There is no need for a priori distribution of digital certificates, the UE can enter a new area and immediately construct and use the public *ID* key. This allows for fast set-up and for improved flexibility in the context binding.

3.3   Secure Multi-part Computation

The Point Inclusion Problem. The problem we are going to study in this section is known as the *point inclusion problem* [19, 20]. It can be defined as following: Alice has a point z and Bob has a polygon P. The problem is to have a decision procedure for determining whether z is located within the polygon P such that Alice does not have to disclose any information about the point z to Bob or that Bob does not have to disclose information on the polygon P to Alice. The only fact to be revealed through the procedure is the answer to the problem. The problem is a special case of the general secure multi-party computation problem and can be solved by using circuit evaluation protocol [22]. However such solution is impractical because of high communication complexity. Therefore special solutions of the problem has been proposed in the literature [19, 20, 21]. They are more efficient but still impractical to be used in the framework described in this paper with respect to consumed computational resources, the number of signaling rounds trips required, and the volume of data exchanged.

Secure Two-Party Location Inclusion Protocol based on homomorphic public-key cryptosystems. We propose a secure two-party privacy-preserving protocol that has lower communication complexity than described in literature [19, 20, 21]. As it has been mentioned in [21] efficient solutions for 2-party model are usually difficult to find. Let us select a public-key cryptosystem with homomorphic property where encryption and decryption are denoted as $E(\bullet)$ and $D(\bullet)$ respectively. That is, there is an operation on encrypted data, denoted $\oplus$, that can be used to perform addition of the data without decryption. That is we assume that $E(x) \oplus E(y) = E(x + y)$. Many such systems have been proposed in the literature [24, 25, 26]. Further, since $E(x) \oplus E(y) = E(x + y)$.,
then $E(2x) = \underbrace{E(x) \oplus E(x)}_{2}$ and $E(xy) = \underbrace{E(x) \oplus \cdots \oplus E(x)}_{y}$. So we can mul-
tiply encrypted data if one of the multipliers is known. This is what we need in the protocol described later in this section. To simplify further notation and make our protocol independent of particular selected homomorphic public-key cryptosystem we assume that operations $\oplus$ and $\otimes$ on encrypted data are defined as following:

$$E(x) \oplus E(y) = E(x + y)$$
$$E(x) \otimes E(y) = E(xy)$$

In order to perform the second operation we need one of multipliers in decrypted form, since $E(x, y) = E(\underbrace{x + x + \cdots + x}_{y}) = \underbrace{E(x) \oplus \cdots \oplus E(x)}_{y}$. Note that generally the expression $\underbrace{E(x) \oplus \cdots \oplus E(x)}_{y}$ does not mean either $E(x) \cdot y$ or $E(y) \otimes y$.

We assume that polygon P can be presented as a set of functions $\{f_i(x, y) \,|\, i = 1, 2, ..., n\}$ where $f_i(x, y) = 0$ represents the equation of the line boundary of the polygon P. We can also assume that functions $\{f_i(x, y) \,|\, i = 1, 2, ..., m\}$ represent the edges of the lower part of the boundary and $\{f_i(x, y) \,|\, i = m + 1, ..., n\}$

represent the edges of the upper part of the boundary. Therefore a location $z = (\alpha, \beta)$ is inside the polygon P if $f_i(\alpha, \beta) > 0$, $i = 1, 2, ..., m$ and $f_i(\alpha, \beta) < 0$, $i = m+1, ..., n$. Further in the paper we assume that the polygon $P = \{g_i(x, y) \,|\, i = 1, ..., n\}$, where

$$g_i(x, y) = \begin{cases} f_i(x, y) & \text{for } i = 1, 2, ..., m \\ -f_i(x, y) & \text{for } i = m+1, ..., n \end{cases}$$

Thus location $z = (\alpha, \beta)$ is inside P if and only if $g_i(\alpha, \beta) > 0$ for all $i = 1, 2, ..., n$. It is easy to see that $g_i(x, y) = a_i x + b_i y = (a_i, b_i) \cdot (x, y)$, that is $g_i(\alpha, \beta)$ can be calculated as a scalar product of (a_i, b_i) and (α, β). Therefore $g_i(x, y)$ can be defined by (a_i, b_i). We assume that Alice (**SN**) knows location z and Bob (**HS**) knows polygon P, and they don't want to disclose information about P and z to each other. However, for home control reasons, Bob wants to know whether the location reported by Alice is inside the polygon.

Protocol: (*Secure Two-Party Location Inclusion Protocol (S2PLIP)*)
Inputs: Alice has a location $z = (\alpha, \beta)$, and Bob has a polygon $P = \{(a_i, b_i) \,|\, i = 1, 2, ..., n\}$; Both Alice and Bob use the same homomorphic public-key cryptosystem (E, D).
Outputs: Bob gets information whether z inside P without knowing more about z and without disclosing P to Alice.

1. Bob generates a key pair for a homomorphic public key cryptosystem and sends the public key to Alice. The corresponding encryption and decryption are denoted as $E(\bullet)$ and $D(\bullet)$, respectively.
2. Bob sends polygon $E(P) = \{(E(a_i), E(b_i)) \,|\, i = 1, ..., n\}$ and $E(\bullet)$ to Alice.
3. Alice calculates encrypted values of $E(g_i(\alpha, \beta))$ without decrypting g_i and encrypting z as following:

$$\begin{aligned} E(g_i(\alpha, \beta)) &= (E(a_i), E_k(b_i)) \cdot (E(\alpha), E_k(\beta)) \\ &= E(a_i) \otimes E(\alpha) \oplus E(b_i) \otimes E(\beta) \\ &= E(a_i \alpha) \oplus E(b_i \beta) \\ &= E(a_i \alpha + b_i \beta) = r_i \end{aligned}$$

Note that α, β are known to Alice but not to Bob. The result is $\{r_1, r_2, ..., r_n\}$.

4. Alice generates a random value v, calculates $\widehat{v} = (r_{i_1} \oplus E(v))$, and asks Bob to decrypt $\widehat{v} = E(g_{i_1}(\alpha, \beta)) \oplus E(v) = E(g_{i_1}(\alpha, \beta) + v)$, where i_1 is a random element from $\{1, 2, ..., n\}$.
5. Bob returns $D(\widehat{v}) = D(E(g_{i_1}(\alpha, \beta) + v)) = g_{i_1}(\alpha, \beta) + v$ to Alice
6. Alice calculates $D(r_{i_1}) = g_{i_1}(\alpha, \beta) = D(E(g_{i_1}(\alpha, \beta) + v)) - v$
7. Alice permutes $r_1, r_2, ..., r_n$ into $r_{i_1}, r_{i_2}, ..., r_{i_n}$, find $D(r_{i_1})$ and calculates

$$\begin{aligned} e_1 &= r_{i_1} + r_{i_2} + ... + r_{i_n} \\ &= E(g_{i_1}(\alpha, \beta)) + E(g_{i_2}(\alpha, \beta)) + ... + E(g_{i_n}(\alpha, \beta)) \\ &= E(g_{i_1}(\alpha, \beta) + g_{i_2}(\alpha, \beta) + ... + g_{i_n}(\alpha, \beta)) \end{aligned}$$

and

$$e_j = D\left(r_{i_1}\right) r_{i_j} = D\left(E(g_{i_1}\left(\alpha, \beta\right))\right) E(g_{i_j}\left(\alpha, \beta\right))$$
$$= g_{i_1}\left(\alpha, \beta\right) E(g_{i_j}\left(\alpha, \beta\right))$$
$$= E(g_{i_1}\left(\alpha, \beta\right) g_{i_j}\left(\alpha, \beta\right)), \text{ for } j = 2, ..., n$$

8. Alice permutes $e_1, e_2, ..., e_n$ into $e_{i_1}, e_{i_2}, ..., e_{i_n}$ and sends its to Bob.
9. Bob decrypts $e_{i_1}, e_{i_2}, ..., e_{i_n}$ and concludes that Alice is inside the polygon P if all decrypted values are positive, that is $D(e_{i_j}) > 0$.

3.4 Diffie-Hellman Exchange

We use a Diffie-Hellman exchange between the SN and the HS to derive the medium-term security context shared secret, but observe that the DH-secret is to be used between SN and UE. This avoids the capacity restrictions on the A-interface. Since the shared secret may be used multiple times during the lifetime of the security context, we propose to use a 256 bit shared secret. For a conventional DH-exchange this will require approx. 15K bit parameters.

4 The PP3WAKA Protocol

4.1 Outline of the PP3WAKA Protocol

The purpose of the *Privacy Preserving 3-Way Authentication and Key Agreement (PP3WAKA)* protocol is to establish a medium-term security context. This includes establishment of a context identity $(CRID)$ and a temporary alias identity $(TAID)$. The $CRID$ shall live for the duration of the medium-term security context. The $TAID$ is assigned in confidentiality protected form.

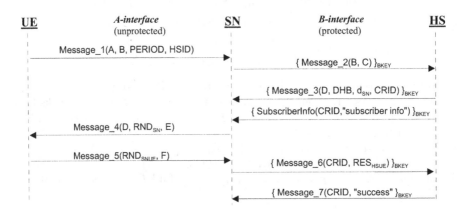

Fig. 2. Overview of the PP3WAKA protocol

4.2   The PP3WAKA Step-by-Step

The PP3WAKA protocol steps:

1. UE prepares to initiate the PP3WAKA sequence
   (a) Generate context reference identity $(CRID)$ and context validity period. $CRID$ is a pseudo-random value and $PERIOD$ is a time interval.
   (b) Generate random challenge and response (CH_{UE}, RES_{UE}) towards the HS (using a key derivation function and the long-term shared key (LSK)).
   (c) Generate shared keys for $CRID$ context for UE-HS communication.
   $KeyGen_{LSK}(CH_{UE}) \rightarrow K_{UEHS}$
   (d) Protect $UEID$, $CRID$ and CH_{UEHS} with HS public IBE key (HSK)
   $HSK = HSID\|SNID\|LONG\_TERM\_PERIOD$
   $Encrypt_{HSK}(UEID, CRID, CH_{UEHS}) \rightarrow B$
   (e) Generate ID and hashed area code $(Hash(CRID, AC) \rightarrow HAC)$.
   $ID = HSID\|SNID\|HAC\|PERIOD$
   $Encrypt_{ID}(CRID) \rightarrow A$

Message 1: $UE \rightarrow SN : (A, B, PERIOD, HSID)$

2. SN prepares to forward data to HS over the protected B-interface (using $BKEY$).
   (a) SN sees message 1. SN observes UE location (x, y) and area code (AC).
   (b) S2PLIP: SN generates $\widehat{v}$
   (c) SN generates DH public key (DHA)
   (d) $C = PERIOD\|HAC\|\widehat{v}\|DHA$

Message 2: $SN \rightarrow HS : \{(B, C)\}_{BKEY}$

3. HS responds. Private IBE keys are not UE specific, and may already be available.
   (a) HS sees (B, C), and verifies validity of $C.PERIOD$. HS constructs ID. If necessary: HS generates private key d_{ID} corresponding to ID.
   (b) HS generates DH public key (DHB), and computes the DH-secret (s)
   (c) If necessary: HS generates private key d_{HSK} corresponding to to HSK.
   (d) $Decrypt_{d_{HSK}}(B) \rightarrow UEID, CRID, CH_{UEHS}$
   (e) HS now knows $UEID$ and computes the response (RES_{UE})
   (f) HS generates challenge and response to UE (CH_{HS}, RES_{HS})
   (g) Generate shared key (K_{UEHS}) for $CRID$ context for UE-HS communication
   (h) S2PLIP: HE computes $D(\widehat{v})$
   (i) HS prepares data to UE
   $Encrypt_{K_{UEHS}}(CH_{HS}, RES_{UE}, s) \rightarrow D$

Message 3: $HS \rightarrow SN : \{(D, DHB, D(\widehat{v}), d_{ID}, CRID)\}_{BKEY}$

4. SN receives message 3 from HS
   (a) $Decrypt_{d_{ID}}(A) \rightarrow CRID$
   (b) SN compares $CRID$ values from UE and HS. SN computes DH-secret (s), and a pseudo-random value for session key generation (RND_{SN}).
   (c) SN generates unidirectional session keys (K_{SN}).
   $KeyGen_s(CRID, RND_{SN}) \rightarrow K_{SN}$
   (d) SN creates the alias identity $(TAID)$, encrypts it and binds it to the $CRID$
   $Encrypt_{K_{SN}}(CRID, TAID) \rightarrow E$

Message 4: $SN \rightarrow UE : (D, RND_{SN}, E)$

5. UE receives message 4 from SN
   (a) UE sees (D, RND_{SN}, E) and decrypts D
       $Decrypt_{K_{UEHS}}(D) \rightarrow CH_{HS}, RES_{UE}, s$
   (b) UE verifies the HS response RES_{UE} and computes response RES_{HS}
   (c) UE generates session keys (K_{SN}) for $(SN \rightarrow UE)$ using DH-secret s and SN
       key deriv. data RND_{SN}. UE also generates RND_{UE} and session keys K_{UE}.
       $KeyGen_s(CRID, RND_{SN}) \rightarrow K_{SN}$
       $KeyGen_s(CRID, RND_{UE}) \rightarrow K_{UE}$
   (d) Using the session keys, the UE decrypts E to verify $CRID$ and get $TAID$
       $Decrypt_{K_{SN}}(E) \rightarrow CRID, TAID$
   (e) UE demonstrates possession of K_{SN} and K_{UE} (this proves possession of s).
       $Encrypt_{K_{UE}}(TAID, RES_{HS}) \rightarrow F$

Message 5: $UE \rightarrow SN : RND_{UE}, F$

6. SN receives the message 5 from UE
   (a) SN computes session keys (K_{UESN}) and decrypts the remaining message
       $Decrypt_{K_{UE}}(F) \rightarrow TAID, RES_{HS}$
   (b) SN verifies $TAID$ and forwards RES_{HS}
   (c) S2PLIP: SN computes $e_{i_N} = e_{i_1}, e_{i_2}, ..., e_{i_n}$

Message 6: $SN \rightarrow HS : \{(CRID, RES_{HS}, e_{i_N})\}_{BKEY}$

7. HS receives the message 6 from SN
   (a) HS verifies the $CRID, RES_{HS}$
   (b) S2PLIP: HS verifies e_{i_N}

Message 7: $HS \rightarrow SN : \{CRID, "success"\}_{BKEY}$

8. SN receives the message 7 from HS

   The context is now established. UE has not yet received HS confirmation of the response, but the UE does not need this information. A "next" protected event provides the UE with assurance that the SN has received the HS acknowledge.

The A-interface session keys (K_{UE} and K_{SN}) are symmetric keys. Separate keys are required for confidentiality and integrity.

5   Analysis of the PP3WAKA Protocol

5.1   Security and Complexity Analysis

The communication and computation complexity of the protocol is overall quite high, but not infeasible. We have taken steps to limit the amount of data transported over the A-interface and to reduce the instantaneous computational requirements. We shall focus on the privacy aspects in our analysis. We have established that the use of privacy protected temporary identities has eliminated the eavesdropping weakness of 2G/3G. We have furthermore ensured that the SN will only know location and (anonymous) temporary identities. The HS will know the permanent identity, but will not learn the exact location. For more on the security and complexity of IBE please refer to [18].

An Informal Security Argument. The mutual challenge-response between UE and HS is relatively standard. We expect no problems with this construct. The DH secret s is constructed online between SN and HS over an authenticated/protected channel. The SN therefore believes that s is fresh and suitable for key derivation. The UE receives s in protected form from the HS, which has jurisdiction over UE. The $CRID$ binding assures UE that s is fresh. The UE is therefore compelled to believe that s is suitable for key derivation. The session keys are generated using local/individual key derivation data ($RND_{SN/UE}$) and s. In message 4 and 5, the SN and UE respectively proves possession of s. So UE and SN are inclined to believe that the opposite entity is recognized by the HS.

In the S2PLIP protocol, Bob sends encrypted polygon P to Alice and Alice will never disclose her position to Bob. Let us evaluate communication cost of this protocol. We assume that polygon P has n angles and selected cryptosystem has l bits keys. We assume, for simplicity, that each coefficient can be presented as l bits number. The following steps will affect its communication complexity:

1. Bob sends encrypted P and public key to Alice. ($2nl$ bits send and communication complexity is $2n$)
2. Alice asks Bob to help to decrypt $g_{i_1}(\alpha, \beta)$ ($2l$ bits send and communication complexity is 1)
3. Alice sends result $e_{i_1}, e_{i_2}, ..., e_{i_n}$ to Bob ($2nl$ bits send and communication complexity is $2n$)

Thus, communication complexity is $4n+1$ or $O(n)$, and no more than $2l(2n+1)$ bits need to be sent between Alice and Bob. We note that the best algorithm for point location within polygon is $O(\log n)$. However it doesn't take into account privacy concerns. Secure two-party point-inclusion protocol proposed in [19] has computational complexity $O(n)$. However in the setting considered here the communication complexity is a bottle-neck. Analyzing the communication complexity of that protocol we can see that protocol utilizes Secure Two-Party Scalar Product Protocol (S2PSPP) and Secure Two-Party Vector Dominance Protocol (S2PVDP) (see [19] for more details). The more efficient S2PSPP for smaller n has communication complexity of is $4nm$ where m is a security parameter such n^m is large enough. It is clear that our protocol is more efficient then S2PSPP. But we should remember that in addition to S2PSPP we must use also S2PVDP. S2PVDP involves between others Yao's Millionaire Comparison Protocol [27] which has communication complexity that is exponential in the number of bits of the involved numbers. By involving untrusted third party (that even can misbehave) the communication complexity can be improved to $O(n)$ where n is the number of bits of each input number. The communication inefficiency of proposed solution has been acknowledged in the literature [20], and new modified solution has been with improved performance has been proposed [21]. The idea is that user can accept some weakening of security for the sake of better performance. The proposed secure scalar product protocol based on commodity-server model [23] has communication cost $4n$, and S2PSPP has communication cost only $2n$ (with significant increasing of computational cost). However communication cost of S2PVDP should still be improved.

5.2   Future Work

The PP3WAKA protocol is complex, and to get more experience with it we plan to develop a prototype implementation. We also intend to develop formal models for at least parts of the protocol and formally verify these models.

6   Summary and Conclusion

In this paper we have analyzed the location and identity privacy of the current 2G/3G systems and found it wanting. We have also seen that the 2G/3G security architecture do not capture modern trust, privacy and control requirements. The security needed for modern cellular systems must include a hierarchical security context model. To enhance privacy we have found that the UE must be the protocol initiator. We have further found that the use of Identity-Based Encryption is ideal for fast set-up in new roaming areas. We have also found a need for spatial control and location privacy that we have resolved with Secure Multiparty Computation methods. Given this, we have designed a *Privacy Preserving 3-Way Authentication and Key Agreement* protocol. The PP3WAKA protocol is more complex than existing cellular security AKA protocols, but it is reasonably fast and provides credible privacy to the user while providing enhanced spatial control for the home operator.

References

1. 3G TS 03.20: Security related network functions, *3GPP*, Sophia Antipolis, France, 2001
2. 3G TS 33.102: 3G Security; Security architetcure (Release 6), *3GPP*, Sophia Antipolis, France, 2004
3. G.M. Køien, Principles for Cellular Access Security, In *Proceedings of the Ninth Nordic Workshop on Secure IT Systems*, pp.65–72, Espoo, Finland, Nov. 2004
4. G.M. Køien, An Introduction to Access Security in UMTS. *IEEE Wireless Communications Mag.*, Vol.11, No.1, pp.8-18, Feb. 2004
5. G. Rose, G.M. Køien, Access Security in CDMA2000, Including a Comparison with UMTS Access Security. *IEEE Wireless Communications Mag.*, Vol.11, No.1, pp.19-25, Feb. 2004
6. K. Nyberg, V. Niemi, UMTS Security. ISBN 0-470-84794-8, *Wiley*, 2003
7. G.M.Køien and V.A.Oleshchuk, Privacy-Preserving Spatially Aware Authentication Protocols: Analysis and Solutions, In *Proceedings of NORDSEC 2003*, pp.161-173, Gjøvik, Norway, 2003

8. G.M. Køien and V.A. Oleshchuk, Spatio-Temporal Exposure Control; An investigation of spatial home control and location privacy issues, In *Proceedings of the 14th Annual IEEE Symposium on Personal Indoor Mobile Radio Communications (PIMRC)*, pp.2760-2764, Beijing, China, Sep. 2003

9. S. Kent, and R. Atkinson, Security Architecture for the Internet Protocol, RFC 2401, *IETF*, Nov. 1998

10. G.M. Køien, Rethinking Cellular Access Security, In *Proceedings of the Second IASTED Intl. Conf. on Comm. and Computer Networks*, pp.212-218, Cambridge, MA, USA, Nov. 2004

11. 3G TS 33.234: 3G Security; Wireless Local Area Network (WLAN) Interworking Security (Release 6), *3GPP*, Sophia Antipolis, France, 2004

12. G.M. Køien, T. Haslestad, Security Aspects of 3G-WLAN Interworking. *IEEE Communications Mag.*, Vol.41, No.11, pp.82-88, Nov. 2003

13. D. Hofheinz, J. Mller-Quade, and R. Steinwandt, Initiator-Resilient Universally Composable Key Exchange, ESORICS 2003, *LNCS 2808, pp.61–84, Springer-Verlag*, Gjøvik, Norway, 2003

14. A.J. Menezes, P.C van Oorschot, S.A. Vanstone, Handbook of Applied Cryptography (5th printing). ISBN 0-8493-8523-7, CRC Press, June 2001

15. A. Joux, A One Round Protocol for Tripartite Diffie-Hellman, In *Proc. ANTS-IV 2000*, LNCS 1838, Springer-Verlag, 2000

16. A. Shamir, Identity-based cryptosystems and signature schemes, In *Proc. CRYPTO 1984*, pp.47-53, LNCS 196, Springer-Verlag, 1984

17. K. Lauter, The Advantages of Elliptic Curve Cryptography for Wireless Security. *IEEE Wireless Communications Mag.*, Vol.11, No.1, pp.62-67, Feb. 2004

18. D. Boneh, M. Franklin, Identity-Based Encryption from the Weil Pairing. In *Advances in Cryptology - CRYPTO 2001*, LNCS 2139, Springer, 2001

19. M.J. Atallah and W. Du, Secure Multy-Party Computational Geometry. In *WADS2001: 7th International Workshop on Algorithms and Data Structures*, pp.165-179, USA, Aug. 8-10, 2001

20. W. Du and M.J. Atallah. Secure Multy-Party Computation Problems and Their Applications: A Review and Open Problems, *NSPW'01*, pp. 13–21, Sep. 10-13, 2002

21. W.Du and Z. Zhan, A Practical Approach to Solve Secure Multi-Party Computational Problems. In *Proceedings of New Security Paradigms Workshop*, Sep. 23-26, 2002

22. O.Goldreich, S.Micali and A.Wigderson. How to Play Any Mental Game. In *Proceedings of the 19th Annual ACM Symposium on Theory of Computing*, pp. 218–229, 1998

23. D. Beaver, Commodity-Based Cryptography. In *Proceedings of the 29th Annual ACM Symposium on the Theory of Computing*, 1997

24. D. Naccache and J. Stern. A New Cryptosystem Based on Higher Residues. In *Proceedings of the 5th ACM Conference on Computer and Communication Security*, pp.59–66, 1998

25. T. Okamoto and S. Uchiyama. An Efficient Public-Key Cryptosystem as Secure as Factoring. In *Advanced in Cryptography - EUROCRYPT'98*, LNCS 1403, pp. 308–318, 1998

26. P. Paillier. Public-Key Cryptosystems Based on Composite Degree Residuosity Classes. In *EUROCRYPT'99*, LNCS 1592, pp. 223–238, 1999

27. A.C. Yao. Protocols for Secure Computations, In *Proceedings of the 23th Annual IEEE Symposium on Foundations of Computer Science*, 1982

28. S. Goldwasser. Multi-party computations: Past and present, In *Proceedings of the 16th Annual ACM Symposium on Principles of Distributed Computing*, Santa Barbara, CA USA, Aug. 21-24, 1997

29. 3G TS 23.271: Functional stage 2 description of Location Services (LCS), *3GPP*, Sophia Antipolis, France, 2004

Appendix A: Main Cellular Procedures

To simplify matters we only consider the most basic procedures. For 2G/3G we have four main procedures:

- **Registration:** The UE listens to the system beacon (broadcast) channel. Upon detecting a new SN and/or location area code (LAC), the UE accesses the SN and requests to be registered in the new area. The request may include the UE identity in cleartext. The SN forwards the location updating request to the HS (this is not needed if the new area is within the same SN area). The HS cancels any previous location (and informs the previous SN/node) and transfers subscriber data to the SN. The registration procedure can only be initiated by the UE. No services are provided until the UE has registered.

- **Data to UE:** A UE in idle position will listen for *paging* on the paging broadcast channel. The paging is in cleartext and the UE identity will be visible to all entities within the paging area (the location area). The UE will then access the system, identity itself (still in clear) and be assigned a dedicated channel. Here the system will request authentication and assign a protected traffic channel.

- **Data from UE:** This procedure is almost identical to the "Data to UE" procedure, except that here the procedure is initiated be the UE.

- **Handover:** The procedure consists of system controlled seamless switching between radio-channels during active transfer.

We note that UE identity is presented in clear for three of the four procedures.

Appendix B: Internal 2G/3G Subscriber Identities

In 2G/3G one has a primary subscriber identity, the IMSI (ITU-T E.212). The IMSI is not public per see, but it cannot be regarded as private either. The IMSI identity should not be confused with public addresses like the ITU-T E.164 MSIDSN (telephone) number. Identity presentation for *Initial Registration* is by means of the permanent IMSI identity. The IMSI is presented in clear over the radio interface every time the subscriber registers with a new SN operator and possibly also when the subscriber moves from one SN server to another. The IMSI is a composite information element (IE), and it contains sufficient information to allow the SN to derive an address to the HS. During emphInitial Registration, the SN requests the HS to register the user. This includes forwarding of subscriber information and security credentials. The HS will update its register such that subsequent calls/packets to the UE are forwarded to the

SN. The claimed IMSI must then be authenticated. The 2G/3G systems deploys a delegated challenge-response authentication mechanism(fig.1) where it is the SN that executes AKA procedure. The AKA procedure includes key agreement for access link confidentiality and integrity protection. The SN will then issue a temporary identity (TMSI). The TMSI, which should appear to be independent of the IMSI, is an unstructured 32-bit wide variable unilaterally decided by the SN. The TMSI is issued in ciphertext form and will only be used in cleartext. The privacy protection relies on subsequent use of the TMSI instead of the IMSI. However, an active attacker can easily provoke the UE to reveal the IMSI simply by requesting it. Furthermore, there are no formal requirements on how to construct the TMSI value. The TMSI may therefore be assigned in a sequential fashion. An adversary may then be able to deduce the TMSI-IMSI association.

Appendix C: Location Determination

The principal driver for location measurement in 2G/3G networks have been the emergency requirements (the so-called E112/E911 requirements). These requirements are mandatory in most markets. Adding to the momentum is the location services, where the network provides location based services to the subscribers. There are two main methods of measuring the UE position. For the E112/E911 requirements the network must be able to provide the UE position when the user is dialing the emergency services. The network must be able to do this without UE assistance. To achieve the required precision for E112/E911 positioning, the network may need to measure UE signal from multiple source (access points) and use triangulation methods to calculate the position. For the user based location services on may also have the user provide the position, and in 3G one have standardized support for GPS in the UE.

- **Radio access information:** The access points (APs) are stationary and have well-known fixed positions. During UE-AP communication, the AP will be able to measure signal propagation delays, phase angles of the signal etc.
- **Augmented radio access information:** A common strategy to cater for the emergency (E911/E112) requirements is to have multiple APs do the measurements, and then to compute a more accurate position [29].
- **Independent measurement infrastructure:** Satellite positioning is the most common method, but terrestrially based system also exists. The independent methods may receive kick-start assistance from the network (for instance GPS satellite configuration information)

Note that the UE must trust the location provider, and this is also true for network independent providers.

Appendix D: Abbreviations and Identifiers

The main abbreviations and *Identifiers*.

Abbreviation	Explanation
AC	Area Code
AKA	Authentication and Key Agreement
AP	Access Point (also called basestation (GSM) and Node B (UMTS))
BTS	Base tranceiver station (GSM name, also called basestation)
CH_{HS}	Pseudo-random Challenge, issued by HS
CH_{UE}	Pseudo-random Challenge, issued by UE
$CRID$	Context Reference Identity
HAC	Hashed Area Code
HS	Home Server
$HSID$	HS Identity
IBE	Identity-Based Encryption
ID	SN public IBE key (UE $\rightarrow$ SN)
LAC	Local Area Code XXXXX
LSK	Long-term Shared Key (UE-HS)
MM	Mobility Management (control plane sublayer at the link layer)
$PERIOD$	Medium-term security context validity interval
PKG	Private Key Generator (IBE function)
PP3WAKA	Privacy Preserving 3-Way Authentication and Key Agreement
RES_{HS}	Response, corresponding to CH_{HS}
RES_{UE}	Response, corresponding to CH_{UE}
RND_{SN}	Pseudo-random value for session key derivation (SN $\rightarrow$ UE), issued by SN
RND_{UE}	Pseudo-random value for session key derivation (UE $\rightarrow$ SN), issued by UE
RRM	Radio Resource Management (lower control plane sublayer at the link layer)
SMC	Secure Multi-party Computation
SN	Serving Network
$SNID$	SN Identity
$TAID$	Temporary Alias Identity
UE	User Entity
$UEID$	UE Identity (permanent private identity)
VA	Validity Area (not related to Area Code)

Towards Modeling Wireless Location Privacy

Leping Huang[1,2], Hiroshi Yamane[2], Kanta Matsuura[2], and Kaoru Sezaki[2]

[1] Nokia Research Center Japan, 1-8-1, Shimomeguro, Meguro-ku, Tokyo, Japan
[2] University of Tokyo, 4-6-1 Komaba, Meguro-ku, Tokyo, Japan

Abstract. The lack of a formal model in wireless location privacy protection research makes it difficult to evaluate new location privacy protection proposals, and difficult to utilize existing research results in anonymous communication into this new problem. In this paper, we analyze a wireless location privacy protection system (WLP^2S), and generalize it to a MIX based formal model, which includes a MIX, a set of MIX's user, and a intruder of MIX. In addition, we also use information theory approach to define anonymity and measures of this model, and describe the characteristics of observation process in WLP^2S in detail. Two benefits arise from our model. Firstly, it provides a means of evaluating the privacy level of proposed location privacy protection protocols. We use the measures of proposed formal model to study the performance of our novel silent period technique. Simulation results reveal the role of many parameters-such as users' mobility pattern and intruders' tracking accuracy- on users' privacy level. The results shed more light on improving our defense protocol. Secondly, our approach provides a link between existing defense and attack protocols in MIX research and the new location privacy protection problem. By utilizing the formal model, we conducted preliminary studies in identifying potential attacks, and improve the performance of existing defense protocol. This study results an extension of existing defense protocols. Those simulation and analytical results demonstrates the promising potential of our model.

1 Introduction

Recent technological advances in wireless location tracking have presented unprecedented opportunities for monitoring the movements of individuals. While such technology may support many useful location-based services (LBSs), which tailor their functionality to a user's current location, privacy concerns might seriously hamper user acceptance. Within those technologies, the positioning systems that utilized short-range radio such as Bluetooth and Wireless local area network (WLAN) have been receiving great attention recently. Due to their short-range characteristics, tracking system based on them [1, 2] achieves very high accuracy up to one meter. However, some of those systems track users' movement by eavesdropping on their communication. Eavesdropping is invasive and does not require the cooperation or approval of the users. Therefore it may present a serious location privacy problem to users of wireless communication.

In this paper, we concentrate on *location privacy*, a particular type of information privacy that we define as *the ability to prevent other parties from learning*

G. Danezis and D. Martin (Eds.): PET 2005, LNCS 3856, pp. 59–77, 2006.
© Springer-Verlag Berlin Heidelberg 2006

one's movement. The only difference to the definition given by Beresford in [3] is that we more concentrate on one's continuous movement than one's position at discrete time instant. Some solutions to the location privacy problem have already been proposed for both Bluetooth and WLAN [2, 4], which are based on the idea of periodic address updates. In our previous works [5], we identified that such solutions cannot protect users from advanced tracking methods including correlation attack. Correlation attack is a method of utilizing the temporal and spatial correlation between the old and new pseudonym of nodes. In addition, we proposed a solution called silent period to circumvent the correlation attack. Preliminary simulation results show that a longer silent period increases the average time that a node is being tracked continuously. A silent period is defined as a transition period between the use of new and old pseudonyms, when a node is not allowed to disclose either of them.

Although such informal expression is essential to the understanding of privacy protection proposals, it will only allow the informal investigation of a system. The privacy level of a complicated system, particularly a wireless location privacy system, the focus of our interest, is affected by many parameters. Unless we have a generalized model for such a system, it will be difficult to study the effect of a system's parameters on users' privacy level.

This paper generalizes a wireless location privacy protection system into a MIX based anonymity model. The model offers two insights: a way of evaluating location privacy protection systems; and serving as a bridge between the new location privacy protection problem and existing defense and attack approaches in the MIX related research.

The rest of the paper is organized as follows. Section 2 reviews existing work in wireless location tracking, privacy threats, MIX and its formal model. Section 3 first describes the results of our background work on location privacy threats and defense protocol, and then proposes a general model for WLP^2S which includes an abstracted framework of system, information-theory based definitions of anonymity and measures, and detailed description about the observation process. Section 4 describes two wireless location privacy protection systems with different tracking algorithms, and evaluate the performance of this two systems by using proposed measures. Simulation results reveal the effect of many parameters of a WLP^2S on users' privacy level. Section 5 utilizes our formal model to identify potential protocol threats and suggests areas for improving silent period protocol. Section 6 summarizes the paper's contribution and suggests areas for future improvements.

2   Prior Arts

Various techniques have been proposed in the literature for estimating the location of a mobile node [6]. These techniques are broadly classified by signal metric-for example, Angle of Arrival (AOA), Received Signal Strength (RSS), and Time of Arrival (TOA)-or by metric processing-for example, triangulation and pattern matching. Readers can find a survey about latest indoor location tracking technologies in [7]. Latest short-range radio based tracking systems [6] achieves accuracy up to 1 meter. Such a high precision tracking system may erode users' location privacy in the future.

To protect users from potential threat, there are several research studies in commercial radios such as WLAN. Gruteser and Grunwald [8, 9, 10] have worked extensively on protecting location privacy in WLAN. In their works, they presented a middleware architecture and algorithm to adjust the resolution of location information along spatial and temporal dimensions, and enhanced location privacy by frequently disposing of a client's interface identifier. They proposed updating the node's interface identifier whenever a station associates with a new access point (AP). On the other hand, Beresford and Stajano [3] proposed the concept of the MIX zone based on Chaum's [11] MIX. A MIX zone for a group of users is defined as the largest connected spatial region in which none of the users in the area has registered an application callback. They assumed the LBS application providers as hostile adversaries, and suggested that application users hide their own identifier from providers. Because application providers do not receive any location information when users are in a MIX zone, the users' identities are *mixed*. The defects of those proposals in the context of WLP^2S are described in [5].

Many modern anonymity systems are based on the MIX concept first proposed by Chaum in [11]. MIX is a set of servers that serially decrypt or encrypt lists of incoming messages. These messages are sent out in a random order, in such a way that an attacker cannot correlate output messages with input messages without the aid of MIX (i.e., when several messages are sent out in a different order than they are received). There are many anonymous applications based on MIX such as untraceable electronic transactions, electrical voting, anonymous mailer and anonymous web surfing.

Increasing attention has been paid to the development of a formal method to verify and evaluate privacy protocol recently. Diaz et al. [12] and Serjantov and Danezis [13] proposed an information theoretical approach to measure the level of anonymity of a system. In these papers, the authors identified that not all nodes involved in anonymous communication contribute the same degree of anonymity to the system. Neither can the size of anonymity set precisely describe the degree of anonymity a system provides. In their proposals, they take into account the entropy of users sending and/or receiving messages as a measure of the anonymous system. In addition, Diaz and Serjantov [14] presented a simple function to generalize different types of mixes: a function that is based on the number of messages inside the MIX to the fraction of message to be flushed. By using ACP-style process algebra, Mauw et al. [15] proposed a formal definition of the notation of anonymity in the presence of an observing intruder, and validate this definition by analyzing a well-known anonymity preserving protocol *Onion Routing*[16]. On the other hand, Steinbrecher and Kopsell [17] chose information theory and equivalence class to describe unlinkability because it allows an easy probabilistic description. Hughes and Shmatikov [18] proposed a new specification framework for information hiding properties such as anonymity and privacy. This framework is based on the concept of a function view, which is a concise representation of the attacker's partial knowledge about the function.

3   Modeling of Wireless Location Privacy Protection System

In this section, we first give an informal description of the Wireless Location Privacy Protection System (WLP^2S), including correlation attack and our proposed defense protocol: *silent period*. After that, we describe the formal anonymity model for a WLP^2S.

3.1   Informal Description of WLP^2S

A system is conceptualized to comprise four types of node: authentication server (AS), access point (AP), station (STA), and eavesdropper (E). AP, STA, and E nodes are incorporated with the WLAN radio interfaces operating at identical frequencies. In commercial hotspot WLAN services, users of STA nodes always contract with one service provider. This service provider controls at least one AS. The area around users may be covered by other APs not controlled by the station's contracted service provider. The eavesdropper is capable of capturing all frames with some radio metric transmitted in the channel within its proximity, and estimating the position of frame sender based on measured radio metric. We also assume that all regions that the STA may visit are covered by adequate number of eavesdroppers for position tracking. By capturing frames continuously, the eavesdropper continuously tracks the user's movement. This greatly violates the user's location privacy.

As noted in the previous section, several schemes are currently available that attempt to protect a user's wireless location privacy by periodically updating its *medium access control* (MAC) address. However, we think that with enough temporal and spatial precision, it may be possible for an adversary to correlate two pseudonyms that are moving through space, which may be sent separately from the same device. Temporal correlation may be used because the period in which stations change their pseudonyms may be small. Spatial correlation may be used if it is assumed that a station will generally continue in the same direction, with the same speed as it traveled in the past. This attack is called correlation attack in this paper. The left-side graph of Fig.1 gives an example of correlation attack. In this figure, a node moves from the upper right to the lower left corner. The node changes address from A to A' in the middle. Because there is a strong correlation between trajectories A and A', it is easy for the eavesdropper to guess that the frames with id A and A' are sent by the same node.

To protect users from correlation attack, we proposed in [5] a method called silent period. A silent period is defined as a transition period between using new and old pseudonyms in which a station is not allowed to disclose either the old or the new pseudonym(s). As a result, the silent period introduces ambiguity when

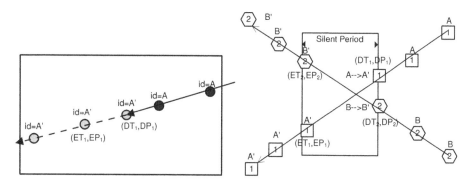

Fig. 1. (left) Correlation Attack, (right) Silent Period

determining the time and/or place at which a change of anonymous address has occurred. This makes it more difficult to associate two separately received pseudonyms with the same station, because the silent period disrupts the temporal and/or spatial correlation between two separately received pseudonyms, and obscures the time and place where a pseudonym changed. From the perspective of anonymous communication, this creates a temporal and spatial MIX to mix the identities of nodes. The right-side graph of Fig.1 shows an example of a silent period algorithm. The effects of the silent period are illustrated near the intersection of the path of both nodes in the figure. Both nodes update their addresses, and then enter silent period. From the perspective of an adversary, either of two identifiers A' and B' may be the new identifier of node 1. As a result, this method obscures the spatial correlation between new and old pseudonyms as a consequence of *mixing* the pseudonyms of the nodes. In addition, the silent period also contains a variable part, which is used to mix the temporal relationship between nodes. Suppose nodes 1 and 2 enter the silent period at different times as shown in the right-side graph of Fig.1. Then the order of time when nodes leave the silent period is guaranteed if the silent period is fixed. This order may be disturbed if the variable silent periods of nodes overlap. In essence, the effect of the variable period is to mix the temporal relationship between the nodes' disappearing and emerging times. For clarity, we define lifetime as the duration the user use one identifier continuously. The ratio of silent period to lifetime, called silent period ratio indicates how much time user spends on privacy protection. In general, larger silent period ratio results lower communication quality.

3.2   Formal Description of WLP^2S

The silent period model with preliminary simulation results is reported in [5]. In this report, we recognized that it is difficult to evaluate and enhance our proposal unless we clearly generalize this problem into a formal model. Our aim therefore is to generalize wireless location privacy protection system into a formal anonymity model. We describe this model in three steps. First, we map different roles of nodes of a WLP^2S into a MIX based system $\mathcal{S}$, including a MIX $\mathcal{M}$, a

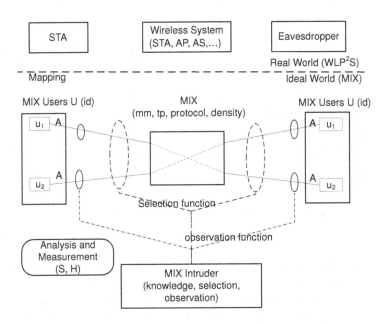

Fig. 2. Formal model of a wireless location privacy protection system

set of MIX's users $\mathcal{U}$ and MIX's intruder $\mathcal{I}$. Concisely, $\mathcal{S} = \{\mathcal{U}, \mathcal{I}, \mathcal{M}\}$. Then, we use equivalence relation to define anonymity set and measures for the generalized WLP^2S. Finally, we analyze the features–mainly accuracy–of a intruder's observation process in detail. Process algebra-based approach defined in [15] is used in step one and three; while information-theory based approach proposed in [17] is used in step two. Our model does not include a formal protocol validation module because we only addressed global passive attacks(GPA) now. Future work may consider adding protocol validations against active attacks if deemed necessary.

To help readers understand our formal model, we first give a visual overview of the model in Fig.2. A WLP^2S is abstracted into three entities (a set of MIX users $\mathcal{U}$, MIX Intruder $\mathcal{I}$, MIX $\mathcal{M}$), functions between those entities(selection function σ, action $\mathcal{A}$, observation function ω). A MIX user u participates in MIX by executing a series of actions $\mathcal{A}$; while a MIX intruder $\mathcal{I}$ observes each of those actions through an observation function ω. This observation function causes loss and bias on the observed actions. Intruder uses selection function σ and a prior knowledge about MIX $k_{\mathcal{M}}$ to find out the correlation between observed actions. This can be seen as a passive attack on the MIX. The *analysis and measurement* blocks in Fig.2 indicate a set of tools for analyzing the generalized system. In current system, we only use size $\mathcal{S}$ and entropy $\mathcal{H}$ of MIX as measures. Explanation of notations used in this paper are listed in table 2 in Appendix.

After preliminary analysis, we noticed that every STA has two roles in the system. Firstly, a user of the MIX u executes a series of actions $\mathcal{A}$(i.e. send a frame). Each STA has one identifier id uniquely identified by others within a specific period of time, and use this identifier as sender id when transmitting a frame. Secondly, a set of STAs and other entities(i.e., AP, AS) in the system forms a MIX between STAs by utilizing their features such as STAs' mobility pattern mm, traffic pattern tp, privacy protection protocol $protocol$. The limits of an intruder's knowledge $k_{\mathcal{M}}$ about some of those features helps creating this MIX. Here, we generalize the first role of a STA to a MIX user $u \in \mathcal{U}$, which contains only one parameter: user identifier id, or concisely: $u = \{id\}$. In WLAN, identifier id is a 48bits MAC address. We also define a set of identifiers $\mathcal{ID}$. Reader should notice that although a set of users $\mathcal{U}$ and a set of identifiers $\mathcal{ID}$ are related with each other, but they are not identical. In a WLP^2S, it is allowed that a user utilizes different identifiers at different period of time; while a identifier is used by different user at different period of time. To avoid address collision–which will seriously disturb normal communication–we assume that one address is not used by multiple users simultaneously. This property can be guaranteed by some form of Duplicate Address Detection(DAD) protocol such as [19].

In a MIX system, users normally execute a series of actions $\mathcal{A}$. Some of those actions are used by intruder $\mathcal{I}$ to attack the system. In a WLP^2S, we think there are three types of actions: node movement $\mathcal{A}_m$, frame transmission $\mathcal{A}_t$ and frame reception $\mathcal{A}_r$. Or concisely $\mathcal{A} := \mathcal{A}_m \| \mathcal{A}_t \| \mathcal{A}_r$. We classify those actions into observable actions $\mathcal{A}_{obs}$ and invisible actions $\mathcal{A}_{inv}$. $\mathcal{A}_m$ represents the actions that a node roams within a geographical area. As an intruder utilizes only the radio metrics in captured frames to estimate a node's position, the movement of the node itself is considered invisible to the intruder. $\mathcal{A}_r$ represents the actions that a node receives a frame targeted to itself. According to WLAN specification, nodes do not need to transmit any signals for frame reception. Consequently, $\mathcal{A}_r$ is also invisible to the intruder. Only $\mathcal{A}_t$ action is observable to the intruder because sender should explicitly send radio signal for each frame transmission. Considering the feature of a WLAN tracking system, we generalize a frame transmission action $a_t = id_s \| id_r \| msg \| t \| sm \| pos$. It means that one message msg is sent from user with id_s to user with id_r with signal metric sm at position pos and time t, while $id_s, id_r \in \mathcal{ID}$. In addition, we also define a function $id(a)$ on $\mathcal{A}_t$, which returns sender id id_s of an action a_t, and another function $time(a_t)$, which returns an action a_t's time instant t when it is generated. Most of tracking algorithms analyze the correlations between groups of actions with same identifiers to track node's movement. For clarity, we define trajectory T_i as set of all $a_t \in \mathcal{A}_t$ with same sender id i, $T_i = \{a_t | id(a_t) = i\}$. One thing we want to emphasize here is that we define trajectory not for users , but for identifiers. $\mathcal{T}$ is defined as set of all trajectories $\mathcal{T} = \{t_i\}$. we notice that set of trajectory is a subset of observable actions: $\mathcal{T} \subseteq \mathcal{A}_{obs}$.

Besides, a group of STA and other entities(i.e., AS, AP) in a WLP^2S forms the MIX. Because intruder lacks knowledges about some features of MIX, it will have some ambiguity(anonymity) when associating users and its actions. The knowledge $k_{\mathcal{M}}$ that may affect the ambiguity of intruder includes randomness of user's behaviors such as mobility pattern mm, traffic pattern tp, privacy protection protocol $protocol$ and number of MIX users $density$.

On the other hand, eavesdroppers use observed actions to attack the unlinkability of MIX. We generalize the behaviors of eavesdroppers into a intruder $\mathcal{I} := \{k_{\mathcal{M}}, \omega, \sigma\}$, while $k_{\mathcal{M}}$ is an abstraction of intruder's prior knowledge about $\mathcal{M}$, ω is an observation function, and σ is a selection function. The intruder $\mathcal{I}$ first observes a set of actions $\mathcal{A}$ generated by a set of users $\mathcal{U}$ by an observation function $\omega : \mathcal{A} \to \mathcal{A}_{obs}$. Only part of the actions $\mathcal{A}_{obs}$ are observable to intruder $\mathcal{I}$, and only fraction of each observable action are understood by intruder. Then, based on the a prior knowledge $k_{\mathcal{M}}$ and observed actions $\mathcal{A}_{obs}$, the intruder uses some selection functions σ to link actions with different ids.

The objective of selection function σ is to find out the relationship between trajectories $\mathcal{T}$. Following the approach described in [17], the relationship between trajectories $\mathcal{T}$ can be expressed as as equivalence relation $\sim_\sigma$ on $\mathcal{T}$. A prior intruder should not know anything about the structure of $\mathcal{T}$, but by utilizing a prior knowledge about MIX $k_{\mathcal{M}}$ and observed action, intruder may know more about it. For a random variable X, let $P(T_i \sim_\sigma T_j) = P(X = (T_i \sim_\sigma T_j))$ denotes the attacker's a posteriori probability that given two trajectories T_i and T_j, X takes the value $(T_i \sim T_j)$. Following the approach used in [13, 17], we define our anonymity model.

Definition 1. *Given an intruder I, a finite set of trajectory $\mathcal{T}$, and a set of identifiers $\mathcal{ID}$'s equivalence relation $\sim_\sigma$, we define a set of discrete probability distribution function $\mathcal{P}$. Let $\mathcal{P}_i \in \mathcal{P}$ be the attacker's a-posteriori probability distribution for a trajectory T_i that T_i is equivalent to trajectories $T_j \in \mathcal{T}$ with respect to equivalence relation $\sim_\sigma$. Each value $p_{i,j} \in \mathcal{P}_i$ is defined as $p_{i,j} = P(T_i \sim_\sigma T_j)$*

In other words, this model defines a function $p : \mathcal{T} \times \mathcal{T} \to [0, 1]$, each value $p_{i,j}$ indicates the linkability between two trajectories T_i and T_j. And mathematically this function satisfy following condition. $\forall i \in I, \sum_{j \in I} p(i, j) = 1$.

The role of a location tracking algorithm is to track nodes' movement by associating trajectories with different identifiers to the same node. Considering with the discussion about the objective of selection function several paragraphs above, we know that a selection function σ is the abstraction of a location tracking algorithm. Two tracking algorithms (implementations of selection function) are discussed in detail in next section.

We can find more features about function $\mathcal{P}_i$ by considering the features of a WLP^2S. In the system, we assume that nodes do not use two identifiers simultaneously, and one identifier is used by at most one user at a time. If the address update time of a node we are interested is t_0, we can easily derive following features of function $p(i, j)$. First, if one trajectory T_j contains actions both before and after time t_0, it means that node with id id_j does not change its identifier at time t_0. Consequently, its linkability with other nodes are zero. Or mathematically,

$$\exists a_1, a_2 \in T_j, time(a_1) < t_0 \wedge time(a_2) > t_0 \to \forall T_i \in \mathcal{T} \wedge T_i \neq T_j, p(i, j) = 0.$$

Besides, if two trajectories T_i, T_j contains actions actions either before or after address update time t_0 at the same time, the probability between this two trajectories $p(i, j)$ is zero.

$$\exists a_i \in T_i, a_j \in T_j, time(a_i) > t_0 \wedge time(a_j) > t_0 \rightarrow p(i, j) = 0.$$

$$\exists a_i \in T_i, a_j \in T_j, time(a_i) < t_0 \wedge time(a_j) < t_0 \rightarrow p(i, j) = 0.$$

With this probability distribution $p(i, j)$ in mind, we are ready for the definition of the anonymity set. Instead of defining the anonymity group of users $\mathcal{U}$, we define the anonymity set of identifier set $\mathcal{ID}$.

Definition 2. *Geographical Anonymity Set(GAS) of a identifier: Given an identifier $i \in \mathcal{ID}$ and its trajectory T_i, the anonymity set–which is called as Geographical Anonymity Set–is defined as a subset of $\mathcal{ID}$, which satisfy following conditions.*

$$GAS(i) = \{j | j \in \mathcal{ID}, \exists T_i, T_j \in \mathcal{T}, p(i, j) \neq 0\} \tag{1}$$

It means that GAS includes all identifiers whose trajectory may be equivalent to T_i. We define the size of a identifier i's GAS $\mathcal{S}_i$ as one measure of identifier i's location privacy.

$$\mathcal{S}_i = |GAS(i)| \tag{2}$$

In addition, we also define entropy of identifier i's GAS $\mathcal{H}_i$ as another measure.

$$\mathcal{H}_i = - \sum_{j \in \mathcal{ID}} p_{i,j} \times \log_2(p_{i,j}) \tag{3}$$

Based on the measures for a specific user, we can also measure the privacy level of the whole system by using some statistical tools. In this paper, we define two system-wide measures: GAS size $\mathcal{S}$ and GAS entropy $\mathcal{H}$ for all observed identifiers as equations below. Other statistical measures such as minimum, maximum of all identifiers' measure (size, entropy) can also be used here depending on different applications.

$$\mathcal{S} = \frac{\sum_{i \in \mathcal{ID}}(\mathcal{S}_i)}{|\mathcal{ID}|} \tag{4}$$

$$\mathcal{H} = \frac{\sum_{i \in \mathcal{ID}}(\mathcal{H}_i)}{|\mathcal{ID}|} \tag{5}$$

Where $|\mathcal{ID}|$ is the size of identifier set $\mathcal{ID}$.

The relationships between those abstracted entities in a MIX system are also summarized in Fig.2 at the beginning of this sub-section.

One major difference between a communications system and a WLP^2S is on their observation functions. In a communications network such as the Internet, although an intruder may observe only a fraction of the actions (e.g., communication of frames between routers) and understand only part of each action (e.g., frame header only), the part of each action (e.g., frame) understood by an intruder is exactly the same as what a user takes. However, in a WLP^2S, the action observed by an intruder is not exactly the same as what a user executes due to the errors introduced in the location observation process. Normally, a location estimation process is composed of two steps. The first step is to measure the set of frame transmission actions $\mathcal{A}_t$. In the measurement process, position pos of each transmission action a_t is invisible to intruders; signal metric sm' received by intruder is smaller than that sent by sender due to the radio attenuation; but other fields are captured correctly. The second step is to estimate node's position pos' based on the observed actions with the same identifier and at same time t. The output of this step a'_t includes an estimation of position pos' of where this action is executed. We notice that set of all estimation results a'_t is not a subset of original transmission actions, or mathematically $\{a'_t\} \not\subseteq \mathcal{A}_t$. Especially, signal metric sm and position pos of each a_t is modified by estimation process because of the accuracy of tracking system.

In addition, similar to the process in [15], only part of the action a_t can be understood by the intruder due to communication mechanisms such as encryption. In a WLP^2S, we assume that the intruder cannot understand the whole message body msg, because it is protected by some encryption mechanism. This process is called tagging function here. Another feature of WLP^2S is that intruders cannot record traces continuously in many cases because of hardware constraints. Instead, an intruder may record actions at a series of time instant.

In summary, the whole observation function ω of a WLP^2S requires three steps: sampling function, position estimation function, and tagging function. In WLP^2S, ω is affected by (1) accuracy of position estimation function, (2) sampling interval of sampling function. We will evaluate the effect of these two parameters in next section.

4   Simulation Study: Silent Period

In this section, we utilize the formal model and its measures to evaluate the privacy level of silent period protocol and formed WLP^2S.

4.1   Design of Two Protection Systems

There are many variable parts in proposed MIX-based formal model. We need to specify following information to define a WLP^2S: (1) MIX $\mathcal{M}$'s mobility model mm, traffic pattern tp, privacy protection protocol $protocol$ (silent period, lifetime), node density $density$, (2) Intruder $\mathcal{I}$'s selection function σ (tracking algorithm), and observation function ω(including tracking accuracy, sampling interval), knowledge about MIX $k_\mathcal{M}$.

In our simulation, we specified two two systems, the only difference between these two systems is on intruder's selection function σ(location tracking algorithm). A summary of the system specification is listed in Table 1.

We first discuss the specification of MIX $\mathcal{M}$. In our system, MIX is formed only by STAs. AP and AS is not involved in the formation of MIX. First, regarding to traffic pattern tp, for simplicity, we assume that all nodes broadcast their identifiers continuously except for silent period in simulation, and they restart communication just after the end of silent period. This implies that there is no frame collision in the system and the effect of different traffic patterns is not taken into account. Secondly, STA use random walk as its mobility model mm when moving around simulation area. In random walk model, the user first selects one direction between 0 and 2π, and a speed between 0 and 1 m/s, which are maintained for about 10 seconds. Afterward, the user iteratively selects its speed and direction. Silent period protocol proposed in [5] is used as privacy protection protocol. There are three parameters in this protocol: length of fixed silent period sp_{fixed}, length of variable silent period $sp_{variable}$, and address lifetime $lifetime$. We also assume that all nodes update their address independently. Density between $0.04/m^2$ and $1/m^2$ are evaluated in simulation.

Then, we discuss the specification of Intruder $\mathcal{I}$. In our system, Intruder $\mathcal{I}$'s knowledge about MIX $k_{\mathcal{M}}$ includes fixed silent period sp_{fixed}, variable silent period $sp_{variable}$, and mobility model mm.

Besides, two tracking algorithms, *simple tracking* and *correlation tracking* are used as the implementation of selection function σ in our simulations. The objective of tracking algorithms is to associate old and new identifiers of nodes from observed frames. We first introduce the notations used by the tracking system. The node under measurement is called target, and others are called mixers. We use $IDP_{type,time}$ to represent a position of a node. IDP is the position of of node with id ID; we use identifiers TP to represent target position, and MPn to represent mixer n's identifier. Subscript *type* indicates how the information is gathered (m, measured; e, estimated; a, actual position), and the subscript *time* indicates when this sample is captured. In compliance with tracking algorithm notations, we assume that a node enters the silent period at time t_{-1}, and leaves it at time t_0. An illustration of notations is given in Fig.3 below. *Simple tracking* utilize its knowledge about nodes' mobility model and the observed target position $TP_{m,t_{-1}}$ at time t_{-1} to estimate its next position $TP_{e,t}$. Based on Intruder's knowledge about fixed and variable silent period, intruder first calculate the maximum duration by that a node will stay inside MIX. Based

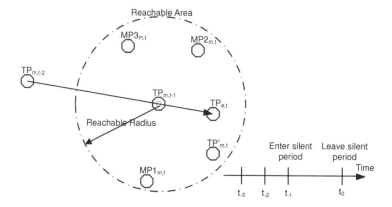

Fig. 3. Notations about positions

on nodes mobility model mm and calculated maximum duration, intruder determines a geographical area *reachable area(RA)* where node may appear with new id. Within a specified time-frame, it is impossible for any nodes to drift out of such reachable area due to the constraint from mobility model; as such, the RA serves as a maximum geographical boundary where a member of the GAS should locate after silent period. Then it chooses a group of nodes who have sent frames with unobserved new identifiers in RA after time t_0 form the GAS of target. This group of nodes forms GAS of target under simple tracking algorithm. Finally, attackers select one node from this group of nodes randomly to associate to target. As a result, the probability that the old and new targets' identifier can be associated correctly is $1/n$ given the size of GAS is n.

Correlation tracking uses the measured position $TP_{m,t_{-2}}$ and $TP_{m,t_{-1}}$ at time t_{-1}, t_{-2}, respectively, to estimate the position TP_{e,t_0} of the target at time t_0. Correlation tracking-algorithm estimates TP_{e,t_0} by assuming that the nodes keep the same speed and direction from time t_{-1} to t_0 exactly like that from time t_{-2} to t_{-1}. Equation (6) is used to calculate TP_{e,t_0}. Based on the estimation result TP_{e,t_0}, the attacker selects one node from new identifiers measured at time t_0, which is nearest to TP_{e,t_0}, as the next identifier of the target.

$$\frac{\overrightarrow{TP_{m,t_{-2}} - TP_{m,t_{-1}}}}{interval} = \frac{\overrightarrow{TP_{m,t_{-1}} - TP_{m,t_0}}}{speriod} \tag{6}$$

In addition, intruder's observation function ω contains two parameters: positioning accuracy and sampling interval. In this simulation, we assume positioning accuracy(error) of observation process follows normal distribution with standard deviation between 0.1 and 2.0. The sampling interval varies between 0.1s to 2s in the simulation.

Finally, we use GAS size $\mathcal{S}$ and GAS entropy $\mathcal{H}$ as measures of these two systems. A summary of the system's configuration is listed in Table 1.

Table 1. Specification of two WLP^2S

Entities	Parameter	Value
$\mathcal{M}$	mobility model mm	random walk(speed: $0 - 1m/s$, step time 10s) node's init position: Uniform distribution
	traffic pattern tp	continuous broadcasting, no frame collision
	protection protocol $protocol$	silent period protocol, fixed silent period(s) sp_{fixed}: $0.1 - 5$ variable silent period(s) $sp_{variable}$: $1.0 - 20$ lifetime(s): $25 - 500$
	$density(/m^2)$	0.04 - 1
$\mathcal{I}$	selection function σ	simple/correlation tracking
	observation function ω	accuracy: normal distribution, std dev. 0.1-2.0 sampling interval(s): $0.1 - 2$
	knowledge $k_{\mathcal{M}}$	sp_{fixed}, maximum value of $sp_{variable}$, mm
Others	simulation area	$20m \times 20m$
	measures	GAS size $\mathcal{S}$, GAS entropy $\mathcal{H}$

4.2   Result analysis

Left side of Fig.4 illustrates the relationship between the size of GAS and the length of the silent period. In the figures, the solid lines denote simulation, while the dotted lines denote analytical calculations. From this figures, we observe that the size of GAS increases proportionately with length of the silent period. This trend can be explained. In the random walk mobility model, the nodes select one direction and speed randomly for a fixed step-time (10 sec in our simulation). The RA of the user is thus a circle centered at the nodes' current position, whose radius is determined by the product of velocity and duration. Because nodes are evenly distributed within the simulation area, the number of nodes that forms the target's GAS can be represented by (7). Equation (7) is plotted, as dotted lines, in left-side of Fig. 4. The comparison between the plots in dotted and solid lines proves the consistency between simulation and theoretical results. The figure between density and size of GAS is omitted because of page limitation. From that figure, we also observe the same trend between density and size of GAS.

$$S(u) = \pi(velocity \times duration)^2 \times density \qquad (7)$$

The right-side graph of Fig.4 illustrates the relationship between entropy of GAS and nodes accuracy, under two tracking algorithms. We observe that the entropy of the system increases proportionately with the nodes' standard deviation of accuracy. In other words, a higher accuracy level of an intruder reduces the privacy level of users. We also observe that the user receives a lower privacy level when a more accurate tracking algorithm is applied. The left-side graph of Fig.5 illustrates the relationship between the sampling interval and entropy of GAS. We observe in this figure that the system's entropy increases proportionally with an increase in the tracking system's sampling interval.

Right-side of Fig.5 shows the performance of the silent period when nodes update their addresses independently. From this figure, we perceive relationship between the silent period ratio and the normalized size of GAS. The silent period ratio is the ratio of the silent period to the lifetime, which represents the

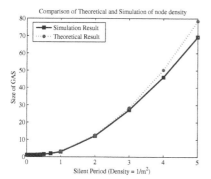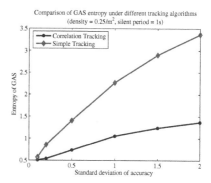

Fig. 4. (left) Comparison of Theoretical and Simulation Results of Silent Period vs. size of GAS, (right) Entropy of GAS vs. accuracy under two tracking algorithms

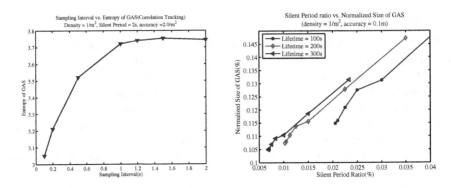

Fig. 5. (left) sampling interval vs. entropy of GAS, (right) silent period ratio vs. normalized size of GAS

share of time a user allocates to protect its privacy. The normalized size of GAS is the ratio of the size of GAS under an independent address update to that under a synchronized address update. The normalized size therefore represents the relative privacy level a user receives when it updates its address independently relative to the synchronized address update. In this figure, we observe that users receive a higher privacy level when they allocate more time to privacy protection. As a result of the preceding analysis, we can conclude that for a higher node density, the longer silent period increases the size of GAS; while a more accurate tracking algorithm and a shorter sampling interval reduces a both entropy and size of GAS. The privacy level decreases sharply when nodes update their addresses independently, but increases when nodes allocate a greater ratio of time to keeping silent. In addition, we guess that less predictable mobility model results in the higher privacy level, but this is still to be verified by simulation.

5   Discussion and Extension

In this section, we utilize the existing results in literatures [20, 17, 21, 14] regarding defense and attack methods on MIX to identify potential threats to the system, and improve the performance of current defense protocols.

Regarding the attack methods, we only consider passive attack based on traffic eavesdropping in current WLP^2S. In addition to this, there are some powerful active and passive attacks such as *blending attack* and *selective attack* introduced in the literatures [20]. Here, we analyze the performance of silent period proposal against these two attacks respectively. First, in a blending attack, intruder floods the MIX with attacker traffic or delay or drop other incoming traffic. Current WLP^2S is robust to such attack because the nodes independently go into silence, the adversary cannot stop the nodes' address update or reduce the anonymity set by adding traffic during the address update. However, this attack should be taken into consideration if variable silent period is decided in the centralized way such as our extension below. Secondly, intruder may use selective attack to reduce the entropy of anonymity group. As discussed in [17], selective attack is a method to exclude other items to be linkable to the items we are interested in. One example of selective attack in WLP^2S is as below. Intruder first tries to link mixers' trajectories before and after silent period, then it exclude all trajectories that has been successfully linked from the GAS of target. Consequently, this method may reduce the size of target's GAS. We think potential advanced tracking algorithm may use this approach to track the target.

On the other hand, we notice that our defense protocol–silent period–can be categorized as a gossip based system. Such systems fundamentally rely on probability to guarantee anonymity. The main representative of this class of anonymity systems is Crowds [22]. One direction to improve our approach is to introduce some deterministic factors in our defense protocol, as a result, defense protocol can provide non-probabilistic anonymity guarantees. The first issue is the address update timing. The simulation results in Sec.4.2 demonstrate that privacy level seriously decreases when nodes update their addresses independently. We suggest that it would be beneficial to add a coordinator to the protection system to help synchronize the address updates. Access point (AP) would be the best-suited node to take such a responsibility because it has connection with all STAs it is serving. Because of page limitation, we only introduce the basic idea of this protocol. STA first registers itself to AP whenever it requests to update its new address, AP schedules the timing of address update for all registered STA, and then notify them when the time arrives by broadcasting some control packets. To prevent compromised AP from leaking the links between old and new identifiers of STA, STA should register itself with new identifier to AS after each address update. This prevent AP from knowing the old identifier of STAs who will go silence.

The second issue is the variable part of silent period. Variable silent period is proposed to mix the temporal relationship between MIX's users. In current system, each node randomly decide the length of variable silent period from a range of value. In simulation, we also assume that two nodes are fully mixed if there are some overlapped variable period between nodes. In comparison with existing MIX research results, we notice that the length of overlapped period *do* affects anonymity level. We think silent period length is analogical to the delay a message experienced in a MIX; and the algorithm to determine silent period length is analogical to batching algorithms used in a MIX. Batch algorithm determines the delay a message should experience for passing through a MIX. Our variable silent period algorithm is similar to the timed MIX, in which all messages are flushed by the MIX in the time of flushing. As discussed in [14], timed MIX are subject to the many attacks. To utilize more robust MIX such as those proposed in [14], we suggest that it would be beneficial to assign AP the responsibility of deciding the length of variable period for all STAs,or in other words, to assign AP the responsibility of batching for all STAs. The benefit of this change is that length of silent period can be decided based on the current status of MIX (i.e., number of nodes in silent period). We expect that when this change

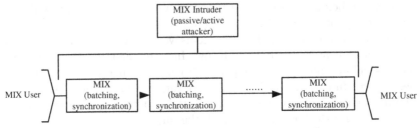

Fig. 6. Illustration of extension for WLP^2S

is applied, user needs to allocate less share of time on variable silent period for the same privacy level as before. Finally, we also propose to utilize a cascade of MIX nodes in WLP^2S. There are two notable advantages for the construction, namely: avoidance of a single point of failure when one MIX is compromised; and improvement of the privacy level by connecting multiple stages of mixes, which allows repeated entry of users in the silent period. Although an intruder may keep tracking a user for one round, it will lose tracking finally if the user enters MIX repeatedly. Mixes in this case may be one or multiple APs in the same serving area.

By conducting a preliminary study based on formal model, we identified the potential attacks to WLP^2S, and extended our current defense protocol. These results demonstrates the effectiveness and promising potential of proposed formal model as a bridge between new location privacy protection problem and existing research results in anonymity research. A summary of those extensions are illustrated in Fig. 6.

6   Conclusion

In this paper, we analyzed wireless location privacy protection system formally, and then generalized it into a formal model based on MIX. Two measures, size and entropy of MIX's anonymity group are proposed. Use of these measures to analyze our system revealed that higher node density, longer silent period increases user's privacy level; while a more accurate tracking algorithm and a shorter sampling interval reduces the privacy level. Besides, user receives much lower privacy when nodes update their addresses independently. On the other hand, based on the formal model, we utilized existing research results in MIX to identify potential threat and improve efficiency of current defense protocol. We also discussed the possibility of introducing deterministic factors into the protocol to improve the protocol efficiency and provide non-probabilistic anonymity guarantee. The result of simulation and preliminary analytical study demonstrated the effectiveness and promising potential of formal model.

We think correlation attack is a common problem for all identity-based wireless communication system. The model and solutions described in this paper is not only applicable for location privacy problem in WLAN and Bluetooth system, but also would be applicable for the very important problem of location privacy in many other areas such as Vehicle ad-hoc networks(VANETs), ubiquitous computing. We will study the feasibility of extending current proposals to those application areas. We also noticed that current model lacks a model check and protocol verification module. Latest research results regarding model checking for probabilistic system [23] as well as deterministic system [15] is a good reference and starting point for us. In addition, we would evaluate those extensions proposed in this paper by more accurate mobility models.

Acknowledgments

We would like to thank Radhakrishna Sampigethaya, Mingyan Li from University of Washington and anonymous reviewers for their comments and advices on this paper. Meanwhile, we would also like to thank Dr. Tracy Camp and Toilers Group from Colorado School of Mines [24] for providing the source code of their mobility model.

References

1. Bandara, U., Hasegawa, M., Inoue, M., Morikawa, H., Aoyama, T.: Design and implementation of a bluetooth signal strength based location sensing system. In: Proc. of IEEE Radio and Wireless Conference (RAWCON 2004), Atlanta, U.S.A (2004)
2. Bahl, P., Padmanabhan, V.: Radar: an in-building rf-based user location and tracking system. In: Proc. of IEEE INFOCOM 2000. Volume 2., Tel-Aviv, Israel (2000) 775–784
3. Beresford, A.R., Stajano, F.: Location privacy in pervasive computing. IEEE Pervasive Computing **2** (2003) 46–55
4. Bluetooth SIG: Bluetooth 1.2 draft 4 (2003)
5. Huang, L., Matsuura, K., Yamane, H., Sezaki, K.: Enhancing wireless location privacy using silent period. In: Proc. of IEEE Wireless Communications and Networking Conference (WCNC 2005), NL, U.S. (2005)
6. Guvenc, I., Abdallah, C., Jordan, R., Dedeoglu, O.: Enhancements to RSS based indoor tracking systems using kalman filter. In: Proc. of Intl. Signal Processing Conf.(ISPC), Dallas, TX, U.S. (2003)
7. Pahlavan, K., Li, X., Makela, J.: Indoor geolocation science and technology. IEEE Communications Magazine **40** (2002) 112–118
8. Gruteser, M., Grunwald, D.: Enhancing location privacy in wireless LAN through disposable interface identifiers: a quantitative analysis. In: Proc. of first ACM international workshop on Wireless mobile applications and services on WLAN hotspots(WMASH 2003), San Diego, CA, USA (2003)
9. Gruteser, M., Grunwald, D.: A methodological assessment of location privacy risks in wireless hotspot networks. In: Proc. of 1st Intl. Conf. on Security in Pervasive Computing(SPC 2003). Volume 2802 of LNCS., Boppard, Germany, Springer (2003)

10. Gruteser, M., Grunwald, D.: Anonymous usage of location-based services through spatial and temporal cloaking. In: Proc. of ACM MobiSys 2003, San Francisco, CA, USA, USENIX (2003) 31–42

11. Chaum, D.: Untraceable electronic mail, return addresses, and digital pseudonyms. Communications of the ACM **24** (1981) 84–88

12. Diaz, C., Seys, S., Claessens, J., Preneel, B.: Towards measuring anonymity. In: Proc. of Privacy Enhancing Technologies, Second International Workshop(PET 2002). Volume 2482 of LNCS., Springer (2002)

13. Serjantov, A., Danezis, G.: Towards an information theoretic metric for anonymity. In: Proc. Privacy Enhancing Technologies, Second International Workshop (PET 2002). Volume 2482 of LNCS., Springer (2002)

14. Diaz, C., Serjantov, A.: Generalising mixes. In: Proc. of Privacy Enhancing Technologies, Third International Workshop(PET 2003). Volume 2760 of LNCS., Dresden, Germany, Springer (2003)

15. Mauw, S., Verschuren, J., Vink, E.d.: A formalization of anonymity and onion routing. In: Proc. of 9th European Symposium on Research Computer Security(ESORICS 2004). Volume 3193 of LNCS., Sophia Antipolis, France, Springer (2004)

16. Syverson, P., Tsudik, G., Reed, M., Landwehr, C.: Towards an analysis of onion routing security. In: Proc. of Workshop on Design Issues in Anonymity and Unobservability, Berkeley, CA, USA (2000)

17. Steinbrecher, S., Kopsell, S.: Modelling unlinkability. In: Proc. of Privacy Enhancing Technologies, Third International Workshop(PET 2003). Volume 2760 of LNCS., Dresden, Germany, Springer (2003)

18. Hughes, D., Shmatikov, V.: Information hiding, anonymity and privacy: A modular approach. Journal of Computer Security **12** (2004) 3–36

19. Yamazaki, K., Sezaki, K.: Spatio-temporal addressing scheme for mobile ad hoc networks. In: Proc. of IEEE TENCON 2004, Chiang Mai, Thailand (2004)

20. Serjantov, A., Dingledine, R., Syverson, P.: From a trickle to a flood: Active attacks on several mix types. In: Proc. of 5th International Workshop on Information Hiding(IH 2002). Volume 2578 of LNCS., Noordwijkerhout, Netherlands, Spinger (2002)

21. Chaum, D.: The dining cryptographers problem: unconditional sender and recipient untraceability. Journal of Cryptology **1** (1988) 65–75

22. Reiter, M., Rubin, A.: Crowds: Anonymity for web transactions. ACM Transactions on Information and System Security **1** (1998) 66–92

23. Shmatikov, V.: Probabilistic model checking of an anonymity system. Journal of Computer Security **12** (2004) 355–377

24. Toilers Group, [Online]: http://toilers.mines.edu/

Appendix: Summary of Notations

Table 2. Notations used in this paper

Notation	Description
u	a MIX user
$\mathcal{U}$	set of all MIX users $\mathcal{U} = \{u\}$
a	an action executed by a MIX user
$\mathcal{A}$	set of all action $\mathcal{A} = \{a\}$
$\mathcal{I}$	MIX's intruder
$\mathcal{M}$	MIX in abstracted MIX system
$\mathcal{S}$	THE system, an abstraction of WLP^2S, $\mathcal{S} = \{\mathcal{U}, \mathcal{I}, \mathcal{M}\}$
id	MIX user' identifier
$\mathcal{ID}$	set of all identifiers $\mathcal{ID} = \{id\}$
T_i	identifier i's trajectory, set of all a_t with same sender id i, $T_i = \{a_t | id(a_t) = i\}$
$\mathcal{T}$	set of all trajectories $\mathcal{T} = \{T_i\}$, $\mathcal{T} \subseteq \mathcal{A}_{obs}$
a_t	a transmission action, $a_t = id_s \| id_r \| msg \| time \| sm \| pos$
$\mathcal{A}_m$	set of all movement actions
$\mathcal{A}_t$	set of all transmission actions $\mathcal{A}_t = \{a_t\}$
$\mathcal{A}_r$	set of all reception actions
$\mathcal{A}_{obs}$	set of all observable actions
$\mathcal{A}_{inv}$	set of all invisible actions
$k_{\mathcal{M}}$	$\mathcal{I}$'s knowledge about $\mathcal{M}$
σ	$\mathcal{I}$'s selection function $\sigma : \mathcal{T} \times \mathcal{T} \to P$
ω	$\mathcal{I}$'s observation function $\omega : \mathcal{A} \to \mathcal{A}_{obs}$
$\sim_\sigma$	selection function σ's equivalence relation on $\mathcal{T}$
$p_{i,i}$	probability that T_i and T_j are equivalent based on equivalence relation $\sim_\sigma$
$\mathcal{P}_i$	attacker's a-posteriori probability distribution function for t_i
$\mathcal{P}$	set of all identifiers' a-posteriori probability distribution function $\{\mathcal{P}_i\}$
msg	an a_t's message payload
$time$	time when a_t is executed
sm	signal metric of a_t
pos	position where a_t is executed
mm	mobility pattern of $\mathcal{M}$
tp	traffic pattern of $\mathcal{M}$
$protocol$	privacy protection protocol used in $\mathcal{M}$
$density$	number of MIX users in $\mathcal{M}$, $density = |\mathcal{U}|$
$GAS(id)$	geographical anonymity set(GAS) of identifier id
$\mathcal{S}_{id}$	identifier id's GAS size
$\mathcal{H}_{id}$	identifier id's GAS entropy
$\mathcal{S}$	GAS size of THE system $\mathcal{S}$
$\mathcal{H}$	GAS entropy of THE system $\mathcal{S}$
$id(a_t)$	identifier of a transmission action a_t
$time(a_t)$	time instant of a transmission action a_t
$\{x\}$	a set of elements
$x \| y$	x concatenated to y

Failures in a Hybrid Content Blocking System

Richard Clayton

University of Cambridge, Computer Laboratory, William Gates Building,
15 JJ Thomson Avenue, Cambridge CB3 0FD, United Kingdom
richard.clayton@cl.cam.ac.uk

Abstract. Three main methods of content blocking are used on the Internet: blocking routes to particular IP addresses, blocking specific URLs in a proxy cache or firewall, and providing invalid data for DNS lookups. The mechanisms have different accuracy/cost trade-offs. This paper examines a hybrid, two-stage system that redirects traffic that might need to be blocked to a proxy cache, which then takes the final decision. This promises an accurate system at a relatively low cost. A British ISP has deployed such a system to prevent access to child pornography. However, circumvention techniques can now be employed at both system stages to reduce effectiveness; there are risks from relying on DNS data supplied by the blocked sites; and unhappily, the system can be used as an *oracle* to determine what is being blocked. Experimental results show that it is straightforward to use the system to compile a list of illegal websites.

1 Introduction

There are a number of mechanisms for blocking Internet access to content. Barring particular IP addresses makes entire sites unavailable, but this can cause significant collateral damage when other websites share the same address. It is also possible to subvert the DNS so that websites cannot be located. Barring access to particular URLs is a more precise technology in that it can make specific parts of sites unavailable. However, it is much more expensive, requiring stateful inspection of packet contents within a firewall or the use of web proxies that interpose themselves between the requestor and the remote content.

In Britain there has been considerable interest in blocking indecent images of children (so-called "child pornography"). It has been illegal to "take" these images since 1978, illegal to "possess" them since 1988 and illegal to "make" them since 1994 [5]. The Internet Watch Foundation (IWF) operates a UK hotline for reporting illegal material found on the Internet. It collates the information it receives, and then informs the appropriate authorities. To avoid duplication of effort, the IWF maintains a database of URLs that have been inspected and keeps a record of when they led to illegal material. In particular, it became apparent to the IWF that although some countries took down illegal content promptly, some websites remained accessible for a considerable time.

BT is one of the largest UK ISPs, operating under brand names such as "BT Openworld", "BT Yahoo!", "BT Click" etc. In late 2003 they decided to create

G. Danezis and D. Martin (Eds.): PET 2005, LNCS 3856, pp. 78–92, 2005.

an innovative blocking system, internally dubbed "CleanFeed".[1] Their aim was to prevent their Internet customers from accessing, either by accident or design, any of the illegal images of children listed in the IWF database. The existence of the system was leaked to the press [1] shortly before it became live in June 2004. The CleanFeed system is a hybrid design, incorporating both redirection of traffic and the use of web proxies. It is intended to be extremely precise in what it blocks, but at the same time to be low cost to build and operate.

This paper is arranged as follows: content blocking mechanisms are reviewed in more detail in Section 2 along with details of their worldwide deployment and previous studies of their effectiveness; the BT system is described in Section 3 and its effectiveness is considered in Section 4; the use of a hybrid system as an *oracle* to reveal which sites it is blocking is presented in Section 5 along with some actual results from the BT CleanFeed system.

2   Content Blocking Systems

2.1   Basic Mechanisms

There are three basic methods of blocking content available to ISPs and network operators. These are packet dropping (which operates at OSI layer 3), content filtering (operating at higher protocol layers), and DNS poisoning (to prevent any connection to the site being made at all).

Packet dropping systems are conceptually very simple. A list is created of the IP addresses of the websites to be blocked. Packets destined for these IP addresses are discarded and hence no connection can be made to the servers. The discarding mechanism can take note of the type of IP traffic, for example, it could just discard HTTP (`tcp/80`) packets and leave email alone.

The main problem with packet dropping is the collateral damage that it causes because *all* of the web content on the particular IP address will become inaccessible. This can be very significant. Edelman [4] obtained a list of all the `.org`, `.com` and `.net` domains and tried to resolve the conventional website address for each of them by prefixing the domain name with `www` and looking this up in the DNS. His paper shows that 87.3% of such sites share IP addresses with one or more other sites and 69.8% with 50 or more other sites. There is no reason to presuppose that content that might be suppressed is hosted in any special way, so his conclusion was that there is a significant risk of "overblocking" with schemes that suppress content by methods based solely on IP addresses.

DNS poisoning systems work by arranging that DNS lookups for the hostnames of blocked sites will fail to return the correct IP address. This solution also suffers from overblocking in that no content within the blocked domain remains available. Thus it would not be an appropriate solution for blocking content hosted somewhere like `geocities.com`; blocking one site would also block about

---

[1] The official name for the project is the BT Anti-Child-Abuse Initiative.

three million others. However, the overblocking differs from that identified by
Edelman in that it does not extend to blocking other domains that are hosted on
the same machine. There is also some "underblocking" in that a URL containing
an IP address, rather than a hostname, would not be affected; because a browser
would simply use the IP address and would not consult the DNS at all.

DNS poisoning can also affect other services, such as email. The blocking of
right-wing and Nazi material mandated by the regional government in North-
Rhine-Westphalia in Germany has been studied by Dornseif [3]. He found that
the majority of local providers had opted for DNS poisoning but had made significant implementation errors. Although `www.stormfront.org` was (correctly)
blocked by all of the ISPs he checked, only 15 of 27 ISPs (56%) also blocked
`stormfront.org` as they should have done, and he believes that all but 4 of them
only blocked it accidentally. Further, just 12 of 27 ISPs (44%) permitted access to
`kids.stormfront.org`, which was not subject to a blocking order. Email should
not have been blocked at all, but nevertheless 16 of 27 ISPs (59%) caused it to
fail for some domains; and in the case of `postmaster@www.stormfront.org`,
every one of the ISPs studied were (incorrectly) blocking email.

Content filtering systems will not only block entire websites but can also
be used to block very specific items, such as a particular web page or even a
single image. They determine that the URL being accessed is one of those to be
blocked and then ensure that the corresponding content is not made available.
This type of system is extremely accurate in blocking exactly what is on the list
of URLs, no more, no less, and hence there should be no overblocking – provided,
of course, that the list of URLs was correct in the first place.

Quite clearly, web proxies are ineffective at blocking content if their usage
is optional. Hence it must be arranged that all customer traffic passes through
the proxy, leading to a considerable expense in providing equipment that can
handle the load. Also, to prevent a single point of failure, the equipment must
be replicated, which considerably increases the cost. The bottom line for most
ISPs considering blocking systems is that although content filtering is the most
precise method, it is also far more expensive than the alternatives.

2.2   Existing Content Blocking Schemes

A number of content blocking schemes are known to have been deployed in various countries [13]. In China the current method appears to be a firewall scheme
that resets connections [10]. Saudi Arabia operates a web proxy system with
a generic list of banned sites, from a filtering software provider, augmented by
citizen reported URLs [7]. In Norway, the child pornography blocking system
introduced in October 2004 by Telenor and KRIPOS, the Norwegian National
Criminal Investigation Service, serves up a special replacement web page "containing information about the filter, as well as a link to KRIPOS" [11].

In Pennsylvania USA, a state statute requiring the blocking of sites adjudged
to contain child pornography was struck down as unconstitutional in September
2004. The evidence presented to the court was that ISPs had, for cost reasons,

been implementing blocking by means of packet dropping and DNS poisoning. Careful reading of the court's decision [12] shows that the resulting overblocking was by no means the only relevant factor; no evidence had been presented to the court that the blocking had "reduced child exploitation or abuse"; and procedural mechanisms for requesting blocking amounted to "prior restraint", which is forbidden under the First Amendment to the US Constitution. However, the mechanisms actually deployed were significant, since the court determined that it was also "prior restraint" that future content at a website would in practice be suppressed, even though the abusive images of children had been removed.

3   Design of the CleanFeed System

The exact design of the BT CleanFeed system has not been published. This description is based on several separate accounts and although it is believed to be substantially correct, it may be inaccurate in some minor details.

The scheme is a hybrid, involving a first stage mechanism that resembles packet dropping, except that the packets are not discarded but are instead routed to a second stage content filtering system. The system is shown diagrammatically in Figure 1. The first stage examines all traffic flowing from customers (along the path labelled a in the figure). If the traffic is innocuous then it is sent along path b to its destination in the normal way. If the traffic is for a suspect site, parts of which may be blocked, then it is redirected along path c to the second stage filter. This first stage selection of traffic is based on the examination of the destination port number and IP address within the packets. The second stage filtering is implemented as a web proxy that understands HTTP requests. When the request is for an item in the IWF database a 404 (page unavailable) response is returned, but all other, innocuous, requests are relayed to the remote site along path d and the material returned to the customer in the reverse direction.

The IP addresses used by the first stage are obtained by working through all the entries in the IWF database and translating the hostname into an IP address in the normal way by making a DNS query. The results are amalgamated and used to modify the normal packet routing (controlled by BGP) within the customer-facing portion of the BT network (shaded in the diagram) so that the HTTP packets for these addresses will be routed to the web cache.

The second stage web proxy uses the URLs from the IWF database. Because there are concerns about keeping a human-readable form of the list on the server, it is held in what journalists have called an "encrypted form" (presumably as cryptographic hashes). The request is also "encrypted" (hashed) and a check for a match is then made. When there is no match, the proxy issues a request to the remote site in the usual way and then presents the response to the requestor. It is unclear, and not especially relevant to this discussion, whether the proxy also acts a cache, serving local versions of recently accessed material.

When compared with the generic solutions outlined in Section 2.1 and the systems deployed elsewhere in the world discussed in Section 2.2, the CleanFeed system has some significant advantages. Although its first stage uses the same

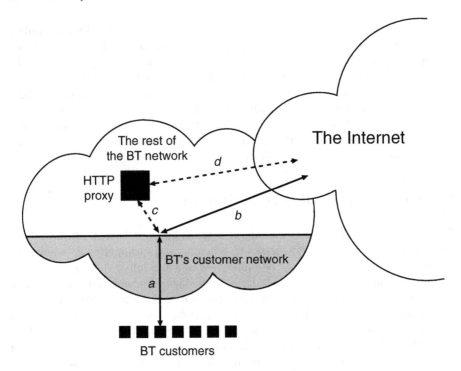

Fig. 1. The BT CleanFeed System

approach as "packet dropping", it does not suffer from overblocking because the second stage web proxy can be as selective as necessary. However, the second stage can use low-cost equipment because it only needs to handle a small proportion of overall traffic. By avoiding DNS poisoning the designers can be sure that only web traffic will be affected and not other protocols such as email.

Therefore CleanFeed is, at first sight, an effective and precise method of blocking unacceptable content. However, there are a number of detailed implementation issues to address as soon as one assumes that content providers or content consumers might start to make serious attempts to get around it.

4   Circumvention of the CleanFeed System

4.1   Identifying the IWF and CleanFeed

If a content provider can identify that an access is being made by the IWF then they can provide information that is specific to that access. For example, they might provide innocuous images to the IWF and illegal images to everyone else. If they can do this successfully, the IWF will never blacklist their site and so it will not be blocked by CleanFeed. It is possible that some content providers already take this approach, since the IWF report that only 33% of hotline reports are

substantiated as potentially illegal [6]. Identifying accesses by CleanFeed itself (in particular, components that do DNS lookups) also gives the content
provider the opportunity for denial-of-service attacks as outlined in Section 4.3
below.

Table 1 summarises how a content provider might detect IWF/CleanFeed
activity, along with the countermeasures that could negate these:

Table 1. Detecting content access by the IWF or the CleanFeed system

Content Provider Strategy	Countermeasure
Recognise the accessing IP address.	Access via web proxies.
Recognise source of DNS requests.	Use DNS proxies for name resolution. Ensure that CleanFeed access is random rather than a regular occurrence.
Anonymously report a sacrificial website to the IWF. Anyone who arrives to look at it must be the IWF or, later on, the police. Bar similar access in future.	Choose proxies and anonymous access systems likely to be used by genuine customers so that content provider will bar them as well.
Serve active content to run on viewer's machine and reveal their identity.	Disable Java, JavaScript, etc.
Serve cookies (from a central site) to tie visits to disparate sites together.	Refuse to return cookies (and/or clear cookie cache before browsing a new site).
Serve content with a request it be cached. Failing to refetch indicates a repeat visit.	Clear cache before browsing a new site.
Ensure unique URLs are used in advertising spam. A second access from a new IP address will be the IWF acting upon a report from the public.	Discard any obvious tracking information appended to URLs. Avoid starting visits in the "middle" of a website, but follow the links from the front page.

4.2 Evading CleanFeed

There are generic ways a content requestor (a customer) can avoid content blocking, such as tunnelling traffic via proxies that can access the content directly
without any intervention. Dornseif [3] discusses this and a number of other techniques. For the hybrid CleanFeed system it is obviously effective to evade either of the two stages. However, CleanFeed's countermeasures can involve the
first stage being less precise about traffic selection because the second stage
will provide accurate blocking. Table 2 gives examples of some possible evasion
strategies.

4.3 Attacking CleanFeed

Content providers could also actively attack the CleanFeed system, with a view
to having it closed down. Example strategies and countermeasures are sum-
marised in Table 3. Some build upon being able to identify CleanFeed system
accesses and provide bogus information to them (see Table 1).

Table 2. Evading the CleanFeed system

Content Requestor Strategy	Countermeasure
Use a tunnelling technique, or proxy system, such as Tor, JAP, etc.	Also block the tunnels and the proxies (this is unlikely to be scaleable).
Use IP source routing to send traffic via routes that will evade the blocking.	Discard all source routed packets (often Best Practice anyway).
Encode requests (perhaps by using %xx escapes) so that they are not recognised.	Ensure URLs are put into a canonical form before they are checked.
Add specious characters to URLs (such as leading zeroes) to avoid recognition.	Ensure URLs are put into a canonical form before they are checked.
Provide specious HTTP/1.1 `Host:` details for an HTTP/1.0 site.	Check whether remote site acts upon `Host:` information.

Content Provider Strategy	Countermeasure
Move site to another IP address.	Regular updates of IP addresses.
Change port used for access (harder to track than address change, but may disrupt users as well as the blocking system).	Redirect other ports (paying careful attention if ports such as `tcp/53` (DNS) need to be intercepted).
Accept unusually formatted requests.	Extend canonicalisation to reflect what server accepts (which may be hard to do).

Table 3. Attacking the CleanFeed system

Content Provider Strategy	Countermeasure
Change location (IP address) of content very rapidly and often so that first stage routing "flaps".	Add addresses quickly, but remove slowly. No harm in sending extra traffic to the second stage unless it is overloaded.
Return specious DNS results referring to high traffic third-party websites. Hope to overwhelm the second stage web cache.	Avoid automating changes of IP address, and run sanity checks on returned values.
Return specious DNS results implicating BT customer or service machines, hoping thereby to create traffic loops.	Discard all results for external sites that claim to be inside the BT network.
Overload system by creating large numbers of addresses to block (eg by distributing content, perhaps by hijacking innocent machines to host the material [2]).	Unlikely to hit any limits in second stage web cache. In first stage, stop considering single addresses but redirect entire subnets. Provided cache can cope with traffic volume, no faults will be visible.

---

[2] The simplest way of providing content on large numbers of IP addresses is by means of a proxy network. In October 2003 Wired reported [9] that a Polish group were advertising "invisible bulletproof hosting" by exploiting a network of 450 000 end-user machines on which they had covertly planted their own software. Surreptitiously obtaining service from tens of thousands of machines is quite conceivable, so the Polish claim is not entirely outrageous, although without independent verification it cannot be seen as entirely trustworthy.

4.4   Blocking Legitimate Content

In a handful of special cases, the content provider can arrange for legitimate content to be blocked. Besides the inconvenience to those requiring access to this content, the effect is to bring the blocking system into disrepute and it must therefore be seen as an important attack.

Systems sometimes provide links based on IP addresses rather than by host-names. This often occurs when linking to back-end database systems that serve query results or extracts from atlases. For example, a link to the Google cache of "the snapshot that we took of the page as we crawled the web" might be of the form `http://66.102.9.104/search?q=cache:FFKHU5mkjdEJ:www.cl.cam.ac.uk/users/rnc1/`. If so, then by ensuring that an illegal image at `http://www.example.com/search` was blocked by CleanFeed (using an anonymous hotline report) then the owner of the DNS for `www.example.com` can arrange for Google's cache to become inaccessible by serving `66.102.9.104` as a possible IP address for `www.example.com`.

The countermeasure is to ensure that whenever a DNS lookup yields new IP addresses they are checked for accuracy. However, if many IP address changes are being made by content providers in the hope of avoiding CleanFeed blocking altogether, it will be too expensive to manually check every change. Automated processes will be required for the testing that determines whether the content is the same but accessed via a different address. Unfortunately, an automated process cannot be relied upon to distinguish between an illegal website changing both content and IP address, and a spuriously supplied IP address. Hence, automation could lead to CleanFeed's users finding some legitimate sites blocked and this in turn would lead to a devaluing of the system's reputation.

5   Real-World Experiments

This paper has briefly discussed a number of attacks that might be made on the effectiveness or integrity of the CleanFeed system – and then explained how they might be countered. It would clearly be useful to determine which of the attacks are effective in practice and which are defeated either because the CleanFeed system already contains a countermeasure or because of some other aspect of the design that is not immediately apparent. However this is not possible, as will now be explained.

5.1   Legal Issues When Experimenting upon CleanFeed

Most experiments upon the CleanFeed system would require an attempt to access the sites containing the illegal material that the system is intended to block. If an evasion method was attempted and was successful in evading the blocking, then, under UK law, a serious criminal offence would be committed by fetching indecent images of children. Although there are statutory defences to inadvertent access, these could not apply to an explicit access attempt.

Experimenting with the techniques available to a content provider would involve working with the providers of illegal content, which would be ethically questionable, even if it was not directly a criminal offence. Even demonstrating that the IWF's access was easy to distinguish (a pre-requisite for some of the attack techniques) would involve submitting a false report and thereby wasting some of their analysts' time by causing them to examine websites unnecessarily, which is undesirable.

There is a method by which experimentation could be done, without these legal and ethical problems. If a test site, containing completely legal images, was added to the IWF database then it would be possible to perform all the necessary experiments on user and content provider strategies – and, as countermeasures were added, assess their effectiveness. However, permission to add such a site has been refused, so the only people running experiments will be the consumers or providers of illegal content and they are unlikely to report their results.

Nevertheless, it was possible to experimentally demonstrate that a user can exploit CleanFeed to construct lists of illegal websites. This is undesirable and unexpected, and should be taken into account when discussing the public policy issue of whether to encourage this method of content blocking.

5.2   Locating Blocked Websites Using the CleanFeed System

The CleanFeed system redirects traffic for particular IP addresses to a web proxy that then determines whether a particular URL should be blocked. It is possible to detect the first stage action, construct a list of redirected IP addresses, and to then determine which websites are located at those IP addresses – and hence use the system as an *oracle*[3] for locating illegal images.

The list of redirected IP addresses is created by a special scanning program. This sends out multiple TCP packets, each to a different address, with the destination port set to 80 and a TTL (time-to-live) value that is sufficient to reach the CleanFeed web proxy, but insufficient to reach the destination IP address (thus it will not unnecessarily trip intrusion detection systems at a remote site). If the IP address is not being redirected then the TTL will be decremented to zero by an intermediate router that will report this event via ICMP. If the IP address is being redirected then the packet will reach the web proxy. If the outgoing packet is sent with a SYN flag then the web proxy will respond with a packet containing SYN/ACK (the second stage of the TCP three-way handshake) and forging the IP address of the destination site. If the IP address is sent without a SYN flag then the proxy should respond with a packet with the RST flag set (because there is no valid connection).

The program was instructed to scan a /24 subnet (256 addresses) of a Russian web-hosting company (of ill-repute), with the results shown in Figure 2. Note that for this scan the SYN bit was set in the outgoing packets, when the SYN bit was absent the same pattern was visible but the RST packet was discarded by a local firewall!

---

[3] *oracle* is being used in the sense of Lowe [8] as a system that will accurately answer any number of questions posed to it without regard to the consequences.

```
17:54:27  Starting scan of [~~~.~~~.191.0] to [~~~.~~~.191.255] (TTL 8)
17:54:27  Scan: To [~~~.~~~.191.0]  : [166.49.168.13], ICMP
17:54:27  Scan: To [~~~.~~~.191.1]  : [166.49.168.5],  ICMP
17:54:27  Scan: To [~~~.~~~.191.2]  : [166.49.168.5],  ICMP
17:54:27  Scan: To [~~~.~~~.191.3]  : [166.49.168.5],  ICMP
17:54:27  Scan: To [~~~.~~~.191.4]  : [166.49.168.9],  ICMP
17:54:27  Scan: To [~~~.~~~.191.5]  : [166.49.168.9],  ICMP
17:54:27  Scan: To [~~~.~~~.191.6]  : [166.49.168.13], ICMP
17:54:27  Scan: To [~~~.~~~.191.7]  : [166.49.168.13], ICMP


... and similar responses until


17:54:28  Scan: To [~~~.~~~.191.39] : [166.49.168.1],  ICMP
17:54:28  Scan: To [~~~.~~~.191.40] : [~~~.~~~.191.40], SYN/ACK
17:54:28  Scan: To [~~~.~~~.191.41] : [166.49.168.13], ICMP
17:54:28  Scan: To [~~~.~~~.191.42] : [~~~.~~~.191.42], SYN/ACK
17:54:28  Scan: To [~~~.~~~.191.43] : [166.49.168.9],  ICMP
17:54:28  Scan: To [~~~.~~~.191.44] : [166.49.168.5],  ICMP
17:54:28  Scan: To [~~~.~~~.191.45] : [166.49.168.9],  ICMP
17:54:28  Scan: To [~~~.~~~.191.46] : [166.49.168.13], ICMP
17:54:28  Scan: To [~~~.~~~.191.47] : [166.49.168.9],  ICMP
17:54:28  Scan: To [~~~.~~~.191.48] : [166.49.168.9],  ICMP
17:54:28  Scan: To [~~~.~~~.191.49] : [~~~.~~~.191.49], SYN/ACK
17:54:28  Scan: To [~~~.~~~.191.50] : [~~~.~~~.191.50], SYN/ACK
17:54:28  Scan: To [~~~.~~~.191.51] : [166.49.168.9],  ICMP
17:54:28  Scan: To [~~~.~~~.191.52] : [166.49.168.5],  ICMP
17:54:28  Scan: To [~~~.~~~.191.53] : [166.49.168.9],  ICMP
17:54:28  Scan: To [~~~.~~~.191.54] : [166.49.168.5],  ICMP
17:54:28  Scan: To [~~~.~~~.191.55] : [~~~.~~~.191.55], SYN/ACK
17:54:28  Scan: To [~~~.~~~.191.56] : [166.49.168.1],  ICMP
17:54:28  Scan: To [~~~.~~~.191.57] : [166.49.168.5],  ICMP
17:54:28  Scan: To [~~~.~~~.191.58] : [166.49.168.1],  ICMP
17:54:28  Scan: To [~~~.~~~.191.59] : [166.49.168.1],  ICMP
17:54:28  Scan: To [~~~.~~~.191.60] : [166.49.168.13], ICMP
17:54:28  Scan: To [~~~.~~~.191.61] : [166.49.168.1],  ICMP
17:54:28  Scan: To [~~~.~~~.191.62] : [~~~.~~~.191.62], SYN/ACK
17:54:28  Scan: To [~~~.~~~.191.63] : [166.49.168.9],  ICMP
17:54:28  Scan: To [~~~.~~~.191.64] : [166.49.168.5],  ICMP
17:54:28  Scan: To [~~~.~~~.191.65] : [166.49.168.9],  ICMP
17:54:28  Scan: To [~~~.~~~.191.66] : [~~~.~~~.191.66], SYN/ACK
17:54:29  Scan: To [~~~.~~~.191.67] : [166.49.168.13], ICMP
17:54:29  Scan: To [~~~.~~~.191.68] : [166.49.168.13], ICMP
... etc
```

Fig. 2. Results of Scanning for IP Addresses Redirected by CleanFeed

These results (the high order octets of the IP addresses have been intentionally suppressed) show responses of either an ICMP packet (for TTL expired) from one of BT's routers in their `166.49.168/24` subnet, or a SYN/ACK packet, apparently from the remote site, but in reality from the CleanFeed web cache machine. The results clearly show that the CleanFeed system is intercepting traffic to a number of websites hosted at the Russian supplier. The full results show a total of seventeen IP addresses being redirected to the web cache.

Of course, knowing the IP address of a website does not allow one to view the content (unless it is using HTTP/1.0 or the server selects one main site to serve when just the IP address is present). However, reverse lookup directories exist that provide a mapping from IP address to web server name (they are constructed by resolving entries from the list of top level domain names). One such directory is sited at `whois.webhosting.info` and this was used to check out the IP addresses that CleanFeed was blocking.

Typical results (again there has been some intentional obfuscation) were:

```
˜˜˜.˜˜˜.191.40    lolitaportal.****
˜˜˜.˜˜˜.191.42    no websites recorded in the database
˜˜˜.˜˜˜.191.49    samayhamed.****
˜˜˜.˜˜˜.191.50    amateurs-world.****
                  anime-worlds.****
                  boys-top.****
                  cute-virgins.****
                  cyber-lolita.****
                  egoldeasy.****
                  ... and 27 more sites with similar names
```

and in total there were 91 websites on 9 of the 17 IP addresses. No websites were reported as using the other 8 IP addresses that were being blocked. This may be because the content has moved and the IWF have yet to update their information, or it may be because they were sites hosted in other top level domains, such as `.ru`, that the reverse lookup database does not currently record.

Checking the other IP addresses, not blocked by CleanFeed, showed a higher proportion of nil returns, but similar looking names. It is not possible to say whether these sites are innocuous or just not known to the IWF at present.

For the reasons explained above, *none* of these sites have been examined to determine what sort of content they actually contain, but it is fairly clear that if one was deliberately setting out to view illegal material then the Clean-Feed system provides a mechanism that permits one to substantially reduce the effort of locating it. Further, since domain names can misrepresent the content (purveyors of pornography do not follow a truth-in-advertising code) it permits such a viewer to weed out superficially alluring website names and only select the ones that the IWF has already determined will contain illegal material.

Experiments showed that scans could be conducted at rates up to 98 addresses/second using a simple dialup connection. At this rate it would take 500 days to scan the entire 2^{32} address space – or, more realistically, 160 days to scan the 32% of the address space currently routable.[4] To scan just Russian IP addresses (and the IWF claim that 25% of all the websites they know of are located in Russia) then this is approximately 8.3 million addresses, which would take just under 24 hours. A suitable "BT Yahoo!" dialup account that is filtered by CleanFeed is available for free and the phone call will cost less than £15.

5.3 Countering the Oracle Attack

The oracle attack described in the previous section works by determining the path the packets take towards their destination. It is hard to counter in practice. The packets being sent by the end user can be made indistinguishable from normal TCP traffic – so they cannot just be discarded by a simple packet filtering system. The responses are either ICMP packets or SYN/ACK packets, again the latter must be permitted to pass, so discarding the former would not do anything especially useful.

If a web proxy is deployed in the network before the first stage at which a routing decision is made (which currently seems to be the case with the "BT Click" pay-as-you-go connectivity product) then the oracle attack fails (the web proxy treats all the packets the same, whether or not they will be candidates for redirection). However, this is an expensive fix, and BT have been removing compulsory (transparent) web caches from their products for marketing reasons.

The scanning attack is defeated if the first stage proxy does not redirect the packets to the web proxy unless their TTL setting is sufficient to reach the remote site. However, this would be complex to configure and would require specialised hardware, rather than standard routers running standard implementations of BGP. Even with this fix, it would almost certainly still be possible to distinguish web cache responses by examining the detail of what was returned.

An alternative approach is to make the scan less accurate. If the CleanFeed system redirected traffic destined for more IP addresses than the minimum necessary, then the scan results would contain even more innocuous websites than at present. It may be entirely practical to redirect /24 subnets rather than individual /32 addresses, the only question being whether or not there would be a substantial increase in traffic to the web caches.

Another way of reducing accuracy would be to make the first stage redirection less predictable by introducing a statistical element. If sites were sometimes blocked and sometimes not, then the scan would take longer to be sure of its results. However, this might not be a viable option with existing equipment and it is rather perverse to defend a blocking system against attack by arranging that sometimes it fails to operate.

The easiest way of dealing with the oracle attack would be to detect it occurring, most simply by examining logs at the web proxy, and then treating it as "abuse" and disconnecting the customer. It would probably take an attacker some time (and a number of terminated accounts) to determine how to reduce the activity sufficiently to avoid being detected.

---

[4] source: http://www.completewhois.com/statistics/index.htm

6 Conclusions

BT's CleanFeed was designed to be a low cost, but highly accurate, system for blocking Internet content. At first sight it is significant improvement upon existing schemes. However, CleanFeed derives its advantages from employing two separate stages, and this hybrid system is thereby made more fragile because circumvention of either stage, whether by the end user or by the content provider, will cause the blocking to fail.

This paper has described attacks on both stages of the CleanFeed system and set out various countermeasures to address them. Some attacks concern the minutiae of comparing URLs, while others address fundamentals of the system architecture. In particular, the CleanFeed system relies on data returned by the content provider, especially when doing DNS lookups. It also relies on the content provider returning the same data to everyone. All of this reliance upon the content providers' probity could well be entirely misplaced.

The CleanFeed design is intended to be extremely precise in what it blocks, but to keep costs under control this has been achieved by treating some traffic specially. This special treatment can be detected by end users and this means that the system can be used as an oracle to efficiently locate illegal websites. This runs counter to its high level policy objectives.

Although legal and ethical issues prevent most experimentation at present, the attacks are extremely practical and would be straightforward to implement. If CleanFeed is used in the future to block other material, which may be distasteful but is legal to view, then there will be no bar to anyone assessing its effectiveness. It must be expected that knowledge of how to circumvent the system (for all material) will then become widely known and countermeasures will become essential.

An important general conclusion to draw from the need for a manual element in many of the countermeasures is that the effectiveness of any blocking system, and the true cost of ensuring it continues to provide accurate results, cannot be properly assessed until it comes under serious assault. Thinking of these systems as "fit-and-forget" arrangements will be a guarantee of their long-term failure.

Postscript

A few days after this paper was presented at the PET Workshop, Brightview (a subsidiary of Invox plc) announced [2] that the oracle attack it describes was also effective against "WebMinder", their own two stage content filtering system, used by the UK ISPs that they operate. Their design is architecturally similar to that of CleanFeed, but they are employing Cisco's proprietary Web Cache Communication Protocol version 2 (WCCPv2) to redirect suspect traffic to a number of patched `squid` proxy servers.

In their announcement, Brightview also claimed that although their system had been vulnerable, they had now made the oracle attack "no longer effective". What they had done was to change stage one of the system to discard all packets with a TTL of less than 24. This means that the scanning program has to use higher TTLs; and hence both the web proxy and remote sites will receive the packets and return SYN/ACK responses – and, it was claimed, that would prevent the two sites from being distinguished.

It is true that the exact method of attack described above is defeated (and was achieved with just a one line change to the WCCPv2 configuration). It is also true that the fix is rather more elegant than just described in Section 5.3 which was envisaged to involve using different TTL limits for every possible destination. Nevertheless, as had been predicted, it remains straightforward to distinguish the web proxy from the remote site whose content it is filtering. A simple technique is to send the scans with a high TTL (such as 128)[5], to evade the countermeasure, and then examine the TTL in the returned packets.

Consider this scanning example of the /24 subnet to which the Russian sites listed above have now moved (with some other internal renumbering):

```
Scan: To [~~~.~~~.234.51] : [~~~.~~~.234.51], TTL=49 RST
Scan: To [~~~.~~~.234.52] : [~~~.~~~.234.52], TTL=49 SYN/ACK
Scan: To [~~~.~~~.234.53] : [~~~.~~~.234.53], TTL=49 SYN/ACK
Scan: To [~~~.~~~.234.54] : [~~~.~~~.234.54], TTL=49 SYN/ACK
Scan: To [~~~.~~~.234.55] : [~~~.~~~.234.55], TTL=49 SYN/ACK
Scan: To [~~~.~~~.234.56] : [~~~.~~~.234.56], TTL=49 SYN/ACK
Scan: To [~~~.~~~.234.57] : [~~~.~~~.234.57], TTL=59 SYN/ACK
Scan: To [~~~.~~~.234.58] : [~~~.~~~.234.58], TTL=49 SYN/ACK
Scan: To [~~~.~~~.234.59] : [~~~.~~~.234.59], TTL=49 SYN/ACK
Scan: To [~~~.~~~.234.60] : [~~~.~~~.234.60], TTL=49 RST
Scan: To [~~~.~~~.234.61] : [~~~.~~~.234.61], TTL=49 SYN/ACK
Scan: To [~~~.~~~.234.62] : [~~~.~~~.234.62], TTL=49 RST
Scan: To [~~~.~~~.234.63] : [~~~.~~~.234.63], TTL=59 SYN/ACK
Scan: To [~~~.~~~.234.68] : [~~~.~~~.234.68], TTL=49 RST
Scan: To [~~~.~~~.234.69] : [~~~.~~~.234.69], TTL=49 SYN/ACK
Scan: To [~~~.~~~.234.70] : [~~~.~~~.234.70], TTL=59 SYN/ACK
Scan: To [~~~.~~~.234.71] : [~~~.~~~.234.71], TTL=49 SYN/ACK
Scan: To [~~~.~~~.234.72] : [~~~.~~~.234.72], TTL=49 RST
Scan: To [~~~.~~~.234.73] : [~~~.~~~.234.73], TTL=49 SYN/ACK
Scan: To [~~~.~~~.234.74] : [~~~.~~~.234.74], TTL=49 SYN/ACK
Scan: To [~~~.~~~.234.75] : [~~~.~~~.234.75], TTL=49 SYN/ACK
Scan: To [~~~.~~~.234.78] : [~~~.~~~.234.78], TTL=49 RST
Scan: To [~~~.~~~.234.79] : [~~~.~~~.234.79], TTL=59 SYN/ACK
```

The results show RSTs from machines that are not running web servers (and there is no response where the IP address is unused). All the other IP addresses respond with SYN/ACK, but the TTL is 59 (64 − 5) for the nearby WebMinder web proxy and 49 (64 − 15) for the Russian sites that were ten hops further away. In practice the Russian sites returned a range of TTL values such as 45, 46, 47 (reflecting minor network connection differences) and 113, 238

---

[5] Setting a high TTL means that the packets will reach the hosting sites, which may detect a "port scan"; hence this attack is more "visible" than the original version.

(reflecting alternative operating system choices for the initial TTL values), but the web proxy value was constant and very different from any value returned by any real site.

Clearly, there are steps that Brightview could now take to obfuscate this latest hint, and an arms race could result as ever more complex methods are used to distinguish a server running `squid` in a UK service centre from machines running many different types of web server in other countries. However, it is a general principle that, in situations like this, hiding your true nature is impossible. So the best that can be hoped for is to make the oracle attack arbitrarily difficult rather than defeating it altogether.

Acknowledgments

This work was supported by the Cambridge MIT Institute (CMI) via the project: "The design and implementation of third-generation peer-to-peer systems".

References

1. Bright, M.: BT puts block on child porn sites. Observer, 6 June 2004.
   `http://observer.guardian.co.uk/uk_news/story/0,6903,1232422,00.html`
2. Brightview Internet Services Ltd: WebMinder, a configuration for restricting access to obscene sites identified by the Internet Watch Foundation. 9 Jun 2005, 21pp.
3. Dornseif, M.: Government mandated blocking of foreign Web content. In: von Knop, J., Haverkamp, W., Jessen, E. (eds.): Security, E-Learning, E-Services: Proceedings of the 17. DFN-Arbeitstagung über Kommunikationsnetze, Düsseldorf 2003, Lecture Notes in Informatics, ISSN 1617-5468, 617–648.
4. Edelman, B.: Web Sites Sharing IP Addresses: Prevalence and Significance. Berkman Center for Internet and Society at Harvard Law School, Feb 2003.
   `http://cyber.law.harvard.edu/people/edelman/ip-sharing/`
5. Her Majesty's Stationery Office: Protection of Children Act 1978.
6. Internet Watch Foundation: Annual Report 2003. 22 Mar 2004.
   `http://www.iwf.org.uk/documents/20050221_annual_report_2003.pdf`
7. King Abdulaziz City for Science and Technology: Local Content Filtering Procedure. Internet Services Unit, KACST, Riyadh, 2004.
   `http://www.isu.net.sa/saudi-internet/contenet-filtring/`
   `filtring-mechanism.htm`
8. Lowe, G.: An Attack on the Needham-Schroeder Public-Key Authentication Protocol. Information Processing Letters, **56(3)** (1995) 131–133.
9. McWilliams, B.: Cloaking Device Made for Spammers. Wired News, 9 Oct 2003.
   `http://www.wired.com/news/business/0,1367,60747,00.html`
10. OpenNet Initiative: Google Search & Cache Filtering Behind China's Great Firewall. Bulletin 006, OpenNet Initiative, 30 Aug 2004.
    `http://www.opennetinitiative.net/bulletins/006/`
11. Telenor Norge: Telenor and KRIPOS introduce Internet child pornography filter. Telenor Press Release, 21 Sep 2004.
12. US District Court for the Eastern District of Pennsylvania: CDT, ACLU, Plantagenet Inc v Pappert, Civil Action 03-5051, 10 Sep 2004.
13. Zittrain, J., Edelman, B.: Documentation of Internet Filtering Worldwide. Harvard Law School. 24 Oct 2003. `http://cyber.law.harvard.edu/filtering/`

Anonymity Preserving Techniques in Trust Negotiations

Indrakshi Ray[1], Elisa Bertino[2], Anna C. Squicciarini[2], and Elena Ferrari[3]

[1] Computer Science Department,
Colorado State University, Fort Collins, Co, USA
`iray@cs.colostate.edu`
[2] CERIAS and Computer Science Department Purdue University,
West Lafayette, IN, USA
{`bertino, squiccia`}`@cs.purdue.edu`
[3] Dipartimento di Scienze della Cultura, Politiche e Informazione,
Universitá degli Studi dell'Insubria, Como
`elena.ferrari@uninsubria.it`

Abstract. Trust negotiation between two subjects require each one proving its properties to the other. Each subject specifies disclosure policies stating the types of credentials and attributes the counterpart has to provide to obtain a given resource. The counterpart, in response, provides a disclosure set containing the necessary credentials and attributes. If the counterpart wants to remain anonymous, its disclosure sets should not contain identity revealing information. In this paper, we propose anonymization techniques using which a subject can transform its disclosure set into an anonymous one. Anonymization transforms a disclosure set into an alternative anonymous one whose information content is different from the original one. This alternative disclosure set may no longer satisfy the original disclosure policy causing the trust negotiation to fail. To address this problem, we propose that trust negotiation requirements be expressed at a more abstract level using *property-based policies*. Property-based policies state the high-level properties that a counterpart has to provide to obtain a resource. A property-based policy can be implemented by a number of disclosure policies. Although these disclosure policies implement the same high-level property-based policy, they require different sets of credentials. Allowing the subject to satisfy any policy from the set of disclosure policies, increases not only the chances of a trust negotiation succeeding but also the probability of ensuring anonymity.

1 Introduction

Most of the interpersonal transactions, carried out in any application environment we may think of, are contingent upon relevant attributes of the involved parties, like nationality, age, job function, financial resources. In the digital world, such interactions have been historically handled out-of-band using alternative means or simply avoided. The increasing use of Internet in a variety of distributed multi-party interactions and transactions with strong real-time requirements has however pushed the search for solutions to the problem of attribute-based digital interactions. A promising solution to this problem is represented by automated trust negotiation systems [1, 9, 15, 16].

A trust negotiation system addresses the problems associated with classical authentication and authorization schemes by allowing subjects outside a local security domain

G. Danezis and D. Martin (Eds.): PET 2005, LNCS 3856, pp. 93–109, 2006.

to securely access protected resources and services [2, 15, 16]. It makes it possible for two parties to carry on secure transactions by first establishing trust through a bilateral, iterative process of requesting and disclosing digital credentials and policies. Digital credentials can be considered the equivalent, in the digital world, of paper credentials. Credentials often contain multiple attributes, for example, the name and the birth date of an individual, and can be used to verify identification information, professional qualifications, and association memberships, etc. Credentials are digitally signed by an issuing authority and assert the veracity of certain attributes of the owner. The use of public key encryption guarantees that these credentials are both unforgeable and verifiable. The other relevant component of any trust negotiation system is represented by policies, protecting sensitive resources, and even other policies from unauthorized access. By specifying necessary credentials a party must possess, and attribute conditions a party must verify in order to access a specific resource, policies provide a means by which any subject may be granted or refused access to a resource in real-time. Such policies are referred to as disclosure policies.

Trust negotiation systems, however, by their very nature may represent a threat to privacy. Credentials, exchanged during negotiations, often contain sensitive personal information that thus needs to be selectively released. Also, a user may want to minimize the released information, thus enforcing the need to know principle in disclosing his credentials to other parties. In other situations, a user may want to carry out negotiations that cannot be linked to him; we refer to such a requirement as non-linkability.

Even though a comprehensive solution to the problem of privacy in trust negotiation systems is quite articulated and requires the combination of different techniques, we believe that a feature that should be provided as part of a privacy-preserving trust negotiation is the anonymization of disclosed information. Such feature is crucial in order to address the non-linkability requirement. The goal of this paper is to develop a solution supporting anonymization in trust negotiation systems. To the best of our knowledge this is the first time such concept is proposed in the framework of trust negotiation systems.

We argue that specifying trust requirements using disclosure policies is too restrictive for trust negotiations requiring anonymity. Since these policies are expressed in terms of specific credential types and attributes, failure to provide the requested credentials and attributes causes the negotiation to fail. We propose that trust negotiation requirements should be specified in terms of high level properties needed to obtain a given resource. These property-based policies can be translated into a number of disclosure policies, each of which requires different disclosure sets containing different credentials. Failure to provide a specific disclosure set no longer causes the negotiation to fail. If a specific disclosure set compromises anonymity, the subject can provide an alternative one. If this anonymous disclosure set satisfies an alternative disclosure policy that implements the same property-based policy as the original one, then the trust negotiation can proceed.

Ideally, each credential and/or attribute disclosed should reveal only the crucial information required to satisfy the corresponding policy without compromising anonymity. Unfortunately, this cannot be always realized in practice. To reach our goal we revisit substitution and generalization techniques [8, 11, 12] presented in previous work and adapt them for use in the trust negotiation context. We propose a novel technique for substitution and generalization of data conveyed in credentials and attributes by use of an ad-hoc data structure, called a concept graph. The concept graph is able to capture semantic relationships among data conveyed in different credentials. The rest of the paper is organized as follows. Section 2 describes our notion of trust negotiation policies and their specification. Section 3 introduces the anonymity property and illustrates how generalization and specialization techniques can be used to ensure it. Section 4 discusses the related work. Section 5 concludes the paper with pointers to future directions. The appendix presents the details of the algorithms for achieving anonymity.

2 Specification of Trust Negotiation Policies

Trust negotiation requirements can be expressed at different levels of abstraction. In what follows, we refer to the subject who requests the credential as *requester* and the subject who submits the credential as *submitter*.[1] The requester begins by expressing its high-level trust requirements in the form of property-based policies. These property-based policies are then refined into disclosure policies. Before discussing these, we introduce our notion of credentials and attributes because they form the basis of trust negotiation requirements.

2.1 Credentials and Attributes

A credential associated with a subject is a digitally signed document containing attributes that describe properties of the subject. Examples of attributes that may be contained in a credential are birth date, name, professional qualifications, and association memberships. Since credentials are encrypted and digitally signed by an issuing authority, they are unforgeable and verifiable. By providing the credentials listed in the disclosure policies, the submitter proves the properties required by the requester.

Like previous work on trust negotiations [2], we consider credentials as instances of credential types. The notion of credential type provides a template for encoding credentials having a similar structure and collecting the same attributes. We denote credential types using the notation CT_i, CT_j, etc. Each credential type CT_i contains a set of attributes denoted as AS_{CT_i}.[2] A credential contains a number of attributes together with values defined for each of these attributes. Often the requester is interested in some, but not all, of the attributes of the requested credentials. Ideally, a submitter would want to provide information on a need-to-know basis and would be reluctant to disclose information that is not requested. In other words, it would like to selectively disclose attributes contained in a credential. One approach currently available to allow partial disclosure of credentials relies on the use of the bit commitment technique [10], which enables users to communicate a value without revealing it. By exploiting this technique on digital credentials it is possible to actually send credentials by revealing only the

---

[1] In trust negotiation a subject may act as a submitter in one step of the negotiation and as a requester in another step.

[2] Typically, credential types will have other information, such as, digital signatures. But these are not relevant for our present discussion.

minimal set of attributes required during the negotiation. The ability to blind one or more attributes in a credential generates different *views* of the credential. Views of the same credential differ with respect to the number of hidden attributes. A requester might be interested in some attributes contained in the credential or the possession of the credential itself. For proving credential possession, we assume that the submitter must provide some attributes contained in the credential that indicates credential possession. When a credential requester requests an attribute *attr* contained in credential *cred*, the submitter will provide the view in which *attr* is not hidden but a maximum number of other attributes are blinded. When a requester requests credential *cred* without mentioning the attributes, then a view of the credential is provided in which the attributes indicating credential possession are not blinded but most of the other attributes are hidden. Henceforth, we will not distinguish between requested attributes and requested credentials. The difference lies in the specific attributes of the credentials that are of interest.

Credential types provide a syntactic structure of information but do not specify anything about the interpretation of the attributes contained in the credential types. This makes it impossible to automatically detect relationships between attributes belonging to different credentials. To solve this problem of semantic conflicts, we borrow some ideas from the work on ontologies [7, 14]. An ontology consists of a set of concepts together with relationships defined among the concepts. The concepts and their relationships are described using a formal language. We propose an ontology for credentials and attributes and express a *concept* as follows.

Definition 1. [Concept]: *A concept C_i is a tuple of the form $< KeywordSet_{C_i}, LangSet_{C_i} >$, where $KeywordSet_{C_i}$ is a set of keywords and $LangSet_{C_i}$ is a set of attributes. $KeywordSet_{C_i}$ is the set of all possible keywords used to describe concept C_i. Each attribute in $LangSet_{C_i}$ implements concept C_i.*

For each concept C, we require that the $KeywordSet_C$ and $LangSet_C$ should be non-empty and finite. For any two distinct concepts C and C', $KeywordSet_C \cap KeywordSet_{C'} = \{\}$ and $LangSet_C \cap LangSet_{C'} = \{\}$. In other words, any keyword belongs to exactly one concept. Similarly, each attribute of a credential is associated with exactly one concept. We use the notation C_{ak} to indicate the concept associated with ak where ak denotes an attribute or a keyword. We assume that each concept is unique. However, concepts may be related using generalization/specialization relationships. We use the notation $C_i \subset C_j$ to indicate that the concept C_i is a generalization of concept C_j and the notation $C_i \subseteq C_j$ to indicate that C_i either equals C_j or is its generalization. For instance, the concept *address* is a specialization of the concept *country of residence*. We specify this as *country of residence* $\subset$ *address*. We assume that there are a finite number of such well-defined concepts in the ontology. An example of a concept is $C =< \{sex, gender\}, \{passport.gender, drivingLicense.sex\} >$. The concept known as *sex* or *gender* can be implemented by the attribute *passport.gender* or the attribute *drivingLicense.sex*. Thus, a concept can be implemented by attributes of different credentials. The different attributes implementing a particular concept are semantically equivalent. The attributes in $LangSet_{C_i}$ are semantically equivalent but they may have different domains. To compare the values of two semantically equivalent attributes, we need functions that convert the value of one attribute to a corresponding value for the semantically equivalent attribute. Similarly, a condition specified over an attribute may need to be translated to a condition defined over a semantically equivalent attribute. These requirements motivate us to propose the notion of translation functions.

Definition 2. [Translation Function]: *The translation function associated with a concept C_i, denoted as Π_{C_i}, is a total function that takes as input a condition A_{pq} op k ($A_{pq} \in LangSet_{C_i}$) and an attribute A_{rs} ($A_{rs} \in LangSet_{C_j}$) and produces an equivalent condition defined over attribute A_{rs}. This is formally expressed as follows. Π_{C_i} : $Cond_{C_i} \times LangSet_{C_j} \rightarrow Cond_{C_j}$ where $Cond_{C_i}$ is the set of all valid conditions specified over the attributes in $LangSet_{C_i}$ and $C_i \subseteq C_j$.*

Since the translation function is total, for every given valid condition and attribute there exists an equivalent condition defined on the given attribute. Several steps are involved in developing the translation function. Let us illustrate this with an example. To express A_{pq} *op* k in terms of A_{rs}, we need to first convert the value k to an equivalent value that is in the domain of A_{rs}. This step is performed by conversion functions which converts the value of one attribute to an equivalent value of another attribute. The second step is to convert the operator op into an equivalent operator op' that is suitable for the domain of A_{rs}. The definition of the conversion function together with the domain of the attribute can determine how the operator must be changed. The details of the translation functions are domain dependent but an example will help to illustrate how they can be specified. Consider the two attributes *passport.age* and *driversLicense.yearOfBirth*. Suppose we want to translate *passport.age* > 25 to an equivalent condition defined over *driversLicense.yearOfBirth*. The first step is to convert *passport.age* = 25 to an equivalent value defined over *driversLicense.yearOfBirth*. Converting *passport.age* to *driversLicense.yearOfBirth* is done by the function: *driversLicense.yearOfBirth* = *currentYear* − *passport.age*. For *passport.age* = 25, this function returns *driversLicense.yearOfBirth* = 1974. Since *driversLicense.yearOfBirth* and *passport.age* are inversely related (that is, *passport.age* increases as *driversLicense.yearOfBirth* decreases) the operator > is inverted to obtain <. The results obtained by the Π function in this case will be *driversLicense.yearOfBirth* < 1979. We use the ⇒ operator to indicate that one condition implies another. For instance *driversLicense.yearOfBirth* < 1979 ⇒ *passport.age* > 25 and *passport.age* > 25 ⇒ *driversLicense.yearOfBirth* < 1979.

2.2 Property-Based Policies

In a trust negotiation each entity is interested in obtaining information and verifying properties about the counterpart. Requestors may adopt different strategies for obtaining this information. One such strategy is the *open strategy*. In this strategy, the information requested from the counterpart who wants some resource is specified in the form of *property-based policies*. A property-based policy, specified at a higher level of abstraction, lists the properties the counterpart has to provide and the conditions it must satisfy in order to obtain some resource.

Definition 3. [Property-Based Policy]: *A property-based policy (PbP for brevity) for a resource R is a pair $(R, properties, conditions)$, where R denotes a target resource, and properties is the set of property names, conditions is the set of conditions defined over one or more properties listed in properties.*

An example of property-based policy is *(Drug, {age, residence, person identifier}, {age > 25})*. This states that the counterpart has to prove that its age is above 25, and give its residence and identifier information in order to obtain the resource *Drug*. In a property-based policy, the requester needs to enumerate all the properties it is interested in. Sometimes it may not be willing to divulge such information to the counterpart. In such cases, the counterpart adopts the *closed strategy* and expresses only *disclosure policies*.

2.3 Disclosure Policies

A disclosure policy lists the attributes and credential types needed to obtain a given resource. Thus, they do not directly reveal the properties that a requester is interested in. Disclosure policies also speed up the process of trust negotiation because the submitter knows precisely the requested credentials and attributes.

Definition 4. [Disclosure policy]: *A disclosure policy is expressed as*
$R \leftarrow T_1, T_2, \ldots T_n, n \geq 1$, *where:*

1. *R denotes a target resource;*
2. *T_i ($1 \leq i \leq n$) denotes an expression, called term, of the form $CT_i()$, $CT_i(A_{ij})$, or $CT_i(A_{ij}\ op\ k)$ where CT_i refers to a credential type, A_{ij} is an attribute contained in CT_i, $A_{ij}\ op\ k$ is a condition on attribute A_{ij} that is contained in the credential type CT_i;*
3. *$\forall T_i, T_j \in \{T_1, T_2, \ldots, T_n\}$ where $i \neq j$, $C_{T_i} \not\sqsubseteq C_{T_j}$ and $C_{T_j} \not\sqsubseteq C_{T_i}$.*

According to such a formalization, because of condition 3, we have that concepts corresponding to the terms in a disclosure policy cannot be equal or related by a generalization/specialization relationship. This condition ensures that no duplicate information is being requested. The goal of the requester is to formulate disclosure policies that implement some property-based policy.

Definition 5. [Implement disclosure policy]: *A disclosure policy $DP : R' \leftarrow T_1, \ldots, T_h$ is said to* implement *a property-based policy $PbP : (R, properties, conditions)$ if the following holds:*

1. *$R = R'$*
2. *$\forall p \in properties \bullet (\exists T_i \in \{T_1, \ldots, T_h\} \mid T_i = CT_i()$ or $CT_i(A_{ij})$ or $CT_i(A_{ij}\ op\ k) \bullet (CT_i()$ or $CT(A_{ij})) \in LangSet_{C_x} \wedge C_p \subseteq C_x))$*
3. *$\forall (p\ op\ k) \in conditions \bullet (\exists T_i \in \{T_1, \ldots, T_h\} \mid T_i = CT_i(A_{ij}\ op\ k) \bullet (CT_i(A_{ij}) \in LangSet_{C_x} \wedge C_p \subseteq C_x \wedge A_{ij}\ op'\ k' \Rightarrow p\ op\ k)$*

Condition 1 states that the disclosure policy *DP* and the property-based policy *PbP* must refer to the same resource. Condition 2 states that each property p in *PbP* should be implemented by a credential or attribute in *DP* and the concept corresponding to the credential or attribute should be equal to or a specialization of the concept corresponding to the property p. Condition 3 states that each condition in *PbP* should be translated into an appropriate condition on the corresponding attribute in *DP*. Not all property-based policies can be implemented by disclosure policies. A property-based policy is implementable if there exists one or more disclosure policies that implements it. We next define the conditions required of property-based policies that make them implementable. The first is that the conditions in the property-based policy should not contradict each other. The second is that each property p in PbP must be associated with some concept y. Since the $LangSet$ of a concept is non-empty, this ensures that each property can be implemented by some attribute. The third states that each condition in PbP should be translated into a condition on the corresponding attribute such that the attribute condition implies the condition stated in the PbP. This ensures that there is an attribute condition corresponding to every condition listed in the PbP.

Definition 6. [Property-based policy implementability]: *A property-based policy* PbP: (R, properties, conditions) *is implementable if the following holds:*

1. $conditions = \{c_1, c_2, \ldots, c_n\} \Rightarrow c_1 \wedge c_2 \wedge \ldots c_n \neq \phi$
2. $\forall p \in properties \bullet (\exists C_y \bullet p \in KeywordSet_{C_y})$
3. $\forall (p \ op \ k) \in conditions \bullet (\exists A_{ij} \in LangSet_{C_x} \bullet (C_p \subseteq C_x \wedge A_{ij} \ op' \ k' \Rightarrow p \ op \ k))$

A single property-based policy can be implemented by a number of disclosure policies as the following example illustrates. Let *PbP: (loan, {MaritalStatus, Country}, {country=USA})* be a property-based policy. Let *{MarriageCertificate (possess), HealthInsurance(MaritalStatus), id_card(maritalStatus)}* and *{id_card (country), ResidenceCert(country), drivingLicense(country)}* be the corresponding *LangSet* components of concepts corresponding to *MaritalStatus* and *Country*, respectively. Some disclosure policies implementing *PbP* are: (1) *loan ← MarriageCertificate(), id_card(country=USA)*, (2) *loan ← id_card(maritalStatus), id_card (country = USA)*, (3) *loan ← HealthInsurance(MaritalStatus), HealthInsurance(Provider), id_card(country = USA)*. These disclosure policies require different sets of credentials. This is possible because a property listed in a property-based policy can be proved by different credentials. For example the property *married* can be demonstrated by giving the credential *MarriageCertificate()* or the attribute *Driving_License(maritalstatus=married)*. Thus a credential submitter not willing to disclose a particular credential can satisfy an alternate disclosure policy and continue with the negotiation process. Next we formalize which alternative disclosure policies will be accepted by the requester. For this we need the notion of the stronger than relation for disclosure policies.

Definition 7. [Stronger than relation]: *Let* $DP1 : R \leftarrow T_a, T_b, \ldots, T_n$ *and* $DP2 : R' \leftarrow T_p, T_q, \ldots, T_y$ *be two disclosure policies.* DP1 *is said to be stronger than* DP2, *denoted by* $DP1 \succ DP2$, *if the it satisfies the following:*

1. $R = R'$
2. $\forall T_j \in \{T_p, T_q, \ldots, T_y\} \bullet (\exists T_i \in \{T_a, T_b, \ldots, T_n\} \bullet C_{T_j} \subseteq C_{T_i})$
3. $\forall T_j \in \{T_p, T_q, \ldots, T_y\} \mid T_j = CT_j(A_{jm} \ op \ p) \bullet (\exists T_i \in \{T_a, T_b, \ldots, T_n\} \mid T_i = CT_i(A_{in} \ op' \ q) \bullet A_{in} \ op' \ q \Rightarrow A_{jm} \ op \ p)$

Condition 1 says that *DP*1 and *DP*2 must refer to the same resource. Condition 2 says that for each term T_j in *DP*2 there is a term T_i in *DP*1 such that the concept associated with T_i is equal to or a specialization of the concept associated with T_j. Condition 3 says that for each term T_j in *DP*2 that contains an attribute condition $A_{jm} \ op \ p$, there is a term in T_i in $DP1$ that has some attribute condition A_{in} op' q, such that the attribute condition A_{jm} op p can be derived from the attribute condition A_{in} op' q.

Theorem 1. *For any two given disclosure policies, DP1 and DP2, evaluating whether DP1 is stronger than DP2 is decidable.*

Definition 8. [Equivalence relation]: *Two disclosure policies DP1 and DP2 are said to be equivalent, denoted DP1 $\equiv$ DP2, if DP1 $\succ$ DP2 and DP2 $\succ$ DP1.*

For two disclosure policies $DP1$ and $DP2$ to be equivalent, each term T_i in $DP1$ must have a corresponding term T_j in $DP2$, such that $C_{T_i} = C_{T_j}$.

The following example helps explain these relations. Consider the following disclosure policies: (i) *DP1: loan $\leftarrow$ Marriage_Cert(), id_card(age $>$ 25), id_card(country=USA)*, (ii) *DP2: loan $\leftarrow$ Marriage_Cert(), id_card(age $>$ 25)*, (iii) *DP3: loan $\leftarrow$ id_card(MaritalStatus=married), id_card(age $>$ 25)*, (iv) *DP4: loan $\leftarrow$ Marriage_Cert(), id_card(age $>$ 25), id_card(city=Fort Collins, USA)*. The following relations hold on the disclosure policies: $DP2 \equiv DP3$, $DP1 \succ DP2$, $DP4 \succ DP1$. Note that, all these disclosure policies implement the same property-based policy *(loan, {maritalstatus,age}, {maritalstatus=married,age >25})*.

We use the notation $DP2 \succeq DP1$ to denote that $DP2$ is either stronger than or equivalent to $DP1$. Suppose the requester requires a disclosure policy $DP1$, and the submitter provides credentials that satisfy an alternate disclosure policy $DP2$. If $DP2 \succeq DP1$, then the submitter has the assurance that the trust negotiation will proceed. This is formally proved by the following theorem.

Theorem 2. *For any two disclosure policies, DP1 and DP2, that are related by DP2 $\succeq$ DP1, any property-based policy PbP that is implemented by DP1 will also be implemented by DP2.*

2.4 Disclosure Sets

Depending on the trust negotiation strategy, the requester either provides a disclosure policy implementing a property-based policy for the negotiated resource or the property-based policy itself. The submitter, in turn, has to provide credentials to satisfy such a request. Each submitter has a *profile* of credentials. The submitter consults its profile to create a disclosure set which it submits to the requester. Disclosure set is a set of credentials, some of which may contain attributes that are blinded. The trust negotiation can proceed if the disclosure set completely or partially satisfies a disclosure policy or a policy that is stronger than or equivalent to the given one. But first, we define what it means for a disclosure set to completely satisfy a disclosure policy.

Definition 9. [Disclosure policy satisfaction]: *Let DP be a disclosure policy of the form $R \leftarrow T_1, T_2, , T_n$, $n \geq 1$. The disclosure set DSet, consisting of unblinded attributes given by AS_{DSet}, satisfies DP if $\forall$ $T_i \in \{T_1, .., T_n\}$ one of the following conditions hold depending on the form of T_i.*

case $T_i = CT_i()$: $\exists CR_{ij} \in DSet$
case $T_i = CT_i(A_{ik})$: $CR_{ij}.A_{ik} \in AS_{DSet}$

case $T_i = CT_i(A_{ik} \ op \ p)$: $CR_{ij}.A_{ik} \in AS_{DSet} \ \wedge \ CR_{ij}.V_{A_{ik}} \ op \ p$ where $CR_{ij}.V_{A_{ik}}$ denote the value of attribute A_{ik} in credential CR_{ij}.

The definition requires that each term specified in DP be satisfied by at least one credential or attribute in the set $DSet$. Intuitively a disclosure policy is satisfied if the submitter provides credentials that are instances of credential types listed in the disclosure policy, and the attributes of the credentials satisfy the conditions specified in the disclosure policy. Note that if a disclosure policy specifies credentials, attributes or attribute conditions, we provide the most blinded view of the credential that will meet the requirements of the disclosure policy. In some cases, a disclosure set provides some, but not all, of the credentials requested in a disclosure policy. We then say that the disclosure set *partially satisfies* the disclosure policy. In these circumstances, the requester, instead of rejecting the request, can ask for the remaining credentials and attributes needed to completely satisfy the policy and proceed with the negotiation.

A disclosure set $DSet$ satisfying a disclosure policy $DP : R \leftarrow T_1, T_2, \ldots, T_n$ contains two kinds of attributes: *requested* and *non-requested*. A requested attribute A_{jk} is one which is mentioned in some term $T_j = CT_j(A_{jk})$ where $1 \leq j \leq n$ in the disclosure policy DP. An attribute that is not explicitly requested in the disclosure policy but is present because it cannot be blinded is a non-requested attribute.

Consider the disclosure policy: $R \leftarrow$ *Marriage_Certificate(), id(age > 25)*. To satisfy this disclosure policy, the subject can either provide the disclosure set $DSet_1 = \{Marriage\_Certificate, \ id.age, \ id.country\}$ or it can provide $DSet_2 = \{Marriage\_Certificate, \ id.age\}$. The subject will provide $DSet_2$ if it can blind all other attributes of *id*. The subject may provide $DSet_1$ if the most blinded view containing age also reveals *id.country*. In this case *id.age* is a requested attribute and *id.country* is a non-requested one.

A disclosure set complies with a property-based policy if it satisfies any disclosure policy implementing the property-based policy.

Definition 10. [Property-based policy compliance]: *A disclosure set DSet complies with (satisfies) a property-based policy PbP if there exists a disclosure policy DP implementing PbP such that DSet satisfies DP.*

Note that a property-based policy is considered satisfied only when the disclosure set (completely) satisfies the corresponding disclosure policy. If a disclosure policy is partially satisfied, then several rounds of negotiation may be needed to satisfy the underlying property-based policy. When this occurs we say that the negotiation has succeeded.

3   Ensuring Anonymity of Disclosure Sets

As trust negotiations often occur between strangers, anonymity may represent an important requirement for negotiating subjects. For instance, Alice may not want to reveal her identity while bidding in an online auction. To formalize anonymity, we need the concept of identity disclosure. An identity disclosure is said to occur for the submitter if the data released to the counterpart contain attributes and credentials that uniquely identify him/her. Intuitively, identity disclosure happens when either the identity of an individual is directly revealed or it can be derived from the released data. For instance, if the released data contains the social security number, then the identity is directly revealed. If the released data contains name and address, then the identity of the individual can be inferred.

Other researchers, such as Samarati and Sweeney [11], have addressed the issue of protecting one's anonymity in the context of database systems. They classify attributes into three categories: (i) *identifiers* – attributes containing explicitly identifying information, (ii) *quasi-identifiers* – attributes that do not contain explicit identifying information, but that can be linked with other attributes to cause identity disclosure, and (iii) attributes that do not contain any identifying information. Identifiers and quasi-identifiers can be automatically determined in the context of databases, where data content is available. There are several aspects in which we differ from Sweeney's work. First, we define identifiers and quasi-identifiers not on the basis of attributes but on the basis of concepts. Second, we need the notion of *set of quasi-identifier groups*. A quasi-identifier group is a set of quasi-identifiers with the following property: the release of all quasi-identifiers in a quasi-identifier group results in identity disclosure. In Sweeney's work, each table is associated with only one quasi-identifier group and so this concept is not needed. But in the context of trust negotiation, we may have different quasi-identifier groups. Third, the submitter trying to protect its anonymity has no knowledge about the information possessed by the requester. Thus, it may be impossible for the submitter to exactly determine the set of attributes that cause identity disclosure for a given case.

Examples of quasi-identifier groups are {*employeeId, company name*} and {*lastname, address*}. In the first set, *employeeId* by itself does not reveal the identity of the individual, but *employeeId* together with the company name does. In the second set the last name does not uniquely identify the subject but when linked to its address, it does. {*employeeId, lastname*} is not a quasi-identifier group because disclosing both of them do not breach anonymity.

Definition 11. [Anonymity-preserving disclosures]: *Let DSet be a set of disclosures, and CS_{DSet} be the set of concepts associated with DSet. Let $Id = \{I_1, \ldots, I_k\}$ be a set of identifiers and let $Q\_Id = \{Q\_I_1, \ldots, Q\_I_n\}$ be a set of quasi-identifier groups. DSet is anonymity-preserving if the following holds:*

– $\forall I \in Id \bullet (I \notin CS_{DSet})$
– $\forall Q\_I \in Q\_Id \bullet (\exists I \in Q\_I \bullet (I \notin CS_{DSet}))$

Condition 1 ensures that identifiers are not present in the set of concepts associated with the disclosure set. Condition 2 ensures that for every quasi-identifier group, there is at least one element that is not present in the set of concepts associated with the disclosure set.

3.1   Concept Graphs

Our anonymization techniques make use of a data structure called *concept graph*. This is a directed acyclic graph in which each node n_i corresponds to a concept and each edge (n_i, n_j) indicates that the concept represented by node n_j is a generalization of the concept represented by node n_i. Since concepts may be unrelated, we may have multiple concept graphs. Unrelated concepts correspond to nodes in different concept graphs. Each concept corresponds to only one node in the set of concept graphs. Figure 1 gives an example of a concept graph. We denote the concept graph associated with concept C_i as CG_{C_i}.

Definition 12. [**Concept Graph**]: *A concept graph* $CG = \langle \mathcal{N}, \mathcal{E} \rangle$ *of a subject having the profile* $Prof$ *is a directed acyclic graph satisfying the following conditions.*

- *$\mathcal{N}$ is a set of nodes where each node n_i is associated with a concept C_i and is labeled with $Prof_{C_i}$. $Prof_{C_i}$ is the credentials belonging to the user that contain unblinded attributes describing the concept C_i. Note that $Prof_{C_i} = LangSet_{C_i} \cap Prof$.*
- *$\mathcal{E}$ denotes a set of directed edges. For each edge $(n_i, n_j) \in \mathcal{E}$, the concept C_j corresponding to node n_j is a generalization of concept C_i corresponding to node n_i.*

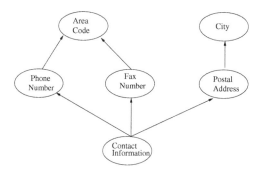

Fig. 1. Example of a Concept Graph

3.2 Using Substitution and Generalization to Achieve Anonymity

A disclosure set *DSet* satisfying a disclosure policy *DP* may cause a breach of anonymity. This may happen if the credentials or attributes contained in the disclosure set releases an identifier or quasi-identifiers. Identity disclosure may occur because of requested or non-requested attributes contained in *DSet*. If a requested attribute causes an identity disclosure, this attribute must be generalized. Alternately, if a requested attribute does not cause an identity disclosure but some other attribute contained in the same credential does, then the requested attribute needs to be substituted with an alternate one.

Consider the disclosure set *DSet* = {*id.age, id.country*} where *id.age* is a requested attribute and *id.country* is a non-requested one. Recall that *id.country* is present in the disclosure set because it cannot be blinded. Assume that *id.country* is a quasi-identifier and disclosing it will reveal the identity of the subject. To ensure anonymity we must remove *id.country* from *DSet*. This is only possible if the credential containing *id.age* is removed from the *DSet*. Since *id.age* is a requested attribute, this will cause the trust negotiation to fail. In such a scenario, we need to substitute *id.age* with an alternate attribute, say *birthCert.dob*, such that $C_{id.age} = C_{birthCert.dob}$. We also need to ensure that all attributes visible in the credential *birthCert* do not cause an identity disclosure.

The process of substitution replaces each requested attribute contained in an identity revealing credential with an alternative equivalent attribute contained in an anonymous credential. Since each alternative attribute is equivalent to the original replaced attribute, it satisfies the same property of the property-based policy as the original one. Substitution, if successful, not only guarantees anonymity but also ensures that the underlying property-based policy will be satisfied.

Sometimes the disclosure policies request attributes or credentials, the disclosure of which causes identity disclosure. In such cases, substituting the attribute with an alternative one belonging to the same concept is not useful because the alternative attribute reveals the same concept as the original one. For such cases, we use the technique of generalization. In generalization we also choose an alternative attribute. However, unlike substitution, this alternative attribute belongs to the language set of the concept that is a generalization of the concept corresponding to the original attribute. Let us explain this with an example. Suppose $id.address$ is a requested attribute that causes an identity disclosure. The generalization technique will replace the requested attribute $id.address$ with an alternative attribute, say $id.city$ where $id.city$ belongs to the concept $city$ that is a generalization of the concept $address$. Since we are not disclosing $id.address$, anonymity is preserved. On the other hand since the alternative attribute contains some but not all information about $id.address$, the negotiation may or may not succeed with the alternative attribute. The negotiation will succeed if the underlying property in the corresponding property-based policy corresponds to the generalized concept $city$. The negotiation will not succeed if the underlying property in the property-based policy corresponds to the concept associated with $address$.

4   Related Work

In this section we briefly review related approaches, which fall in two categories: trust negotiation systems and techniques for information disclosure control. Researchers have investigated trust negotiations for web-based applications and have developed a number of systems and prototypes [2, 3, 5, 15, 16, 13]. However, to the best of our knowledge, these approaches do not consider different levels of abstractions for trust negotiation policies. Nor do they focus on anonymity. Winsborough and Li[15] have also addressed how sensitive credentials can be protected during trust negotiation. They formalize the notion of safety in the context of automated trust negotiations. The definition of safety is based upon third parties ability to infer information about the profiles of the negotiating parties. They do not address any issues pertaining to anonymity in particular. The problem of releasing data so that individuals who are the subjects of the data cannot be identified has been explored by works on *k-anonymity* [11, 12], statistical databases [6] and deductive databases [4]. Most of this work focuses on limiting the information that can be released in response to multiple queries. These schemes require history information to be maintained so that multiple interactions with the same parties can be correlated. We borrow the notion of identifier and quasi-identifier from Sweeney's work [12]. However, as outlined in Section 3, there are several aspects in which we differ.

5   Conclusion

Trust negotiation is a promising approach for establishing trust among subjects in open systems. Each subject specifies disclosure policies that list the credentials and attributes necessary to obtain its protected resources. The counterpart, in response, provides a disclosure set containing the necessary credentials. If the counterpart wants to remain anonymous, its disclosure set should not contain identity revealing information. We show how a subject can verify whether the disclosure-set preserves anonymity, and, if not, how it can use generalization and substitution techniques to transform its disclosure set to an anonymous one. The anonymous disclosure set may no longer satisfy the original disclosure policy. However, if it satisfies an alternate disclosure policy that implements the same property-based policy as the original one, the trust negotiation can proceed.

In future, we plan to propose the notion of k-anonymity-safe disclosure which ensures that the disclosure set submitted by a user is indistinguishable from the disclosure sets of k other subjects. We plan to develop crowd formation protocols that minimize the reliance on trusted third parties, and explore the use of incentives to obtain disclosure sets from other subjects.

References

1. E. Bertino, E. Ferrari, and A. Squicciarini. Trust Negotiations: Concepts, Systems and Languages. To appear in IEEE -CISE, Computing and Science Engineering.
2. E. Bertino, E. Ferrari, and A. Squicciarini. Trust-X a Peer to Peer Framework for Trust Establishment. To appear in IEEE TKDE, Transactions on Knowledge and Data Engineering.
3. E. Bertino, E. Ferrari, and A. C. Squicciarini. Privacy Preserving Trust Negotiations. In *4th International Workshop on Privacy Enhancing Technologies, Toronto, Canada*, May 2004.
4. P. Bonatti and S. Kraus. Foundations on Secure Deductive Databases. *IEEE TKDE, Transactions on Knowledge and Data Engineering, 7(3)*, pages 406422, 1995.
5. P. Bonatti and P. Samarati. Regulating Access Services and Information Release on the Web. *7th ACM Conference on Computer and Communications Security, Athens, Greece*, November 2000.
6. J. Domingo-Ferrer. *Inference Control in Statistical Databases from Theory to Practice.* Volume 2316. Springer, 2002.
7. T. R. Gruber. A translation approach to portable ontology specifications. *Knowledge Acquisition*, 5(2):199220, 1993.
8. V. S. Iyengar. Transforming Data to Satisfy Privacy Constraints. *Eighth ACM SIGKDD International Conference on Knowledge Discovery and Data Mining, Edmonton, Canada*, July 2002.
9. T. Yu K.E. Seamons, M. Winslett. Requirements for Policy Languages for Trust Negotiation. *Third IEEE International Workshop on Policies for Distributed Systems and Networks, Monterey, CA*, June 2002.
10. M. Naor. Bit Commitment Using Pseudorandomness. *Advances in Cryptology- 89*, 435, 1990.
11. P. Samarati and L. Sweeney. Generalizing Data to Provide Anonymity when Disclosing Information. *In Seventeenth ACM SIGACT-SIGMOD-SIGART Symposium on Principles of Database Systems, Seattle, Washington.* ACM Press, June 1998.

12. L. Sweeney. *k*-anonymity: A Model for Protecting Privacy. *International Journal on Uncertainty, Fuziness and Knowledge-based Systems, 10(5)*, pages 557570, 2002.
13. K. E. Seamons T. Yu, M. Winslett. Supporting Structured Credentials and Sensitive Policies through Interoperable Strategies for Automated Trust Negotiation. *ACM Transactions on Information and System Security, (6)1*, feb 2003.
14. M. Uschold and M. Gruninger. Ontologies: Principles, methods, and applications. *Knowledge Engineering Review 11(2)*, pages 93155, 1996.
15. M. Winsborough and N. Li. Safety in Automated Trust Negotiation. *IEEE Symposium on Security and Privacy*, May 2004. Oakland, CA.
16. T. Yu and M. Winslett. A Unified Scheme for Resource Protection in Automated Trust Negotiation. *IEEE Symposium on Security and Privacy*, May 2003. Oakland, CA.

Appendix – Algorithms for Ensuring Anonymity

In this appendix we give detailed algorithms pertaining to anonymity. Table 1 gives a table that lists the notations that we use in our algorithms.

Table 1. Notations used in algorithms

Notation	Meaning
ANC_{C_i}	Set of ancestors of C_i obtained from CG_{C_i}
AS_{DSet}	Unblinded attributes in *DSet*
$C_{A_{ij}}$	Concept associated with attribute A_{ij}
CG_{C_i}	Concept graph containing node associated with concept C_i
CR_{ij}	Credential of type CT_i
CS_{DSet}	Concept set associated with unblinded attributes in *DSet*
$CS_{CR_{ij}}$	Concept set associated with unblinded attributes in CR_{ij}
DSet	Disclosure Set
IDSet	Set of identifier concepts
PCSet	Set of previously disclosed concepts
$Prof_{C_i}$	Credentials in profile containing unblinded attributes corres. to C_i
QIDSet	Set of quasi-identifier groups

Algorithm 1. *Get Attributes Causing Identity Disclosure*
Input: *(i) DSet – the disclosure set that must be evaluated for identity disclosure, (ii) IDSet – set of identifier concepts, and (iii) QIDSet – set of Q_Id_Groups*
Output: *IdDiscAttr – set of attributes causing identity disclosure*

Procedure $GetIdDiscAttr(DSet, IDSet, QIDSet)$
begin
    $IdConDisc = CS_{DSet} \cap IDSet$
    for *each* $Q\_Id\_Group \in QIDSet$
      if $Q\_Id\_Group \cap CS_{DSet} = Q\_Id\_Group$
        $IdConDisc = IdConDisc \cup (Q\_Id\_Group \cap CS_{DSet})$
    for *each* $C_i \in IdDiscCon$
      $IdDiscAttr = AS_{DSet} \cap LangSet_{C_i}$
    return *IdDiscAttr*
end

The algorithm *GetIdDiscAttr* checks whether a disclosure set *DSet* contains attributes that cause identity disclosure. The first step finds the identifier concepts contained in CS_{DSet} which is the set of concepts associated with *DSet*. The second step finds the quasi-identifier concepts in CS_{DSet} that cause identity disclosure. The final step is to find the attributes corresponding to the identifier and the quasi-identifier concepts found in the earlier two steps. These set of attributes cause identity disclosure and are returned to the caller.

Algorithm 2. *Anonymize Disclosure Set Using Generalization/Substitution*

Input: *(i) DSet – the original disclosure set that must be made anonymous, (ii) IDSet – set of identifier concepts, and (iii) QIDSet – set of Q_Id_Groups*

Output: *returns DSet' – anonymous disclosure set or an empty set if anonymity cannot be achieved*

Procedure *Anonymize(DSet, IDSet, QIDSet)*
begin
        $IdDiscAttr = GetIdDiscAttr(DSet, IDSet, QIDSet)$
        for *each attribute $A_{ij} \in IdDiscAttr$*
        $DSet' = DSet - \{CR_{im}\}$
          for *each requested attribute A_{ik} of CR_i*
            if $A_{ik} \in IdDiscAttr$ /* A_{ik} *caused identity disclosure* */
            generalize = true
            for *each element $p \in AS_{DSet'}$*
              if $C_{A_{ik}} \subseteq C_p$ *or* $C_p \subseteq C_{A_{ik}}$
              generalize = false
            if *generalize*
            $CR_{rs} = SelectAncCred(DSet', IDSet, QIDSet, C_t)$
            if $CR_{rs} \neq NULL$
              $DSet' = DSet' \cup \{CR_{rs}\}$
            else
              return *NULL*
          else /* A_{ik} *did not cause identity disclosure* */
            substitute = true
            for *each element $p \in AS_{DSet'}$*
              if $C_{A_{ik}} \subseteq C_p$
              substitute = false
            if *substitute*
            $CR_{rs} = SelectBestCand(DSet', IDSet, QIDSet, C_t)$
            if $CR_{rs} \neq NULL$
              $DSet' = DSet' \cup \{CR_{rs}\}$
            else
              return *NULL*
        return *DSet'*
end

The algorithm *Anonymize* works as follows. It first gets the attributes causing identity disclosure by calling *GetIdDiscAttr*. For each attribute A_{ij} causing an identity disclosure, the corresponding credential CR_{im} is removed from the disclosure set. This causes the requested attributes A_{ik} contained in CR_{im} to be removed as well. If A_{ik} caused an identity disclosure, then A_{ik} must be generalized unless an attribute corresponding to a generalized or specialized or same concept is already present in the remaining disclosure set. To generalize, we call the function *SelectAncCred* that returns an anonymity preserving credential corresponding to one of its ancestor concepts. If such a credential cannot be found, then the algorithm returns with a null value. On the other hand if the requested attribute A_{ik} did not cause an identity disclosure but some other attributes contained in CR_{im} did, then A_{ik} does not need to be generalized. In such cases, if an attribute exists in remaining $DSet'$ that belongs to the same or more specialized concept as A_{ik}, we do not have to look for a substitution for A_{ik}. If no such attributes exist, we call *SelectBestCand* that selects an anonymity preserving credential that contains an unblinded attribute corresponding to the concept $C_{A_{ik}}$. If no such credential can be found, the function returns with a null value. The process is repeated for every attribute causing identity disclosure. The function returns the anonymized disclosure set at the end or null if anonymization is not possible.

Algorithm 3. *Selecting the Best Candidate from a Concept*
Input: *(i) DSet – the disclosure set to which the new credential must be added, (ii) IDSet – set of identifier concepts, and (iii) QIDSet – set of Q_Id_Groups, (iv) C_j – the concept from which the best credential must be selected.*
Output: *returns CR_r – the most suitable credential or null if none can be found*

Procedure *SelectBestCandidate(DSet, IDSet, QIDSet, C_j)*
begin
        $minm = infinity$
        $min = NULL$
        for *each* $CR_{im} \in Prof_{C_j}$
            if $GetIdDiscAttr(CR_i \cup DSet, IDSet, QIDSet) = \{\}$
                $QIDrelease_{im} = QIDSet \cap CS_{CR_{im}}$
                if $minm > QIDrelease_{im}$
                    $minm = QIDrelease_{im}$
                    $min = CR_{im}$
        return *min*
end

The algorithm *SelectBestCandidate* selects a credential present in the subject's profile corresponding to a given concept. The objective of the algorithm is to select a candidate credential from the set of credentials in $Prof_{C_j}$. To qualify for a candidate the credential together with the given disclosure set ($DSet$) should not cause an identity disclosure. From the set of candidates, we use a heuristic to determine the best choice. The heuristic chooses the candidate that will cause minimum number of quasi-identifiers to be revealed.

Algorithm 4. *Selecting an Ancestor Concept Credential*
Input: *(i) DSet – the original disclosure set that must be made anonymous, (ii) IDSet – set of identifier concepts, (iii) QIDSet – set of Q_Id_Groups, and (iv) C_i – the concept whose ancestor credential must be selected.*

Output: *returns DSet' – anonymous disclosure set or an empty set if anonymity cannot be achieved*

Procedure *SelectAncCred(DSet, IDSet, QIDSet, C_i)*
begin

      minm = infinity
      cred = NULL
      for *each* $t \in ANC_{C_i}$
          $CR_{rm} = SelectBestCandidate(DSet', IDSet, QIDSet, C_t)$
          if $CR_{rm} \neq NULL$
             $count_t = QIDSet \cap CS_{CR_{rm}}$
             if $count_t < minm$
                $minm = count_t$
                $cred = CR_{rm}$
      return *cred*
end

The above algorithm selects a credential corresponding to an ancestor concept. From all the ancestors, it tries to select the best credential that minimizes the number of disclosure of quasi-identifiers.

Unmixing Mix Traffic*

Ye Zhu and Riccardo Bettati

Department of Computer Science
Texas A&M University
College Station TX 77843-3112, USA
zhuye@tamu.edu, bettati@cs.tamu.edu

Abstract. We apply blind source separation techniques from statistical signal processing to separate the traffic in a mix network. Our experiments show that this attack is effective and scalable. By combining the flow separation method and frequency spectrum matching method, a passive attacker can get the traffic map of the mix network. We use a non-trivial network to show that the combined attack works. The experiments also show that multicast traffic can be dangerous for anonymity networks.

1 Introduction

In this paper, we describe a class of attacks on low-latency anonymity networks. These attacks, which we will call *flow separation* attacks, aim at *separating* (as opposed to *identifying*) flows inside a network, based on aggregate traffic information only.

Since Chaum [1] pioneered the basic idea of the anonymous communication systems, researchers have developed various mix-based anonymity systems for different applications. One of the main functions of the mix network is to mix the traffic flows and so render senders or receivers anonymous. Mix networks typically achieve this by perturbing the traffic in (a) the payload domain (through encryption), (b) in the route domain (through re-routing) and (c) in the timing domain (through batching and link padding). By using the flow separation attack, an attacker can separate the flows based on passively collected traffic data. Further attacks by frequency spectrum matching or time domain cross-correlation [2] can then easily determine the path of a flow in the mix network if additional knowledge about the flow is available or determine the traffic directions in the mix network.

The flow separation attack employs the *blind source separation* model [3], which was originally defined to solve *cocktail party problem*: The blind source separation algorithms can extract one person's voice signal given the mixtures of voices in a cocktail party. Blind source separation algorithms solve the problem based on the independence between voices from different persons. Similarly, in a mix network, we can use blind source separation algorithms to separate independent flows.

---

* This work is supported in part by the Texas Information Technology and Telecommunication Task Force.

G. Danezis and D. Martin (Eds.): PET 2005, LNCS 3856, pp. 110–127, 2006.
© Springer-Verlag Berlin Heidelberg 2006

The contributions of this paper can be summarized as follows:

- We propose a new class of anonymity attacks, which can *separate* the flows through a mix. Further attacks can make use of the information about the separated flows and so be very effective in reducing anonymity.
- We use experiments to show that flow separation attacks are effective for both single mixes and mix networks.
- We analyze the effect of multicast/broadcast traffic on the flow separation attack. In contrast to intuition, our analysis and experiments show that the presence of multicast/broadcast traffic significantly helps the attacker to more precisely separate the flows.
- We discuss the possible use of flow separation attack in other anonymity network settings and pros and cons of counter-measures.

The remainder of this paper is organized as follows: Section 2 reviews the related work. Section 3 outlines our mix network model and the threat model. In Section 4, we introduce the flow separation attack. We will also describe the frequency spectrum matching that we will use to evaluate the quality of flow separation. The same method is used in the Flow Correlation Attack described in [4]. In Section 5 and 6, we use ns-2 simulation experiments to show the effectiveness of the flow separation attack. We evaluate the flow separation attack against a non-trivial mix network in Section 7. Section 8 discusses the application of flow separation attack in different network settings and countermeasures for flow separation attack. We conclude this paper in Section 9, by remarking on extensions of this work.

2 Related Work

Chaum [1] pioneered the idea of anonymity in 1981. Since then, researchers have applied the idea to different applications, such as message-based email and flow-based low-latency communications, and they have invented new defense techniques as more attacks have been proposed. For anonymous email applications, Chaum proposed to use relay servers, called mixes, that re-route messages. Messages are encrypted to prevent their tracking by simple payload inspection.

Low-latency anonymity systems have been developed recently for the dominant flow-based traffic in the Internet. A typical example is Tor [5], the second-generation onion router, developed for circuit-based low-latency anonymous communication. It can provide perfect forward secrecy.

In contrast to the traditional message-based anonymity attacks [6], several flow-based anonymity attacks have been proposed. Examples are intersection attacks [7], timing attacks [2], Danezis's attack on continuous mixes [8], and the flow correlation attack [4]. The timing attack [2] uses time domain cross-correlation to match flows given the packet timestamps of the flow. Danezis's attack on the continuous mix [8] uses likelihood ratios to detect a flow in aggregate traffic. The flow correlation attack [4] employs statistical methods to detect TCP flows in aggregate traffic. The flow separation attack proposed in this paper belongs to the class of flow-based anonymity attacks.

3   Models

3.1   Mix and Mix Network

A mix is a relay device for anonymous communication. A single-mix network can achieve a certain level of communication anonymity: The sender of a message attaches the receiver address to a packet and encrypts it using the mix's public key. Upon receiving a packet, the mix decrypts the packet using its private key. Different from an ordinary router, a mix usually will not relay the received packet immediately. Rather, it will attempt to perturb the flows through the Mix in order to foil an attacker's effort to link incoming and outgoing packets or flows. It does this, typically, in three ways: First, it re-encrypts the packet to foil attacks that attempt to match packets in the payload data domain. Then, it *re-routes* the packet to foil correlation attacks that rely on route traceback. Finally, it perturbs the flows in the time domain through *batching, reordering*, and *link padding*. Batching collects several packets and then sends them out in a *batch*. The order of packets may be altered as well. Both these batching techniques are important in order to prevent timing-based attacks. Different batching and reordering strategies are summarized in [6] and [4].

But in real world, most low-latency anonymity systems do not employ mixing strategies for different reasons. For example, Onion Router [9], Crowds [10], Morphmix [11], P5 [12], and Tor [5] do not use any batching and reordering techniques.

A network may consist of multiple mixes that are inter-connected by a network such as the Internet. A mix network may provide enhanced anonymity, as payload packets may go through several mixes so that if one mix is compromised, anonymity can still be maintained.

3.2   Threat Model

We assume a passive adversary, whose capabilities are summarized as follows:

1. The adversary observes a number of input and output links of a mix, collects the packet arrival and departure times, and analyzes them. This type of attack is *passive*, since traffic is not actively altered (by, say, dropping, inserting, and/or modifying packets during a communication session), and is therefore often difficult to detect. This type of attack can be easily staged on wired and wireless links [13] by a variety of agents, such as governments or malicious ISPs [14].
2. For simplicity of discussion, we assume a *global* adversary, i.e. an adversary that has observation points on all links between mixes in the mix network. While this assumption seems overly strong, it is not, as the attacker will naturally aggregate mixes for which it has no observation points into *super-mixes*.
3. The adversary cannot correlate (based on packet timing, content, or size) an individual packet on an input link to another packet on an output link based on content and packet size. This is prevented by encryption and packet padding, respectively.
4. We focus on mixes operating as simple proxy. In another word, no batching or reordering is used. Link padding (with dummy packets) is not used either. This follows the practice of some existing mix networks such as, Tor [5].

5. Finally, we assume that the specific objective of the adversary is to identify the path of a flow in a mix network if there is some knowledge about the flow, or to determine a map of traffic directions in the mix network.

4 Flow Separation in Mix Networks

In this section, we will first define the problem in the context of blind source separation and then describe how to apply the flow separation method in a mix network.

4.1 Blind Source Separation

Blind source separation is a methodology in statistical signal processing to recover unobserved "source" signals from a set of observed mixtures of the signals. The separation is called "blind" to emphasize that the source signals are not observed and that the mixture is a black box to the observer. While no knowledge is available about the mixture, in many cases it can be safely assumed that source signals are independent. In its simplest form [15], the blind source separation model assumes n independent signals $F_1(t), \cdots, F_n(t)$ and n observations of mixture $O_1(t), \cdots, O_n(t)$ where $O_i(t) = \sum_{j=1}^{n} a_{ij} F_j(t)$. The goal of blind source separation is to reconstruct the source signals $F_j(t)$ using only the observed data $O_i(t)$, the assumption of independence among the signals $F_j(t)$. A very nice introduction to the statistical principles behind blind source separation is given in [15]. The common methods employed in blind source separation are minimization of mutual information [16, 17], maximization of nongaussianity [18, 19] and maximization of likelihood [20, 21].

4.2 Flow Separation as a Blind Source Separation Problem

In this paper, we define a *flow* as a series of packets that are exchanged between a pair of hosts. Typically, such a flow is identified by a tuple of source/destination addresses and port numbers. Similarly, we define an *aggregate flow* at the *link-level* to be the sum of the packets (belonging to different flows) on the link. We define the aggregate flow at *mix-level* as sum of packets through the same input and output port of a mix. Unless specified, otherwise the word "flow" in the remaining of this paper means "mix-level aggregate flow" for brevity.

We will show in this paper that, for the attacker who tries to break the anonymity of a mix, it is very helpful to *separate* the flows through the mix based on the observation of the link traffic. The separation of the flows through the mix can recover the traffic pattern of flows, which can be used in further attacks, such as the frequency spectrum matching attack described in Section 4.3 or the time domain cross-correlation attack [2].

In this paper, we are interested in the traffic pattern carried in the time series of packet count during each sample interval T. For example, in Figure 1, the attacker can get a time series $O_1 = [o_1^1, o_2^1, \cdots, o_n^1]$ of packet counts by observing the link between Sender S_1 and the mix. We use n to denote the *sample size* in this paper. The attacker's objective is to recover the packet count time series $F_i = [f_1^i, f_2^i, \cdots, f_n^i]$ *for each flow*. For the simplest case, we assume that (a) there is no congestion in mix and that (b) the

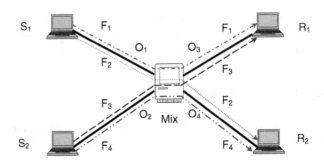

Fig. 1. An Example for Flow Model

time series can be synchronized. (We will relax both assumptions in later sections.) In the example of Figure 1, the time series F_1 is contained in both time series O_1 and O_3 i.e. $O_1 = F_1 + F_2$, $O_3 = F_1 + F_3$. For a mix with j input ports, k output ports and m mix-level aggregate flows, we can rewrite the problem in vector-matrix notation,

$$
\begin{pmatrix} O_1 \\ O_2 \\ \vdots \\ O_{j+k} \end{pmatrix} = \mathbf{A}_{(j+k) \times m} \begin{pmatrix} F_1 \\ F_2 \\ \vdots \\ F_m \end{pmatrix}
\tag{1}
$$

where $\mathbf{A}_{(j+k) \times m}$ is called *mixing matrix* in the blind source separation problem [3].

The flow separation can be solved using a number of blind source separation techniques. The rationale for blind source separation relies on the fact that the aggregate flows through a mix are independent from each other, since the aggregate flows are from different sources. Even the flows from a same host, such as F_1 and F_2, can be regarded as independent as they follow different paths and controlled by different sockets. This independence assumption is of course only valid as long as Sender S_1 is not heavily overloaded, since otherwise one flow would influence the other. Given the observations $O_1, O_2, \cdots, O_{j+k}$, blind source separation techniques estimate the independent aggregate flows $F_1, F_2, \cdots, F_m$ by maximizing the independence between estimated aggregate flows. In the following, we need to keep in mind that flow separation often is not able to separate individual flows. Rather, mix-level aggregates flows that share the links at the observation points form the minimum separable unit.

Issues about Blind Source Separation Method. Basic blind source separation algorithms require the number of observations to be larger than or equal to the number of independent components. For flow separation, this means that $j+k \geq m$, where j and k denote the number of observations at the input and output of the mix, respectively, and m denotes the number of flows. Advanced blind source separation algorithm [22, 23] target over-complete bases problems and can be use for the case where $m > j + k$. But they usually require that m, the number of independent flows, be known. Since all the mix traffic is encrypted and padded, it is hard for the attacker to estimate m. In this paper, we assume that $m = j + k$. The cost of the assumption is that some independent flows can not be separated, that is, they are still mixed. We will see that this is not a severe constraint, in particular not in mix networks where flows that remain mixed in some separations can be separated using separation results in neighbor mixes.

Unless there is multicast or broadcast traffic through the mix, the $j + k$ observations will have some redundancy, because the summation of all the observations on the input ports are equal to the summation of all the observations on the output ports. In other words, the row vectors of the mixing matrix are linearly dependent. Again, the cost of the redundancy is that some independent flows are not separated.

The flow estimation generated by blind source separation algorithms is usually a lifted, scaled version of the actual flow (of its time series, actually). Sometimes, the estimated flow may be of different sign than the actual flow. Both lifting and scaling does not affect the frequency components of the time series, and so frequency matching can be used to further analyze the generated data.

Furthermore, since the elements of the estimated mixing matrix are not binary, it is not straightforward to tell the direction of each aggregate flow. Some heuristic approach can be used, but we leave this to further research.

In the rest of this paper, we will show that the issues identified above can be largely solved with the use of appropriate frequency matching.

4.3   Frequency Matching Attack

After the flows have been separated, a number of flows, each with a given time series of packet counts, has been determined to traverse the mix.

Frequency spectrum matching has shown to be particularly effective to further analyze the traffic. The rationale for the use of frequency matching is four-fold: First, the dynamics of a flow, especially a TCP flow [24], is characterized by its periodicities. By matching the frequency spectrum of a known flow with the frequency spectrums of estimated flows obtained by blind source separation techniques, we can identify the known flow with high accuracy. Second, frequency matching can easily remove the ambiguities introduced by the lifting and scaling in the estimated time series by removing the zero-frequency component. Third, frequency spectrum matching can also be applied on the mix-level aggregate flows, since the different frequency components in each individual flows can characterize the aggregate flow. Fourth, the low frequency components of traffic are often not affected by congestion as they traverse multiple switches and mixes. This is particularly the case for TCP traffic, where the frequency components are largely defined by the behavior at the end hosts. In summary, frequency spectrum analysis has excellent prerequisites to be highly effective.

Even if no information is available about individual flows, the attacker can easily determine if there is communication between two neighboring mixes. Matching the estimated aggregate flows through the neighboring mixes can give attackers more information, such as how many aggregate flows are going through the next mix. In a mix network, an aggregate flow through a mix may split into aggregate flows of smaller size, multiplex with other aggregate flows, or do both. By matching the estimated aggregate flows through neighboring mixes, the attacker can detect the split and multiplex. Based on the information gathered, the attacker can eventually get a detailed map of traffic in a mix network. In Section 7, we show a traffic map obtained from the aggregate flow matching.

The sample interval T is important to the frequency spectrum matching. The averaging effect of sample interval T on frequency spectrum matching results can be modeled as low-pass filtering. If we are matching TCP flows, it is important to select a proper sample interval to avoid filtering out interesting TCP frequency components such as round trip time (RTT), time-out frequencies. More details on selecting T and modeling of the effect of T can be found in [24].

In the following, we will be using frequency matching of the *separated* flows against the *actual* flows in the network to measure the accuracy of the flow separation. The rationale for this method is that a highly accurate flow separation will result in good matching with the component flows, whereas a poor separation will generate separated flows that can not be matched with the actual ones.

5   Evaluation on Single Mix with Different Combinations of Traffic

In this section, we will evaluate the performance of the flow separation for a single mix. We use the blind source separation algorithm proposed in [25] to separate the flows. The accuracy of separation will be measured using frequency matching with actual flows.

5.1   Experiment Setup

Figure 2 shows the experimental network setup for single mix. We use ns-2 to simulate the network. The links in the figure are all of $10Mbit/s$ bandwidth and $10ms$ delay[1] if not specifically mentioned. In the series of experiments in this section, the mix under study has two input ports and two output ports and four aggregate flows passing through the mix, as shown in Figure 1. We will study mixes with more than two ports in Section 6. Unless specified otherwise, we will use time observation intervals of $32second$ length and sample interval of $10ms$ length, resulting in time series of size $n = 3200$. Similar results were obtained for shorter observations as well.

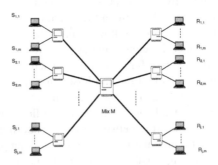

Fig. 2. Experiment Setup for Single Mix

---

[1] Senders and receivers can be at a large distance from the mix, potentially connecting through several routers and switches.

5.2 Metrics

In the following, we will adopt two metrics to evaluate the accuracy of the flow separation. Both metrics are based on a comparison of the separated flows with the actual flows in the mix.

As first performance metric, we use *mean square error (MSE)*, a widely used performance criterion in blind source separation research. Let
$F_A = [f_1^A, f_2^A, \cdots, f_n^A]$ represent the time series of the actual flow and $F_B = [f_1^B, f_2^B, \cdots, f_n^B]$ represent the time series estimated by the blind source separation algorithm. To match the time series F_A with F_B, we first need to scale and lift F_B so that they have the same mean and variance.

$$F_B' = \frac{std(F_A)}{std(F_B)} \cdot (F_B - mean(F_B) \cdot [1, 1, \cdots, 1]) + mean(F_A) \cdot [1, 1, \cdots, 1] \ , \quad (2)$$

where $std(F)$ and $mean(F)$ denote the standard deviation and average of the time series F, respectively. The *mean square error* is defined as follows:

$$\varepsilon_{A,B} = \frac{\|F_A - F_B'\|^2}{n} \ . \quad (3)$$

Since the times series F_B can also be a flipped version of F_A, we also need to match F_A with $-F_B$.

As the second metric, we use what we call *frequency spectrum matching rate*. We define the matching rate to be probability that the separated flow F_B has the highest frequency spectrum cross-correlation with the actual flow F_A.

We note that while the mean square error captures the accuracy of the separation in the time domain, the matching rate captures the effectiveness of the separation in the frequency domain.

5.3 Different Types of Traffic

In this experiment, four aggregate flows, including one FTP flow, one sequence of HTTP requests, and two on/off UDP flows, are passing through the mix. The parameters for the flows are as follows: Flow 1: FTP flow, with round trip time around $80ms$. Flow 2: UDP-1 flow, on/off traffic, with burst rate $2500kbit/s$, average burst time $13ms$ and average idle time $6ms$. Flow 3: HTTP flows, with average page size 2048 byte. Flow 4: UDP-2, on/off traffic with burst rate $4000kbit/s$, average burst time $12ms$ and average idle time $5ms$. All the random parameters for the flows are exponentially distributed. The flows are passing through the mix as shown in Figure 1.

Figure 3 shows portions of the actual times series (Figure 3(a)) and of the estimated time series (Figure 3(b)). From the figures, it is apparent that the flipped version of the actual flow 3 (HTTP flows) is contained in the estimated flow 2. We also observe the resemblance between actual flow 1 (FTP flow) and estimated flow 4. Estimated flow 1 is clearly not close to any actual flows. This is caused by the redundancy contained in the observations, as described in Section 4.2.

Figure 4 shows the separation accuracy using the two metrics defined earlier. We note in Figure 4(b) that both the separated flow and its flipped time series is compared

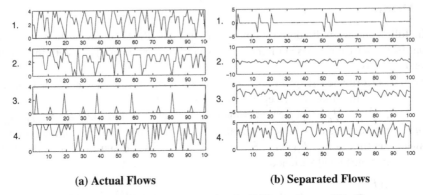

(a) Actual Flows   (b) Separated Flows

Fig. 3. Example of Flow Separation for Different Types of Traffic

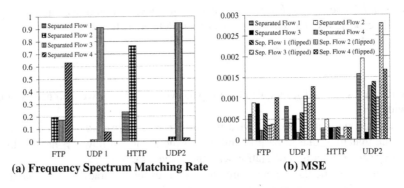

(a) Frequency Spectrum Matching Rate   (b) MSE

Fig. 4. Performance of Flow Separation for Different Types of Traffic

against the actual flows. Both metrics can identify the FTP flow, HTTP flows and one UDP flow. But the two metrics disagree on the other UDP flow. This is because of the redundancy in the observations, and the two UDP flows can not be separated. MSE fails for this case since it is designed for one-to-one flow matching while frequency spectrum matching is more suitable for matching of flows against aggregates. The latter case is more common in the context of flow separation.

5.4 Different Types of Traffic with Multicast Flow

In this experiment, the flow UDP-1 in the previous experiment is multicast to both output ports.

Portions of the actual flows and the estimated flows are shown in Figure 5. We observe the correspondence between the actual flows and estimated flows easily. In comparison with the previous experiment, we can conclude that multicast flows can help the flow separation. The reason is that in this experiment, there is no redundant observation when the multicast flow is passing through the mix.

MSE performance metrics in Figure 6 identify the flows successfully. Frequency spectrum matching successfully determine the FTP and HTTP flows, but does not

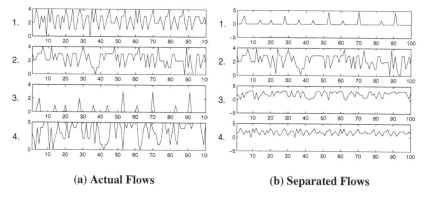

| (a) Actual Flows | (b) Separated Flows |

Fig. 5. Example of Flow Separation for Different Types of Traffic (with Multicast Traffic)

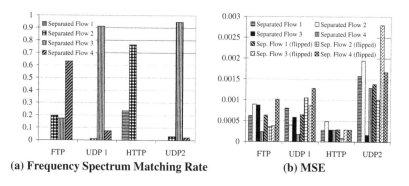

(a) Frequency Spectrum Matching Rate   **(b) MSE**

Fig. 6. Performance of Flow Separation for Different Types of Traffic (with Multicast Traffic)

perform well on the UDP flows. This is because the two UDP flows have approximately same period and the periodical behavior is not strong for exponential on/off traffic.

5.5   TCP-Only Traffic

Since most of the traffic in today's network is TCP traffic, we focus on TCP traffic in the next series of experiments. All the flows in this experiment are FTP flows. To distinguish the flows, we vary the link delays between the sender and mix, with S_1 having $10ms$ link delay to the mix, and S_2 having $15ms$ delay.

Figure 7 shows the flow separation performance. Since there is no multicast traffic, the redundancy in observations results that TCP Flow 1 and TCP Flow2 are still mixed. But the flows are identified successfully, especially by the frequency spectrum matching method.

5.6   TCP-Only Traffic with Multicast Flow

In this experiment, we change one FTP flow in the previous experiment to a multicast UDP flow. The UDP flow is exponential on/off traffic with the same parameter as UDP-1 in the experiment of Section 5.3.

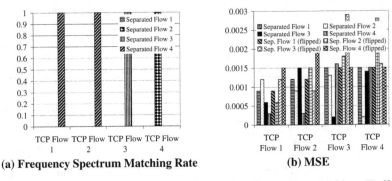

(a) Frequency Spectrum Matching Rate   (b) MSE

Fig. 7. Performance of Flow Separation for TCP-Only Traffic (without Multicast Traffic)

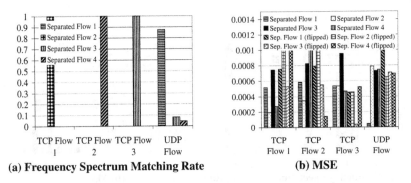

(a) Frequency Spectrum Matching Rate   (b) MSE

Fig. 8. Performance of Flow Separation for TCP-Only Traffic (with Multicast Traffic)

Figure 8 shows the flow separation performance. Similarly to the effect of multicast flow on different types of traffic, the four flows are separated completely since there are no redundant observations. We can also observe that the frequency spectrum method identifies the FTP flows successfully. But the performance on the exponential on/off UDP flow is not as good as FTP flows because exponential traffic flow's frequency signature is very weak.

6   Evaluation of Scalability of Flow Separation

We performed a series of experiments to evaluate the scalability of flow separation. We did this with respect to (a) increasing the number of flows in mix-level aggregate flows (the number of aggregate flows remains constant), (b) increasing the number of mix-level aggregate flows, and (c) increasing the number of ports per mix.

These experiments focus on a single mix. We use frequency spectrum matching results as performance metrics. Please refer [26] for more details of the experiments and results. Following are the observations for this series of experiments.

In general, the performance of flow separation remains good when we increase the number of flows in mix-level aggregate flow, increase the number of mix-level aggregate flow, and increase the number of ports per mix. For example, with 20 flows per aggregate, the lowest matching for 100Mbit/s link and 0.05 second sample interval is still above 65%.

We note that, as we increase the size of aggregate flows, the congestion caused by TCP flows will cause some performance decrease of flow separation attack. However, this can be compensated by increasing sample interval due to higher signal noise ratio.

Increasing the number of aggregate flows may lead to some flows not being separable due to a shortage of observations. Nevertheless, the frequency matching rate remains high. Same applies to experiments on increasing number of ports per mix.

In summary, it can be safely said that blind source separation performs well in large systems as well.

7   Evaluation for Mix Networks

Flow separation can also be used in mix networks when assuming a global passive attacker. The attacker can do flow separation at each mix according to observations obtained at that mix. Then the attacker can correlate the separated aggregate flows to derive the traffic map of the whole mix network.

7.1   Experiment Setup

Figure 9 shows the network setup in this experiment. Eight FTP flows from senders on the left side are traversing the mix network. To distinguish these eight FTP flows, we incrementally add $5ms$ delay to link connected to each sender. To simulate the cross traffic in the mix network, four larger aggregates of flows are added to the mix network. According to the self-similar nature of the network traffic [27], the high-volume cross traffic is Pareto distributed. The configuration of the flows is shown in Table 1.

In the center of the mix network, the traffic volume ratio between link-level aggregate traffic and each individual flow from senders is at least $7 : 1$. We assume the attacker can observe links connected to Mix $M_1, M_2, \cdots, M_{12}$. Thus, a flow originating from S_1 can take 2^6 possible paths.

Table 1. Flow Configuration

Flows	Path	Parameters	Throughput (packets/s)
1	$S_1 \rightarrow M_1' \rightarrow M_1 \rightarrow M_3 \rightarrow M_5 \rightarrow M_7 \rightarrow M_9 \rightarrow M_{11} \rightarrow M_5' \rightarrow R_1$	FTP	106.125
2	$S_2 \rightarrow M_1' \rightarrow M_1 \rightarrow M_4 \rightarrow M_5 \rightarrow M_8 \rightarrow M_9 \rightarrow M_{12} \rightarrow M_7' \rightarrow R_5$	FTP	100.791
3	$S_3 \rightarrow M_2' \rightarrow M_1 \rightarrow M_3 \rightarrow M_5 \rightarrow M_7 \rightarrow M_9 \rightarrow M_{11} \rightarrow M_6' \rightarrow R_3$	FTP	95.936
4	$S_4 \rightarrow M_2' \rightarrow M_1 \rightarrow M_4 \rightarrow M_5 \rightarrow M_8 \rightarrow M_9 \rightarrow M_{12} \rightarrow M_8' \rightarrow R_7$	FTP	91.541
5	$S_5 \rightarrow M_3' \rightarrow M_2 \rightarrow M_3 \rightarrow M_6 \rightarrow M_7 \rightarrow M_{10} \rightarrow M_{11} \rightarrow M_5' \rightarrow R_2$	FTP	87.531
6	$S_6 \rightarrow M_3' \rightarrow M_2 \rightarrow M_4 \rightarrow M_6 \rightarrow M_8 \rightarrow M_{10} \rightarrow M_{12} \rightarrow M_7' \rightarrow R_6$	FTP	83.858
7	$S_7 \rightarrow M_4' \rightarrow M_2 \rightarrow M_3 \rightarrow M_6 \rightarrow M_7 \rightarrow M_{10} \rightarrow M_{11} \rightarrow M_6' \rightarrow R_4$	FTP	80.483
8	$S_8 \rightarrow M_4' \rightarrow M_2 \rightarrow M_4 \rightarrow M_6 \rightarrow M_8 \rightarrow M_{10} \rightarrow M_{12} \rightarrow M_8' \rightarrow R_8$	FTP	77.357
9	$\rightarrow M_3 \rightarrow M_5 \rightarrow M_8 \rightarrow M_{10} \rightarrow$	Pareto	319.317
10	$\rightarrow M_3 \rightarrow M_6 \rightarrow M_8 \rightarrow M_9 \rightarrow$	Pareto	318.558
11	$\rightarrow M_4 \rightarrow M_5 \rightarrow M_7 \rightarrow M_{10} \rightarrow$	Pareto	321.806
12	$\rightarrow M_4 \rightarrow M_6 \rightarrow M_7 \rightarrow M_9 \rightarrow$	Pareto	323.36

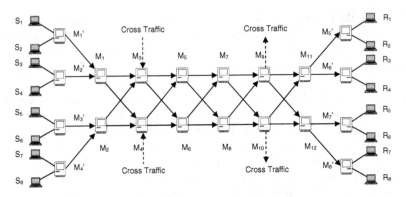

Fig. 9. Experiment Setup of Mix Network

7.2 Performance Metrics

To evaluate the performance of detecting a flow in the network, we introduce a network-level performance metrics, which is based on the entropy-based anonymity degree proposed in [28, 29]. Suppose we are interested in flow F_x. The attacker can suspect the flow F_x taking a path P_i with probability p_i based on the information gathered from the anonymity attack on the mix network. Assuming there are h possible paths that can be suspected as the path taken by the flow F_x, we define the anonymity degree as

$$D = -\sum_{i=1}^{h} p_i \log_2 p_i \quad . \tag{4}$$

Suppose a flow originated from S_1 in Figure 9 is suspected to use each of 2^6 possible paths with equal probability. Then the anonymity degree $D = 6bit$.

7.3 Performance

Figure 10 shows the mean value of cross correlation using frequency spectrum matching method among the first four FTP flows and separated flows recovered from Mix $1 - 12$. The cross-correlation values less than 0.1 are marked as white. Please note that the cross-correlation values between separated flows recovered from the same mix are also marked as white. This includes the cross-correlation (auto-correlation) for the same separated flow or FTP flow.

From the cross-correlation map shown in Figure 10, we can easily figure out the traffic direction in the mix network.

Figure 11 shows an algorithm to detect a flow say F_x in the network based on flow separation attack and frequency spectrum matching method. The main idea behind the algorithm is to first use the aggregate flow F_{tmp}, which is determined to be on the path previously to match the separated flows on the neighboring mixes. The threshold $threshold\_1$ is used to determine the Candidate array which includes the separated flows that have some components of the identified aggregate flow F_{tmp}. Then we

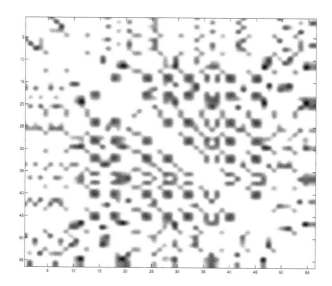

Fig. 10. Mean Value of Cross Correlation between Four FTP flow and Estimated Flows

match the flow F_x with the separated flows in the Candidate array to determine the most closely matching flow on the next hop. The process continues until the correlation is too weak, which is determined by the threshold $threshold\_2$. Thresholds $threshold\_1$ and $threshold\_2$ can be determined by online learning based either on data collected by attacker or on some heuristics setting. The algorithm works in dynamic programming way. It can be further improved by considering more possible routes and select the one has the largest overall possibilities.

We set the Thresholds $threshold\_1$ to zero and $threshold\_2$ to 0.1 heuristically. The result is based on the observations of 32 seconds of traffic. Our data indicates that similar results can be obtained with significantly smaller observation intervals. Our results indicate that the attack is very effective. In most cases, the anonymity was reduced from 6 bit to zero bit, while in one case, it was reduced form 6 bit to about 0.5 bit.

8   Discussion

In this paper, we focus on simple proxy mixes because of their popular use in practical anonymity systems. But flow separation can also be used to attack mixes using other batching strategies, such as the timed mix. Timed mixes batch the packets and release them every t seconds. So packets arriving at a timed mix in one batch will depart in the next batch. In turn, the noise in the observation at the output ports caused by queuing delays is zero as long as the timed mix is not congested. This helps the flow separation attack.

Flow separation attacks can also be used in wireless ad-hoc anonymity networks such as ANODR [30]. ANODR assumes that the packets in wireless anonymity network are encrypted and sender uses broadcast to avoid MAC address disclosure. Flow

$F_{tmp}=F_x$
$M_{tmp}=M_x$
while (mix M_{tmp} is not a dead-end) do {
      empty Candidate array
      for each mix M_i connected to M_{tmp} {
            for each flow F'_y separated by flow separation attack on M_i {
                  matching(F_{tmp}, F'_y)=Cross-correlation coefficient of the frequency
                  spectrums of F_{tmp} and F'_y
                  if matching$(F_{tmp}, F'_y)>$ threshold_1
                        record (F'_y, M_i) into array Candidate
            }
      }
      find the element (F'_{max}, M_{max}) in candidate array, so that
      matching$(F_x, F'_{max}) \geq$matching(F_x, F'_y), for any F'_y in Candidate array
      if matching$(F_x, F'_{max}) <$threshold_2
            break
      $F_{tmp}=F'_{max}$
      $M_{tmp}=M_{max}$
      record M_{max} as a mix on the flow path
}

Fig. 11. Flow Detection Algorithm

separation attack is more powerful in wireless anonymity network for two reasons: First, the passive attacker can get more observations easily in a wireless setting than in wired network by simply placing more wireless receivers in the wireless anonymity network. In order to eliminate redundant observations, the locations of these wireless receivers will depend on the transmission range of the wireless transmitters in the wireless anonymity network. Second, the attacker can execute flow separation attack not only on the basis of packet count time series but also on the physical strength of the wireless signal.

The countermeasures to flow separation attack are intuitive.

- Padding the links so that the observations obtained by the passive attacker are identical, or at least mostly redundant.
- Use pool-mix like batching strategies. Pool mixes fire packets with a certain probability p. If the probability p is small enough, the aggregate flows at the output ports can be significantly different from aggregate flows at the input ports. Adding noise in the passive attacker's observations can degrade the performance of flow separation attacks. But the cost will be increased packet transfer latency and lower throughput, especially for TCP traffic.
- Increase the dependency among flows by adding dependent dummy traffic flows to the mix-level aggregate flows.
- Padding each aggregate flow so that the distribution of the packet count is Gaussian. Most blind source separation algorithms fail when the signals mixed are Gaussian distributed. But different classes of blind source separation algorithm that make use of the time structure of the signals can still separate the flows e.g., [31, 32].

In general, it can be said that blind source separation algorithms coping with noisy delayed signals, over-complete base problems are still active research topics in blind source separation research. Flow separation attacks will be more powerful when more advanced algorithms become available.

9   Conclusion and Future Work

We proposed a new anonymity attack, called the *flow separation attack* which can be used either alone or in conjunctions with other attacks to significantly reduce the effectiveness of anonymous communication systems. Flow separation attack is based on the blind source separation algorithms widely used to recover individual signals from mixtures of signals. Our experiments show that the anonymity attack is effective and scalable. With the aid of further attack such as frequency spectrum matching attack, flow separation attack can be used to detect the path taken by a flow in a mix network. Flow separation attack can also be used to simply recover the traffic map of the anonymity network. We discuss the possible usage of flow separation attack in different anonymity network settings, and we elaborate on criteria for its countermeasures.

Our future work will focus on the usage of the attack in the wireless and ad-hoc anonymity networks. We also planning to analytically model the effectiveness of the attack.

References

1. D. Chaum, "Untraceable electronic mail, return addresses, and digital pseudonyms," *Communications of the ACM*, vol. 4, February 1981.
2. B. N. Levine, M. K. Reiter, C. Wang, and M. K. Wright, "Timing attacks in low-latency mix-based systems," in *Proceedings of Financial Cryptography (FC '04)* (A. Juels, ed.), Springer-Verlag, LNCS 3110, February 2004.
3. C. Jutten and J. Herault, "Blind separation of sources, part 1: an adaptive algorithm based on neuromimetic architecture," *Signal Process.*, vol. 24, no. 1, pp. 1–10, 1991.
4. Y. Zhu, X. Fu, B. Graham, R. Bettati, and W. Zhao, "On flow correlation attacks and countermeasures in mix networks," in *Proceedings of Privacy Enhancing Technologies workshop (PET 2004)*, May 2004.
5. R. Dingledine, N. Mathewson, and P. Syverson, "Tor: The second-generation onion router," in *Proceedings of the 13th USENIX Security Symposium*, August 2004.
6. A. Serjantov, R. Dingledine, and P. Syverson, "From a trickle to a flood: Active attacks on several mix types," in *Proceedings of Information Hiding Workshop (IH 2002)* (F. Petitcolas, ed.), Springer-Verlag, LNCS 2578, October 2002.
7. G. Danezis and A. Serjantov, "Statistical disclosure or intersection attacks on anonymity systems," in *Proceedings of 6th Information Hiding Workshop (IH 2004)*, LNCS, (Toronto), May 2004.
8. G. Danezis, "The traffic analysis of continuous-time mixes," in *Proceedings of Privacy Enhancing Technologies workshop (PET 2004)*, LNCS, May 2004.
9. D. Goldschlag, M. Reed, and P. Syverson, "Onion routing for anonymous and private internet connections," *Communications of the ACM (USA)*, vol. 42, no. 2, pp. 39–41, 1999.

10. M. Reiter and A. Rubin, "Crowds: Anonymity for web transactions," *ACM Transactions on Information and System Security*, vol. 1, June 1998.
11. M. Rennhard and B. Plattner, "Introducing MorphMix: Peer-to-Peer based Anonymous Internet Usage with Collusion Detection," in *Proceedings of the Workshop on Privacy in the Electronic Society (WPES 2002)*, (Washington, DC, USA), November 2002.
12. R. Sherwood, B. Bhattacharjee, and A. Srinivasan, "P5: A protocol for scalable anonymous communication," in *Proceedings of the 2002 IEEE Symposium on Security and Privacy*, May 2002.
13. J. D. Howard, "An analysis of security incidents on the internet 1989 - 1995," tech. rep., Carnegie Mellon University Dissertation, 1997.
14. F.B.I, "Carnivore diagnostic tool." http://www.fbi.gov/hq/lab/carnivore/carnivore2.htm, 2003.
15. J. Cardoso, "Blind signal separation: statistical principles," vol. 9, no. 10, pp. 2009–2025, 1998. Special issue on blind identification and estimation.
16. P. Comon, "Independent component analysis, a new concept?," *Signal Process.*, vol. 36, no. 3, pp. 287–314, 1994.
17. Z. He, L. Yang, J. Liu, Z. Lu, C. He, and Y. Shi, "Blind source separation using clustering-based multivariate density estimation algorithm," *IEEE Trans. on Signal Processing*, vol. 48, no. 2, pp. 575–579, 2000.
18. A. Hyvärinen, "Fast and robust fixed-point algorithms for independent component analysis," *IEEE Transactions on Neural Networks*, vol. 10, no. 3, pp. 626–634, 1999.
19. A. Hyvärinen and E. Oja, "A fast fixed-point algorithm for independent component analysis," *Neural Comput.*, vol. 9, no. 7, pp. 1483–1492, 1997.
20. M. Gaeta and J.-L. Lacoume, "Source separation without prior knowledge: the maximum likelihood solution," in *Proc. EUSIPCO'90*, pp. 621–624, 1990.
21. D.-T. Pham, P. Garrat, and C. Jutten, "Separation of a mixture of independent sources through a maximum likelihood approach," in *Proc. EUSIPCO*, pp. 771–774, 1992.
22. A. Hyvärinen and M. Inki, "Estimating overcomplete independent component bases for image windows," *J. Math. Imaging Vis.*, vol. 17, no. 2, pp. 139–152, 2002.
23. A. Hyvärinen, R. Cristescu, and E. Oja, "A fast algorithm for estimating overcomplete ICA bases for image windows," in *Proc. Int. Joint Conf. on Neural Networks*, (Washington, D.C.), pp. 894–899, 1999.
24. Y. Zhu, X. Fu, B. Graham, R. Bettati, and W. Zhao, "Correlation attacks in a mix network," *Texas A&M University Computer Science Technical Report*, February 2005.
25. S. A. Cruces-Alvarez and A. Cichocki, "Combining blind source extraction with joint approximate diagonalization: Thin algorithms for ICA," in *Proc. of the Fourth Symposium on Independent Component Analysis and Blind Signal Separation*, (Nara, Japan), pp. 463–468, Apr. 2003.
26. Y. Zhu and R. Bettati, "Unmixing mix traffic," *Texas A&M University Computer Science Technical Report*, February 2005.
27. K. Park and W. Willinger, "Self-similar network traffic: An overview," 1999.
28. A. Serjantov and G. Danezis, "Towards an information theoretic metric for anonymity," in *Proceedings of Privacy Enhancing Technologies Workshop (PET 2002)* (R. Dingledine and P. Syverson, eds.), Springer-Verlag, LNCS 2482, April 2002.
29. C. Diaz, S. Seys, J. Claessens, and B. Preneel, "Towards measuring anonymity," in *Proceedings of Privacy Enhancing Technologies Workshop (PET 2002)* (R. Dingledine and P. Syverson, eds.), Springer-Verlag, LNCS 2482, April 2002.
30. J. Kong and X. Hong, "Anodr: anonymous on demand routing with untraceable routes for mobile ad-hoc networks," in *MobiHoc '03: Proceedings of the 4th ACM international symposium on Mobile ad hoc networking & computing*, pp. 291–302, ACM Press, 2003.

31. L. Tong, R.-W. Liu, V. C. Soon, and Y.-F. Huang, "Indeterminacy and identifiability of blind identification," *Circuits and Systems, IEEE Transactions on*, vol. 38, no. 5, pp. 499–509, 1991.

32. L. Molgedey and H. G. Schuster, "Separation of a mixture of independent signals using time delayed correlations," *Physical Review Letters*, vol. 72, pp. 3634–3637, June 1994.

Mix-Network with Stronger Security

Jan Camenisch[1] and Anton Mityagin[2]

[1] IBM Research, Zurich Research Laboratory
Säumerstrasse 4, CH-8803 Rüschlikon, Switzerland
jca@zurich.ibm.com
[2] Department of Computer Science, University of California, San Diego
9500 Gilman Drive, Dept. 0114, La Jolla, CA 92093-0114, USA
amityagin@cs.ucsd.edu

Abstract. We consider a mix-network as a cryptographic primitive that provides anonymity. A mix-network takes as input a number of ciphertexts and outputs a random shuffle of the corresponding plaintexts. Common applications of mix-nets are electronic voting and anonymous network traffic. In this paper, we present a novel construction of a mix-network, which is based on shuffling ElGamal encryptions. Our scheme is the first mix-net to meet the strongest security requirements: it is robust and secure against chosen ciphertext attacks as well as against active attacks in the Universally Composable model. Our construction allows one to securely execute several mix-net instances concurrently, as well as to run multiple mix-sessions without changing a set of keys. Nevertheless, the scheme is efficient: it requires a linear work (in the number of input messages) per mix-server.

1 Introduction

Mix-networks were introduced by Chaum [10] in the early 80-ies and have been extensively studied since then. However, most of the cryptographic constructions found in the literature are ad-hoc constructions often without or only hand-waving security proofs. In fact, the area has a history of proposing, breaking, and fixing schemes [19, 21, 1, 14, 15, 16, 3, 24].

A mix-network could be viewed as a public key cryptographic primitive that takes as input a number of ciphertexts, decrypts and shuffles them and finally outputs a random permutation of plaintexts. To ensure anonymity, a mix-network is implemented by multiple mix-servers and the secret permutation is shared between the servers. Therefore, even if one or several of the servers are corrupted, it remains hidden which ciphertext corresponds to which plaintext.

The most widespread definition of security of a mix-network is called unlinkability or anonymity. Unlinkability definition typically considers a single run of a mix-session and it says that an adversary (who might corrupt some users and some servers) cannot find a match between a plaintext and a ciphertext any better than by guessing it at random.

A step towards developing a stronger security notion was taken only recently by Abe and Imai [3] who presented a definition of anonymity under chosen ciphertext attacks (CCA-anonymity). CCA-anonymity allows an adversary to use

G. Danezis and D. Martin (Eds.): PET 2005, LNCS 3856, pp. 128–146, 2006.

multiple mixing rounds to mount a chosen ciphertext attack on the mix-net. However, the authors did not provide any scheme satisfying their definition. Indeed, prior to our work, no mix-network was proved to achieve CCA-anonymity.

The latest and the only known work so far that constructs a mix-network which is proved to achieve a stronger security notion than unlinkability is the recent result of Wikström [25]. He presents a security definition for a mix-network in the Universally Composable model [7] together a construction of it, which is secure against blocking adversaries. Although it provides strong provable security, the protocol has some drawbacks. The complexity of the protocol is high — it requires quadratic work per mix-server, i.e., each mix server has complexity proportional to the total number of mix-servers times the total number of messages. Also, his protocol is not robust and misbehavior even of a single mix-server can cause all the other parties to abort already initiated mixing.

Our Results. We present a novel construction of a mix-network, which is based on ElGamal public key encryption and straight-line extractable zero-knowledge proofs. Our protocol uses the following building blocks: threshold ElGamal encryption, proof of equality of ElGamal plaintexts *PfEqual*, proof of decryption to a given plaintext *PfDec*, proof of knowledge of a decryption *PfPtxt* and proof of correctness of a shuffle *PfShuf*.

Our construction is robust and achieves both CCA-anonymity and UC security. This is the first mix-network in the literature to achieve all these properties. Our construction allows one to securely execute several mix-net instances concurrently, as well as to run multiple mix-sessions without changing the keys. Nevertheless, the scheme is efficient: it requires from mix-server work linear in the number of input messages. Our mix-network is also optimistic: it gains efficiency assuming the number of misbehaving parties is small.

We assume the existence of a trusted authority who verifies that the parties follow the protocol. We stress that the role of a trusted authority is minimal: he is not allowed to possess any secrets and his role is limited only to generating public random coins for zero-knowledge proofs of correctness. Without loss out security, the trusted authority can be replaced by a secure multi-party protocol. Our protocol is robust and secure provided that at least one server is not corrupted (trusted authority model) or the majority of servers are not corrupted (no trusted authority, common reference string model).

In contrast to [25], we consider the UC model with guaranteed message delivery (also called security against non-blocking adversaries, see [4, 7, 22]). In this model adversary (who is responsible for the delivery of messages) is not allowed to cancel any messages sent between the parties. This gives stronger security guarantees and, in particular, UC-security a mix-network with guaranteed message delivery implies robustness, while UC-security without guaranteed message delivery does not.

Organization. The paper is organized as follows. In Section 2 we review cryptographic primitives which we will use in the construction of our protocol. In Section 3 we define a mix-net primitive and give our construction of a mix-network.

In Section 4 we consider mix-networks in Universally Composable model: we introduce Ideal Functionality for a mix-net and prove that our construction securely realizes it. Finally, in Section 5 we discuss the simulation-based model and show robustness and CCA-anonymity of our mix-net.

2 Preliminaries

2.1 (n out of n) Threshold ElGamal Encryption

A threshold public key cryptosystem uses a single public key for encrypting messages but the corresponding secret key is shared among a set of n decryption servers $D_1, \ldots, D_n$ in a way such that at least t of them must cooperate to decrypt a message. Such cryptosystems are called t out of n threshold cryptosystems. The decryption of a ciphertext is done using decryption shares. That is, given a ciphertext, each decryption server responds with a decryption share and proves its validity. After collecting valid shares from t decryption servers, anyone can combine these shares to obtain the decryption of the ciphertext.

In our mix-network construction we will use the n out of n threshold ElGamal cryptosystem ThEG which uses Shamir's secret sharing scheme [23]. Let $\mathfrak{G}$ be a multiplicative subgroup of prime order q of $\mathbb{Z}_p^*$, where p is also a prime. Let g be a generator of $\mathfrak{G}$. We denote by $E_y(m; r)$ the ElGamal encryption $(g^r, m \cdot y^r)$ of message m under the public key y using the random coins r; if we do not want to specify the random coins we write $E_y(m)$.

Threshold ElGamal encryption scheme ThEG:

- **Key Generation.** The key generation algorithm G picks a set of n decryption secret keys $x_1, \ldots, x_n$ at random from $\mathbb{Z}_q$. The keys are given to decryption servers and the corresponding verification keys $y_1 \leftarrow g^{x_1}, \ldots, y_n \leftarrow g^{x_n}$ are announced. The public key is $y \leftarrow y_1 \cdot \ldots \cdot y_n$.
- **Encryption.** The encryption algorithm $E_y(\cdot)$ is identical to the original ElGamal cryptosystem. Encryption algorithm picks a random element r from $\mathbb{Z}_q$ and returns $E_y(m; r) = (g^r, m \cdot y^r)$.
- **Share Decryption.** The share decryption algorithm $D_{x_i}(\cdot)$, given as input a ciphertext $(a, b) = (g^r, m \cdot y^r)$ and a secret key x_i, returns a decryption share $s_i \leftarrow a^{x_i}$.
- **Share Verification.** The share verification protocol $SV(s_i, (a, b), y_i, D_i, V)$ involves a decryption server D_i and a verifier V. A common input is a ciphertext (a, b), a share s_i and a verification key y_i. A server D_i is also given a secret key x_i. The protocol is realized by a Chaum-Pedersen proof [11] of discrete logarithm equality $log_a s_i = log_g y_i$:
  - D_i picks $s \in \mathbb{Z}_q$ at random and announces (a^s, g^s).
  - V sends back a random challenge $c \in \mathbb{Z}_q$.
  - D_i replies with $t \leftarrow s + cx_i$.
  - V accepts if both $a^t = a^s \cdot s_i^c$ and $g^t = g^s \cdot y_i^c$ and rejects otherwise.

– **Combining Algorithm.** Given a ciphertext $c = (a, b)$ and secret shares $s_i = a^{x_i}$ for $i = 1, \ldots, n$, the combining algorithm $C((a,b), s_1, \ldots, s_n)$ computes a plaintext $m =\leftarrow b \cdot s_1^{-1} \cdot \ldots \cdot s_n^{-1}$.

The ElGamal threshold encryption scheme has a homomorphic property. For for any two messages m_1 and m_2, any public key pk, and any random coins r_1 and r_2 we have $E_{pk}(m_1; r_1) \cdot E_{pk}(m_2; r_2) = E_{pk}(m_1 \cdot m_2; r_1 + r_2)$. The following fact is not hard to show.

Theorem 1. *Under the decisional Diffie-Hellman assumption in the group $\mathfrak{G}$, ThEG achieves IND-CPA security against a static adversary who can corrupt all the decryption servers except one.*

2.2   Proof of a Correct Shuffle

A major building block of our mix-network is a zero-knowledge proof of a correct shuffle. Let $L_0 = \{c_1^0, \ldots, c_n^0\}$ and $L_1 = \{c_1^1, \ldots, c_n^1\}$ be lists of size n of ElGamal ciphertexts under a public key y. A proof of correct shuffle $PfShuf(y, L_0, L_1, P, V)$ allows a prover P to prove in zero-knowledge that lists of plaintexts corresponding to these ciphertexts are permutations of each other. A witness of P is a permutation $\pi : \{1, \ldots, n\} \rightarrow \{1, \ldots, n\}$ and a list of random coins $\{r_1, \ldots, r_n\}$ such that

$$\forall\, i = 1, \ldots, n \quad c_i^1 = c_{\pi^{-1}(i)}^0 \cdot E_y(1; r_{\pi^{-1}(i)}).$$

We refer the reader to the work of Groth [13] for efficient zero-knowledge proof of correctness of a shuffle of ElGamal ciphertexts. The protocol [13] is proved to achieve Special Honest Verifier Zero-Knowledge. Due to the lack of space, we are not giving the details of it in this paper and just recall that the protocol requires 7 round of communication between the prover and the verifier each of which have to perform $6n$ exponentiations in the group $\mathfrak{G}$ used for the encryption scheme.

2.3   Proof of Equality of ElGamal Plaintexts

Another building block for our protocol is a zero-knowledge proof of equality of two ElGamal ciphertexts. Again, all the operations are in a group $\mathfrak{G}$ with a generator g. A proof of equality of ElGamal plaintext $PfEqual(c_1, c_2, pk_1, pk_2, P, V)$ is a proof that two given ciphertexts c_1 and c_2 under two given public keys pk_1 and pk_2 decrypt to the same plaintext. The witness for $PfEqual(c_1, c_2, pk_1, pk_2, P, V)$ consists of decryptions of c_1, c_2 and random coins used in the encryptions. Let $c_1 = (a_1, b_1)$ and $c_2 = (a_2, b_2)$. Then $PfEqual(c_1, c_2, pk_1, pk_2, P, V)$ is a proof for the NP-relation $R_{PfEqual}((a_1, b_1), (a_2, b_2), pk_1, pk_2)$:

$$\exists\, r_1, r_2 \text{ s.t. } a_1 = g^{r_1} \wedge a_2 = g^{r_2} \wedge b_1 \cdot b_2^{-1} = pk_1^{r_1} \cdot pk_2^{-r_2}.$$

Standard techniques allow one to construct a constant round honest-verifier zero-knowledge proof $PfEqual$ that requires a constant number of exponentiations both for the prover and for the verifier.

2.4   Straight-Line Extractable HVZK Proofs

In our mix-network construction we will use honest verifier zero-knowledge proofs of knowledge with an extra property. Specifically, a cheating verifier (simulator) should be able to extract a witness for the proof without rewinding a prover and he should do it unnoticeable to the prover. This is a special case of straight-line extractable proofs and a deeper discussion on the topic could be found in [20].

Definition 1. *Let $Pf_R(x, P, V)$ be a honest-verifier zero-knowledge proof protocol for NP-relation $R(x)$ of the form "$\exists \ w$ s.t. $Q(x, w)$" (for some poly-time relationship Q). In the protocol x is a common input of the parties and the prover is also given a witness w s.t. $Q(x, w) = 1$. We say that Pf_R achieves straight-line extractability for a function $f(\cdot)$, if there exists a (malicious) verifier V^* such that for any prover P^* and for any common input x: if the honest verifier V accepts P^*'s proof w.r.t. x with some probability p, then V^* after interaction with P^* must be able to extract $f(w')$ (for some witness w' s.t. $Q(x, w') = 1$) with probability at least p minus some negligible quantity. We also require V^* to behave indistinguishably from the honest verifier V.*

In our construction some proofs need to be straight-line extractable while other proofs do not. We will explicitly mention if we require a proof to have straight-line extractability property.

2.5   Straight-Line Extractable Proof of Knowledge of a Discrete Log

We describe a straight-line extractable zero-knowledge proof of knowledge of a discrete logarithm. We construct such a proof using the Camenisch-Shoup verifiable encryption scheme for discrete logarithms [6]. Let $PfDec(y, c, pk, P, V)$ denote the proof that the discrete logarithm of y is contained in the ciphertext c that was created under public key pk provided by Camenisch and Shoup [6]. Let $Enc_{pk}(m; r)$ denote the encryption algorithm of Camenisch-Shoup scheme (it takes input a public key pk, a message m and random coins r). The witness for $PfDec$ consists of a discrete logarithm of y and random coins used to construct a ciphertext. Then the following protocol $PfLog(y, P, V)$ is a straight-line extractable proof of knowledge of a discrete logarithm of y:

Protocol $PfLog(y, P, V)$:

- Common input of P and V is (y, g), P is also given the witness $x = \log_g y$.
- V picks a public key pk (for Camenisch-Shoup encryption) at random and sends it to P. Note that V doesn't know the secret key corresponding to pk.
- P picks random coins r, encrypts $x = \log_g y$ under public key pk to get a ciphertext $c \leftarrow Enc_{pk}(m; r)$ and sends c to V.
- P and V execute a proof $PfDec(y, c, pk, P, V)$. V outputs "1" if it accepts a proof $PfDec$ and "0" otherwise.

Proof of the following lemma is standard:

Lemma 1. *If PfDec is honest verifier zero-knowledge proof, then PfLog is a straight-line extractable honest verifier computational zero knowledge proof under DDH assumption in the group $\langle g \rangle$.*

2.6 Straight-Line Extractable Proof of Knowledge of a Plaintext

We use the techniques by Naor and Yung [18] to construct a straight-line extractable zero-knowledge proof of knowledge of a plaintext of an ElGamal encryption. That is we require the prover to encrypt the same message twice, each time under a different public key and then to prove that the two ciphertexts decrypt to the same message (using the protocol provided in Section 2.3). Let $PfEqual(c_1, c_2, pk_1, pk_2, P, V)$ be a proof that two given ciphertexts c_1 and c_2 under two given public keys pk_1 and pk_2 decrypt to the same plaintext. Then the following protocol $PfPtxt(c, pk, P, V)$ is a straight-line extractable proof of knowledge of a decryption of c under pk. We denote the decryption of c by m.

Protocol $PfPtxt(c, pk, P, V)$:

- A verifier V picks a random public key pk^* and sends pk^* to P.
- P encrypts a message m with a public key pk^* to get a ciphertext c^*, and sends c^* to V.
- P and V execute a proof $PfEqual(c, c^*, pk, pk^*, P, V)$. Verifier outputs "1" if it accepts a proof $PfEqual$ and "0" otherwise.

The following is not hard to show.

Lemma 2. *Provided that PfEqual is sound and honest-verifier zero-knowledge, then PfPtxt is a straight-line extractable public-coin honest-verifier zero knowledge proof.*

3 Mix-Network Protocol

3.1 High-Level Description and Communication Model

Participants. A mix-network protocol is executed by 2 groups of parties: users $U_1, \ldots, U_k$ and mix-servers $M_1, \ldots, M_m$. All the parties are considered to be polynomially bounded interactive Turing machines.

In our mix-net protocol, all communication is done via an authenticated bulletin board BB. Any party can post messages to the BB in authenticated manner and as well read all the information from it. No one can cancel or modify any information once written to the BB.

Procedures of a Mix-Network.
The purpose of the mix-network is to shuffle messages and it processes messages in batches. In each mix-session, all the k users encrypt their messages and send the resulting ciphertexts to a mix-net. The mix-network decrypts and shuffles

the ciphertexts in a distributed manner and outputs a random permutation of plaintext messages.

In general, a mix-network protocol could be described by three interactive multi-party protocols. They are: a key-generation protocol $\mathbb{M}.Gen(\cdot)$, an encryption protocol $\mathbb{M}.Enc(\cdot)$, and a distributed shuffle/decryption protocol $\mathbb{M}.Exec(\cdot)$. First, the servers and the authority execute $\mathbb{M}.Gen(\cdot)$, then they jointly compute a public key and announce it via the BB and as well each of the servers generates its own secret key.

For each mix-session each user U_i chooses a message m_i, encrypts it under the mix-net's public key using $\mathbb{M}.Enc(\cdot)$, and submits a the resulting ciphertext to the bulletin board. The list of correctly submitted messages $K = \{m_1, \ldots, m_{k_h}\}$, is called "input" of a mix-network. Note that this list might contain some messages chosen and submitted by the adversary.

Then all the servers jointly execute the $\mathbb{M}.Exec(\cdot)$ protocol. They shuffle and decrypt the ciphertexts input distributedly and in the end output a list of plaintexts $\tilde{K} = \{\tilde{m}_1, \ldots, \tilde{m}_k\}$ to the BB. The output $\tilde{K}$ contains a random permutation of a list K of input messages.

Adversary. We consider a polynomially bounded adversary A who can read all the communications between the parties (but cannot modify it) and who can corrupt some of the users and some of the servers. The adversary can corrupt a party in two ways: passively and actively. For a passively corrupted party, the adversary can see all the secret information of the party as well as all the internal state of the party at each moment of time, while the corrupted party still follows the protocol. We say that an adversary actively corrupted a party if this party is fully controlled by the adversary. I.e., the adversary not only has access to the party's secrets but it also can send any messages on behalf on this party. We distinguish between static and adaptive adversaries. The static adversary chooses the corrupted parties before the execution of the protocol while the adaptive adversary can corrupt parties during the execution of the protocol.

In the analysis of our mix-network we will consider a static adversary who can actively corrupt arbitrary all except one mix-server and all except one decryption server.

3.2   Our Mix-Network Construction: $\mathbb{MIX}$

Our mix-network protocol $\mathbb{MIX}$ involves k users $U_1, \ldots, U_k$, m mix-servers M_1, $\ldots, M_m$, n decryption servers $D_1, \ldots, D_n$, the trusted authority V, and the bulletin board BB.

Key Generation. The key generation algorithm $\mathbb{MIX}.Gen(\lambda)$ is essentially the key generation algorithm of threshold ElGamal scheme. The authority V selects a group $\mathfrak{G}$ of prime size q ($|q| \approx \lambda$) and a generator $g \in \mathfrak{G}$. He publishes a description of $\mathfrak{G}$ together with g to the bulletin board. Each decryption server D_i, $i = 1, \ldots, n$, chooses a random secret key $x_i \in \mathbb{Z}_q$ and computes a public verification key $y_i \leftarrow g^{x_i}$. Then D_i publishes y_i to BB and executes a straight-line extractable proof $PfLog(y_i, D_i, V)$ to the authority V (see Section 2.5 for a construction of $PfLog$). If the proof is accepted, V authorizes D_i to work as a decryption server. After all the decryption servers published their verification keys, the authority computes the encryption public key $y \leftarrow y_1 \cdot \ldots \cdot y_n$, which is the product of all the authorized verification keys[1] and publishes y on the BB together with a list of the authorized decryption servers.

Encryption. The authority starts each mix-session by publishing an initiating message together with the session id to the BB. At every mix-session each user sends a single encrypted message using the encryption procedure $\text{MIX}.Enc_y(m)$ which consists of encrypting a message m by ElGamal under public key y and producing a proof $PfPtxt$ that is verified by the authority V. That is, each user U_i, on input a message m_i picks a random $r_i \in \mathbb{Z}_q$ and encrypts m_i with a public key y: $c_i^0 \leftarrow (g^{r_i}, m_i \cdot y^{r_i})$. Furthermore, U_i sends a ciphertext c_i^0 to the bulletin board and executes the proof $PfPtxt(c_i^0, pk, U_i, V)$ of correct encryption (cf. Section 2.6). The authority V verifies the proofs and writes to BB a list L_0 of all the accepted ciphertexts. We will call the list of correctly submitted plaintext messages $K = \{m_1, \ldots, m_{k_h}\}$ the *input to the mix-network* in a given mix-session.

Shuffling. The protocol $\text{MIX}.Exec$ does both shuffling and decryption operations. After L_0 appeared on the bulletin board, mix-servers one-by-one do the shuffling. The i-th mix-server M_i reads a list $L_{i-1} = \{c_1^{i-1}, \ldots, c_{k_h}^{i-1}\}$ from the bulletin board, chooses a permutation π_i at random and forms a list $L_i = \{c_1^i, \ldots, c_{k_h}^i\}$, where each

$$c_j^i \leftarrow c_{\pi^{-1}(j)}^{i-1} \cdot E_{pk}(1).$$

M_i submits L_i to BB and executes the proof $PfShuf(L_{i-1}, L_i, M_i, V)$ of a correct shuffle (see Section 2.2) to a verifier V. If the authority V does not accept the proof, L_i is discarded, V sets $L_i = L_{i-1}$ and announces M_i to be cheating.

Decryption. After the last mix-server M_m outputs a list $\tilde{L} = \{\tilde{c}_1, \ldots, \tilde{c}_{k_h}\}$, each of the decryption servers outputs decryption shares for each message and proves correctness of each share. Specifically, a decryption server D_i for each message $(a, b) \in \tilde{L}$ computes a share $s_i \leftarrow a^{x_i}$ and executes a share verification proof $SV(s_i, (a, b), y_i, D_i, V)$. If D_i crashes or fails to prove correctness of some decryption share, V announces that D_i cheated and re-runs the protocol, following the re-run procedure described below. He continues re-running the protocol until all the decryption shares are accepted. Then V combines shares for all the ciphertexts from $\tilde{L}$, computes a list of plaintexts $\tilde{K} = \{\tilde{m}_1, \ldots, \tilde{m}_{k_h}\}$ and writes $\tilde{K}$ to the BB. $\tilde{K}$ is called the *output of a mix-network* in a given mix-session.

---

[1] For notational convenience we will assume that all n decryption servers are authorized.

Re-run. If some decryption server D_i is announced to be cheating, the mix-session is re-run from the scratch. First, the server who cheated is "eliminated" and he will not participate neither in a re-run of the mix-session nor in any future session. The authority computes a new public key $y' \leftarrow y \cdot y_i^{-1}$ and all the parties are updated to use a new encryption key y'. Then all the users re-submit their messages to BB. Note that they must submit the same messages as in the original run. Each user U_i picks random coins $r_i' \in \mathbb{Z}_q$, sends $c_i'^0 \leftarrow (g^{r'}, m_i \cdot y'^{r'})$ to BB and executes a proof $PfEqual(c_i, c_i', y, y', U_i, V)$ (see Section 2.3) that he submits the same message as before. Then, the mix-network proceeds with shuffling and decryption as in the original execution.

Discussion. As we will show later, the protocol is secure provided that at least 2 users, 1 mix-server and 1 decryption server are honest. Note that if a decrypting server is found to be cheating and the protocol is re-run, messages are re-encrypted only under the keys of remaining servers. Thus it remains secure if there is at least 1 honest decryption server.

3.3   Efficiency

At the encryption stage each of the k users spends a constant number of modular multiplications to compute a ciphertext and to prove it's correctness. At the shuffling stage, each of the m mix-servers needs $O(k)$ modular multiplications to compute a shuffled list and to prove the correctness. At the decryption stage each decryption server needs a constant number of modular multiplications to compute a share for each of the ciphertexts and to prove a correctness of the share. Therefore, the total complexity of a mix-session assuming that no re-runs take place is

$$O(k) + O(m \cdot k) + O(n \cdot k) = O(k \cdot (n + m))$$

modular multiplications. Each re-run requires the same work as the whole mix-session. The total number of re-runs in all the mix-sessions does not exceed the number of corrupted decryption servers, which is less than n. Thus the average complexity of a mix-session with total d mix-sessions is at most

$$\left(1 + \frac{n}{d}\right) \cdot O(k \cdot (n + m)).$$

3.4   Honest Majority Model with Secure Initialization

Our mix-network could be easily modified to work in the Common Reference String Model [5] with honest majority of the parties, when no trusted authority V is available or wanted.

In the Honest Majority model all the operations of V can be done by a majority vote of all the parties.

First, the parties would initially choose public keys of an encryption scheme to be used for the straight-line extractable proofs. These keys could then be used for all the proofs.

The verification of the proofs is done as follows: each time a prover asks for a random challenge from V, all the parties execute a secure coin tossing algorithm [9] to compute the random challenge. A prover uses this random challenge and outputs a proof to the bulletin board. Then each party verifies the proof and outputs either "accept" or "reject". The proof is accepted if the majority of the parties returned "accept" and rejected otherwise.

Alternatively, one could resort to the random oracle model/Fiat-Shamir heuristic to make the proofs non-interactive. In this case, the parties would need to interact only for the initial set-up of the public keys and for the implementation of the bulletin board.

4   Security of Our Protocol in the UC Framework

The goal of this section is to prove that our mix-network $\mathbb{MIX}$ is secure in the Universally Composable framework. We start by giving a brief overview of the UC framework; we refer our reader to Canetti [7] for the comprehensive study of the UC model. We show how to adopt an arbitrary mix-net protocol in the UC framework and give the ideal functionality of a mix-network $\mathrm{IF}_{\mathrm{MIX}}$. Our functionality is a different from the one in Wikström's paper [25] in that it can handle crashes of corrupted parties. Then, we discuss the security concerns that arise in this model and prove that our mix-network $\mathbb{MIX}$ meets the notion of UC-security.

4.1   Universally Composable Framework

We assume our reader to be familiar with a concept of Universally Composable Framework [4, 7, 22]. In this paper we consider communication model, where communication is asynchronous and ideally authenticated with guaranteed delivery. We consider security against static active adversary.

The Universally Composable framework consists of the two models of computation: a Real World model, that corresponds to an actual multi-party cryptographic protocol and an Ideal World model, that corresponds to a desired functionality of the cryptographic primitive. These two models have the identical sets of parties, however in the Real World model the computation is done by the actual protocol while in the Ideal world all the parties hand their data to a trusted party called *Ideal Functionality* who does the desired computation. There is a special party Z called *the Environment* which is located outside the models and who chooses all the input data of the parties: e.g., messages users send to each other. A protocol Π is said to *securely realize an ideal functionality* IF or Π is said to be *UC-secure*, if no environment can distinguish if it is interacting in with the real world parties who runs Π or with ideal world parities interacting via the ideal functionality IF. Composition theorems guarantee [4, 7, 22] that if a protocol is secure in the universally composable setting then several instances of the protocol could be executed concurrently and arbitrarily interleaved without any loss in security.

4.2 Communication Model

We assume that the communication is asynchronous and ideally authenticated with guaranteed delivery. Although Universally Composable model without guaranteed delivery is more common in the literature, we argue that the guaranteed delivery model both seems to be more natural for the case of mix-networks and provides stronger security guarantees.

We stress that in the case of mix-networks the difference between these security notions is crucial. First, UC-security with guaranteed delivery implies robustness of the mix-net protocol, this holds because the ideal adversary is guaranteed to deliver all the communication and thus it cannot break robustness. On the other hand, there exist mix-net protocols (e.g. [25]) which are not robust and UC-secure in the model without guaranteed delivery.

Second, UC-security in the guaranteed delivery model automatically implies CCA-anonymity. In turn, it is not clear whether it is true in the model without guaranteed delivery. The straight-forward reduction fails because the blocking ideal world adversary is capable of breaking anonymity of the ideal mix-network protocol. He can do it by not delivering some of the messages sent by the honest parties.

4.3 Bulletin Board

All the mix-network protocols use an ideally authenticated bulletin board without erasures as a communication channel between the parties. Surprisingly, such a bulletin board turned out to be a hard primitive to construct in UC model. A result of Lindell, Lysyanskaya, and Rabin [17] establishes that one cannot have a secure authenticated bulletin board unless more that $2/3$ of parties are honest. The construction of a secure bulletin board is out of the scope of this paper and we assume that it is implemented as by the ideal functionality IF_{BB} who simply broadcasts all the data it receives together with the identities of the senders [25]. In practice, a bulletin board could either be implemented by a trusted party or by a secure distributed protocol.

Ideal functionality IF_{BB}:

- Upon receiving (Announce, M), where $M \in \{0,1\}^*$ from some party P, send (Broadcast, P, M) to all the parties and to the adversary.

4.4 Ideal Functionality for a Mix-Network

We consider the ideal functionality IF_{MIX} for a mix-network which captures the possible re-runs of a protocol. The involves parties are m mix-servers, n decryption servers, k users, and an adversary A We will assume that these roles are already assigned to the parties in UC framework. These parties receive their inputs from the environment and send their outputs to the environment. Furthermore, they interact with the ideal functionality IF_{MIX}. That is, the ideal functionality takes as input a collection of messages from the users, shuffles them, and sends the result to the adversary A. The adversary has the choice to either accept it or to declare one of the corrupted servers as malfunctioning. The later corresponds to an event when some of the decryption servers fails, in this case ideal functionality announces the cheated parties and re-shuffles the messages. When the adversary accepts the shuffle, IF_{MIX} returns shuffled messages to all the parties and to the environment.

Ideal functionality IF_{MIX}:

1. When first activated, wait until m values of the form ($\texttt{Mix-server}, id$) are received from $M_1, \ldots, M_m$ and n values ($\texttt{Decryption-Server}, id, D_i$) from $D_1, \ldots, D_n$. Whenever a message ($\texttt{Decryption-Server}, id, D_i$) is received, forward it to all parties. Make a list D of all the decryption servers.
2. Select a new session ID sid. Send ($\texttt{Open}, id, sid$) to all parties.
3. Construct empty lists K and U. Wait until k values are received from users $U_1, \ldots, U_k$, each of the form ($\texttt{Send}, id, sid, m_i$). On the receipt of each value, add a message m_i to the list K, a user ID U_i to the list U, and send ($\texttt{Send}, id, sid, U_i$) to all parties.
4. Choose a random permutation π. Apply π to a list K to get a permuted list $\tilde{K}$. Give $\tilde{K}$ to the adversary. Adversary responds either with a message ($\texttt{ok}$) or with ($\texttt{re-shuffle}, D_i, U^*$), where D_i is some corrupted server in D and U^* — some subset of corrupted users in U.
5. If adversary answered $\texttt{re-shuffle}$, erase D_i from D, erase all the users of U^* from U and erase messages sent by these users from K. Repeat step (4).
6. When the adversary answers $\texttt{ok}$, send ($\texttt{Output}, id, sid, \tilde{K}, U$) to all the parties.
7. Repeat the process starting from the step (2).

Definition 2. *A mix-network protocol* $\mathbb{M}$ *is called UC-secure against a class of adversaries* $\mathfrak{A}$*, if for any Real World adversary* $A \in \mathfrak{A}$ *there exists an Ideal World adversary* B *such that no environment could distinguish if it is interacting with Real World implementation of* $\mathbb{M}$ *and* A *or if it is interacting with* IF_{MIX} *and* B*, any better that with probability* $negligible(\lambda)$*.*

The following theorem establishes UC-security of our mix-network construction $\mathbb{MIX}$. We use the hybrid model, where the bulletin board in the real protocols is implemented by the ideal functionality IF_{BB}. The proof of Theorem 2 can be found in Appendix A.

Theorem 2. *Under DDH assumption in a group* $\mathfrak{G}$*, our mix-network* $\mathbb{MIX}$ *securely realizes* IF_{MIX} *against a class of adversaries that could actively corrupt any number of users, all except one mix-server and all except one decryption server.*

5   Security of $\mathbb{MIX}$ in the Simulation Based Model

In this section we will survey security definitions for mix-networks in a simulation based model. We will state the existing definitions of anonymity and also present a novel definition of anonymity against chosen ciphertext attacks. We prove that our mix-network satisfies all the known simulation based security definitions. Most of the security results in this section will be corollaries of the Universally Composable security of our mix-net proved in Theorem 2.

There are two major security properties of mix-networks: *robustness* and *anonymity*. Loosely speaking, anonymity means that an adversary cannot guess which user sent which message, while robustness means that an adversary, who can abuse the parties in any way he wants, cannot crash the mix-network. I.e., the mix-network outputs a permutation of the input messages even when under an adaptive attack. We stress that in the case of an active adversary, the anonymity notion makes sense only for robust mix-networks. Furthermore, if an adversary corrupts the parties only passively, robustness come for free and one has to show only the anonymity property. Now we proceed to the formal security definitions.

Correctness. To define robustness, we need to have a notion of a correct execution of a mix-session. Let a mix-network M execute some mix-session sid with input $K = \{m_1, \ldots, m_{k_h}\}$ and let it produce output $K' = \{m'_1, \ldots, m'_k\}$. We say that a given mix-session was *executed correctly* or that it *produced correct output* if $K \subseteq K'$ taking into account multiplicities of the elements.

Robustness. Robustness of a mix-network protocol is only taken into account for active adversaries. Robustness means that even in the presence of an active adversary, the mix-net returns the correct output with overwhelming probability. Consider any mix-network M and any active adversary A who corrupts some of the servers and all the users except $U_1, \ldots, U_{k_h}$. We associate with them an experiment ROB.

Experiment ROB(M, A):

- The mix-network M runs a key-generation algorithm.
- The following is repeated a polynomial number of times:
  - The adversary A selects a list of plaintext messages $K = \{m_1, \ldots, m_{k_h}\}$.
  - M executes the next mix-session, where all the honest users are given corresponding messages from K. A can submit anything on behalf of actively corrupted users, while for passively corrupted users he only selects the plaintext messages.
- The adversary A tries to sabotage execution of the mix-network M. He wins the game if M failed to execute correctly any of the mix-sessions. The advantage of the adversary A in the ROB experiment is $Adv_M^{ROB}(A) = Pr[A \text{ wins ROB game}]$.

A mix-net M achieves *robustness* against a class of adversaries $\mathfrak{A}$ if all the adversaries from this class succeed in the game ROB with probability at most $negligible(\lambda)$.

Lemma 3. *Our mix-network construction* MIX *achieves robustness against a class of adversaries who can actively corrupt an arbitrary number of the users and all except one mix-server.*

Proof. The proof of the lemma is straight-forward from Theorem 2. Assume there exists an efficient adversary A who breaks robustness of $\mathbb{MIX}$. Note that in the UC model there exists an environment that plays the ROB experiment an adversary. The environment plays the challenger role in the experiment and the adversary has to break correctness of execution of some mix-session. The real world adversary A has non-negligible probability of breaking the robustness of $\mathbb{MIX}$ although it is information-theoretically impossible for a ideal adversary. This allows the environment to distinguish between the real world and ideal world executions. In turn, this contradicts the UC-security of $\mathbb{MIX}$.

Anonymity: ANON. The anonymity property of a mix-network says that an adversary who observes all the public information of the protocol including a shuffled list of output messages, cannot tell which user sent which message. Most of the literature on mix-networks uses this notion as the major anonymity property of a mix-network. Some of the papers refer to it as anonymity and some as unlinkability. Consider an adversary A who corrupts all except k_h users and some of the servers. The adversary might corrupt some of the parties actively and some of them passively. Without loss of generality, assume that the non-corrupted users are $U_1, \ldots, U_{k_h}$. Anonymity is defined by the following experiment ANON played by an adversary A against a mix-network M:

Experiment ANON($\mathbb{M}$, A):

- The mix-network $\mathbb{M}$ generates secret/public keys using key-generation procedure $\mathbb{M}.Gen(\cdot)$ and public keys are posted to the bulletin board.
- The adversary A computes and outputs two lists of messages for non-corrupted parties: $M_0 = \{m_1^0, \ldots, m_{k_h}^0\}$ and $M_1 = \{m_1^1, \ldots, m_{k_h}^1\}$, which are permutations of each other.
- Choose a bit $b \in \{0,1\}$ at random. Secretly give messages from the list M_b to the corresponding honest users. The users encrypt their messages with $\mathbb{M}.Enc(\cdot)$ and post ciphertexts c_i's to the bulletin board. The adversary submits arbitrary ciphertexts on behalf of the corrupted users.
- The mix-network processes all the ciphertexts written to the bulletin board with a procedure $\mathbb{M}.Exec(\cdot)$ and outputs a shuffled list of messages $M' = \{m_1', \ldots, m_k'\}$.
- The adversary tries to distinguish which of the lists was selected and outputs a bit $b' \in \{0,1\}$. Advantage of the adversary in this game is

$$Adv_{\mathbb{M}}^{ANON}(A) = |2 \cdot Pr\,[b' = b] - 1| \ .$$

A mix-net achieves *anonymity* against a class of adversaries $\mathfrak{A}$ if all the adversaries from this class succeed in this game with probability no better than *negligible*(λ).

Chosen Ciphertext Attack Anonymity: ANON-CCA. Recently Abe and Imai in [3] presented a stronger anonymity requirement for a mix-network, called chosen ciphertext (CCA) anonymity. They regard a mix-network as a batch decryption algorithm of a public key encryption scheme with encryption algorithm

M.$Enc(\cdot)$ and distributed batch decryption M.$Exec(\cdot)$. The adversary in their model is given an additional power with respect to the standard anonymity definition — it can launch a kind of chosen ciphertext attack on a mix-net. The adversary is allowed to run a mix-network for an arbitrary number of times on arbitrary input messages both before and after an execution of a challenge mix-session. A mix-network is said to achieve CCA-anonymity if adversary who launches a chosen ciphertext attack on a mix-net still cannot guess senders of non-corrupted messages in the challenge execution any better than guessing them at random. We present our definition of CCA-anonymity which will be slightly different from the one in [3].

Consider an adversary A who corrupts all except k_h users and some of the servers. Without loss of generality, assume that the non-corrupted users are $U_1, \ldots, U_{k_h}$. CCA-anonymity is defined by the experiment ANON-CCA played by an adversary A against a mix-net M.

Experiment ANON-CCA(M, A):

- The mix-network generates secret/public keys using key-generation procedure M.$Gen(\cdot)$ and public keys are posted to the bulletin board.
- The adversary is allowed to invoke the mix-network M with arbitrary input messages for an arbitrary (polynomially bounded) number of times (i.e., A could use a mix-network as a decryption oracle).
- A computes the two lists of challenge messages $M_0 = \{m_1^0, \ldots, m_{k_h}^0\}$ and $M_1 = \{m_1^1, \ldots, m_{k_h}^1\}$, where M_1 is a permutation of M_0.
- Choose a bit $b \in \{0, 1\}$ at random. Secretly from A, give messages from the list M_b to the corresponding honest users. Users encrypt their messages with M.$Enc(\cdot)$ and post the ciphertexts c_i's to the bulletin board.
- The mix-network processes all the ciphertexts written to the bulletin board with procedure M.$Exec(\cdot)$ and outputs a shuffled list of messages $M' = \{m_1', \ldots, m_n'\}$.
- The adversary again is allowed to invoke the mix-network. Note that he is allowed to use as inputs arbitrary messages for the honest parties and arbitrary ciphertexts for the corrupted parties.
- Finally, the adversary tries to distinguish between the cases $b = 1$ and $b = 0$ and he outputs a bit $b' \in \{0, 1\}$. The adversary wins the game if $b = b'$. The advantage of the adversary in this game is

$$Adv_{\mathbb{M}}^{ANON-CCA}(A) = \mid 2 \cdot Pr\left[A \text{ wins}\right] - 1 \mid .$$

A mix-net achieves CCA-anonymity against a class of (polynomial time) adversaries $\mathfrak{A}$, if no adversary from this class has an ANON-CCA advantage better than $negligible(\lambda)$.

Lemma 4. *Our mix-network construction* $\mathbb{MIX}$ *achieves CCA-anonymity against a class of adversaries who can actively corrupt arbitrary number of the users and all except one mix-server.*

Proof. The lemma follows from Theorem 2. Assume there exists an efficient adversary A who breaks CCA-anonymity of MIX with non-negligible advantage δ. In the Universally Composable model, there exists an environment Z which plays the ANON-CCA experiment with the adversary. The real world adversary A wins the experiment with probability $1/2 + \delta/2$ although all ideal world adversaries information-theoretically cannot guess the correct bit with probability better than $1/2$. Therefore the environment Z is able to distinguish between real world and ideal world executions with non-negligible probability.

Acknowledgements

Part of Jan Camenisch's work reported in this paper is supported by the European Commission through the IST Programme under Contract IST-2002-507932 ECRYPT and by the IST Project PRIME. The PRIME projects receives research funding from the European Community's Sixth Framework Programme and the Swiss Federal Office for Education and Science. The information in this document reflects only the authors' views, is provided as is and no guarantee or warranty is given that the information is fit for any particular purpose. The user thereof uses the information at its sole risk and liability.

References

1. M. Abe. Mix-Networks on Permutation Networks. *ASIACRYPT '99*, LNCS Vol. 1716, K. Lam, E. Okamoto and C. Xing ed., Springer-Verlag, 1999
2. M. Abe and F. Hoshino. Remarks on Mix-Network Based on Permutation Networks. *Public-Key Cryptography '01*, LNCS Vol. 1992, K. Kim ed., Springer-Verlag, 2001
3. M. Abe and H. Imai. Flaws in Some Robust Optimistic Mix-Nets. *Proceedings of the 2003 ACISP*, LNCS Vol. , ed., Springer-Verlag, 2003
4. Michael Backes, Birgit Pfitzmann, and Michael Waidner. A general composition theorem for secure reactive systems. In Moni Naor, editor, *TCC 2004*, volume 2951 of *LNCS*, pages 336–354. Springer, 2004.
5. M. Blum, P. Feldman and S. Micali. Non-Interactive Zero-Knowledge and Its Applications. *Proc. of the 20th ACM STOC*, ACM, 1988
6. J. Camenisch, V. Shoup. Practical Verifiable Encryption and Decryption of Discrete Logarithms. *CRYPTO '03*, LNCS Vol. , D. Boneh ed., Springer-Verlag, 2003
7. R. Canetti. Universally Composable Security: A New Paradigm for Cryptographic Protocols. *Proc. of the 42nd IEEE FOCS*, IEEE, 2001
8. R. Canetti, E. Kushilevitz and Y. Lindell. On the Limitations of Universally Composable Two-Party Computation Without Set-Up Assumptions. *EUROCRYPT '03*, LNCS Vol. 2656, E. Biham ed., Springer-Verlag, 2003
9. R. Canetti, Y. Lindell, R. Ostrovsky and A. Sahai. Universally composable two-party and multi-party secure computation. *Proc. of the 34th ACM STOC*, ACM, 2002
10. D. Chaum. Untraceable electronic mail, return addresses, and digital pseudonyms. *Communications of the ACM*, v.24 n.2, p.84-90, Feb. 1981

11. D. Chaum and T. Pedersen. Wallet databases with observers. *CRYPTO '92*, LNCS Vol. 740, E. Brickell ed., Springer-Verlag, 1992
12. P. Feldman. A practical scheme for non-interactive verifiable secret sharing. *Proc. of the 28th* IEEE FOCS, IEEE, 1987
13. J. Groth. A Verifiable Secret Shuffle of Homomorphic Encryptions. *Public-Key Cryptography '03*, LNCS Vol. 2567, Y. Desmdedt ed., Springer-Verlag, 2003
14. M. Jakobsson. A Practical Mix. *EUROCRYPT '98*, LNCS Vol. 1403, K. Nyberg ed., Springer-Verlag, 1998
15. M. Jakobsson and A. Juels. An optimally robust hybrid mix network. *PODC '01*
16. P. Golle, S. Zhong, D. Boneh, M. Jakobsson, and A. Juels. Optimistic Mixing for Exit-Polls. *ASIACRYPT '02*, LNCS Vol. 2501, Y. Zheng ed., Springer-Verlag, 2002
17. Y. Lindell, A. Lysyanskaya and T. Rabin. On the Composition of Authenticated Byzantine Agreement. *Proc. of the 34th* ACM STOC, ACM, 2002
18. M. Naor and M. Yung. Public-key Cryptosystems Provably Secure against Chosen Ciphertext Attacks. *Proc. of the 22nd* ACM STOC, ACM, 1990
19. C. Park, K. Itoh, K. Kurosawa. Efficient anonymous channel and all/nothing election scheme. *EUROCRYPT '93*, LNCS Vol. 765, T. Helleseth ed., Springer-Verlag, 1993
20. R. Pass. On Deniabililty in the Common Reference String and Random Oracle Model. *CRYPTO '03*, LNCS Vol. , D. Boneh ed., Springer-Verlag, 2003
21. B. Pfitzmann. Breaking Efficient Anonymous Channel. *EUROCRYPT '94*, LNCS Vol. 950, A. De Santis ed., Springer-Verlag, 1994
22. B. Pfitzmann and M. Waidner. A model for asynchronous reactive systems and its application to secure message transmission. In *Proceedings of the IEEE Symposium on Research in Security and Privacy*, pages 184–200. IEEE Computer Society Press, 2001.
23. A. Shamir. How to Share a Secret. *Communications of ACM* 22(11): 612-613, 1979.
24. D. Wikström. Five Practical Attacks for Optimistic Mixing for Exit-Polls. *Selected Areas of Cryptography 2003*
25. D. Wikström. A Universally Composable Mix-Net. Appears in Naor, editor, *TCC 2004*, LNCS 2951, 2004

A   Proof of UC Security of $\mathbb{MIX}$

Consider an arbitrary Real World Adversary A. We are going to construct an Ideal World Adversary B such that no environment Z could not distinguish if it is interacting with the real world parties or with ideal world parties.

In the Ideal World, B corrupts the same set of parties as A does in the Real World. Without loss of generality, assume that users $U_1, \ldots, U_{k_h}$, decryption server D_1 and a mix-server M_{i*} are honest and the rest of the parties (except V and BB) in the simulated mix-network are controlled by A.

Furthermore, B is given blackbox access to A and simulates all honest real world parties towards A. Also, B forwards all the communication from A to the Environment Z and visa versa. Finally, both A and B are connected to the BB.

Construction of the Adversary B

Consider B's behavior in the set-up phase. Let $\mathcal{D}$ be an empty list.

There is two kinds of messages B can receive in this phase. The first one is a message (Decryption-Server, id, D_i) from IF_{MIX}: Upon the reception of such a message, B generates a key y_i, sends y_i to A via the BB. Also, B sets $\mathcal{D} = \mathcal{D} \cup \{D_i\}$. The second kind of messages are those received from A, i.e., from a corrupted decryption server via the BB: When some corrupted party D_j sends a public key and executes a proof $PfLog(y_j, D_j, V)$ of knowledge of a secret key x_j, B extracts a secret key x_j using the straight-line extractability of $PfLog$. If this worked, B sends the message (Decryption-server, id, D_j) to IF_{MIX} and sets $\mathcal{D} = \mathcal{D} \cup \{D_j\}$.

When the key-generation is complete, B sends (Mix-server, id) to IF_{MIX} on behalf of all the corrupted mix-servers.

Now, when IF_{MIX} outputs (Open, id, sid), B computes $y = \prod_{j: D_j \in \mathcal{D}} y_j$ and publishes y together with the list $\mathcal{D}$ on behalf of V on bulletin board BB. Furthermore, B sends a message for the initiation of the first mix round and sid to BB. Note that B knows the secret keys of all the authorized decryption servers.

In the encryption phase B can receive again two kinds of messages: one kind is messages from IF_{MIX} saying that some honest user submitted a ciphertext and the other one is messages over the BB from A, i.e., a corrupted user who submitted a ciphertext. Let L_0 be an empty list. We next treat these two cases. Upon reception of (Send, id, sid, U_j) from IF_{MIX}, the ideal world adversary B sends an encryption c'_j of the message $m'_j = 1$ and the proof $PfPtxt$ on behalf of honest user U_j to the BB and sets $L_0 = L_0 \cup \{c'_j\}$.

Whenever B receives from A a ciphertext c_i on behalf of a corrupted user U_i who also proves knowledge of a plaintext, B extracts the plaintext m_i using the straight-line extractability of $PfPtxt$. B sends (Send, id, sid, m_i) on behalf of U_i to IF_{MIX} and sets $L_0 = L_0 \cup \{c_i\}$.

At some point, IF_{MIX} will shuffle the plaintexts and send the list $\tilde{K}$ to B. Thus, B, on behalf of V, sends the list L_0 to the BB.

We now enter the mixing stage where the mix-servers $M_1, \ldots, M_m$ are invoked one-by-one. Here, B participates as M_{i*} in the real world shuffling protocol. Eventually the last mix-server outputs a shuffled list of ciphertexts L_m.

Next, we move to the decryption stage.

Knowing the targeted output list $\tilde{K}$ and secret keys of the decryption servers, B computes fake decryption shares for the entries in the list L_m in such that the list decrypts to list $\tilde{K}$. To this end, B computes for each encryption $(a_i, b_i) \in L_m$, the fake share for D_1 as

$$s_1 = b_i \cdot m_i^{-1} \cdot a^{-x_2} \cdot \ldots \cdot a^{-x_n} \ ,$$

where m_i is the i-th entry in $\tilde{K}$, and a *simulated* share verification proof SV $((a_i, b_i), s_1, y_1, D_1, V)$. B sends these values on D_1's behalf to BB. On behalf of decryption servers, B runs the protocol as specified.

If some corrupted decryption server D_i fails to provide a correct decryption share, our mix-net protocol prescribes that a re-run is required. To this end, B re-runs the protocol as described above. B submits encryptions of 1 on behalf of the honest users. After the encryption phase of the rerun, B puts all corrupted users who did not successfully resubmit their input to a list U^* (i.e., the users who fail to prove *PfEqual*). Then, B sends (**re-run**, D_i, U^*) to IF_{MIX}, getting a new list $\tilde{K}$ with which B repeats the shuffling and decryption procedures as described above.

If at some point the decryption phase is finished successfully, B sends (**ok**) to IF_{MIX} and sends the final list $\tilde{K}$ to the BB.

After this, B is ready to engage in the next mixing session: whenever IF_{MIX} sends (**Open**, id, sid) to B, it sends a message initiating the next mixing round and sid to BB. It will then continue with the encryption phase as described above.

This concludes the description of B.

Indistinguishability to Z. It remains to argue that the environment cannot distinguish whether it interacts with the ideal or the real world parties.

It is not hard to see that this is the case if B did successfully simulate the real world parties towards A. That is, we have to show that A cannot tell that B deviated from the protocol, i.e., that it did

- encrypt 1's instead of real messages in the encryption phase and
- provide false decryption shares and fake the proof of correctness of these shares.

The first deviation is not noticed because of the semantic security of ElGamal encryption. The second deviation is not noticed because, first, in the real world M_{i*} is honest and thus enforces a random permutation, second, because of the semantic security of ElGamal, and, third, because of the simulatability of the proof of the correctness of the decryption shares. Proving all of this is not hard and is omitted here.

Covert Channels in IPv6

Norka B. Lucena, Grzegorz Lewandowski, and Steve J. Chapin

Syracuse University, Syracuse NY 13244, USA
{norka, chapin}@ecs.syr.edu,   grlewand@syr.edu

Abstract. A covert channel is a communication path that allows transferring information in a way that violates a system security policy. Because of their concealed nature, detecting and preventing covert channels are obligatory security practices. In this paper, we present an examination of network storage channels in the Internet Protocol version 6 (IPv6). We introduce and analyze 22 different covert channels. In the appendix, we define three types of active wardens, *stateless*, *stateful*, and *network-aware*, who differ in complexity and ability to block the analyzed covert channels.

Keywords: covert channel, IPv6, active warden, stateless, stateful, IPsec.

1 Introduction

When analyzing the security of computer systems, it is important to evaluate both overt and covert communication channels. An *overt* channel is a communication path within a computer system or network designed for the authorized transfer of data. Authorized data transmission involves the existence of security policies as well as mandatory and discretionary access controls that restrict the flow of information. A *covert* channel, in contrast, is a communication path that allows an unauthorized process to transfer information in a way that violates a system security policy [1]. Because of the concealed nature of covert channels, detecting and preventing them are obligatory practices in multilevel security systems (MLS) where most of the processes carry classified information [2].

Covert channels are primarily classified as storage or timing channels. A *storage* channel concerns "the direct or indirect writing of a storage location by one process and the direct or indirect reading of it by another" [3]. A *timing* channel involves signaling mechanisms based on modulation of system resources such as CPU or time in a way that the change in response time observed by a second process conveys information. This paper focuses in the study of covert storage channels in the Internet Protocol version 6 (IPv6) (also called the Next Generation Internet Protocol or IPng). This initial examination is a specification-based analysis, to identify redundancies and ambiguities in the protocol semantics that could potentially be used to carry covert data.

Network-based covert channels can be used both as a means of private communication and as a means to coordinate distributed denial of service or other kinds of attacks [4]. In addition, hackers favor network storage channels over timing channels because of the synchronization issues and significantly lower bandwidth of the latter. Our research aims to generate discussion of such channels, and also to raise issues for consideration by implementors of IPv6 protocol stacks and firewalls that handle IPv6 traffic.

G. Danezis and D. Martin (Eds.): PET 2005, LNCS 3856, pp. 147–166, 2006.

The remainder of this document is organized as follows. Section 2 summarizes the work done in network covert channels detailing the findings corresponding to storage channels. Section 3 presents the adversary model under which the existence of covert channels will be analyzed. Section 4 discusses potential covert channels in IPv6 as well as issues regarding security.Finally, section 5 draws some conclusions and points out directions for future work. Appendix A analyzes the defined covert channels in a network monitored by several types of active wardens.

2 Related Work

Previous research in network covert channels [4] focuses on Internet Protocol version 4 as well as other related protocols such as TCP, ICMP, and HTTP[4,5,6,7,8,9,10,11,12, 13,14,15,16,17,18,19,20] . The study of network storage channels[9,10,11,12,13,14,15, 16] is broader than its counterpart of network timing channels [4, 5, 6, 7, 8], presumably because of the synchronization issues present in timing channels and their low bandwidth in comparison to storage channels. This work aims to analyze storage channels in the new generation of the Internet Protocol, IPv6.

Handel and Sandford [9] pioneers covert channels within network communication protocols. It describes different methods of creating and exploiting hidden channels in the OSI network model, based on the characteristics of each layer. Szczypiorski [10] describes a hidden communication system at the data link layer of the OSI network mode that takes advantage of imperfections in the transmission medium, such as interferences and noise. Rowland [11], Dunigan [12], and Rutkowska [13] present examples of implementation of covert channels that exploit header fields of the TCP/IP protocol suite (for IPv4). These three papers focus their attention in the network and transport layers of the OSI network model.

Abad [14] describes how to embed data in the IP checksum using selected hash collisions. The IPv4 checksum can be exploited because the algorithm used to calculate it is susceptible to collision attacks. In IPv6, checksums are calculated by keyed message authentications codes (MAC) based on symmetric encryption algorithms such as DES or on one-way hash functions such as MD5 or SHA-1. One-way hash algorithms will reduce, but probably not eliminate because of recent MD5 collisions [15, 16], the possibility of existence of similar channels in IPv6.

Giffin et al. [17] analyzes a low-bandwidth covert channel that uses TCP timestamps. The channel is based on a modification of a TCP header field, in particular, the low order bit of the timestamp option. In a slow connection, this channel is harder to detect than the ones described in [12, 11] because under such network conditions the low order bit of the timestamp appears randomly distributed facilitating the transmission of encrypted messages.

Ahsan and Kundur [5, 6] proposes five covert channel approaches: four of them based on manipulations of the TCP, IGMP, and ICMP protocol headers and one of them based on packet sorting within the IPsec protocol. The former are storage channels while the latter is a timing channel. The network timing channel works by sorting packets by the sequence number field present in both the authentication header (AH) and the encapsulated security payload header (ESP) defined in IPsec. The hidden information is the difference between the original sequence of packets and the sorted sequence.

Project Loki[1] [18, 19] explores the concept of ICMP tunneling, exploiting covert channels through the data portions of the ICMP_ECHO and ICMP_ECHOREPLY packets. The Loki client allows a remote attacker to wrap and transmit commands in ICMP payloads. Lokid, the Loki server, unwraps and executes the commands, sending the results back wrapped in ICMP packets. Back Orifice 2000 with the BOSOCK32 plug-in also implements covert channels via ICMP. Firewalls can disallow entirely the passing of ICMP traffic, preventing the existence of tunneling. Project Loki also runs over UDP on port 53, simulating DNS traffic. Sneakin [20] provides an incoming shell through outgoing Telnet-like traffic.

Currently, the most effective defensive mechanisms against network storage channels for IPv4 are protocol scrubbers [21], traffic normalizers [22], and active wardens [23]. Both protocol scrubbers and traffic normalizers focus on eliminating ambiguities found in the traffic stream presumably created by a skilled attacker with the purpose of evading network intrusion detection systems. Fisk et al. [23] defines two classes of information in network protocols: *structured* and *unstructured* carriers. Structured carriers present well-defined, objective semantics, and can be checked for fidelity en route (e.g., TCP packets can be checked to ensure they are semantically correct according to the protocol). Unstructured carriers, such as images, audio, or natural language, lack objectively defined semantics and are mostly interpreted by humans rather than computers. Analyzing the Linux and OpenBSD implementation of the TCP/IP protocol stack, Murdoch and Lewis [24] shows that fields commonly used for steganography, such as the IP identification field and the TCP initial sequence number, exhibit enough structure and nonuniformity to facilitate detection.

3   Adversary Model

In the context of the "classical" prisoners' problem [25], *Alice* and *Bob* are two agents who wish to communicate covertly (see Figure 1). As described in [26], Alice and Bob exploit an already existing communication path, corresponding to two arbitrary communicating processes: the *sender* and the *receiver*. *Wendy* is a warden, located somewhere along the communication path, monitoring all possible messages exchanged by Alice and Bob.

The dotted boxes in Figure 1 indicate that Alice and Bob could either act as sender and receiver, or could modify the messages in transit [26]. From Wendy's point-of-view, these situations are indistinguishable.

In this framework, Wendy always acts as an *active* warden [23, 27, 28]. Active wardens can modify the content of the network traffic with the purpose of eliminating any form of hidden communication. When modifying network packets, active wardens should maintain the syntactic and semantic integrity of the packet to avoid breaking the overt communication. They reinforce protocol specifications through mechanisms such as zeroing reserved fields, randomizing ID numbers, and requiring or prohibiting the use of option fields.

---

[1] Loki is pronounced "low-key", and is named for the Norse god of trickery.

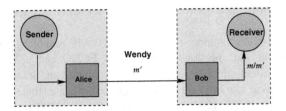

Fig. 1. Framework for Covert Communication

4   Potential IPv6 Covert Channels

The IPv6 header structure has a fixed length of 40 bytes. Five fields from IPv4 were removed (header length, identification, flags, fragment offset, and header checksum). Options are defined as extension headers. A packet can have more than one extension header. When present, the headers are layered in order. The IPv6 protocol specification, RFC 2460 [29], defines six extension headers [30]:

- Hop-by-Hop Options header
- Routing header
- Fragment header
- Destination Options header
- Authentication header (AH)
- Encapsulating Security Payload (ESP) header

The last two extension headers and their functionality are described in separate RFCs as part of the IP security framework (IPsec): RFC 2401 [31], RFC 2402 [32], and RFC 2406 [33]. The security architecture for the Internet protocol, RFC 2401, establishes that the AH and ESP header can be used in two modes: transport mode and tunnel mode. In *transport* mode, encryption or authentication are applied to the payload contained in all IP packets related to particular end-to-end connection. In *tunnel* mode, authentication and encryption mechanisms are defined between two security gateways[2], surrounding both the IP header and the payload with a "wrapper" IP packet.

Our analysis of potential covert channels in IPv6 includes a specification-based covert channel discovery and an informal bandwidth estimation. The presence of AH and ESP headers in any of the modes affects some of the presented covert channels. The examination also points out such effects. Covert channels are described by header and identified with a letter from the Greek alphabet.

4.1   IPv6 Header

Figure 2 shows the fields in the IPv6 header as well as the plausible covert channels observed.

---

[2] An intermediate system that implements the IPsec framework, e.g. a firewall implementing IPsec.

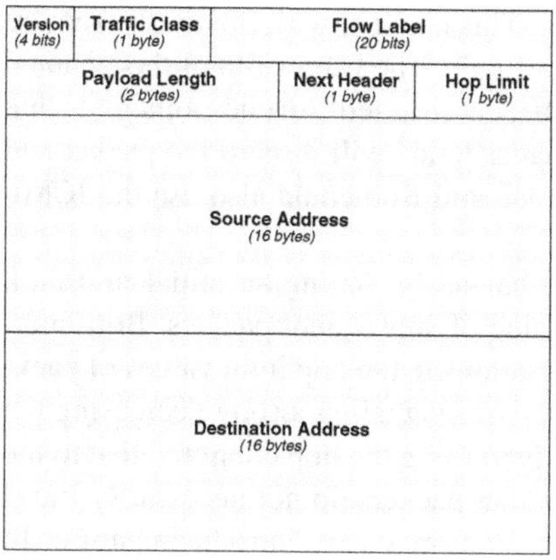

Version (4 bits)	Traffic Class (1 byte)	Flow Label (20 bits)	
Payload Length (2 bytes)		Next Header (1 byte)	Hop Limit (1 byte)
Source Address (16 bytes)			
Destination Address (16 bytes)			

ID	Field	Covert Channel	Bandwidth
α	Traffic Class	Set a false traffic class	8 bits/packet
β	Flow Label	Set a false flow label	20 bits/packet
γ	Payload Length	Increase value to insert extra data[3]	Varies
δ	Next Header	Set a valid value to add an extra extension header[3]	Varies
ϵ	Hop Limit	Increase/decrease value	$\approx$ 1 bit/packet
ζ	Source Address	Set a false source address	16 bytes/packet

(a)   (b)

Fig. 2. Covert Channels in the IPv6 Header. (a) IPv6 Header Format, (b) Identified covert storage channels.

α Alice can set a false *traffic class* value. The bandwidth of this channel varies up to 8 bits per packet, depending on whether or not the field is modified by intermediate nodes. The IPv6 specification allows the intermediate nodes to change the value of the traffic class field as they forward the packet. For example, Differentiated Services traffic conditioner [34] might modify the traffic that passes through it. Therefore, when Alice and Bob communicate using this covert channel, they have to be prepared to handle disturbances. Additionally, intermediate nodes might use this field to make decisions about packet processing, thus covert channel that manipulates the value of this field might have an unpredictable effect on the network.

β Fabricating a *flow label*, Alice can send 20 bits of data per packet. Authentic flow labels are pseudo-randomly and uniformly selected numbers, ranging from 1 to FFFFF hex. Alice needs to preserve the same conditions when creating a fake flow label.

γ Alice can increase the value of the *payload length* and append extra data at the end of the packet. The bandwidth of this channel varies depending on the size of the original packet, but the modified packet cannot be larger than 65536 bytes. If encryption is used without authentication, stego techniques like the ones described in [26] are appropriate. If authentication is used, Alice and Bob need to take extra steps to maintain the covertness of the channel because the payload length is included in the calculation of the integrity check value (ICV). The ICV is a field of the Authentication Extension Header calculated over several fields from the IP header and from the extension headers, when present, used to verify whether a packet was corrupted or modified in transit. See subsection 4.6 for details.

δ Because extension headers are not examined nor processed by intermediate nodes of an end-to-end communication path, Alice can change the *next header* content

---

[3] This covert channel, when authentication is used, requires recalculating or circumventing the integrity check value (ICV). See subsection 4.6 for details.

to insert an entire extension header covertly. This channel will, obviously, require that Alice increases the payload length accordingly. The bandwidth of this channel depends on the total length of the extension header inserted. An end-point node that does not recognize the value in the *next header* field[4] will discard the packet and send an ICMP notification to the source. Alice and Bob could also use the ICMP reply as a means of covert communication.

ϵ Alice can initiate a covert communication channel by setting an initial *hop limit* value, h, and manipulating the *hop limit* value of subsequent packets. Bob interprets the covert message by checking the variations in the hop limit values of packets traversing his location. One scheme has Alice signaling a 0 by decreasing the hop count from the prior packet, and a 1 by increasing the hop count relative to the prior packet. A drawback of this channel is that packets do not necessarily travel the same route, so the number of intermediate hops may vary, introducing noise. To overcome this, Alice can choose a δ that is greater than the expected noise, and use hop counts less than $h - \delta$ signal a 0, and hop counts greater than $h + \delta$ to signal a 1. Bob then compares the received hop count to h to deduce the bit. The bandwidth of this channel is limited. Alice needs to modify n packets to send $n - 1$ bits of information.

ζ Alice can forge the source address field to send 16 bytes of covert data. Detection of this channel is however very likely because of the existing security mechanisms that detect source address spoofing.

4.2   Hop-By-Hop Options Header

The hop-by-hop options header carries optional information that needs to be checked by every node the packet traverses. Because of its different option types, both defined and undefined, and its variable length, this extension header offers possibilities for high-bandwidth covert channels. As described in the protocol specification [29], the *option type* field is an octet structure that has three subfields: the first two bits specify what action should be taken when an unrecognized option is received; the next bit determines whether or not the option data can change in route; the last five bits represent the option number[5]. The analysis introduced below discusses relevant types of option such as the padding, jumbogram, and routing alert options (see Figure 3). When authentication is used, most of the covert channels in the hop-by-hop header may require recalculating or circumventing the ICV (see discussion in subsection 4.6).

α Jumbograms are IPv6 packets with payload length longer than 65535 bytes. Alice can use jumbograms as a means of covert communication in two ways. The first one relies on modifying an existing jumbogram length with the purpose of appending covert data (this mechanism relates to the δ channel is subsection 4.1). The second method involves converting a regular datagram into a jumbogram and filling in the extra bytes with hidden content. It will be necessary, consequently, to change the payload length in the IPv6 header. Jumbograms are discarded by intermediate

---

[4] The Protocol Numbers document [35] lists of all possible *next header* field values.

[5] These last five digits are also called "option type" or "rest". However, the option type is fully specified only when using the entire octet.

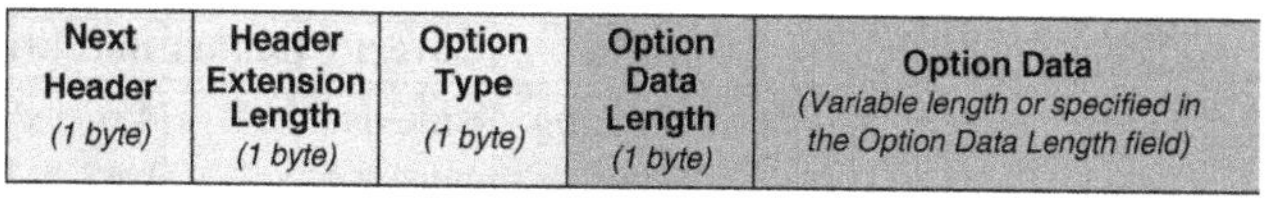

Next Header (1 byte)	Header Extension Length (1 byte)	Option Type (1 byte)	Option Data Length (1 byte)	Option Data (Variable length or specified in the Option Data Length field)

(a)

ID	Field	Covert Channel	Bandwidth
α	Option Type: Jumbogram	Insert or create a jumbogram	Varies
β	Option Type: Router Alert	Set a false router alert	2 bytes/packet
γ	Option Type: PadN	Set a false padding value	Up to 256 bytes/packet
δ	Option Type: Unknown	Fabricate one or more options	Up to 2038 bytes/packet

(b)

Fig. 3. Covert Channels in the Hop-by-Hop Options Extension Header. (a) Format of the Hop-by-Hop Options Header, (b) Identified covert storage channels.

nodes that do not support them. Therefore, Alice and Bob need to make sure that all nodes in the communication path understand jumbograms.

β Router alert options contain a 2-byte *reserved* field where Alice can embed data to establish a covert communication. Alice could also add an entire router alert option type, if it does not exist. That alternative will require readjustment of the packet length in the IPv6 header.

γ Individual options in the option data field need to preserve header alignment. Two types of padding are defined for that: Pad1 and PadN. Pad1 inserts a single octet, PadN appends two or more bytes as an individual option type. Alice can exploit any of the padding types, but γ focuses only in the PadN *option type*. A simple form of using this option is to embed covert data in an already-existing padding. The bandwidth of that channel will depend then in the length of the padding option. A more crafted way would be inserting a padding option when the header does not contain one. Alice could send this way up top 256 bytes/packet because the PadN option has a maximum length of 256 bytes. The last alternative, illustrated in Figure 4, requires modification of the IPv6 payload length.

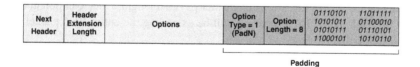

Next Header	Header Extension Length	Options	Option Type = 1 (PadN)	Option Length = 8	01110101 11011111 10101011 01100010 01010111 01110101 11000101 10110110

Padding

Fig. 4. δ Covert Channel in the Hop-by-Hop Options Extension Header

δ Alice can fabricate an option type, different from the ones listed in [36], as long as she maintain the semantics of the field described at the beginning of the subsection. She needs to make the first two bits of the *option type* equal to 00. That will dictate intermediate nodes to "skip and continue processing" when they do not recognize the option type [29]. The maximum length of option data is 256 bytes. Therefore,

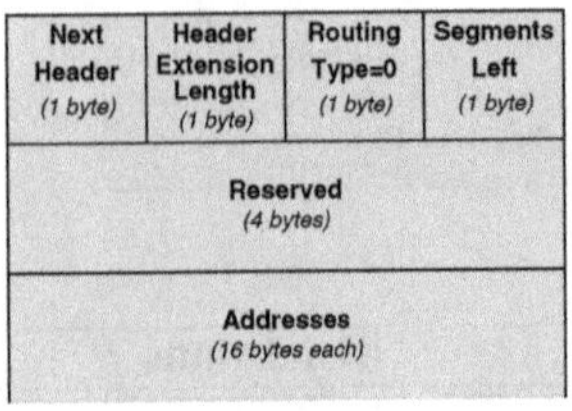

Next Header (1 byte)	Header Extension Length (1 byte)	Routing Type=0 (1 byte)	Segments Left (1 byte)
Reserved (4 bytes)			
Addresses (16 bytes each)			

(a)

ID	Field	Covert Channel	Bandwidth
α	*Routing Type: 0 - Reserved*	Hide data in unused bits	4 bytes/ packet
β	*Routing Type: 0*	Set one or more false addresses[7]	Up to 2048 bytes/packet

(b)

Fig. 5. Covert Channels in the Routing Extension Header. (a) Format of the Routing Header, (b) Identified covert storage channels.

up to 256 bytes of covert data can be inserted that way. Moreover, because the hop-by-hop header can include many options, by repeating the insertion with different option type values, up to 2,038 bytes can be added in total[6]. Inserting new options increases the total length of the IPv6 packet.

4.3   Routing Header

The routing extension header contains a list of intermediate nodes a packet in transit should visit on the way to its destination. The IPv6 Parameters document [36] enumerates three different types of routing, but only one of them, *Type 0*, is fully described in the specification [29]. Figure 5 shows the format of the routing header when routing type is 0 and its possible channels.

α There exists a *reserved* field in routing header structure when the *routing type* is 0. Alice can hide 4 bytes of covert data per packet using this channel.

β When the *routing type* is 0, Alice can fabricate "addresses" out of arbitrary data meaningful to Bob. She appends the covert data and sets the *segments left* field to 0 to prevent any node to attempt processing the fake addresses. Figures 6 and 7 display two different types of embedding:

  - one where Alice chooses to create a new routing extension header of routing type 0 to send Bob 48 bytes of covert information
  - another one where she takes advantage of an already existing routing extension header of routing type 0 to embed a covert message of 32 bytes.

Based on the maximum extension header payload length, Alice can potentially insert up 2048 bytes. Therefore, she will be extending the entire IPv6 packet by the same amount of bytes.

4.4   Fragment Header

As in IPv4, fragmentation of packets occurs when the MTU of a link is not large enough to handle a packet of a particular size. Unlike IPv4, IPv6 packets are not fragmented by

---

[6] The length of the header payload is 2054 bytes, which can be filled by 7 options carrying 256 bytes each and 1 option of 246 bytes considering that the headers of individual options will require 16 bytes.

[7] This covert channel, when authentication is used, requires recalculating or circumventing the ICV. See subsection 4.6 for details.

Fig. 6. α. **Covert Channel in the Routing Extension Header.** When Alice creates fake addresses in a packet that did not originally a routing extension header.

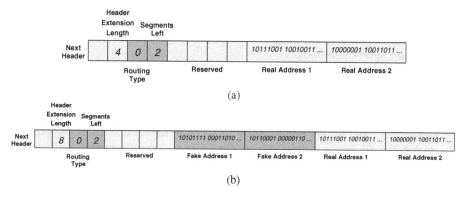

Fig. 7. α. **Covert Channel in the Routing Extension Header.** When Alice inserts fake addresses in a packet already containing a routing extension header. (a) Original routing extension header, (b) Routing header after Alice inserts the covert data.

routers along the path. Sending hosts use path MTU discovery to determine the allowed maximum packet size on the way to a specific destination. Sending hosts fragment packets accordingly, when necessary. Destination hosts reassemble them.

An important consideration regarding fragmented packets is that they are themselves IPv6 packets, thus all previously described covert channels exist in fragments as well. In addition, because the number of packet fragments is presumably greater than the original number of packets to be sent by a host, the opportunities for information hiding also increase. On the other hand, new covert channels appear when a large packet is fragmented. Channel γ is an example of such case.

Figure 8 displays the format of the Fragment Extension Header and its potential covert channels.

α Alice can transmit 8 bits of covert data using the first *reserved* field of the header. This field is initialized to zero by the sending host, but it is ignored by the destination. Therefore, at the receiving end a value different from zero makes no difference.

β 2-bit *reserved* field has the same treatment as the 8-bit reserved field, so Alice can exploit it taking a similar approach.

γ The reassembly process at the destination host takes into account only the *next header* value of the first fragment as a reference. Also, it ignores the *next header* values of fragments that differ. Those conditions give Alice the opportunity to em-

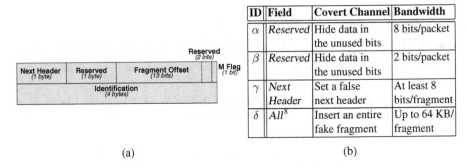

ID	Field	Covert Channel	Bandwidth
α	Reserved	Hide data in the unused bits	8 bits/packet
β	Reserved	Hide data in the unused bits	2 bits/packet
γ	Next Header	Set a false next header	At least 8 bits/fragment
δ	All[8]	Insert an entire fake fragment	Up to 64 KB/ fragment

(a)   (b)

Fig. 8. Covert Channels in the Fragment Extension Header. (a) Format of the Fragment Header, (b) Identified covert storage channels.

bed 8 bits of covert data per fragment as long as she keeps the next header value of the first fragment untouched.

δ Alice can potentially insert an entire fragment exploiting *all* fields of the fragment header. To avoid having this fragment included in the reassembly of the original packet, she can assign an invalid fragment ID field, so that the receiver will discard it. The bandwidth of this channel depends on the size of the fragment. Figure 9 shows a graphical representation of this channel.

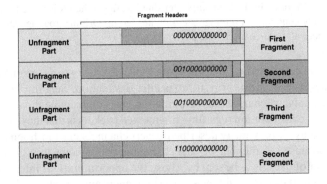

Fig. 9. δ Covert Channel in the Fragment Extension Header. Alice inserts a fake fragment in the fragments stack, setting a *fragment offset* value that causes its data to be overwritten in reassembly.

4.5 Destination Options Header

The Destination Options Header carries optional information only relevant to the destination nodes. It may appear twice in the IPv6 headers stack: a) after the hop-by-hop header when has options that need to be processed by the first destination in the IPv6 header and the ones listed in the router header; and b) after all other extension headers when it carries options to be processed only by the final destination.

---

[8] This covert channel, when authentication is used, requires recalculating or circumventing the ICV. See subsection 4.6 for details.

Because options of both extension headers, hop-by-hop and destination, follow the same option format, the covert channels identified are similar to those shown in Figure 10. Details of how to exploit those channels are described in subsection 4.2. In addition, the Swiss Unix User Group reports an implementation of the covert channel α [37].

Next Header (1 byte)	Header Extension Length (1 byte)	Option Type (1 byte)	Option Data Length (1 byte)	Option Data (Variable length or specified in the Option Data Length field)

(a)

ID	Field	Covert Channel	Bandwidth
α	Option Type: Unknown	Fabricate one or more options[9]	Up to 2038 bytes/packet
β	Option Data: Padding	Set a false padding value[10]	Up to 256 bytes/packet

(b)

Fig. 10. Covert Channels in the Destination Options Extension Header. (a) Format of the Destination Options Header, (b) Identified covert storage channels.

4.6 Authentication Header

The Authentication Extension Header (AH) is the one of the two headers that compose IPsec. It provides connectionless integrity and data origin authentication of individual IP packets. It does so by calculating an integrity check value (ICV) per packet based on particular fields from other extension headers and from the IPv6 header as well. Whether a header field is actually used in the ICV computation or not depends on its mutability in transit. Only fields whose values do not change or change in a predictable way along the communication path are included in the computation. Other fields that may vary en-route, such as the *option data* field in options headers, are set to zero before being included calculation to avoid modifications in length or alignment. If a covert channel technique involves modifying a *immutable* or *mutable predictably* header field protected by authentication, Alice and Bob need to take special actions so their covert communication is not broken. This subsection discusses both potential covert channels in the authentication header and possible solutions the agents can apply when using previously discussed channels over authenticated headers. Figure 11 shows the structure of the authentication header and its potential covert channels.

α This channel is similar to the channel α from subsection 4.4. It has however twice as much bandwidth.

β When the authentication header is not present, Alice can fabricate one and insert it in the stack of extension headers. Alice has to set appropriate values for the *next header, payload length, security parameters index*, and *sequence number* to avoid detection. She places the covert data in the field that apparently contains *authentication data*. Obviously, the fake authentication header will not pass the IPsec integrity

---

[9] These channels involve changing the packet total length, which affects the ICV, when authentication is present. Subsection 4.6 describes that situation.

	Next Header (1 byte)	Payload Length (1 byte)	Reserved (2 bytes)
	Security Parameters Index (SPI) (4 bytes)		
	Sequence Number Field (4 bytes)		
	Authentication Data (Variable length)		

ID	Field	Covert Channel	Bandwidth
α	Reserved	Hide data in the unused bits	2 bytes/packet
β	All	Insert an entire fake header	Up to 1022 bytes/packet

(a)   (b)

Fig. 11. Covert Channels in the Authentication Extension Header. (a) Format of the Authentication Header, (b) Identified covert storage channels.

check at the receiving end. Therefore, Bob needs to strip it before the packet authentication check. Alice can send Bob up to 1022 bytes per packet through this channel (see Figure 12) Notice that this channel also involves modifying the size of the original packet, but this time the *payload length* in the IPv6 is not actually authenticated because there is no real AH.

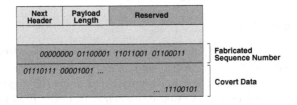

Fig. 12. β **Covert Channel in the Authentication Header.** Alice inserts fake authentication header in the stack of headers, simulating a *sequence number* to defeat active wardens.

Issues with the Authentication Header Integrity Check Value (ICV): The ICV computation consists of applying message authentication code (MAC) algorithms over immutable and mutable but predictable fields from the IPv6 header and its extension headers. Several of the proposed covert channels involve changing values of some of those protected fields. The existence of this channel can cause failure of the integrity check, which triggers an auditable event in IPv6. That may cause both immediate detection of the channel and disruption of the overt communication. Alice and Bob must take actions to avoid such situations. The following, Table 1, table summarizes the affected covert channels and notes the nature of the field protected by the ICV.

To avoid a failed check on the ICV, Alice must either be the sender, and therefore compute the ICV including the covert data, or Bob must intercept the packet before it reaches its destination, and remove the covert data, as described in [29].

4.7 Encapsulating Security Payload Header

Also part of IPsec, the Encapsulating Security Payload (ESP) Header provides confidentiality for all data transmitted end-to-end in IP packets. The general structure of the ESP header and its plausible covert channels are illustrated in Figure 13.

Table 1. Covert Channels Affected by the ICV Calculation

Affected Covert Channel	Protected Field
γ channel in 4.1	*Payload Length* (immutable)
δ channel in 4.1	*Next Header* (immutable)
α, β, γ, and δ channels in 4.2, when changing packet size	*Payload Length* (immutable)
α 4.3, when changing the size of original packet	*Payload Length* (immutable)
δ 4.4, when changing the size of original packet	*Payload Length* (immutable)
α and β channels in 4.5, when changing packet size	*Payload Length* (immutable)

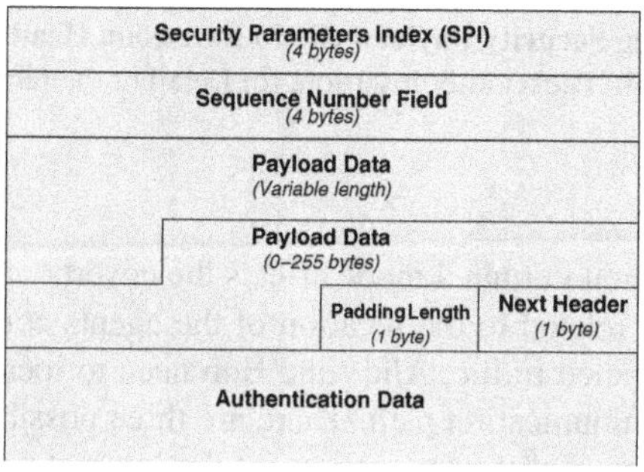

ID	Field	Covert Channel	Bandwidth
α	*Padding*	Set a false padding value	Up to 255 bytes/packet
β	*All*	Insert an entire fake header	Up to 1022 bytes/packet

(a)   (b)

Fig. 13. Covert Channels in the Encapsulating Security Payload (ESP) Extension Header.
(a) Format of the ESP Header, (b) Identified covert storage channels.

α Although the *padding* field in the ESP header is optional, all IPv6 must support them. Alice can send up to 255 bytes per packet exploiting this channel.

β When the ESP header is not present, Alice can fabricate an entire ESP-like header to transmit covert information. Because the ESP header is an encapsulating header, she will need to include the original payload when creating her own. As in channel β of the AH, a fake ESP header will not pass through the IPsec verification. Therefore, Bob needs to remove it, restoring the packet to its original form, before the packet reaches the final destination. Figure 14 shows an example of this channel.

Effects of the Encapsulated Security Payload Header: As shown in Figure 13(a), the ESP header includes an authentication field. However, the ESP integrity check applies only to the ESP internal fields, the encapsulated headers, and the payload. That implies that, in transport mode, the presence of the ESP header does not affect the covert channels previously described, with exception of the ones belonging to the destination options header because that header is placed after the ESP header (i.e., it is encapsulated). To exploit the destination options header channels, Alice and Bob need access to the encryption keys. In tunnel mode, the "inner" IP header and all its extensions are encapsulated from source to destination in the "outer" IP header. However, ESP tunnels can still be used for secret communication if Alice piggybacks an encrypted covert message to the "outer" header payload [29].

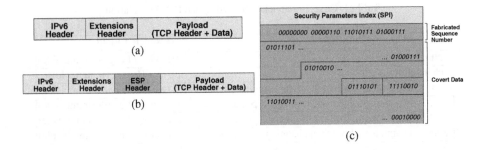

Fig. 14. β **Covert Channel in the Encapsulating Security Payload (ESP) Extension Header.** (a) Packet before inserting the fake ESP header, (b) Packet after insertion, (c) Detail of the fabricated header.

4.8 Covert Channels in Tunneled Traffic

The use of IPsec authentication and encryption in tunnel mode affects the covert communication. The implications are primarily related to the location of the agents communicating covertly. In the presence of tunneled traffic, Alice and Bob need to locate themselves in particular sprts along the communication path. There are three possible tunnel configurations based on the interaction of different versions of the Internet protocol:

IPv6 Traffic in an IPv6 Tunnel: In this scenario both inner and outer headers follow the IPv6 specification, hence both can carry covert data using the techniques in the described channel. Moreover, both headers provide two independent covers for hiding information.

– An **authenticated tunnel** affects the embedding and extraction of covert data in both inner and outer headers.
  When Alice and Bob are outside the tunnel (see Figure 15), they communicate covertly by modifying field within the inner headers. If Wendy is within the tunnel as in Figure 15(a), any countermeasures might cause a failure in the authentication check, breaking the overt communication as well. On the other hand, if Alice and Bob are within the tunnel, as in Figure 15(b), they most likely modify the outer header. Wendy can block their channel without major implications.

– An **encrypted tunnel** alters the embedding and extraction of data hidden in the inner headers. Because inner headers are encrypted, any agent who wishes to modify them must either have knowledge of the encryption key or hide the data before the tunnel is applied.

IPv6 Traffic in an IPv4 Tunnel: This is the most common case present today. Because our interest is only IPv6, the concern here is with the covert channels present in the inner header. However, the IPv4 tunnel interferes with all agents trying to monitor or modify the inner IPv6 traffic. If the IPv4 tunnel does not use IPsec, Alice, Bob, and Wendy just need to understand both IPv4 and IPv6 headers. If the IPv4 tunnel employs IPsec, the encountered problems are exactly as discussed in the previous scenario.

(a)   (b)

Fig. 15. Location of Alice, Bob, and Wendy under and IPsec Tunneling Mode. (a) Alice and Bob embed and extract, respectively, covert data outside the tunnel; Wendy is within the tunnel, so an attempt to modify the traffic might cause the authentication to fail. (b) Alice, Bob, and Wendy are all inside the tunnel; the warden can prevent covert channels in the outer header.

IPv4 Traffic in an IPv6 Tunnel: In this case, the IPv4 traffic is treated as any other payload within a stream of IPv6 packets.

5   Conclusions

In this paper we have presented a comprehensive overview of covert channels existing in the Internet Protocol version 6. We have found and analyzed 22 covert channels.

We hope that this analysis is useful to implementors of firewalls that understand IPv6 traffic, attracting their attention towards harmful covert channels at the IP level. Especially, considering the recent trend of deep packet inspection firewalls, which evolve towards the application layer.

Our future work will include an analysis of covert channels within the Internet Control Message Protocol (ICMPv6) for the Internet Protocol Version 6, implementation of a software package that demonstrates communication using the covert channels described here, more formal calculation of bandwidth available in the covert channels, statistical analysis of IPv6 traffic carrying covert communication.

Appendix A defines three types of active wardens, *stateless*, *stateful*, and *network-aware*, which differ in complexity and ability to block the covert channels introduced in this paper. Additionally, we discuss the countermeasures active wardens can undertake to detect and defeat those channels.

References

1. Gligor, V.D.: A Guide to Understanding Covert Channel Analysis of Trusted Systems. National Computer Security Center, Meade, MD, USA. Version-1 edn. (1993) NCSC-TG-030.
2. McHugh, J.: Covert Channel Analysis: A Chapter of the Handbook for the Computer Security Certification of Trusted Systems. Portland State University, Portland, Oregon, USA. (1995)
3. of Defense, U.D.: Department of Defense Trusted Computer System Evaluation Criteria. (1985) DOD 5200.28-STD.
4. Cabuk, S., Brodley, C.E., Shields, C.: Ip covert timing channels: Design and detection. In: Proceedings of the 11th ACM Conference on Computer and Communications Security, Washington DC, USA, ACM Press (2004) 178–187
5. Ahsan, K.: Covert channel analysis and data hiding in tcp/ip. Master's thesis, University of Toronto (2002)
6. Ahsan, K., Kundur, D.: Practical data hiding in tcp/ip. In: Proceedings of the ACM Workshop on Multimedia Security at ACM Multimedia. (2002)

7. Servetto, S.D., Vetterli, M.: Codes for the fold-sum channel. In: Proceedings of the 35^{35} Annual Conference on Information Science and Systems (CISS), Baltimore, MD, USA (2001)

8. Servetto, S.D., Vetterli, M.: Communication using phantoms: Covert channels in the internet. In: Proceedings of the IEEE International Symposium on Information Theory (ISIT), Washington, DC, USA (2001)

9. Handel, T., Sandford, M.: Hiding data in the OSI network model. In Anderson, R., ed.: Information Hiding: Proceedings of the First International Workshop. Volume 1174., Cambridge, U.K., Springer (1996) 23–38

10. Szczypiorski, K.: Hiccups: Hidden communication system for coruppted networks. In: Proceedings of the Tenth International Multi-Conference on Advanced Computer Systems ACS'2003, Międzyzdroje, Poland (2003) 31–40

11. Rowland, C.H.: Covert channels in the TCP/IP protocol suite. Psionics Technologies (1996) http://www.firstmonday.dk/issues/issue2_5/rowland/.

12. Dunigan, T.: Internet steganography. Technical report, Oak Ridge National Laboratory (Contract No. DE-AC05-96OR22464), Oak Ridge, Tennessee (1998) [ORNL/TM-limited distribution].

13. Rutkowska, J.: The implementation of passive covert channels in the linux kernel. In: 21st Chaos Communication Congress, Berliner Congress Center, Berlin, Germany (2004) www.ccc.de/congress/2004/fahrplan/ files/223-passive-covert-channels-linux.pdf.

14. Abad, C.: Ip checksum covert channels and selected hash collision. http://grayworld.net/cn/papers/ipccc.pdf (2001)

15. Wang, X., Feng, D., Lai, X., Yu, H.: Collisions for hash functions MD4, MD5, HAVAL-128 and RIPEMID. http://eprint.iacr.org/2004/199/ (2004)

16. Kaminsky, D.: MD5 to be considered harmful someday. http://www.doxpara.com/md5_someday.pdf (2004)

17. Giffin, J., Greenstadt, R., Litwack, P., Tibbetts, R.: Covert messaging through tcp timestamps. In: Second Workshop on Privacy Enhancing Technologies. Volume 2482 of Lectures Notes in Computer Science., San Francisco, CA, USA, Springer-Verlag Heidelberg (2003) 194–208

18. daemon9 (route@infonexus.com): Loki2 (the implementation). Phrack Magazine, 51, article 6 (1997) http://www.phrack.org/show.php?p=51&a=6.

19. daemon9 (route@infonexus.com), alhambra (alhambra@infornexus.com): Project loki. Phrack Magazine, 49, article 6 (1996) http://www.phrack.org/show.php?p=49&a=6.

20. Skoudis, E.: Counter Hack: A Step-by-Step Guide to Computer Attacks and Effective Defenses. Series in Computer networking and Distributed Systems. Prentice Hall, Upper Saddle River, NJ (2002)

21. Malan, G.R., Watson, D., Jahanian, F., Howell, P.: Transport and application protocol scrubbing. In: Proceedings of the IEEE INFOCOM 2002 Conference, Tel-Aviv, Israel (2000) 1381–1390

22. Handley, M., Paxson, V.: Network intrusion detection: Evasion, traffic normalization, and end-to-end protocol semantics. In: Proceedings of the 10th USENIX Security Symposium, Washington, DC, USA, USENIX Association (2001)

23. Fisk, G., Fisk, M., Papadopoulos, C., Neil, J.: Eliminating steganography in Internet traffic with active wardens. In Oostveen, J., ed.: Information Hiding: Preproceedings of the Fifth International Workshop, Noordwijkerhout, The Netherlands, Springer (2002) 29–46

24. Murdoch, S.J., Lewis, S.: Embedding covert channels into TCP/IP. In: Information Hiding: Proceedings of the Seventh International Workshop, Barcelona, Spain, Springer (2005)

25. Simmons, G.J.: The prisoners' problem and the subliminal channel. In Chaum, D., ed.: Advances in Cryptology, Proceedings of CRYPTO '83, Plenum Press (1984) 51–67

26. Lucena, N.B., Pease, J., Yadollahpour, P., Chapin, S.J.: Syntax and semantics-preserving application-layer protocol steganography. Lecture Notes in Computer Science, Toronto, Canada, Springer-Verlag Heidelberg (2004) 164–179

27. Craver, S.: On public-key steganography in the presence of an active warden. In Aucsmith, D., ed.: Information Hiding: Proceedings of the Second International Workshop. Volume 1525., Portland, OR, USA, Springer (1998) 355–368

28. Katzenbeisser, S., Petitcolas, F.A.: Information Hiding: Techniques for Steganography and Digital Watermarking. Artech House, Norwood, MA (2000)

29. Deering, S., Hinden, R.: Internet protocol, version 6 (ipv6) specification (1998) RFC 2460.

30. Hagen, S.: IPv6 Essentials. First edn. O'Reilly & Associates, Inc., Sebastopol, CA (2002)

31. Kent, S., Atkinson, R.: Security architecture for the internet protocol (1998) RFC 2401.

32. Kent, S., Atkinson, R.: Ip authentication header (1998) RFC 2402.

33. Kent, S., Atkinson, R.: Ip encapsulating security payload (esp) (1998) RFC 2406.

34. Kent, S., Atkinson, R.: Definition of the differentiated services field (ds field) in the ipv4 and ipv6 header (1998) RFC 2402.

35. (IANA), I.A.N.A.: Protocol numbers. http://www.iana.org/assignments/protocol-numbers (2004)

36. (IANA), I.A.N.A.: IP version 6 parameters. http://www.iana.org/assignments/ipv6-parameters (2004)

37. Graf, T.: Messaging over ipv6 destination options. http://net.suug.ch/articles/2003/07/06/ip6msg.html (2003)

A   Active Warden Analysis

The channels previously described can be blocked, partially blocked, or remain open depending on the capabilities of the active wardens monitoring the network. The three types of active wardens introduced in section 3, *stateless*, *stateful*, and *network-aware*, apply countermeasures according to their ability.

A.1   Stateless Active Warden

If Wendy is a *stateless* active warden, she knows the protocol syntax and semantics and attempts to verify them. She "sees" one packet at a time. That is, she has no recollection of previous packets nor previously encountered semantic conditions. As a stateless warden, Wendy can perform at two levels of diligence. At the lower one, she checks only that IPv6 headers comply to the specifications. For example, she can ensure that field that are supposed to be zero have exactly that value, otherwise she clears them, enforcing the semantic of the protocol and blocking some possibilities of covert data transmission. This simple stateless active warden can be continuously modifying the traffic without fear of breaking the overt communication. Table 2 shows what Wendy can do to the defined covert channels when she only verifies the protocol semantics.

On the other hand, when Wendy behaves aggressively she also modifies field values that do not necessarily violate the protocol specifications. She can be more effective in blocking covert communication, but may also cause harmful side effects listed in Table 4. The implementation of such active warden requires then careful evaluation of the side effects in the overt communication to avoid a detrimental effect on the network.

A.2   Stateful Active Warden

Wendy acting as a *stateful* active warden can do all the normalizations that a stateless active warden does; she also registers already-observed semantic conditions, and

Table 2. Covert Channels Affected by the Activity of a Stateless Active Warden limited to verifying protocol semantics

Header	Covert Channel	Countermeasure
Hop-by-Hop	γ	Zeroing all *padding* octets
Hop-by-Hop Routing Authentication	α and β α α	Zeroing values of the *reserved* fields

Table 3. Covert Channels Affected by the Activity of a Stateful Active Warden

Header	Covert Channel	Observed Situation	Countermeasure
IPv6	α	Packets exchanged between two hosts have belong to many different *traffic classes*.	Resetting the *traffic class* to zero in packets exchanged between that pair of hosts.
IPv6	β	Packets traveling between a pair of hosts exhibit a large range of *flow label* values.	Resetting the *flow label* to zero in packets interchanged between the two hosts.
IPv6	ϵ	Variations in the *hop limit* values outside certain range. Wendy can expect fluctuations in the hop limit value because not all packet travel the same path, but not too many.	Resetting the *hop limit* value to be the same (e.g. 255).
Routing	β	Significantly different routing headers attached to packets exchanged between two hosts.	Removing the entire routing header in packets interchanged by the two hosts.
Fragment	γ	Fragment *next header* values differ among fragments belonging to the same packet.	Resetting the *next header* value of all fragments to be the same as the one in the first fragment.
Fragment	δ	Fragments overlap when simulating reassembly.	Dropping all the fragments belonging to the same packet.
Authentication	β	*Sequence number* values do not increase monotonically; also SPI values seem semantically incorrect.	Removing the entire authentication header of the suspicious packet.
ESP	β	*Sequence number* values do not increase monotonically; also SPI values seem semantically incorrect.	Removing the entire ESP header of the suspected packet.

applies that knowledge in subsequent monitoring sessions. Because a stateful active warden can remember previously seen packets, she can more effectively and less invasively eliminate the same covert channels destroyed by a stateless active warden. In

Table 4. Covert Channels Affected by the Activity of a Stateless Active Warden who aggressively attempts to block the covert communication

Header	Covert Channel	Countermeasure	Side Effect
IPv6	α	Resetting the *traffic class* to zero in all packets.	Removes any benefits provided by traffic class aware routers.
IPv6	β	Resetting the *flow label* to zero in all packets.	Removes the router ability of using *flow label* functions. In addition, this action violates the protocol specification, which states that *flow label* values cannot be modified in transit. It is unlikely though that doing it so will cause packet delivery problems because intermediate notes will assume the default behavior.
IPv6	γ	Verifying that the *payload length* value matches the actual datagram payload and removing extra data if found.	Violation of the protocol specification that establishes that extra data must be forwarded, causing the packet to fail during the integrity checking.
IPv6	δ	Verifying that the *next header* value is one of the allowed protocol numbers and stripping the entire header, in case of an unknown value.	Violates the protocol specification and essentially disables the IPv6 header extension mechanism, because any extension header will be unusable until active wardens are aware of new extension header definitions.
IPv6	ϵ	Resetting the *hop limit* value to be the same (e.g. 255)	Risks network congestion. When a routing cycle exists, the active warden will reset the *hop limit* value in every cycle and as a result packets could travel endlessly in the network.
Hop-by-Hop	β	Removing all options of type *routing alert*.	Eliminates the mechanism that informs the router about contents of interest, so it can handle any control data accordingly.
Hop-by-Hop	δ	Discarding all options of *unknown* type.	Violates the protocol specification that says that *unknown* options should be handled accordingly to their *option type* value. By ignoring this requirement, active wardens damage the options header functionality until they learn about new option types.
Routing	β	Removing the entire routing header.	Disregards all advantages of a routing header extension, thus packets cannot travel by predefined paths.

addition, a stateful active warden can detect covert channels that a stateless cannot. Table 3 summarizes what a stateful active warden can do to detect the described covert channels.

A.3   Network-Aware Active Warden

A *network-aware* active warden is the most sophisticated type of warden. Wendy is a stateful warden and also a network topologist. That is, she is able to defeat some of the proposed covert channels because of her knowledge of the topology of the surrounding networks.

If Wendy is a network-aware active warden, she can defeat covert channel β of the routing header (see section 4.3). She can do that taking several countermeasures. She can, for example, verify whether or not the address fields are in fact valid IPv6 addresses. At the same time, she can verify that the addresses are not multicast addresses because they are not allowed to be. In addition, if Wendy has knowledge of the topology of the network where the packet originated, she can match the addresses listed in the routing header to the ones the packet has traversed. The location of a network-aware warden is critical. Being placed in the egress gateway of an organization, Wendy can monitor all outgoing packets and verify the IP addresses in the routing header.

Towards Privacy-Aware eLearning

Katrin Borcea, Hilko Donker, Elke Franz,
Andreas Pfitzmann, and Hagen Wahrig

Dresden University of Technology, Dresden, Germany
{borcea, donker, ef1, pfitza, wahrig}@inf.tu-dresden.de

Abstract. Acting in the digital world, such as browsing the Internet, always causes generation of data. However, the average user is not aware that his actions leave traces which might cause privacy risks. Within this paper, we discuss the need for privacy-enhancing application design considering eLearning as example. eLearning is an application area that comprises many use cases which are common in the digital world. Since an eLearning application aims at assisting users, they cannot act in full anonymity. We discuss a possible solution which uses privacy-enhancing identity management (PIM) in order to provide as much anonymity as possible while still enabling assistance.

1 Introduction

In the context of learning and teaching, as in many other application areas, computing systems are of growing importance. eLearning aims at providing a platform for learning based on telecommunication, possibly combined with conventional learning in the real world (i.e., "blended learning"). An important goal of eLearning is to assist each individual user during the learning process. However, the necessary prerequisite for adequate assistance is to collect and evaluate information about the particular user. Computer-based learning systems actually must know more and more details about their individual users in order to improve assistance. Of course, this fact can lead to privacy problems since the collected data can be misused. We cannot be sure that the data are perfectly secure against unintended access unless the computing systems used are "perfect", i.e., correct, dependable, and fault tolerant as well as securely managed. Current systems, however, cannot be expected to be perfect and it is not clear whether such a system will be possible at all.

Obviously, this calls for action. In other application areas such as e-commerce, users are increasingly sensitized for privacy threats. Until now, this is not the case in the area of eLearning. But we expect that privacy problems will imply serious acceptance problems for eLearning applications at a later point in time. Finally, it is a mood question whether eLearning will establish successfully as commonplace way to learn if privacy problems are not solved. A first discussion on the need for user anonymity and identity management within eLearning is given in [7]. We want to enhance this discussion by a detailed exposition of the privacy problems and resulting requirements on privacy w.r.t. relevant use

G. Danezis and D. Martin (Eds.): PET 2005, LNCS 3856, pp. 167–178, 2006.

cases within eLearning. Our aim is to establish awareness for privacy problems occurring in different application areas by discussing the application area of eLearning in depth. We show by means of a conceptual sketch that these privacy problems can be solved by using privacy-enhancing identity management (PIM).

Currently, we investigate privacy-enhancing solutions within the EU project PRIME[1]. This project aims at developing a comprehensive architecture that supports privacy and identity management. The research focuses on solutions for well-defined application scenarios. One of these scenarios is eLearning. The eLearning platform BluES[2] [3] establishes the concrete eLearning application and is the basis for the privacy-enhancing solution described in this paper.

The paper is organized as follows. Sec. 2 shortly summarizes general principles of privacy. After an introduction to the application area *eLearning* in Sec. 3, we discuss privacy threats which occur in the different use cases introduced in Sec. 4. Afterwards, Sec. 5 describes how PIM can be used in order to provide a privacy-aware eLearning environment. Finally, Sec. 6 concludes and gives an outlook.

2   Principles of Privacy and Security

Generally, we cannot exclude the misuse of information once collected. Therefore, a general principle of privacy and security is to store as less personal data as possible, i.e., to ensure data minimization and avoidance. Users must be enabled to determine by themselves which data are stored at all. Furthermore, data should be partitioned instead of managed centrally. Then, there is much less danger that anybody may gain a global view on the information available about a user. The partitioned information must be unlinkable in order to prevent that somebody is able to create user profiles.

PIM provides the required partitioning of data. In this section, we give only a short survey of relevant terms and issues of identity management. A detailed introduction to identity management can be found in [5, 6]. In general, PIM is about enabling users to control by their own which personal information they disclose to others in the digital world. Thereby, PIM enables users to act as they are used to in everyday life: They do not offer all information about them in each situation. Depending on the context, users decide which information is disclosed. Such a subset of information is called a *partial identity*. All partial identities represent the user. The partitioned information, i.e., the data fragments, should not be linkable to the users' real identity. Only users themselves are able to explicitly link different partial identities. For example, this can be desired if they want to build up their own reputation.

Pseudonyms are used as identifiers for partial identities (in general, they are identifiers for subjects or groups of subjects). There are different kinds of pseudonyms known which offer different degrees of anonymity [10]: A *transaction pseudonym* is used only once. Therefore, it provides the maximum degree of

---

[1] www.prime-project.eu.org

[2] www.blues-portal.de

anonymity. Sometimes a user wishes to be recognized by others if acting again in one and the same context. Appropriate pseudonyms for this case are *role pseudonyms* (user is recognized if she acts again in the same role), *relationship pseudonyms* (user is recognized if she communicates with the same communication partner), or *role-relationship pseudonyms* (used for communication with a specific communication partner while acting in a specific role). A *person pseudonym* is used in all contexts. Therefore, it is a simple substitution of the holder's name and offers the least degree of anonymity. In the long run, a person pseudonym identifies the user, i.e., the user can be individualized within a set of users [10].

A pseudonym and the data assigned to it establish a partial identity of a user. PIM supports users to manage their partial identities. This comprises many tasks, for example creating and managing pseudonyms, or management of preferences about disclosure of personal data. The identity manager is used when a communication shall be established in order to negotiate between information required by the communication partner and preferences about disclosure. This negotiation is necessary in order to enforce multilateral security. Multilateral security means that all parties involved in a communication are able to express their own protection goals, that conflicting interests are recognized and negotiated, and that the protection goals agreed are enforced [9].

Partitioning of personal information as well as explicitly linking of some partitioned data is required in the context of eLearning in order to solve the occurring privacy problems. Actually, PIM is a reasonable way to meet these conflicting requirements as discussed in Section 4.2. Thereby, we aim at a solution that realizes the technical design principles stated within the PRIME project [11]:

1. Design must start from maximum privacy.
2. Explicit privacy rules govern system usage.
3. Privacy rules must be enforced, not just stated.
4. Privacy enforcement must be trustworthy.
5. Users need easy and intuitive abstractions of privacy.
6. Privacy needs an integrated approach.
7. Privacy must be integrated with applications.

3   Short Introduction to eLearning

There are already attempts to support distance education for a number of years. Early solutions mainly provided content to learners, such as the transmission of video data in Teleteaching systems [8]. However, providing content is not sufficient to support learning and teaching in a virtual environment. For a couple of years, the need for integrated solutions initiated research in the field of eLearning. Current eLearning systems are complex applications that cover a variety of tasks related to learning. Besides different learning scenarios such as self-study or guided learning, they also support tutoring, communication, evaluation, annotation, and administration. Some of them also support the authoring process of learning modules. These systems enable interactions between users and, therefore, explicitly support cooperative learning.

eLearning obviously offers various advantages: It allows users to learn to a large extent independently from time and location and to be assisted anyway. Multi-media based presentation of information helps learners to understand difficult topics easier. There is an increasing demand for eLearning in both the economical and the educational sector: eLearning solutions can be used in companies, universities, schools, or further education centers. They can support education and studies as well as extension studies, professional training, on-the-job training, and so on. It can be expected that eLearning applications become more and more commonplace. A market study yielded the result that nearly 46% of large-scale enterprises (more than 1000 employees) in Germany provide eLearning, and about 34% of enterprises support learning via Internet or intranet [1]. Therefore, eLearning is an important application area and a research field of increasing interest. However, popular use of eLearning as means for all tasks related to learning is more in an initial phase until now.

Research in the complex application area of eLearning mainly focuses on topics directly related to learning. For example, it is a challenging task to select and realize the learning strategy that is best suited for specific eLearning scenarios. Multimedia-based presentation of information to the users and enabling cooperative learning is very important and requires serious studies. However, it is also very important to consider privacy topics. Every action within a computer-based system implies the accruement of data. Therefore, users leave traces if acting in the system. Monitoring and linking such traces can be used to create detailed profiles of the users, that induce privacy threats. There are some approaches to integrate identity management within eLearning applications. However, these solutions mainly consider authorization of users [7].

4   Privacy Issues Within eLearning

4.1   Roles and Use Cases

In an eLearning application users typically act within diverse roles depending on their goals. Table 1 summarizes roles that are considered within the eLearning application BluES. The table does not include the eLearning provider since he does not act within the application. He is the person or company providing the eLearning environment to users and responsible for this environment from a legal point of view. The technical administrator, who installs the application, owns administrative rights a priori. He must grant initial permissions for content managers, who afterwards grant permissions to authors and tutors. Learners also need permissions to act within the system, but they will get these permissions for the most part during their actions within the system, e.g., after registration or if they have successfully passed an exam. Anonymous users do not need any permission. Of course, they are quite restricted and can only browse.

The eLearning application runs on a server. All persons except from the technical administrator who acts also directly on the server connect to this server using an eLearning client. They install this client in their own trusted

Table 1. Roles within eLearning

Role	Tasks/interests
Technical administrator	Administrates and manages the technical environment (the server), manages policies and grants initial permissions.
Content manager	Provides and manages the overall structure of the eLearning environment, plans new classes and commissions tutors and authors.
Author	Creates informative material and test material.
Tutor	Organizes classes, controls learning paths, gives assistance.
Learner	Gains knowledge, practices and asks, tests his/her knowledge.
Moderator	Moderates discussions in synchronous learning.
Anonymous user	Browses, i.e., informs himself about classes and groups provided by the eLearning environment, but cannot access learning content.

environment, e.g., on their laptop. If they want to access the eLearning application, the client establishes a connection to the eLearning server.

Users should be able to separate acting within the eLearning environment from other roles in their life. However, we need an even finer-grained partitioning of information within the eLearning application itself. First, each user can act within different roles if he owns the needed permissions. For example, a tutor of a class can act as learner in another class. He does not want to be recognized as tutor since he wants to learn without pressure. But role-dependent identity management is also not sufficient since there are a lot of use cases that require a finer partitioning (Fig. 1).

For example, there are a lot of use cases for common working. The eLearning environment shown in this figure supports different learning scenarios. Within a *Guided Class*, a tutor centrally manages learning. He monitors the learning progress of the learners of his class and provides assistance if necessary. In *Self-Study Classes*, learners are not provided assistance by tutors. Both scenarios comprise a number of sub use cases, such as registration, process learning modules, practice, self-tests, and exams. *Dynamic groups* are established by users. They can be assigned to classes, but they can also be established separately, for example, if users came across an interesting topic during their discussions.

Furthermore, the eLearning application provides personal workspaces and shared workspaces for cooperative working (*Annotation*). The latter can be used within dynamic groups, but also for public annotations within a class. Personal workspaces enable users to make private annotations.

Different means to communicate support discussions between users (*Contact/Communication*). Examples are blackboard or chat, as well as access to external communication services such as internet telephony. The eLearning environment also considers the mobility of its users (*Mobile Access*). Users may configure settings for different equipments, such as home/office and travel.

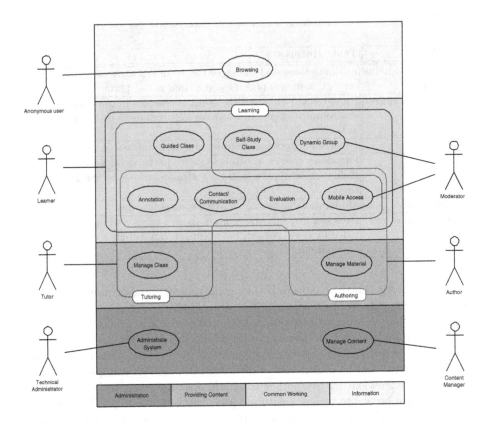

Fig. 1. Use Cases in eLearning

Evaluation is an essential part of an eLearning process. Tutors initiate evaluation in order to get feedback about tutoring. Authors use evaluation in order to improve their material. Learners evaluate their results in comparison to other learners in order to assess their learning progress on their own. Evaluation requires the collection of further data, such as test results of learners, or data about the use of the learning materials by the learners. Just from this very short overview of the use cases result clear consequences concerning requirements on PIM which are discussed in the next section.

4.2   Privacy Threats and Resulting Requirements on PIM

Privacy requirements are obviously important for eLearning, since they establish an unbiased environment. However, users cannot act completely anonymously: An eLearning application aims at assisting learners which obviously requires information about their learning progress. Furthermore, a privacy-aware evaluation of learning is quite a challenging task since it requires information about the actions of learners during learning in order to draw reasonable conclusions. Due to these tasks, the eLearning application necessarily must learn something about its users. It must recognize them, what requires to acquire and to store data describing their activities within the application.

Without PIM, all actions of a user within the eLearning application can be linked to him. This, however, offers the possibility to create detailed user profiles: First, it is recognizable which classes and groups a learner attends. Second, all actions within a class or group can be assigned to the particular user. For example, frequency of learning sessions, average duration of processing learning modules, or results of tests can be observed. Third, this collected information allows drawing conclusions about the learner, for example about interests, learning speed, habits, or equipment. Actually, users have no control about their data. Possible negative consequences may be a biased environment or a lost reputation due to failures. Users may feel restricted and become afraid to disgrace themselves. They might become discouraged to ask and practice.

These threats result in requirements on anonymity posed by learners: They do not want that all of their actions within the eLearning environment can be linked by others. Learners want to be recognizable only if necessary, e.g., in order to enable reasonable discussions with others or to enable the tutor to assist them. If learners start learning in a new class, they want to have the possibility to work in an unbiased environment independently from results of formerly attended classes. Additionally, learners should be able to act under different partial identities — and possibly even anonymously — within one and the same class, e.g., if they practice or ask. Separating activities encourages learners to feel unrestricted and, thus, to learn without pressure. Besides this separation, we also need explicit linking of information. Learners must be able to build up their own reputation by disclosing information about them.

Tutors and authors are interested in building up their own reputation. Therefore, they are not necessarily interested in being anonymous. However, they could also wish to be recognizable for learners only in single classes. For example, they could wish to get an unbiased evaluation of tutoring or authoring that considers only this single class.

To conclude, users must be able to control which information others know about them. As already mentioned, we need a *fine-grained partitioning of personal data* in order to enable reasonable assistance of users or evaluation while enforcing their privacy requirements. Partial identities must be established *depending on the working context* of the user. The *context* describes the situation in which a user has acted. Particularly, the context comprises "role", "use case", "value" of this use case, and "action". For example, a context can contain the information that a user has acted as "learner" in the "guided class" "Principles of Statistics", and that he has processed "practice #1".

Pseudonyms are used as identifiers of the partial identities. If users start working in a new context, they should have the possibility to act under another, possibly newly created pseudonym. If they wish to act anonymously, they will use this pseudonym only once (transaction pseudonym). If they use one pseudonym every time they work in one and the same context, the pseudonym becomes a role-relationship pseudonym.

Despite the need for unlinkability of different partial identities, we need a reasonable access control in order to prevent unauthorized accesses to material, annotations, or evaluation results. Therefore, we consider the use of anonymous credentials as described in [4] for providing evidence of permissions. Anonymous credentials enable users to unlinkably demonstrate possession of certain attributes.

This approach allows reasonable working while ensuring that all information that might be collected at the eLearning server can only be assigned to this specific partial identity. That means, user profiles can only refer to a partial identity. Different partial identities can only be linked by the user they belong to. The next section sketches an architecture that implements these requirements.

5   Sketch of a Privacy-Enhancing Solution Based on PIM

5.1   Overall Structure

Fig. 2 gives an outline of an architecture that enables privacy-enhancing eLearning. The PIM-aware platform provides the necessary functionality such as managing pseudonyms and credentials, and establishing anonymous communication. Users can configure the PIM via a console. Fig. 2 indicates that the eLearning application needs to be extended in order to support a PIM-aware solution. One issue is the intuitive representation of information about the current privacy status, e.g., the visibility of attributes for others. Furthermore, the eLearning application must be enabled to recognize context switches. Users must be informed if starting an action implies a context switch and they must have the possibility to switch their partial identity in this case. Finally, existing functionality needs to be adapted. One example is the registration process that now has to consider pseudonyms and only checks organizational registration rules such as time limits for guided classes. Checking user-related registration rules is delegated to the PIM server component that requests necessary credentials from the PIM client component. Furthermore, Fig. 2 also suggests that the PIM application as well as the eLearning application must be extended by an interface in order to allow them to communicate with each other.

5.2   Selecting a Partial Identity

If users want to access the eLearning server, they start their eLearning client which immediately interacts with the PIM client component. The PIM client offers the user all contexts already known within eLearning. Pseudonyms used are managed internally by the PIM client; they are not presented to the user. This is reasonable since pseudonyms are random bit strings only [2]. The PIM server component can assign random names to these random pseudonyms in order to allow others acting in the system, e.g. the tutor or communication partners, to recognize the user easier.

Users can work again in an existing context under a previously used partial identity, or they can let the PIM client generate a new partial identity for this

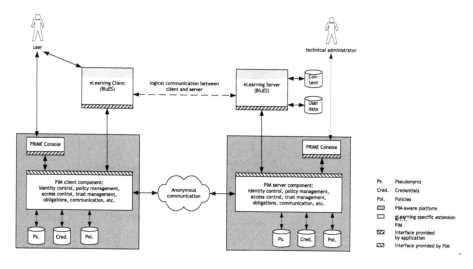

Fig. 2. Privacy-enhancing architecture for eLearning

context. They can also establish a new context and let the PIM client either generate a new pseudonym or select an existing one for acting in this new context. Since all content-related information is stored at server side only, creating a new context will usually require browsing in order to establish this context (especially the "value" of the "use case"). For browsing, it is not necessary to generate a pseudonym. The PIM client also supports configuration of pseudonyms. Configurations may determine which data may be transferred if the user acts under this pseudonym, which credentials may be delivered if requested, and which actions imply a context switch. It must be transparent for users which information others know about them.

The eLearning client receives the generated or selected pseudonym and requests the PIM client to establish an anonymous connection to the eLearning server in order to transmit the pseudonymous service request of the user. The PIM client forwards the service request as well as parameters for this request to the PIM server component, which forwards them to the eLearning server component.

Actions that require permissions imply a negotiation phase. The necessary authorization is initiated by the PIM server component. Permissions are established by means of anonymous credentials [4]. The credential system (considered as part of the PIM) at server side issues credentials that are delivered to clients. The credential system of a PIM client component stores the credentials. It may select a subset of the assertions contained in a credential where the subset is agreed upon in the negotiation phase.

In order to prevent the eLearning client to link different partial identities, a new instantiation of the eLearning client is started after switching partial identities. The server is not able to link these clients since they use anonymous communication channels. However, if the user completely trusts his eLearning

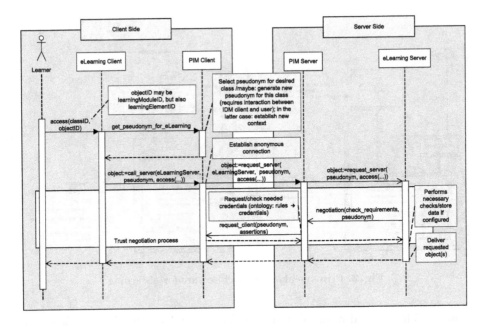

Fig. 3. Process Learning Modules

client, he has not to open a new client if he changes the learning context. In that case, the eLearning client lets the PIM client component establish a new connection to the PIM server component using the new (generated/selected) pseudonym it has received from the PIM client component. It can be expected that this solution increases performance. However, it will not be possible for users to comprehensively check the client software in order to decide whether they can really trust it — even if this software is open source. Therefore, certified assertions by trusted third parties that confirm that the client software fulfills its specifications can be used to increase the trustworthiness of the client software for the users. The ISO/IEC 15408 could be a framework for this. In any case, the user should be able to select client software he trusts.

As a matter of principle, only necessary data should be stored at all. At client side, credentials and pseudonyms as well as policies describing their use are stored (managed by the PIM client component). At server side, the actual contents and necessary user data (assigned to partial identities) are stored.

5.3   Process Learning Modules

We want to have a look at a use case common for learning in a guided or self-study class in order to point out possible interactions between the PIM-aware platform and the eLearning application. Actually, *Process Learning Modules* means to access objects provided by the eLearning server (Fig. 3). The eLearning client interacts with the PIM client in order to select a partial identity or to establish a new one. The latter is only possible if no evaluation should be done for this class or if the learner does not want to participate in the evaluation. The service request is forwarded by the PIM client via the PIM server to the eLearning server that initiates the negotiation process. The learner has to claim that he is registered for this class. His PIM client sends the required credentials to the PIM server in the negotiation phase. If negotiation was successfully finished, the requested objects are delivered.

If the author has configured evaluation of his material in order to improve authoring, data describing the processing of requested material must be collected by the eLearning client and delivered to the server. Evaluation of tutoring also requires collecting information about which material a learner has accessed. Learners must be informed about this evaluation, and they must explicitly agree to data collection. They can also refuse it, since evaluation should not restrict to attend classes.

This example shows some general tasks which are performed by the integrated architecture consisting of a privacy-aware eLearning application on top of a PIM-aware platform. The platform performs all common tasks such as managing pseudonyms or credentials. The application must be extended in order to initiate communication with the PIM-aware platform, e.g., to get a pseudonym, or to establish an anonymous connection. The interfaces must forward requests and responses of the eLearning client or eLearning server, respectively.

6   Summary and Outlook

In this paper, we have discussed privacy issues within eLearning in order to increase the awareness of privacy problems and opportunities. There are conflicting requirements within eLearning since there are clear requirements on anonymity on the one side and necessary data collection in order to provide core functionality on the other side. As discussed in this paper, these conflicts can be solved by using a platform that provides PIM.

At the moment, this approach is pursued within the project PRIME which develops a comprehensive architecture supporting PIM. This provides an opportunity to investigate practical issues such as performance, usability, and — concluding — user acceptance of privacy-aware eLearning. Gaining such practical experiences with privacy-aware applications is an important goal of the PRIME project and work in progress.

Finally, we hope that a privacy-aware eLearning environment can increase awareness of privacy threats as well as understanding of privacy-enhancing mechanisms since eLearning is intended to transfer knowledge. Since this environment has the character of a situation where learning and applying new concepts in order to gain experiences is usual, it can encourage users to really make use of the PIM concepts. This will be further supported by providing eLearning classes about PIM enabling self-reflexive learning, i.e., applying concepts to be learned within the eLearning process itself.

Acknowledgement

We like to thank Mike Bergmann, Sebastian Clauß and Thomas Kriegelstein for fruitful discussions. The information in this document is provided as is, and no guarantee or warranty is given that the information is fit for any particular purpose. The user thereof uses the information at his/her sole risk and liability. The work reported in this paper was supported by the IST PRIME project; however, it represents not necessarily the view of the project. The PRIME project receives research funding from the European Community's Sixth Framework Programme and the Swiss Federal Office for Education and Science.

References

1. P. Bock. Wachstumsmarkt E-Learning — Anforderungen, Akteure und Perspektiven im deutschen Markt (08/2001), 2001. Berlecon Research.
2. K. Borcea, E. Franz, and A. Pfitzmann. Metaphorical representation of pseudonyms. To be published.
3. K. Borcea, O. Neumann, and H. Wahrig. Adapting an internet based learning environment to a hybrid approach. In *Proceedings ED-MEDIA*, 2000.
4. J. Camenisch and A. Lysyanskaya. An efficient system for non-transferable anonymous credentials with optional anonymity revocation. In B. Pfitzmann, editor, *EUROCRYPT 2001*, LNCS 2045, pages 93–118. Springer, Heidelberg, 2001.
5. S. Clauß and M. Köhntopp. Identity management and its support of multilateral security. *Computer Networks*, (37):205–219, 2001.
6. S. Clauß, A. Pfitzmann, M. Hansen, and E. V. Herreweghen. Privacy-enhancing identity management. *The IPTS Report 67*, pages 8–16, September 2002. http://www.jrc.es/pages/iptsreport/vol67/english/IPT2E676.html.
7. M. Hansen. Nutzeranonymität und Identitätsmanagement — auch für E-Learning? In R. Grimm, editor, *E-Learning: Beherrschbarkeit und Sicherheit*, pages 51–62, 2003.
8. J. Kawalek. Acceptance factors for video teaching. In *Workshop on Computer Aided Teaching, Tele-Teaching / Mediafication, Towards a Platform for Teleteaching Teleservices*, 1993.
9. A. Pfitzmann. Multilateral security: Enabling technologies and their evaluation. In R. Wilhelm, editor, *Informatics — 10 Years Back, 10 Years Ahead*, LNCS 2000, pages 50–62. Springer, Heidelberg, 2001.
10. A. Pfitzmann and M. Hansen. Anonymity, unobservability, pseudonymity, and identity management — a proposal for terminology. Draft status: http://dud.inf.tu-dresden.de/literatur/Anon-Terminology_v0.21.pdf, September 2004.
11. PRIME: Description of work — Excerpt. http://www.prime-project.eu.org/public/prime_products/WorkPlan-public.pdf.

Anonymization of IP Traffic Monitoring Data: Attacks on Two Prefix-Preserving Anonymization Schemes and Some Proposed Remedies

Tønnes Brekne[1], André Årnes[1], and Arne Øslebø[2]

[1] Centre for Quantifiable Quality of Service in Communication Systems*
Norwegian University of Science and Technology
O.S. Bragstads plass 2E, N-7491 Trondheim, Norway
{tonnes, andrearn}@q2s.ntnu.no
http://www.q2s.ntnu.no/
[2] Uninett AS, Abels gate 5, Teknobyen, N-7465 Trondheim, Norway
arne.oslebo@uninett.no
http://www.uninett.no/

Abstract. In our search for anonymization solutions for passive measurement data in the context of the LOBSTER passive network monitoring project, we discovered attacks against two initially promising candidates for IP address anonymization. We present a suite of three algorithms employing packet injection and frequency analysis, which can compromise individual addresses protected with prefix-preserving anonymization in multilinear time. We present two algorithms to counter our attacks. These methods support gradual release of topological information, as required by some applications. We also introduce an algorithm that strengthens some hash-based anonymization methods.

1 Introduction

This paper presents three attacks we devised while examining some candidate solutions for anonymization of passive monitoring data in the context of the LOBSTER[1] and SCAMPI[2] projects. We suggest improvements on these schemes in order to provide satisfactory anonymization. We also show how hash-based anonymization of IP-addresses for particular types of traffic can be strengthened. Unless otherwise is stated, discussion of anonymization is done in the specific context of anonymizing IP addresses in IP packet headers.

---

* The "Centre for Quantifiable Quality of Service in Communication Systems, Centre of Excellence" is appointed by The Research Council of Norway, and funded by the Research Council, NTNU and UNINETT.

[1] LOBSTER is a pilot European Infrastructure for large-scale monitoring of broadband Internet infrastructure, see http://www.ist-lobster.org/.
[2] SCAMPI is a EU project for creating a scalable and programmable monitoring platform for the Internet, see http://www.ist-scampi.org/.

G. Danezis and D. Martin (Eds.): PET 2005, LNCS 3856, pp. 179–196, 2006.

Passive measurement of communications networks bases itself on collecting real traffic data. Since collected data can reveal information about corporate or personal habits, it should be anonymized as far as possible. Effective anonymization, however, tends to render information on network structures unusable for analysis applications. Thus there is a case for providing *configurable anonymization*, where a minimum of necessary structural information is preserved, and the data otherwise are anonymized as far as possible.

An overview of available anonymization tools for IP traffic monitoring data is given in appendix B.

1.1   Anonymity Requirements

The anonymization requirements imposed by LOBSTER were our initial motivation for examining prefix-preserving anonymization. In order to support sharing of monitoring data, the data must be *sanitized* so that private and sensitive data are removed or anonymized. The scheme should provide *sender and receiver untraceability* so that unauthorized extraction of identifying data is impossible. To enable network operations and research, we wish to *preserve network topology information*. For this purpose, observations should be *linkable*, so that it is possible to correlate observations.

Some applications demand accountability, which implies that anonymization must be *reversible*[3], by allowing reidentification of anonymized data by authorized parties. Police investigations and abuse handling exemplify such applications. Reversibility can be provided by pseudonymization provided pseudonymization tables or decryption keys are available.

1.2   Reference and Threat Model

We assume an IP network where passive sensors monitor network traffic and anonymize captured data. The sensors are programmable network monitoring cards[4], which capture high-bandwidth traffic, while performing mandatory onboard data anonymization. The anonymized network traces are subsequently made available to other parties.

The main threat is that an adversary acquires private data by reidentifying anonymized network traces. For the purpose of our analysis, we make the following assumptions:

Assumption 1. *The adversary may access all anonymized monitoring data from at least one passive sensor.*

Assumption 2. *The adversary may send forged network traffic with arbitrary source and destination IP addresses.*

In other words, the adversary is capable of performing an attack similar to a cryptographic *chosen plaintext attack*.

Assumption 3. *The adversary has a priori knowledge of the traffic distribution of the observed network.*

This is an assumption similar to that made by Chaum in [1]).

---

[3] Also referred to as revocable anonymization.
[4] Examples of such cards are SCAMPI cards and Endace DAG cards.

2   Anonymization and Pseudonymization Primitives

There is a fine distinction between *anonymization* and *pseudonymization*. In this section, we will consider some of the most common primitives for achieving anonymity and pseudonymity.

2.1   Anonymization

Anonymization tries to achieve "the state of being not identifiable within a set of subjects, the anonymity set" [2]. It may be achieved in several manners, as shown below.

Data removal implies the irreversible deletion of data. This can be implemented by replacing data with a constant.

Randomization of data usually involves a substitution of sensitive information with random information. This provides unlinkability[5] between observations in the same way as data removal.

Generalization is substitution of identifying data with more general data, so that no individuals may be identified. In our case, one example could be the substitution of IP-addresses with their respective AS-numbers[6]. This preserves network topology, but may fail to provide anonymity in the cases where an AS-number may be associated with a single user or a small group.

Truncation is a type of generalization where a fixed number m least significant bits are deleted, while the others are kept in their original form. For example, one may keep the most significant 8 bits of the plaintext IP-address and delete the rest.

2.2   Pseudonymization

In the case of pseudonymization, the actual identity is replaced by an alternate identity (a pseudonym). The issue of using pseudonymous network monitoring traces is discussed in [3, 4]. Pseudonymization implies that the process is reversible, in that it may be possible to uniquely identify plaintext data, given a pseudonym. We have identified the following types of pseudonymization:

Bijective mappings make pseudonymity possible. A pseudonymous entity must be uniquely identifiable. This identifiabililty is also a feature that makes injection attacks possible, where an adversary retrieves address mappings by sending packets and observing their anonymous versions.

Data permutations are permutations of the identifier language from which real identities and pseudonyms are drawn. This type of pseudonymization is reversible for anyone knowing the permutation that has been used.

---

[5] Unlinkability means that "two or more items within a system are no more and no less related than they are related concerning a-priori knowledge" [2].

[6] An Autonomous System (AS) is a collection of IP networks registered by a single entity. A unique AS-number is associated with each AS for routing purposes.

Cryptographic methods for anonymization of network traces are discussed in [5, 6, 7]. Any cryptographic anonymization scheme is subject to attacks on the cryptographic algorithms or the key management system.

Hashing can be considered a pseudonymization scheme, although it is computationally difficult to recover the plaintext data based on a hash value. The hash value is an "initially unlinkable pseudonym" according to the definitions in [2]. We consider hashing an IP-address x with a hash function[7] f. One may also consider a hashing scheme where, for a constant m, the host address x with length n bits is represented by a hash value of the least significant m bits and the most significant $n - m$ bits respectively. This will, like truncation, preserve some topology information. However, the anonymity will be weakened, as the anonymity sets are smaller.

Keyed hashing addresses a weakness with unkeyed hash functions, such as MD5 and SHA1, where any adversary can perform the same computations and build a dictionary for all possible IP addresses. In an experiment, we computed MD5 hashes for the entire IPv4 address space in a matter of hours on a modest PC. Such an attack can be prevented by using a keyed hashing scheme.

3   Prefix-Preserving Pseudonymization

An anonymization scheme is prefix-preserving if, for any two plaintext IP addresses sharing a m-bit prefix, their anonymized versions will also share a m-bit prefix. The tools TCPdpriv, wide-tcpdpriv, and Crypto-PAn are examples of prefix-preserving schemes, as discussed in [6, 7]. Prefix-preserving pseudonymization seems suitable for our purpose, as it preserves network topology. As an example, we will provide a brief description of TCPdpriv.

Example 1. TCPdpriv stores a set of plaintext and anonymized IP address pairs. When a new IP address arrives, it is compared with previous plaintext IP addresses in order to identify the longest prefix match. The new IP address is anonymized by using the same anonymized prefix as that of its match, whereas the remaining part of the address is anonymized with a random value. As new pseudonyms are generated using random values, TCPdpriv is not deterministic, and the pseudonym for a given IP address will differ between TCPdpriv sessions.

3.1   Cryptographic Prefix-Preserving Pseudonymization

Cryptographic prefix-preserving pseudonymization was proposed in [6, 7], and it is an improvement of TCPdpriv in several respects. In particular, it is deterministic, and it allows both consistent prefix-preserving pseudonymization across sessions, as well as distributed processing. Cryptographic prefix-preserving pseudonymization uses a cryptographic algorithm rather than a random value. In

---

[7] We assume that hash functions are preimage resistant, 2nd-preimage resistant, and collision resistant (see pages 323–324 in [8]).

this way, the pseudonymization is uniquely determined by the encryption key K. This scheme has been implemented in the tool Crypto-PAn. Some improvements on Crypto-PAn were proposed in [9].

The form of the anonymization function is (using mostly the notation of [7]):

$$F(a) \leftarrow a'_1 \cdots a'_n, \tag{1}$$

where $a'_i = a_i \oplus f_{i-1}(a_1 \cdots a_{i-1})$ is bit i of the pseudonymized address, and a_i is bit i of the plaintext address. f_{i-1} is an encryption function, which takes as input a bitstring of length $i-1$, and returns a single bit.

4 Attacking Prefix-Preserving Pseudonymization

In this section we consider some weaknesses in prefix-preserving pseudonymization, relevant for both TCPdpriv and Crypto-PAn. We show that these methods do not provide sufficiently strong pseudonymization, at least not for IPv4. Based on this, we will present improvements in the next section.

First note that the set of all IP addresses in use can be represented by a binary search tree, where each leaf node represents a specific IP address. Edges are labeled with address bits, the most significant bits closest to the root node, and the least significant bits on the edges ending in the leaf nodes themselves.

4.1 Packet Injection Attack

Given our threat model (section 1.2), an adversary can send IP packets with arbitrary source and destination IP addresses, for example by spoofing IP addresses or sending packets from a variety of places. By forging a packet header or a traffic pattern in such a way that it is recognizable in its anonymized form, an adversary is able to find an exact match between an plaintext and an anonymized IP address. This is a general problem with pseudonymization schemes. The use of repeated messages for revealing the correspondence between plaintext and anonymized data is discussed by Chaum in [1] and referred to as *flush attacks* by Raymond in [10]. The forging of packet headers for reidentification purposes is related to the *message tagging* attack described by Raymond in [10].

In the case of prefix-preserving pseudonymization, a successful attack also reveals information about the prefix for all other addresses with identical prefixes. Using this, an adversary can build a binary tree mapping pseudonymized to plaintext IP addresses. For a directed attack, the adversary can build such a binary tree only for selected addresses, such as IP addresses associated with a specific person or organization.

4.2 Preparing an Injection Attack

If an adversary wants to find the traffic data associated with k specified IP addresses in a measurement set, there are significant advantages to be gained by carefully designing the injection patterns. The complexity one primarily wants to keep to a minimum in this context is "packet complexity"—the number of packets that need to be successfully injected in order to reach a particular attack goal. We present the algorithm for doing this.

The algorithm first constructs a binary search tree for the selected addresses. Nodes in this tree are capable of storing weights. After constructing the tree, it is recursively traversed to sum weights. This is done so that at each node with two descendants, the weights of each descendant are unbalanced. This allows the use of an algorithm that reveals addresses efficiently by exploiting the unbalanced weights. The algorithm makes use of the following composite data structure :

node=   begin structure
                 node $*a$ Pointer to ancestor node
                 node $*d_0$ Pointer to left descendant node
                 node $*d_1$ Pointer to right descendant node
                 integer w Weight
            end structure

C-style notation is used, with `<type> *<var-name>` defining a pointer of name `<var-name>` to a variable of type `<type>`. `*<var-name>` refers to the contents of the variable referenced by the pointer. `<var-name>` refers to the pointer itself. Assignment has the form `<var-name>←<expression>`.

Example 2. If t is a pointer to an instantiated node, then $*t$ refers to the node, $*t.a$ refers to the pointer to the ancestor node, and $*(*t.a)$ refers to the ancestor node itself.

Algorithm 1 below is used to build a binary search tree for the selected addresses. A more precise version of this pseudocode is given in appendix A. Algorithm 2 computes weights for each leaf node to ensure unbalanced packet distribution at all levels, so that algorithm 3 (see section 4.3) for probabilistic address matching is guaranteed to terminate with a correct result when restricted to the tree constructed by algorithm 1. The weight is the number of times an address must occur in successfully injected packets. More precise versions of algorithms 2 and 3 are given in appendix A.

PSEUDOCODE 1. *build-tree*$(n, k, \{I_i\}_{i=1}^k, b, a)$
IN: address length[8] n, number of addresses k, list of addresses $\{I_i\}_{i=1}^k$, bit depth b, pointer a to ancestor node
OUT: pointer r to local root node of binary tree

$t \leftarrow$ *pointer to newly allocated node*
if $b = 1$ then there is no ancestor, so $*t.a \leftarrow NULL$
if $b < n$ we are not at the bottom of the tree, so:
      split $\{I_i\}_{i=1}^k$ into h_0 with i_0 addresses with bit b equal to zero, and
                   h_1 with i_1 addresses with bit b equal to one.
      $*t.d_0 \leftarrow$ build-tree$(n, i_0, h_0, b+1, t)$
      $*t.d_1 \leftarrow$ build-tree$(n, i_1, h_1, b+1, t)$

---

[8] IP addresses contain either $n = 32$ bits (IPv4) or $n = 128$ bits (IPv6).

else if $b = n$ *we are at the bottom of the tree, so:*
    $*t.d_0 \leftarrow NULL$
    $*t.d_1 \leftarrow NULL$
     $*t.w \leftarrow 1$
end if
return t

PSEUDOCODE 2. *build-weights*(t, δ)
IN: *pointer t to a node in a tree built with build-tree, weight adjustment δ*
OUT: $*t.w$ *total weight of traversed and adjusted binary tree under node $*t$*

if $*t.d_0 = NULL$ *and* $*t.d_1 = NULL$ *then we are at the bottom of the tree, so:*
    increase the node weight by δ: $*t.w \leftarrow *t.w + \delta$
else if $*t.d_0 = NULL$ *and* $*t.d_1 \neq NULL$ *all descendants are to the right, so:*
    $*t.w \leftarrow$ *build-weights*$(*t.d_1, \delta)$
else if $*t.d_0 \neq NULL$ *and* $*t.d_1 = NULL$ *all descendants are to the left, so:*
    $*t.w \leftarrow$ *build-weights*$(*t.d_0, \delta)$
else
    left$\leftarrow$ *build-weights*$(*t.d_0, 0)$
    right$\leftarrow$ *build-weights*$(*t.d_1, \delta)$
    if left=right then the subtrees are equally weighted, so:
        right$\leftarrow$ *build-weights*$(*t.d_1, 1)$
    end if
    Assign weight of t to sum of weights of subtrees: $*t.w \leftarrow$ *left*+*right*
end if
return $*t.w$

After carrying out this preprocessing, the requisite packets must be successfully injected, and an anonymized measurement set, including header information for all these packets, collected. The injected packets are extracted from the measurement set. It is then possible to run algorithm 3 (see section 4.3) on these packets to reveal the desired addresses in worst-case time complexity nk' where n is the address length in bits, and k' is the number of successfully injected packets. In general $k' \geq k/2$, where k is the number of targeted addresses.

Finally note that these algorithms are designed for a scenario where $k \ll 2^n$. If k is of the same magnitude as 2^n, so that the adversary is attempting to find the plaintext versions of *all* anonymized addresses, other approaches are likely to be more efficient. In other words, the attack we have described is a general *system attack* for prefix-preserving pseudonymization algorithms, where a given address a always has only one pseudonym a'.

4.3   Frequency Analysis

A comprehensive overview of traffic analysis issues was given by Raymond in [10]. In this section, we discuss a type of traffic analysis based on the assumption that the adversary has a priori knowledge of the traffic distribution of the observed network. If an adversary a priori knows the traffic distribution relative to the address space, then it is possible to efficiently attack prefix-preserving pseudonymization and compromise selected addresses or subnets. We call this attack frequency analysis.

Denote by p_α the probability that a packet has an address with prefix α. The attack assumes the following:

1. The adversary knows all p_α for the network.
2. The measurements are protected by the same primary pseudonymization key, so that each address has only one pseudonym.

Denote by λ the empty string. Denote by "$\alpha\beta$" the string concatenation of the string α with β. Denote by $|\alpha|$ the length of bitstring α. Denote by $p_{\alpha\beta|\alpha}$ the probability that an address has a prefix $\alpha\beta$, given that it has a prefix α. Denote by $\oplus$ the bitwise exclusive-or operator.

PSEUDOCODE 3. *frequency-analysis*$(n, \{p_\eta\}_{\eta \in \{0,1\}^n}, \{\nu_i\}_{i=1}^{2m}, \omega)$

IN: address length n in bits, the relative frequency p_η at which a prefix η occurs in network traffic, IP addresses $\{\nu_i\}_{i=1}^{2m}$ encrypted with prefix-preserving pseudonymization taken from a measurement set consisting of m packets with in all $2m$ addresses, the plaintext address ω whose traffic data is of interest

OUT: a "decryption key" κ for the pseudonym for ω

set α and κ to the empty string λ
for all i from 1 to n do:
    initialize number of messages with bit i set to 0: $m_0 \leftarrow 0$
    initialize number of messages with bit i set to 0: $m_1 \leftarrow 0$
    for all j from 1 to m do:
        if $\alpha \oplus \kappa$ is a prefix of ν_j then
            increment $m_{\text{bit number } i \text{ from the source address}}$
        end if
    end for
    compute the square q_0 of the difference between $p_{\alpha 0|\alpha}$ and $\frac{m_0}{m_0+m_1}$
    compute the square q_0' of the difference between $p_{\alpha 0|\alpha}$ and $\frac{m_1}{m_0+m_1}$
    if $q_0 < q_0'$ then
        $\kappa \leftarrow \kappa 0$
    else
        $\kappa \leftarrow \kappa 1$
    end if
    append bit i of ω to α
end for
return κ

The pseudonymized address is thus $\kappa \oplus \omega$. The above algorithm has a worst-case running time of $\mathcal{O}(nm)$, assuming that bitstring comparison can be done in a constant number of operations. It is not guaranteed to reach a correct conclusion, especially if there is little difference between prefix probabilities for each possible node (that is: $p_{\alpha 0|\alpha} \approx p_{\alpha 1|\alpha}$).

If this algorithm is used in conjunction with the injection attack described in section 4.1, it is possible to restrict the algorithm to the constructed binary search tree, and compute all p_ηs using the weights in that tree. Finally, note that algorithms 1–3 can be applied to packets pseudonymized with any prefix-preserving pseudonymization system, including TCPdpriv and Crypto-PAn.

5   Strengthening Pseudonymization

The proposed strengthening bases itself on the assumption that the most interesting measurements are carried out on traffic between two parties A and B. Thus identifying individual nodes is not imperative per sé. Rather the identification of *pairs* of addresses is imperative. It is therefore possible to apply a hash or encryption function f to the concatenation of source and destination address. Denote by a the address of A, and by b the address of B.

5.1   Improving Prefix-Preserving Pseudonymization

In this section, we show how prefix-preserving pseudonymization schemes can be strengthened. The strengthening is provided as pseudocode 4, and a more precise version is given in appendix A.

The strengthening exploits the fact that it rarely is necessary to release all topological information. Denote by a the source address, and b the destination address. First of all, applications using traffic measurements often need only parts of the topological information. Second, it may be desirable to allow the regulated release of topological information as a differentiating factor to satisfy legal or business requirements. One way of doing this is to permute the bits of encrypted addresses. This removes any visible structure, but it does so in a reversible manner. This can be expressed as follows:

$$\mathcal{F}(a_1 \cdots a_n) = a'_{g(1)} \cdots a'_{g(n)}, \tag{2}$$

where $g : \{1, \ldots, n\} \longrightarrow \{1, \ldots, n\}$ is a permutation. It is possible to apply this permutation to the concatenation of source and destination addresses simultaneously.

PSEUDOCODE 4. *hardened-pseudonymization-1(n, a, b, g, F)*
IN: address length n in bits, source address a destination addresse b, a permutation function $g : \{1, \ldots, 2n\} \longrightarrow \{1, \ldots, 2n\}$, a prefix-preserving pseudonymization function F
OUT: two n-bit blocks a' and b' replacing the plaintext addresses a and b respectively.

if a lexicographically precedes b
    apply prefix-preserving pseudonymization F to a to get c_a
    apply prefix-preserving pseudonymization F to b to get c_b
    $s \leftarrow 0$
else
    apply prefix-preserving pseudonymization F to a to get c_b
    apply prefix-preserving pseudonymization F to b to get c_a
    $s \leftarrow 1$
end if
concatenate c_a and c_b to get c
permute the pseudonymized bits: $r \leftarrow c_{g(1)} \cdots c_{g(2n)}$
$a' \leftarrow$ first n bits of r
$b' \leftarrow$ last n bits of r
return a', b', s

By employing an injection attack, and repeating frequency analysis with different bits to find a best match, the hardened pseudonymization of algorithm 4 could still be broken in polynomial time, with at worst $\mathcal{O}(n^3 k)$ steps. This is done by first trying to identify imbalances in bit distributions bit-by-bit using the data in the constructed search tree, using a modified frequency analysis algorithm. This has to be done $2n + 2n - 1 + \ldots + 1$ times: $\mathcal{O}(n^2)$ times. Frequency analysis costs $\mathcal{O}(nk)$, so $\mathcal{O}(n^3 k)$ in all. Thus, this does still not provide the degree of protection we desire.

Another improvement is obtained by encrypting as large blocks as possible in one go, while still offering the opportunity to release prefix-preserving pseudonymized address data, if necessary. This can be achieved by splitting addresses into a series of l blocks, each block w_i bits in length. w_1 is the most significant block, and w_l the least significant block. Block l from source and destination are concatenated and encrypted, producing r_l. Block $l - 1$ from source and destination are concatenated, and then concatenated with r_l. This is then encrypted, producing r_{l-1}. This continues, until block 1 from source and destination are concatenated along with r_2, and all $2n$ bits encrypted. This is the essence of algorithm 5, given as pseudocode 5 below, and algorithm 5 in appendix A.

PSEUDOCODE 5.   *hardened-pseudonymization-2*$(n, a, b, l, \{w_i\}_{i=1}^l, e, F)$

IN: address length n in bits, source address a, destination address b, the number l of sub-blocks, a list $\{w_i\}_{i=1}^l$ of sub-block lengths such that $\sum_{i=1}^l w_i = n$, a keyed block encryption function e_k, that encrypts k-bit blocks, a prefix-preserving pseudonymization F

OUT: two n-bit blocks a' and b' replacing the plaintext addresses a and b, one bit s indicating whether a lexicographically precedes b or not

if a lexicographically precedes b
    apply prefix-preserving pseudonymization F to a to get c
    apply prefix-preserving pseudonymization F to b to get d
    $s \leftarrow 0$
else
    apply prefix-preserving pseudonymization F to a to get d
    apply prefix-preserving pseudonymization F to b to get c
    $s \leftarrow 1$
end if
$i \leftarrow l$
while $i > 0$ do:
    $p \leftarrow p - w_i$
    encrypt the concatenation of bits $p + 1, \ldots, p + w_i$ of c and d with
        the last $n - p$ bits from any previous encryption, if any with e_{n-p}
    $i \leftarrow i - 1$
end for
call the resulting cryptotext block r
$a' \leftarrow$ *first n bits of r*
$b' \leftarrow$ *last n bits of r*
return a', b', s

Algorithm 5 encrypts successively longer concatenations of corresponding blocks from source and destination addresses. Thus, each header is now coupled to *both* addresses in a communication. The adversary now sees all pseudonymized pairs.

The adversary is trying to identify the pseudonyms for a list of target addresses $\{I_i\}_{i=1}^{k}$. Since we assume that our injected packets are always recognizeable somehow, the adversary can extract the set of injected packets in their anonymized form. Assuming that all injected packets are in the trace, they can also be sorted in the weighted tree. The adversary can now identify some address pairs (I_i, I_j) or (I_j, I_i). The adversary is now able to identify selected sessions between two target addresses. The adversary cannot, however, recognize any single IP address in general.

Suppose the adversary wants to pick out all pseudonymized packets containing the IP address a in their headers. This assumption implies that the actual "set of interest" is $\{a\}$. To find all packets containing a, the adversary must generate all possible lexicographically sorted pairs (a, b) and (b, a) of ip addresses, where b is an IP address. This set can then be sorted in a binary search tree. The "set of interest" now contains 2^{n-1} elements, and the length of the elements is not n anymore, but $2n$. This results in two problems.

1. The number of packets required to mount an injection attack in conjunction with traffic analysis has become excessive: the adversary must expect that the injections will be noticed. This can be mitigated by executing a distributed injection attack. Of course, there is then the problem of collecting sufficient logs to carry out a subsequent analysis.
2. Even though a search tree has been constructed, only $2p$ out of $2n$ bits, $1 \le p \le n$, are tractably deducible. The rest have been encrypted with a strong block cipher, and should not be deducible using the type of analysis presented here.

5.2   Strengthening the Anonymization of Two-Way Sessions Using Hash Functions

One method of IP-address anonymization is hashing of IP addresses (see also subsection 2.2), which can be done for a large set of distributed measurement sites without any coordination between the sites. A cryptographically strong hash or encryption function f is applied to a (possibly padded) n-bit IP address, and retains the last w bits of the result. Usually $w = n$ to exploit available address fields to their fullest. This yields a unique identifier, that can be computed by any node. One limiting factor with respect to the security of such an anonymization, is the number of bits in an address: n.

Since f operates on ab (the concatenation of a and b's addresses), $2n$ bits of f's output must be retained. The scheme is presented in pseudocode 6.

PSEUDOCODE 6.   *block-anonymization*(n, a, b, f)

IN: address length in bits n, source address a, destination address b, cryptographically strong hash function f generating output at least $2n$ bits long, or keyed encryption function f with blocklength $2n$

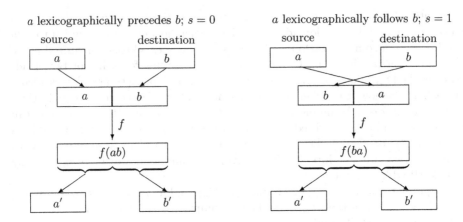

Fig. 1. Illustration of block anonymization shows how it provides bidirectional traffic with a unique hashed identifier, which is equal for both directions

OUT: two n-bit blocks a' and b' replacing the plaintext addresses a and b, respectively. One bit s indicating whether a lexicographically precedes b or not.

if a lexicographically precedes b
 return last 2n bits of $f(ab)$ as two n-bit bitstrings, along with $s = 0$
else
 return last 2n bits of $f(ba)$ as two n-bit bitstrings, along with $s = 1$
end if

A more precise version of pseudocode 6 is given in appendix A. The use of a key or initialization vector or both is implicit. Since a' and b' do not change if the packet's direction between A and B changes, s is used to keep track of the packet direction. If $s = 0$, then a' contains the source's half of the hash and b' the destination's half of the hash. If $s = 1$, then a' contains the destination's half of the hash, and b' the source's half.

The sheme ensures that packets sent between two specific addresses a and b have identical source and destination fields irrespective of packet direction. Packet direction is determined using s. If f is a block cipher, the plaintext addresses can be recovered with the correct key.

The single bit of plaintext search space lost through lexicographical ordering is insignificant. The net effect is to increase the size of the plaintext search space by a factor of 2^{n-1}, and presumably the time complexity of cryptographic attacks (such as the birthday attack) is increased by a factor of approximately $2^{(n-1)/2}$.

6   Conclusions

We have given a brief analysis of some functionally appropriate candidates for anonymization in a passive monitoring infrastructure.

Hashing of IP-addresses preserves linkability and the uniqueness of addresses, but it does not provide topological information. There are concerns that the short length of IPv4 addresses exposes IP address hashes to brute-force attacks. We have proposed a way of strengthening such hashes, while retaining their usefulness for session-oriented analysis. The scheme can be made reversible, depending on the parameter selection. The scheme increases plaintext search space by a factor of 2^{n-1}, and thus resistance to collisions by a factor of approximately $2^{(n-1)/2}$.

Prefix-preserving pseudonymization, such as Crypto-PAn, preserves information about the network topology. This is desirable for network research and operational applications. We have provided three algorithms for attacks which, using packet injection and frequency analysis, enable an adversary to compromise individual addresses in multilinear time.

To address these vulnerabilities, we present two algorithms that provide additional resistance against our attacks. they can be viewed as wrappers "around" the current prefix-preserving algorithms, providing literally an additional layer of protection. Both algorithms can be made reversible.

Acknowledgments

We thank our colleagues Svein J. Knapskog and Karin Sallhammar for their helpful comments. We also thank Mark Burgess at Oslo University College and Geoffrey Canright at Telenor Research and Development for interesting discussions.

References

1. Chaum, D.: Untraceable electronic mail, return addresses, and digital pseudonyms. Communications of the ACM **4** (1981)
2. Pfitzmann, A., Koehntopp, M.: Anonymity, unobservability, and pseudonymity – a proposal for terminology. In: Workshop on Design Issues in Anonymity and Unobservability. (2000)
3. Biskup, J., Flegel, U.: On pseudonymization of audit data for intrusion detection. In: Workshop on Design Issues in Anonymity and Unobservability, Springer-Verlag, LNCS 2009 (2000)
4. Sobirey, M., Fischer-Hübner, S., Rannenberg, K.: Pseudonymous audit for privacy enhanced intrusion detection. In: SEC. (1997) 151–163
5. Peuhkuri, M.: A method to compress and anonymize packet traces. Internet Measurement Workshop (San Francisco, California, USA: 2001) (2001) 257–261
6. Xu, J., Fan, J., Ammar, M., Moon, S.B.: On the design and performance of prefix-preserving ip traffic trace anonymization. In: Proceedings of the ACM SIGCOMM Internet Measurement Workshop 2001. (2001)
7. Xu, J., Fan, J., Ammar, M., Moon, S.B.: Prefix-preserving ip address anonymization: Measurement-based security evaluation and a new cryptography-based scheme. ICNP 2002 (2002)
8. Menezes, A.J., van Oorschot, P., Vanstone, S.: Handbook of Applied Cryptography. CRC Press (1996)

9. Slagell, A., Wang, J., Yurick, W.: Network log anonymization: Application of Crypto-PAn to Cisco Netflows. In: IEEE Workshop on Secure Knowledge Management (SKM). (2004)
10. Raymond, J.F.: Traffic analysis: Protocols, attacks, design issues, and open problems. In: Workshop on Design Issues in Anonymity and Unobservability, Springer-Verlag, LNCS 2009 (2000)
11. Forte, D.: Using tcpdump and sanitize for system security. ;login: **26** (2001)
12. Cho, K., Mitsuya, K., Kato, A.: Traffic data repository at the WIDE project. In: Proceedings of FREENIX Track: 2000 USENIX Annual Technical Conference. (2000) 263–270

A   Algorithms

This section contains a more precise description of the pseudocode algorithms presented in the main body of this article.

Algorithm 1 constructs a binary search tree for a selected list of IP addresses.

ALGORITHM 1. build-tree$(n, k, \{I_i\}_{i=1}^{k}, b, a)$

IN: n address length in bits
     k number of targeted addresses
     $\{I_i\}_{i=1}^{k}$ indexed list of addresses
     b bit depth
     a pointer to ancestor node

OUT: r pointer to local root node of the constructed binary tree

$t \leftarrow$ pointer to new allocated node
if $b = 1$ then
    $*t.a \leftarrow$ NULL
end if
$i_0 \leftarrow 0$
$i_1 \leftarrow 0$
$h(0,) \leftarrow ()$ h is a local two-dimensional array
$h(1,) \leftarrow ()$ Before using h, it must be emptied
if $b < n$ then
    $i \leftarrow 0$
    while $i < k$ do:
        $f \leftarrow$ bit number b in l_i
        if $f = 0$ then
            $i_0 \leftarrow i_0 + 1$
        else
            $i_1 \leftarrow i_1 + 1$
        end if
        $h(f, i_f) \leftarrow I_{i_f}$
    end while
    $*t.d_0 \leftarrow$ build-tree$(n, i_0, \{h(0, i)\}_{i=1}^{i_0}, b + 1, t)$
    $*t.d_1 \leftarrow$ build-tree$(n, i_1, \{h(1, i)\}_{i=1}^{i_1}, b + 1, t)$
else if $b = n$ then

```
    *t.d_0 ←NULL
    *t.d_1 ←NULL
    weight← 1
end if
return t
```

Algorithm 2 takes a binary search tree, and assigns weights to each node such that left descendants always have less weight than right descendants.

ALGORITHM 2. build-weights(t, δ)

IN: t pointer to a node in a tree built with build-tree
       δ weight adjustment

OUT: $*t.w$ total weight of traversed and adjusted binary tree under node $*t$

```
if *t.d_0 =NULL and *t.d_1 =NULL then
    *t.w ← *t.w + δ
else if *t.d_0 =NULL and *t.d_1 ≠NULL then
    *t.w ← build-weights(*t.d_1, δ)
else if *t.d_0 ≠NULL and *t.d_1 =NULL then
    *t.w ← build-weights(*t.d_0, δ)
else
    left← build-weights(*t.d_0, 0)
    right← build-weights(*t.d_1, δ)
    if left=right then
        right← build-weights(*t.d_1, 1)
    end if
    *t.w ←left+right
end if
return *t.w
```

Algorithm 3 takes occurrence probabilites for IP addresses, and extracts a sort of "decryption" key for addresses protected with prefix-preserving anonymization techniques.

ALGORITHM 3. frequency-analysis$(n, \{p_\eta\}_{\eta \in \{0,1\}^n}, \{\nu_i\}_{i=1}^{2m}, \omega)$

IN: n address length in bits, 32 for IPv4, 128 for IPv6
       p_η the relative frequency at which a prefix η occurs in the traffic
       $\{\nu_i\}_{i=1}^{2m}$ IP addresses encrypted with prefix-preserving pseudonymization
                taken from a measurement set consisting of m packets with
                in all $2m$ addresses
       ω the address whose traffic data is of interest

OUT: κ a "decryption key" for the encrypted representation of ω

```
α ← λ
κ ← λ
i ← 0
while i < n do:
```

$i \leftarrow i + 1$
$m_0 \leftarrow 0$
$m_1 \leftarrow 0$
$j \leftarrow 0$
while $j < m$ do:
    if $\alpha \oplus \kappa$ is a prefix of ν_j then
        $k \leftarrow$ bit number i from the source address
        $m_k \leftarrow m_k + 1$
    end if
end while
$q_0 \leftarrow (p_{\alpha 0 | \alpha} - m_0/(m_0 + m_1))^2$
$q_0' \leftarrow (p_{\alpha 0 | \alpha} - m_1/(m_0 + m_1))^2$
if $q_0 < q_0'$ then
    $\kappa \leftarrow \kappa 0$
else
    $\kappa \leftarrow \kappa 1$
end if
append bit i of ω to α
end while
return κ

Algorithm 4 employs a permutation of bits to increase the cost of deducing address bits from addresses pseudonymized with prefix-preserving pseudonymization.

ALGORITHM 4. hardened-pseudonymization-1(n, a, b, g, F)

IN: n address length in bits
       a, b source and destination addresses, respectively
       g a permutation function $\{1, \ldots, 2n\} \longrightarrow \{1, \ldots, 2n\}$
       F a prefix-preserving pseudonymization function

OUT: a', b' two n-bit blocks replacing the plaintext addresses a and b, respectively.

if a lexicographically precedes b
    apply prefix-preserving pseudonymization F to a to get c_a
    apply prefix-preserving pseudonymization F to b to get c_b
    $s \leftarrow 0$
else
    apply prefix-preserving pseudonymization F to a to get c_b
    apply prefix-preserving pseudonymization F to b to get c_a
    $s \leftarrow 1$
end if
$c \leftarrow c_a c_b$
$r \leftarrow c_{g(1)} \cdots c_{g(2n)}$
$a' \leftarrow$ first n bits of r
$b' \leftarrow$ last n bits of r
return a', b', s

Algorithm 5 employs strong encryption in conjunction with a concatenation scheme to both increase the effective plaintext space, and strengthen prefix-preserving pseudonymization.

ALGORITHM 5. hardened-pseudonymization-2$(n, a, b, l, \{w_i\}_{i=1}^l, e_k, F)$

IN: n address length in bits
         a, b source and destination addresses, respectively
         l number of sub-blocks
         $\{w_i\}_{i=1}^l$ sub-block lengths such that $\sum_{i=1}^l w_i = n$
         e_k keyed block encryption function that encrypts k-bit blocks
         F a prefix-preserving pseudonymization function

OUT: a',b' two n-bit blocks replacing the plaintext addresses a and b,
                respectively
       s one bit indicating whether a lexicographically precedes b or not

if a lexicographically precedes b
    apply prefix-preserving pseudonymization F to a to get c
    apply prefix-preserving pseudonymization F to b to get d
    $s \leftarrow 0$
else
    apply prefix-preserving pseudonymization F to a to get d
    apply prefix-preserving pseudonymization F to b to get c
    $s \leftarrow 1$
end if
$i \leftarrow l$
$p \leftarrow n$
while $i > 0$ do:
    $p \leftarrow p - w_i$
    $r_i \leftarrow e_{n-p}(c_{p+1} \cdots c_{p+w_i} d_{p+1} \cdots d_{p+w_i} r_{i+1} \cdots r_l)$
    $i \leftarrow i - 1$
end while
$a' \leftarrow$ first n bits of r
$b' \leftarrow$ last n bits of r
return a', b', s

Algorithm 6 employs a concatenation scheme that increases the effective plaintext space. This increases the time complexity of birthday attacks by a factor of approximately $2^{(n-1)/2}$, where n is the address length in bits.

ALGORITHM 6. block-anonymization(n, a, b, f)

IN: n address length in bits, 32 for IPv4, 128 for IPv6
         a, b source and destination addresses, respectively
         f cryptographically strong hash function generating output at least
                $2n$ bits long, or keyed encryption function with blocklength $2n$

OUT: a',b' two n-bit blocks replacing the plaintext addresses a and b,
                respectively.
       s one bit indicating whether a lexicographically precedes b or not.

if a lexicographically precedes b
    $c \leftarrow ab$
    $s \leftarrow 0$
else
    $c \leftarrow ba$
    $s \leftarrow 1$
end if
$r \leftarrow$ last $2n$ bits of $f(c)$
$a' \leftarrow$ first n bits of r
$b' \leftarrow$ last n bits of r
return a', b', s

B   Anonymization and Pseudonymization Tools

The authors of this article have looked into several tools for IP traffic anonymization. Some of these tools are listed in the following table.

Table 1. Network trace anonymization tools

Tool	URL
Sanitize [11]	http://ita.ee.lbl.gov/html/contrib/sanitize.html
ip2anonip	http://dave.plonka.us/ip2anonip/
tcpdpriv [6, 7]	http://ita.ee.lbl.gov/html/contrib/tcpdpriv.html
wide-tcpdpriv [12]	http://tracer.csl.sony.co.jp/mawi/
Crypto-PAn [6, 7]	http://www.cc.gatech.edu/computing/Telecomm/cryptopan/

Privacy Issues in Vehicular Ad Hoc Networks

Florian Dötzer

BMW Group Research and Technology
Hanauerstrasse 46
80992 Munich, Germany
florian.doetzer@bmw.de

Abstract. Vehicular Ad hoc NETworks (VANETs) demand a thorough investigation of privacy related issues. On one hand, users of such networks have to be prevented from misuse of their private data by authorities, from location profiling and from other attacks on their privacy. On the other hand, system operators and car manufacturers have to be able to identify malfunctioning units for sake of system availability and security. These requirements demand an architecture that can really manage privacy instead of either providing full anonymity or no privacy at all. In this paper we give an overview on the privacy issues in vehicular ad hoc networks from a car manufacturer's perspective and introduce an exemplary approach to overcome these issues.

1 Introduction

A mobile ad hoc network (MANET) consists of mobile nodes that connect themselves in a decentralized, self-organizing manner and may also establish multihop routes. If the mobile nodes are cars this is called Vehicular Ad Hoc Network (VANET). The main difference between VANETs and MANETs is that the nodes move with higher average speed and the number of nodes is assumed to be very large[1]. Apart from that, VANETs will be operated or at least rolled-out by multiple companies and the nodes belong to people within different organizational structures.

One important property that characterizes both MANETs and VANETs is that they are self-organizing and decentralized systems. Successful approaches for security and privacy therefore must not rely on central services or mandatory connections to some fixed infrastructure. However, as connections to central authorities may not be completely inevitable, we assume that in some exactly specified situations such as during production or regular maintenance processes, a car would have access to central services.

1.1 Applications for VANETs

One of the most promising applications in the various car manufacturers' activities are local danger warning messages. In Fig. 1 you can see a simple example of

---

[1] At the moment, there are in the order of some hundreds of millions of cars registered worldwide.

G. Danezis and D. Martin (Eds.): PET 2005, LNCS 3856, pp. 197–209, 2006.

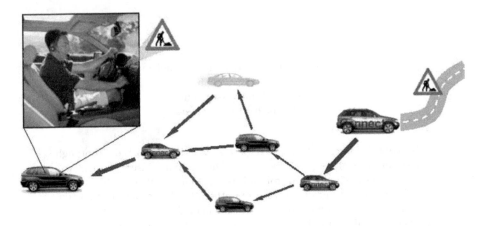

Fig. 1. Local Danger Warning

such a system. The idea is that cars can generate messages about safety related events, such as accidents, road conditions, their own behaviour (e.g. emergency braking) and so on. These messages will then be distributed using wireless communication systems to neighboring cars. If there are no immediate neighbors, cars may also store messages and deliver them by moving along the road until new communication partners are found. The cars' systems can therefore gather information that is relevant for their human drivers. The drivers can then be informed about relevant events, depending on context and situation.

Safety related events are quite different in the way they can be detected, as pointed out in [1]. First, there are events that can be detected by a single car's sensors. In that case local sensor information is aggregated and if there is a matching event, a message will be sent out.[2] Second, there are events such as traffic jams, that may not be detected by a single car, but if multiple cars' position information is aggregated, a car may conclude that it is in or before a traffic jam. In this example, it is easy to understand, that matching the information is critical for reliability, but may also affect privacy.

Other applications are more related to entertainment, media and non-safety information. For example car-to-car messaging, information download at gas stations or public hotspots, and car-to-car information exchange such as points of interest. Some of these applications will be free, while others would require a service subscription or a one-time payment.

In the context of privacy it is important to mention that in order to operate such a network it seems inevitable that nodes exchange neighborhood information on a regular basis. Every node will once in a while send a hello beacon, containing at least an identifier, a timestamp based on a global system time[3] and its position.

---

[2] This is on a logical level. In our system, the number of messages related to one event depends on different environment parameters.

[3] In our case, a global system time is based on satellite navigation

1.2 VANET Privacy in Research Projects and Standardization

Currently, there are some car-to-car network research projects which have operational prototypes, such as FleetNet [2], Carisma [3] and VSC. However, only the VSC project dealt with security, where privacy has only been a minor issue. Out of the ongoing funded research projects, such as VSC-2, NOW, Prevent, Invent VLA, etc. only NOW and VSC-2 made considerable efforts to accomodate privacy so far. Nevertheless, security and privacy are enabling technologies for the applications those projects envision. The Car-to-Car Communications Consortium, which has been founded recently, aims at standardizing car-to-car communications. It strongly encourages privacy enhancing concepts in this context. Other activities, such as IEEE's P1556 working group, have been raising security and privacy concerns and standards bodies like ISO's TC204/WG16 are discussing privacy now.

It seems that privacy has been recognized as an enabler for VANETs. But we are still lacking appropriate technologies and architectures to accomodate the requirements.

In section 2 we will outline several problems related to privacy in VANETS. In section 4 we will present one potential solution and evaluate its advantages and disadvantages. Section 3 will point to related work. In section 5 we will discuss open points and conclude in section 6.

2 Privacy Issues

2.1 Why Is Privacy Important for VANETs?

We live in a world where almost any data is available electronically. What protects us from Orwell's nightmare is mainly the incompatibility of the systems and organizational separation. Cars are personal devices, they are usually kept for a long time and in the future they will probably store lots of personal information as well. In many societies, cars are status symbols and a lot of personal behavior can be derived from the car a person is driving. Last but not least, most of the future's automobiles will be equipped with navigation systems and therefore technically be able to gather complete movement patterns of its user. All of this would not be much of a problem as long as the car is an isolated system. But future cars will have various communication capabilites. Electronic tolling systems, internet access, maintenance systems, software and media download, off-board navigation systems are just some examples why cars will get connected.

Although most people are not aware of the implications information society has on their privacy, their perception is (hopefully) changing over time. Discussions about Radio Frequency Identification Tags have already generated protests in european countries. In the automotive market, customers can choose among a large variety of products and there is a strong competition among automakers. Customers that are concerned about a new technology would probably pick products that reflect their concerns. It is therefore a vital interest of all car manufacturers promoting car-to-car communication technology, to pay close attention to security and privacy of such systems.

A very dangerous and often ignored fact about privacy is that innocent looking data from various sources can be accumulated over a long period and evaluated automatically. Even small correlations of the data may reveal useful information. For instance, the knowledge about specific sensor characteristics may give some hints about the make and the model of car. This in turn may be related to other information to identify a specific car. And once privacy is lost, it is very hard to re-establish that state of personal rights.

Privacy sometimes contradicts with security requirements. While system operators want to find or identify attackers to take proper countermeasures, the ability to do so may be used for less noble reasons. Newsome, Shi, Song and Perrig presented a paper about sybil attacks in sensor networks [4]. One of their proposed countermeasures is registering nodes in the network. This concept is somewhat similar to the idea of electronic license plates. While their approach is absolutely reasonable for sensor networks, registration could turn out to be a major privacy concern in VANETs.

In section 4 we will outline a solution that address both, security and privacy concerns.

2.2 Privacy Threats

During our work, we found a couple of situations, where privacy should be discussed. As mentioned before, sometimes it is not desirable to achieve perfect privacy. But it has to be decided which degree of privacy is necessary under given circumstances and the system has to be designed accordingly.

In the following we will give some examples for the problems we have to tackle in a widespread VANET.

- The police uses hello beacons[4] to calculate driving behavior and issues speeding tickets.
- An employer is overhearing the communications from cars on the company parking lot. After distinguishing which car-identifier belongs to which employee he automatically gets exact arrival and departure dates.
- A private investigator easily follows a car without being noticed by extracting position information from messages and hello beacons.
- Insurance companies gather detailed statistics about movement patterns of cars. In some cases individual persons may be charged for traffic accidents based on gathered movement patterns.
- A criminal organization has access to stationary communication boxes and uses the accumulated information to track law enforcement vehicles. The same technique could be used by a foreign secret service to track VIPs.

As we can see from these examples, most issues are related to position and identifiers. More specifically, either keeping identifiers and relating them to other received identifiers (re-recognition) or correlating the identifier with a real-world

---

[4] Hello beacons are used in mobile ad-hoc networks to maintain information about the nodes' neighborhood.

identity (identification). Analyzing the relations of various position-identifier pairs, a multitude of attacks on privacy can be carried out, where the given examples represent only a small subset.

The first example might be the easiest to resolve, because in most countries a defendant is innocent until it can be proven that he is guilty. In our case that means that the police must be able to prove that the culprit is really the one who was speeding. So instead of using one's original identity in the system, a pseudonym may be used. Unless there is no perfectly provable mapping between the pseudonym and real-world identity, the police would have a hard time issuing a ticket. In the second example this may not be enough, because the employer has other means of correlating real-world identities and car-identifiers. And he may guess as well. In this case, it would be desirable to change the car's identifiers from time to time. In the third example however, even these precautions would not be sufficient. To prevent being followed, the car's identifier would have to be changed while moving. One possible approach are geo-bound pseudonyms, discussed in section 5.2 Note that a concept considering changing identifiers on application layer also means that all lower layers must change their addresses / identifiers at least as often as application layer IDs. This would require frequent changes of MAC-addresses and network addresses for instance. Some simple experiments with our prototypes have shown that this is doable in principle, but remains an extremely challenging task for large systems. In addition this will definitely decrease overall performance due to collisions and/or increased signaling overhead.

In scenarios where a car communicates with a dedicated partner, we assume that in some cases the car's real identity will be required for service usage. In such a case it is obvious that the communication partner has the identity anyway, so the identity must only be protected from neighbors overhearing the communication. In [5] we proposed a vehicle - traffic light communication protocol that keeps the identity of the vehicle hidden from third party observers.

A good thing about mobility is that real (communication-)traffic analysis would probably be hard to do, since nodes usually move at high speed and in large geographic areas. But nevertheless, an attacker might use the properties of communicating vehicles as an aid for tracking a specific car. Even if identifiers are anonymized and addresses are changed frequently, there are ways to distinguish a node from others, such as characteristic packet sizes, special timings, RF-fingerprints [5].

2.3 Privacy Related Requirements

After the previous sections, we now identify a number of requirements to achieve adequate privacy.

1. It is possible to use pseudonyms as identifiers instead of real-world identities.
2. It is possible to change these pseudonyms.

---

[5] An RF fingerprint in this context means that the hardware of a node has a specific signature within the radio spectrum.

3. The number of pseudonym changes depends on the application and its privacy threat model.
4. Pseudonyms used during communication can be mapped to real-world identities in special situations.
5. A set of properties and/or privileges can be cryptographically bound to one or more pseudonyms.

This discusses only the primary requirements with respect to the VANET messaging system. There might be other important things to consider such as user interfaces and usability issues.

3   Related Work

There has been some work in various areas relevant for us. Samfat, Molva and Asokan provide a classification for mobile networks such as GSM and CDPD, where they map privacy requirements to various network entities (home domain, remote domain, legitimate network entities, and eavesdroppers)[6]. They also discuss the effects of these requirements on system design.

Golle, Greene and Staddon have presented a very useful paper [7] on detection and correction of malicious data in VANETs. We share their opinion that comparing the data of different information sources is a fundamental approach to solve problems with aggregation of sensor data. Concerning privacy they point out that there is a tradeoff between privacy and detection of malicious data depending on how often an identifier is changed. Hubaux, Capkun and Luo gave an overview on security and privacy in VANETs in [8]. Others are investigating "Metropolitan Area Ad Hoc Networks" [9] and Yih-Chun Hu has shown how attackers can get privacy-sensitive information in this context.

Weimerskirch and Westhoff presented a protocol [10] that allows nodes that do not have any additional knowledge to re-recognize themselves when meeting again. Their approach allows maximum privacy while still providing immutable and non-migratable identities. There has also been some work on mapping identifiers and cryptographic material. In [11] and [12] the authors describe a way to derive identifiers from pre-existing cryptographic keys in such a way, that they are statistically unique and cryptographically verifiable. Going the other way around and starting with given identities such as email addresses, Shamir presented an identity based signature scheme in [13], but he was unable to do encryption using this concept. It was Boneh / Franklin and Cocks who independently proposed ways to do identity based encryption in [14] and [15] respectively.

4   An Approach to Privacy in VANETs

4.1   Identification and Addressing

An intriguing question in the context of privacy is whether we need identification in a VANET or only some form of addressing. In the latter case, we only have to make sure that messages reach their destination(s), while identification of a sender depends on the application's requirements and must therefore be solved by the application itself. In the case of safety-related messages there is no need for identification. What we need here is an assertion that the sender is equipped with standard-compliant sensors / communication system and that it is working according to specifications.

4.2 Architecture

In our recent work, we have been looking at a trusted third party approach supported by smart cards. A major requirement has been the use of non-interactive protocols, since most security-related messages will be sent in broadcast[6] style.

The fundamental idea in our architecture is that there will be an authority A, that is trusted by all parties participating in the network: customers, manufacturers, system operators, service providers, etc. Gordon Peredo has presented such an architecture in [16]. The authority must be independent from other parties' interests and obtain special legislative protection. Authority A stores real-world identities and maps one or more pseudonyms to each identity. The mapping is kept secret and will only be revealed in exactly specified situations.

4.3 Assumptions

In order for our system to work, we assume that every car will be equipped with a hard-mounted, non-removable tamper resistant device such as a smart card. It offers two main features: secure memory to store secrets and secure computation to execute small programs and cryptographic algorithms. In our prototype implementation we use G&D's Java Card [17], [18]. We further assume that during production of a car a secure connection between this device and authority A is available. This can be realized using Smart Card Management Systems such as Visa's Global Platform [19], which enables "secure channels" from smart cards to backend hardware security modules (HSMs) [20].

4.4 Three Phases of Operation

We distinguish three phases in the lifecycle of a single vehicle. The initialization phase where the systems of a vehicle are set up. The operational phase as the major mode of operation, where vehicles can send messages signed according to a chosen pseudonym. And the credential revocation phase, where predefined situations can lead to the disclosure of a vehicle's real ID and the shutdown of its system.

Initialization Phase. Fig. 2 gives an overview on the entities in this architecture. Each car is equipped with a smart card during its production that is fixed physically and cannot be removed without destruction. The smart card

---

[6] Note broadcast here is on application level. This does not necessarily mean that data link layer transmission is broadcast

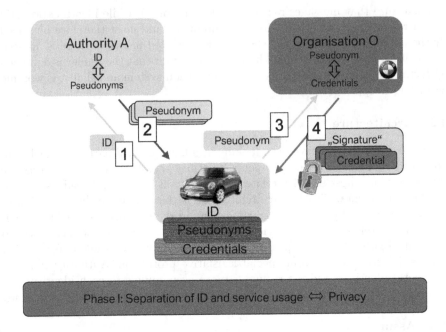

Fig. 2. Phase I

(and therefore also the car) is associated with a unique, immutable and non-migratable electronic ID. A secure communication link is established between the smart card and authority A. The smart card transmits the ID (1) and the authority cryptographically derives a set of pseudonyms from that ID after checking it. The pseudonyms are then transmitted back to the smart card (2). Now the car is ready to subscribe for various services. For every pseudonym (3) the car can get multiple service subscriptions from organization O, typically a car manufacturer. For every pseudonym organization O generates a set credentials, one for each service and sends it back (4). The car is now ready for use.

Operational Phase. During normal operation a car may choose any of its pseudonyms and the related credentials to testify its rights or sign messages, see Fig. 3. A communication partner can therefore always check the credentials in order to verify the car's compliance with common standards, its right to use a service or other properties that have been approved by organization O.

Credential Revocation Phase. Fig. 4 shows what happens if a vehicle sends wrong data. If there is a serious malfunction of a car such as transmission of malicious data (1), other participants of the network will file reports and send their evidence to organization O (2). Organization O must gather the evidence of this malfunctioning unit in order to apply at authority A for identification resolution and service shutdown (3). If the evidence is sufficient to allow for ID disclosure, authority A will compute a reverse mapping from a pseudonym to

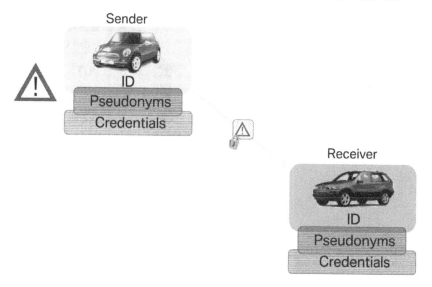

Fig. 3. Phase II

the real identity (4). Thus, organization O can find malfunctioning or malicious nodes and therefore maintain the long-term availability of the system.

Note that during the normal operation, the ID, all pseudonyms and credentials are stored in a tamper resistant smart card and therefore some protection against misuse is provided.

4.5 Evaluation

One alternative to our approach is to use pseudonyms that are not related to a real ID. The downside of this concept is that it is not possible to find a certain malfunctioning or misbehaving nodes. However, in some cases it may be sufficient to guarantee that every device can only use one single pseudonym at a time.

The other extreme, using unique identifiers, does not provide sufficient privacy.

5   Additional Considerations

The approach we presented in section 4 is one of many possible solutions. There are some general issues that we believe have to be solved.

5.1   MIX-Zones

[21] defines anonymity as "the state of being not identifiable within a set of subjects, the anonymity set". That is something to keep in mind when proposing

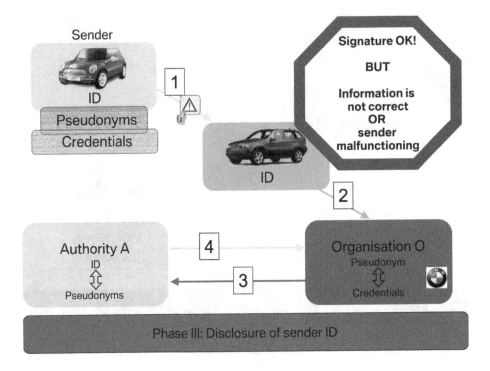

Fig. 4. Phase III

to change pseudonyms on the move. For example if a vehicle using pseudonym A does not want to be tracked and therefore changes its pseudonym to B. If an observer monitors all communication traffic around this vehicle and if this vehicle sends messages during observation (such as beacons), then the observer can relate pseudonym A and B as long as this vehicle is the only one (or one of few) changing its pseudonym. In other words, if you cannot hide in a crowd of pseudonym changing vehicles, you must assume that an observer can link your old pseudonym and your new one, making this process useless.

There are two straightforward approaches to this problem. First, you don't transmit something using your pseudonym for a sufficiently long time before and after a pseudonym change. Or second, the system design specifies times where all cars within a certain region, called MIX-zone, change their pseudonym. Such a region would ideally be a place, where a lot of vehicles are within communications range. There must be a sufficient number of such places to ensure that vehicles can change their pseudonyms frequently. It remains an open question what happens if there are not enough other nodes changing their pseudonyms at the same place.

5.2   Geo-bound Pseudonyms

In some scenarios, where (road-)traffic monitoring and generation of movement patterns are of major concern, we already concluded that it is desirable to change pseudonyms on the move. However, when thinking about decentralized trust in a mobile ad hoc network, for some concepts, such as keeping reputation information, it is necessary to re-recognize cars. This requirements can fortunately be reduced to re-recognition of nodes within a certain area. In such cases, it may be useful to dedicate a set of pseudonyms to predefined regions. That means for every geographic position there is a set of associated pseudonyms available, being a true subset of all pseudonyms used by that single vehicle.

Note that the boundaries of those individually different regions must reflect the arguments of the previous section.

5.3 Feasibility of Organizational Solutions

Apart from purely technological questions, we need to investigate whether organizational solutions such as the one we proposed in section 4 are feasible economically and legally. A company that sells products worldwide has to consider many different legal systems. Especially civil rights are handled quite differently and privacy is something that people cannot rely on in many countries. Regarding our approach, it has to be determined for each country in question whether there are regulatory aspects that require a system operator to provide access to central identification data. The architecture that we presented will only work in a legal environment where authority A is protected from outside access other than specified revocation requests. The incidence documented on [22] shows that even in countries with strong privacy laws such as Germany this is a difficult task and would require intensive lobbying. The problem with a central database is that once it is there, there will always be voices in favor of exploiting it.

Another downside of the proposed solution is that authority A must not be within organizational control of a single (car-) manufacturer. Unfortunately that means that multiple companies must agree on the modes of operation, standards have to be defined and a business model has to be created for the operation of centralized services.

6   Conclusion

In this paper we discussed some threats to privacy in VANETs and argued why privacy is important. We also pointed out that the degree of privacy depends on user preferences, environmental settings, and application requirements and should therefore be adjustable. We proposed a possible solution, based on prototypical experiments that we made and discussed its strengths and weaknesses.

In the future, we will further improve the presented concept and look at alternative approaches more thoroughly. Maybe it is possible to operate a traffic-related car-to-car messaging system without using identifiers and without requiring nodes to send periodic beacons. This would be desirable, not only from a privacy perspective, but also from a complexity and cost viewpoint. At the moment it is unclear if such an approach is feasible.

Acknowledgements

We would like to thank Uwe Baumgarten for inspiring discussions and valuable comments. We would also like to thank the anonymous reviewers, whose comments and suggestions stimulated new thoughts and helped to improve the paper.

References

1. Doetzer, F., Kosch, T., Strassberger, M.: Classification for traffic related inter-vehicle messaging. In: Proceedings of the 5th IEEE International Conference on ITS Telecommunications, Brest, France (2005)
2. Franz, W., Eberhardt, R., Luckenbach, T.: Fleetnet - internet on the road. In: Proceedings of the 8th World Congress on Intelligent Transportation Systems. (2001)
3. Kosch, T.: Local danger warning based on vehicle ad-hoc networks: Prototype and simulation. In: Proceedings of 1st International Workshop on Intelligent Transportation (WIT 2004). (2004)
4. Newsome, J., Shi, E., Song, D., Perrig, A.: The sybil attack in sensor networks: analysis & defenses. In: IPSN'04: Proceedings of the third international symposium on Information processing in sensor networks, ACM Press (2004) 259–268
5. Dötzer, F., Kohlmayer, F., Kosch, T., Strassberger, M.: Secure communication for intersection assistance. In: Proceedings of the 2nd International Workshop on Intelligent Transportation, Hamburg, Germany (2005)
6. Samfat, D., Molva, R., Asokan, N.: Anonymity and untraceability in mobile networks. ACM International Conference on Mobile Computing and Networking (1995)
7. Golle, P., Greene, D., Staddon, J.: Detecting and correcting malicious data in vanets. In: VANET '04: Proceedings of the first ACM workshop on Vehicular ad hoc networks, ACM Press (2004) 29–37
8. Hubaux, J.P., Capkun, S., Luo, J.: Security and privacy of smart vehicles. IEEE Security & Privacy 2 (2004) 49–55
9. Jetcheva, J., Hu, Y.C., PalChaudhuri, S., Saha, A., Johnson, D.: Design and evaluation of a metropolitan area multitier wireless ad hoc network architecture. In: Proceedings of the 5th IEEE Workshop on Mobile Computing Systems & Applications, Monterey, CA, USA, IEEE (2003) 32 – 43
10. Weimerskirch, A., Westhoff, D.: Zero common-knowledge authentication for pervasive networks. In: Selected Areas in Cryptography. (2003) 73–87
11. O'Shea, G., Roe, M.: Child-proof authentication for mipv6 (cam). SIGCOMM Comput. Commun. Rev. 31 (2001) 4–8
12. Montenegro, G., Castelluccia, C.: Statistically unique and cryptographically verifiable (sucv) identifiers and addresses. In: Proceedings of the Network and Distributed System Security Symposium (NDSS). (2002)
13. Shamir, A.: Identity-based cryptosystems and signature schemes. In: Proceedings of CRYPTO '84, Springer-Verlag (1984) 47–53
14. Boneh, D., Franklin, M.: Identity-based encryption from the weil pairing. In: Proceedings of CRYPTO 2001, Springer-Verlag (2001) 213–229
15. Cocks, C.: An identity based encryption scheme based on quadratic residues. In: Proceedings of IMA 2001, Springer-Verlag (2001) 360–363
16. Peredo, G.: Brake-ing news – technologies for inter-vehicle communication (2003)

17. Sun Microsystems: Java card 2.2 runtime environment specification (2002)
18. Sun-Microsystems: Java card 2.2 virtual machine specification (2002)
19. Global Platform: Global platform card specification (version 2.1) (2001)
20. Dötzer, F.: Aspects of multi-application smart card management systems. Master's thesis, Technical University Munich (2002)
21. Pfitzmann, A., Köhntopp, M.: Anonymity, unobservability, and pseudonymity - a proposal for terminology. In Federrath, H., ed.: Proceedings of Workshop on Design Issues in Anonymity and Unobservability, Springer (2001) 1–9
22. Independent Centre for Privacy Protection: First partial success for an.on (2003)
23. Wright, J., Stepney, S., Clark, J., Jacob, J.: Designing anonymity - a formal basis for identity hiding. Internal yellow report, York University, York, UK (2004)

High-Power Proxies for Enhancing
RFID Privacy and Utility

Ari Juels[1], Paul Syverson[2], and Dan Bailey[1]

[1] RSA Laboratories
Bedford, MA 01730, USA
{ajuels, dbailey}@rsasecurity.com
[2] Naval Research Laboratory
Washington, D.C. 20375, USA
syverson@itd.nrl.navy.mil

Abstract. A basic radio-frequency identification (RFID) tag is a small and inexpensive microchip that emits a static identifier in response to a query from a nearby reader. Basic tags of the "smart-label" variety are likely to serve as a next-generation replacement for barcodes. This would introduce a strong potential for various forms of privacy infringement, such as invasive physical tracking and inventorying of individuals.

Researchers have proposed several types of external devices of moderate-to-high computational ability that interact with RFID devices with the aim of protecting user privacy. In this paper, we propose a new design principle for a personal RFID-privacy device. We refer to such a device as a REP (*RFID Enhancer Proxy*).

Briefly stated, a REP assumes the identities of tags and simulates them by proxy. By merit of its greater computing power, the REP can enforce more sophisticated privacy policies than those available in tags. (As a side benefit, it can also provide more flexible and reliable communications in RFID systems.) Previous, similar systems have been vulnerable to a serious attack, namely malicious exchange of data between RFID tags. An important contribution of our proposal is a technique that helps prevent this attack, even when tags do not have access-control features.

1 Introduction

In this paper, we propose the design of a new type of device for protecting consumer privacy with respect to RFID. We refer to this device as a REP (*RFID Enhancer Proxy*). Before explaining the aims and functioning of a REP, we first review background on RFID and its associated privacy problems.

A passive *radio-frequency identification* (RFID) tag is a microchip that is capable of transmitting a static identifier or serial number for a short distance. It is typically activated by a query from a nearby reader, which also transmits power for the operation of the tag. Several varieties of RFID tag are already familiar in daily life. Examples include the ExxonMobil Speedpass^{TM} payment device, the small plaques mounted on car windshields for the purpose of automated toll payment, and the proximity cards used to control physical access to buildings.

G. Danezis and D. Martin (Eds.): PET 2005, LNCS 3856, pp. 210–226, 2006.

The cost of rudimentary RFID tags, sometimes called "smart labels," promises to drop to roughly $0.05/unit in the next several years [19]. Tags as small as 0.4mm × 0.4mm, and thin enough to be embedded in paper are already commercially available [23]. Such improvements in cost and size will mean a rapid proliferation of RFID tags into many areas of use. The United States Department of Defense and major retailers such as Wal-mart have issued mandates to their top suppliers requring RFID deployment starting in 2005.

One goal of RFID-tag development is to see RFID serve ubiquitously as a replacement for barcodes. The main industry consortium advancing this goal is EPCglobal, a joint venture between the UCC and EAN, the organizations overseeing barcode use in the United States and Europe. EPCglobal is the standards-setting body for a system of standardized "electronic product codes" (EPC) analogous to the printed barcode used universally on consumer products today. (See, e.g., [13] for a description of a 96-bit EPC standard.) Broadly speaking, the vision is for RFID tags to serve as unique identifiers. These identifiers may serve as pointers to database entries, thereby allowing the compilation of extensive automated histories for individual items. EPCglobal has recently ratified its Class 1 Generation 2 standard, which will likely dictate basic tag architectures for some time to come.

Improved supply-chain management is the initial goal of major RFID deployments in the next few years. Pallets of goods will carry RFID tags so as to automate inventory tracking.

The present cost of RFID tags is such that prevalent RFID-tagging of individual goods in retail environments will be impractical for some years. Pilots are already afoot, however, and with improved manufacturing processes and larger economies of scale, as well as technological innovations like plastic circuits, item-level tagging seems inevitable.

Basic item-level RFID tagging promises many benefits, allowing flexible and intelligent handling of consumer goods and devices. Among the intruiging possibilities are:

- *Receiptless item returns:* Retailers can record the purchase conditions of an item in a database entry for its attached RFID tag. This would permit customers to return items without receipts. With RFID tags used to record the full lifcycle of an item, retailers would benefit from the ability to track the source of item defects.

- *"Smart" appliances:* With RFID tagging of foodstuffs, refrigerators could alert consumers to the presence of expired or recalled comestibles, and also compile shopping lists automatically based on a scan of their contents. Washing machines could use RFID-tagged articles of apparel to select an appropriate wash cycle. Microwave ovens could use RFID tags on cartons of food to determine an appropriate power setting and cooking regime.

- *Aids to the handicapped:* Researchers at Intel are exploring ways in which RFID may furnish information to aid Alzheimer's patients in navigating their environments.

- *Recycling:* Sorting recyclables is a resource-intensive process. RFID tags could permit automated identification of different types of recyclable plastics and other materials.
- *Smart phones:* Mobile phone manufacturers have plans to embed RFID readers in their handsets [16]. Consumers could use such devices to scan movie posters for showtimes, to scan products so as to make price comparisons, and so forth.

1.1   The Privacy Problem

The impending ubiquity of RFID tags, however, also poses a potentially widespread threat to consumer privacy [14] and likewise to the privacy of corporate data. The initial RFID-chip designs proposed by EPCglobal are geared toward general corporate and consumer use. So as to permit inexpensive manufacture, tags of this kind carry only the most basic functionality, emitting a static, 96-to-256-bit identifier (EPC) on receiving a reader query [19]. Such a system would divulge a large amount of information about ordinary consumers. This threat is twofold: (1) Thanks to their unique identifiers, RFID tags could permit indiscriminate physical tracking of individuals, and (2) As RFID tags may carry product information (as in EPCglobal standards), they would permit surreptitious inventorying of their bearers and could facilitate corporate espionage. An attacker scanning the RFID tags contained in personal items could in principle gather information about a victim's clothing, medications, memberships and financial status (via RFID tags in wallet cards), and so forth. An attacker gaining access to RFID information in warehouses or store shelves can glean valuable corporate intelligence.

The privacy issues raised by RFID tags in the consumer domain have received considerable coverage in the popular press and attention from privacy advocates. Early fuel for these concerns included a purported plan by the European Central Bank to embed RFID tags in Euro banknotes. Public outcry has since forced the postponement or withdrawal of several retail RFID pilot projects. A number of states in the United States, including Utah, California, and Massachusetts have embarked upon legislation to address the problems of RFID privacy. (It should be noted that legislation in California was defeated this year by the California Assembly.) The risks that RFID poses to corporate data have been less well publicized, but have still received some attention [22].

1.2   Why "Killing" Is Insufficient

EPCglobal chip designs address the privacy problem by permitting an RFID tag to be "killed." On receiving a short, specially designated PIN [18], a tag renders itself permanently inoperable. For example, a clothing shop might deploy RFID tags to facilitate tracking of shipments and monitoring of shelf stocks. To protect the privacy of customers, checkout stations might "kill" the tags of purchased goods. The concept is similar to the removal or deactivation of inventory-control tags as practiced today.

There will be many environments, however, in which simple measures like "kill" commands are unworkable or undesirable for privacy enforcement. The several examples above of beneficial consumer uses for RFID illustrate why consumers may not wish to have their tags killed. Likewise, "kill" commands will not protect privacy in cases where RFID tags are deployed to track borrowed items like library books. Libraries are already beginning to deploy RFID [21]. The same will be true for RFID-tagging of rented items, like DVDs. Killing cannot play a role in protecting consumer privacy in these cases.

In the corporate setting, of course, killing is unworkable, as it would negate the benefits of supply-chain visibility that RFID brings to begin with.

1.3 Why Faraday Cages are Insufficient

Another proposed tool for protecting RFID tags is known as a Faraday cage. This is a metal shield, e.g., a piece of alluminum foil, that is impenetrable by radio waves of certain frequencies, including those used by RFID systems. By enclosing an RFID tag in a Faraday cage, one can minimize its vulnerability to unwanted scanning.

In some cases, Faraday cages may indeed prove very effective. For example, to protect an RFID-enabled identity card when not in use, one might store it in a metal-lined case. For general consumer use, for example, the approach is unworkable. One could use a foil-lined bag, for instance, to protect groceries from scanning. As foil-lined bags can be used to evade inventory-control systems (i.e., theft detection systems), retail shops are unlikely to embrace their proliferation. Moreover, this approach will not work for items on one's person, including clothing, handbags, wristwatches, etc.

1.4 RFID-Tag Capabilities

Projections on the likely resources in several years of Class 1 RFID tags with cost in the vicinity of $0.05 include several hundred bits of memory and somewhere between 500 to 5000 logical gates [26], of which a considerable fraction will be required for basic tag functions. Few gates will be available for security functionality. Thus such RFID tags may be expected to perform some basic computational operations, but not conventional cryptographic ones. Even hardware-efficient symmetric-key encryption algorithms like that recently proposed by Feldhofer et al. [2] are well beyond the reach of RFID tags of this kind. At best, low-cost RFID tags may include security functions involving static keys, such as keyed writes, i.e., essentially just PIN-controlled data accesses.

1.5 Our Work

As explained above, we introduce in this paper a new type of RFID-privacy-protecting device known as a REP. The REP works by assuming the identities of RFID tags under its control. In particular, it loads their identifying information and then simulates the tags in the presence of reading devices in order to enforce a privacy policy on behalf of the REP owner. These privacy policies may include the requirement for the reader and the REP to participate in an authentication protocol more sophisticated than an ordinary tag implements. When a tag is no longer to be simulated by a REP, it may have its identity re-implanted.

For consumer applications, we propose that the REP more-or-less continually rewrite the identifiers transmitted by tags under its control. The REP may write either ciphertexts or random pseudonyms to tags. This proposal is similar in flavor to those of of Golle *et al.* [6] and Juels and Pappu [10], which propose re-encryption of ciphertexts on tag identifiers by computationally powerful and potentially untrusted external computing devices. In contrast to these proposals for tag re-encryption, however, we consider the REP as a trusted personal device. This removes the need for a reliance on public-key cryptography, and consequently leads to a different set of architectural choices, as we shall see.

A REP must perform four different operations:

1. *Tag acquisition:* When the owner of a REP and RFID tag wishes the REP to simulate the tag, the REP must acquire all of the necessary tag information and place the tag in a state permitting the REP to act as its proxy. The main technical challenge occurs when the tag has associated secrets, like PINs for access control or "killing," that must be transferred securely.

2. *Tag relabeling (or re-encryption):* The REP changes the identifiers on tags in its control so as to prevent surveillance of these tags. (Tags could instead be put in a "sleep" mode, but this has drawbacks that we discuss later.) Relabeling introduces various integrity problems, particularly the need to prevent adversarial re-writing of tags. Indeed, one of our contributions is a simple technique for preventing an adversary from swapping the identities of two different tags, e.g., swapping the identifiers on two medications with differing dosages. Previous proposals [6] are vulnerable to this type of attack or require special physical prevention mechanisms [10]. The technique we propose, which involves random input from the tag in the creation of pseudonyms, works even when tags do not have access-control features.

3. *Tag simulation:* The REP simulates tags in interaction with readers. The REP may also simulate spurious tags to prevent leakage of information about the number of tags carried by its owner. As a REP is presumed to be a powerful device, it can enforce more-or-less any privacy policy desired by its owner. We do not therefore specify simulation policies in this paper. We note, however, that these could include robust public-key based authentication schemes.

4. *Tag release:* When the owner of a REP wishes it no longer to simulate a tag, the REP must release its control and reimprint the tag with its original identity.

We note that blocker devices as proposed by Juels, Rivest, and Szydlo [11] and the variant proposed in [9] can serve as alternatives to REPs for consumer privacy protection. REPs, however, have a couple of features that make them an attractive alternative to blockers: (1) If a tag temporarily exits the broadcast range of a blocker, it is subject to complete compromise; by contrast, a tag under the control of a REP will merely go without an identity change during this period, and (2) Blocker tags can only be effective as a universal standard implemented on both tags and readers, while a REP requires only tag-based support, and can be compatible with any reading system.

In fact, though, the idea of blocking can be viewed as complementary to the tag-simulation aspect of our REP proposal: A blocker could, for instance, act as a REP under certain circumstances. It might, for instance, simulate tags that it is protecting in its "private" space so as to allow reader access to these tags when policy permits. This "block-and-simulate" approach is conceptually simple, and an attractive alternative to ideas we describe here.

1.6   Organization

In section 2, we briefly describe previous work relevant to our proposal here. We outline our REP proposal in section 3, delineating ideas for the functions of tag acquisition, tag simulation, and re-implantation of tag identities. We conclude in section 4.

2   Previous Work

Researchers have from the outset recognized the limitations of the "killing" approach, and the consequent possibility of privacy threats from physical tracking in the deployment of RFID tags [18]. Several recent papers have proposed ways of addressing the problem. As explained above, the major challenge is that inexpensive RFID tags, the type likely to be deployed most widely, may well be incapable of performing even the most basic cryptographic operations, and also have little memory (just a few hundred bits).

Weis, Sarma, Rivest, and Engels [26] propose a collection of privacy-enforcement ideas for RFID tags in general environments. First, they identify the problem of attacks based on eavesdropping rather than active tag queries. Recognizing that transmission on the tag-to-reader channel is much weaker than that on the reader-to-tag channel, they propose protocols in which tag-identifying information is concealed on the stronger channel. They also propose privacy-preserving schemes for active attacks. One scheme involves the use of a hash function to protect the key used for read-access to the tag. Another includes use of a pseudo-random number generator to protect tag identities. In a nutshell, their idea is for the tag to output the pair $(r, PRNG(ID, r))$, where ID is the secret tag identifier and $PRNG$ denotes a pseudo-random number generator. A verifier must perform an expensive brute-force lookup in order to extract the ID from such an output. The authors note that this drawback probably limits applicability of the idea to small systems. They also note that it is unclear how and when adequate pseudo-random number generators can be deployed on inexpensive RFID tags.

Juels and Pappu [10] consider a plan by the European Central Bank to embed RFID tags in Euro banknotes. They propose a privacy-protecting scheme in which RFID tags carry ciphertexts on the serial numbers of banknotes. These ciphertexts are subject to re-encryption by computational devices in shops, thereby rendering multiple appearances of a given RFID tag unlinkable. Thus tags themselves perform no cryptographic operations. Verification of correct behavior by re-encryption agents in the Juels and Pappu system may be performed by any entity with optical access to banknotes, e.g., shops and banks. Thus, while their scheme involves changes in the identities of RFID tags, they require optical contact for the purpose of authentication, which our scheme does not.

Juels, Rivest, and Szydlo [11] propose a special form of RFID tag called a "blocker." This tag disrupts the protocol used by the reader to establish communications with individual tags among a set of tags. By targeting this disruption selectively, the "blocker" tag aims to protect consumer privacy while permitting normal inventory-control processes to proceed normally. A "blocker" could be a more sophisticated device than an RFID tag, e.g., a mobile phone.

Juels [12] proposes the concept of "minimalist cryptography." This involves a scheme in which RFID tags store a small set of unlinkable pseudonyms. They rotate through these as a privacy-protection measure. To ensure against an attacker exhausting the set of pseudonyms, Juels proposes a form of "throttling," i.e., timed delay on pseudonym changes. The full-blown scheme here includes use of one-time padding to enforce privacy and authentity of tags, and is accompanied by a formal model and analysis.

Molnar and Wagner [15] examine RFID privacy in the special setting of libraries, where tag deactivation is naturally infeasible. They propose a range of schemes. Some of these do not require symmetric-key cryptography on tags; for example, they consider the idea of having tags transmit random strings to readers for use in protecting communications on the stronger reader-to-tag link and the idea of relabelling tags with new identifiers at the time of check-out. As libraries may be in a position to purchase relatively high-cost RFID tags, Molnar and Wagner also consider some schemes that involve pseudo-random number generation on tags.

Garfinkel [5] proposes a different approach based on an "RFID Bill of Rights," which consists of five articles proposed as a voluntary framework for commercial deployment of RFID tags. Included are: (1) the right of the consumer to know what items possess RFID tags, (2) the right to have tags removed or deactivated upon purchase of these items, (3) the right of the consumer to access of the data associated with an RFID tag, (4) the right to access of services without mandatory use of RFID tags, and finally (5) the right to know to when, where, and why the data in RFID tags is accessed. In a similar vein, Floerkemeier et al. consider ways of harmonizing RFID use with the Fair Information Principles of the OECD [4]. They also propose the concept of a "Watchdog Tag," a high-powered device that monitors policy compliance.

In their work on mix networks, Golle et al. [6] and also Danezis and Lysyanskaya [1] independently propose a cryptographic tool known as *universal re-encryption*. Universal re-encryption permits a (semantically secure) public-key ciphertext to be re-encrypted by an entity *without knowledge of the associated public key*. Taking advantage of this property, Golle et al. briefly propose a system in which an RFID tag stores a public-key ciphertext of its unique identifier in a form subject to universal re-encryption. In order to change the appearance of this ciphertext, it is necessary to permit its re-encryption by external agents, namely RFID reader/writers with adequate computational power to perform cryptographic operations.

The Golle *et al.* approach is similar in flavor to that of Juels and Pappu. The major difference, however, is that in the case of banknotes, a single public key may be used for the complete system. In contrast, in a consumer environment, it is likely that many public keys will be employed. Every consumer, for example, may wish to possess an individual key to permit direct management of his or her privacy. Thus, in such an environment, it is important that no public key be involved in the process of re-encryption: The public key itself could otherwise serve as a privacy-compromising identifier. Universal re-encryption provides exactly this feature of public-key concealment, and thereby permits unlimited privacy-preserving re-encryption of the ciphertexts carried by tags. With this approach, one can imagine special privacy-enhancing readers scattered throughout a city to re-encrypt ciphertexts on behalf of the owners of tags.

Golle *et al.* also propose the idea of having privacy-concerned users of RFID-tags carry personal re-encryption devices with them. This is similar in flavor to our REP proposal in this paper. As we shall see, however, by exploiting the fact that a REP is a trusted device, we are able to solve an important integrity problem present in the Golle *et al.* proposal, namely the problem of attackers *swapping* identifiers between tags.

More generally, the idea of small devices communicating through more powerful proxy devices has already proven of value in a number of computing systems. This is a means by which small, embedded computational devices in the Oxygen project at MIT, for example, enforce privacy for users [25], and by which some privacy-preserving systems have operated [17]. Our main contribution in this paper is the application of the idea in the face of the special challenges that the limited computational capabilities, high mobility, and sensitive nature of RFID devices pose.

The "RFID Guardian" project [24], an effort contemporaneous with our own research, aims shortly to build a device similar in flavor to a REP. That project does not at present treat the issues of fine-grained control such as tag acquisition and ownership transfer.

3   How a REP Works

A REP, as we have explained, functions as a proxy for RFID tags. As such, it is able to simulate these tags and therefore enforce privacy policies of more-or-less arbitrary sophistication. Additionally – and quite importantly for many applications – a REP, being a powered device, can serve as a much more reliable interface for transmitting RFID data than an RFID tag. Stated more generally, a REP can serve as a more trustworthy conduit for RFID data than the tags it controls. This can be particularly valuable in, e.g., environments in which there are physical impediments to RFID scanning. Metals and liquids can both interfere with

RFID scanning, for instance; manufacturers have already confronted challenges in scanning such items as cans of drinking soda.

We now offer details on the four processes involved in REP management of tags: Tag acquisition, Tag relabeling, Tag simulation, and Tag release.

3.1 Tag Acquisition

Acquisition of a tag by a REP involves transfer of the complete set of tag data. For tags that simply broadcast identifiers and other public information, this is a straightforward matter: The REP need merely scan the tag. Where it becomes more complicated is when a tag has associated secrets, particularly PINs required to implement secure tag operations such as writing and "killing." The transfer of these data may take place in one of two ways:

1. The tag data may be transfered directly to the REP from a trusted higher powered device such as a reader. In all cases, care should be taken of course to protect the privacy and integrity of data during this transfer.

   At checkout from a shop, for example, private data associated with the tags on purchased products might be communicated by the checkout register directly to the REP via, e.g., a Bluetooth link.

   In a supply chain, before shipment to a supply-chain partner, a pallet of tagged items might itself be tagged with a REP. The REP is programmed with private data about the tags in its pallet from a reader. This data transfer may take place using the RFID data transport or another physical layer such as Bluetooth, ZigBee, or IrDA.

2. The tag data may be released by the tag on suitable out-of-band authentication of the REP to the tag, or this data transfer may take place in an environment with adequate compensating controls. There are several channels by which the RFID reader might authenticate itself to the tag as a trusted device. If tags bear printed keys, then optical scanning of these keys might serve this function [10, 26]. A more convenient alternative might be release of tag data upon physical contact or proximity between the REP and the tag in accordance with the "resurrecting duckling" paradigm of [20]. Indeed, researchers have demonstrated methods by which tags may be able to ascertain (very roughly) whether a reader is in close proximity [3].

3.2 Tag Relabeling

As explained above, we advocate relabeling of tags by the REP as a means of protecting against privacy compromise thorugh direct tag scanning. One way to accomplish this is to have the REP re-encrypt a public-key ciphertext carried by a tag, as proposed in previous work. The setting we consider, however, in which the REP serves as a proxy permits a simpler approach involving the assignment of changing pseudonyms to tags. In particular, for timeslot t, the REP can assign a k-bit pseudonym $p_{t,i}$ to tag i. (Time here would be maintained by the REP alone, as it is infeasible for tags to keep time.) This pseudonym may be generated uniformly at random by the REP and stored in a table in association with the tag identity. Alternatively, it could be computed as a k-bit symmetric-key ciphertext based on a master key σ held by the REP. In particular, we might simply compute $p_{t,i} = E_\sigma[t, i]$.

The approach of re-encryption or more generally, re-naming of tags, however, introduces a serious security problem, that of *data integrity*. Because tags are computationally too weak to authenticate re-writing entities, it is hard to enforce write-control permissions on tags that preclude adversarial tampering. This means that an attacker can corrupt tag data.

Writing of tag data is typically a PIN-protected process in RFID tags. This mitigates the risk of malicious corruption of tag data, but does not eliminate it. An adversary can potentially intercept REP-to-tag communications and thus learn the write PIN for the tag. Alternatively, if attacking at sufficiently close range, the adversary can hijack a write session between the REP and tag. Provided that k is sufficiently large, i.e., pseudonyms are long enough, an attacker has very little chance of being able to forge a pseudonym existentially.

More serious is the possibility of a *swapping attack*, in which an adversary exchanges the ciphertexts $p_{t,i}$ and $p_{t,j}$ between two tags i and j. This can have very serious consequences. It suffices to consider the possibility of an attacker exchanging ciphertexts associated with two medications or two spare aircraft parts. Previous proposals involving re-encryption of ciphertexts have been unable to address this attack, and have indeed left its resolution as an open problem.

In the case where the PIN associated with a tag is locked, i.e., not subject to alteration, the PIN itself can serve as a kind of authenticator for the tag [7]. Thus, a PIN can be used as a mechanism to defend against swapping attacks: If a tag is discovered to carry a pseudonym that does not match its PIN, then it may be presumed that a swapping attack has occurred.

The use of PINs to defend against swapping attacks, however, is twofold. First, as noted above, a frequently-used PIN is subject to compromise. And a compromised PIN is effectively a kind of static identifier. An attacker capable of testing the correctness of a PIN can use it to track a tag. Of course, if a PIN is not used to authenticate the operation of identifier-writing, but only to test periodically for swapping, then the risk of PIN compromise is diminished. A second, more serious problem is the basic one of PIN management. We have already noted that tag acquisition may need to involve out-of-band transfer of tag secrets. In general, management of tag PINs is like the general problem of key management in data-security systems. It is conceptually simple, but operationally thorny. Hence, it seems very likely that consumers will carry RFID tags that do not have associated PINs, or will not know the associated PINs of their tags!

Happily, we are able to provide a simple defense against identifier swapping that works even when write access to tags is universal.

The idea is for a tag i to participate itself in the generation of a given pseudonym $p_{t,i}$. In principle, if the tag itself could perform symmetric-key encryption under an appropriate cipher E, then the data-integrity problem would be solved: The tag would not need to have its pseudonyms updated by the REP.

Cryptography of this kind, however, as we have explained, is well beyond the reach of low-cost tag capabilities.

Tags can, however, generate a certain amount of randomness. We might therefore consider a protocol in which a tag generates a new pseudonym $p_{t,i}$ for a counter t maintained (internally) on the tag. If it receives an "update" command from the REP, along with a valid write key, the tag transmits $p_{t,i}$ to the reader and adopts $p_{t,i}$ as its new pseudonym. (In order to prevent desynchronization due to an interrupted session, a tag might await a final "ack" from the reader before effecting the update.) This approach would render swapping attacks infeasible, as the REP – and thus an adversary – would be unable to dictate tag pseudonyms.

In practice, tags are capable of generating only a limited number of random bits in the course of a given session. Moreover, much of the randomness that a tag generates is already bespoke by other protocol requirements. (See the remark below.) A tag may therefore be unable to generate a full-length random pseudonym in each session.

Even partial generation of a pseudonym by a tag, however, can help alleviate the risk of swapping attacks. In particular, tag might emit a random nonce r of length $k' < k$ before accepting the writing of a new pseudonym. The tag then only accepts a new pseudonym if it "matches" this nonce, e.g., if the last bits of the pseudonym are equal to r. (As an alternative, a tag might simply "declare" the last bits of its pseudonym to be r and accept only the other bits from the reader.) In other words, a tag can participate *partially* in the generation of its pseudonyms. An adversary attempting to swap pseudonyms, then, will be unable to do so unless it can locate a pair of tags simultaneously emitting the same nonces.

The probability of successful attack by an adversary, then, is a function of the number of tags N managed by a REP, the number of timeslots s available to the adversary for its attack, and the bit-length k'. Consider, for instance, a pallet carrying some 100 tags relabelled every minute, and seeking protection against attacks lasting up to one day (1440 minutes), and employing tags that generate 32-bit nonces. The probability that a given tag shares a random pseudonym with any of the 99 others may be crudely bounded above by $99/2^{32}$. Thus the probability of a successful swapping attack in this case is easily seen to be less than $(1 - (1 - 99/2^{32})) \times 1440 < 0.000034$.

Denial-of-service: Even if an attacker cannot successfully initiate a swapping attack, corruption of tag data has a second effect: Denial of service. If an attacker is able to implant a pseudonym in a tag, the tag effectively becomes desynchronized with the REP: The REP no longer recognizes the tag's pseudonym. If the REP were consequently to halt rotation of new pseudonyms into a tag, a breach of privacy could result, since tag identifier would remain static. A REP might alert a user to unexpected de-synchronization events of this kind by emitting a warning tone, for instance. (Alternatively, a REP might continue to relabel tags even if it does not know their true underlying identifiers; the REP can, of course, simply generate temporary identifiers for tags it does not recognize. This might have an undesirable spillover effect if a REP relabels tags that do not belong to its owner!)

A secondary effect of a corruption attack is that the REP cannot properly release tags: If it does not recognize their pseudonyms, it cannot manage them properly. Thus, one of two approaches might be needed for tag restoration: (1) If the REP possesses PINs for the tags in its control, it can try to match tags to PINs via exhaustive search or (2) Some kind of manual intervention on the part of the user might be necessary, e.g., the user might have to key in a printed product code from items that the REP has "lost." Given the current and probably persistent imperfections in RFID, we expect some level of back-up identifer recovery and manual intervention to occur regularly. Since denial-of-service attacks would likely be a rarity, anyway, they would probably constitute little more than a nuisance in our system.

Remarks: Communications on the reader-to-tag (or REP-to-tag) channel, which is often called the *forward channel*, are typically transmitted at a higher power than on the tag-to-reader channel, which is often called the *back channel*. One way to achieve privacy protection of REP-to-tag communications, therefore, is to have the tag generate a random value R and send it on the back channel. The REP can then protect transmission of a message on the forward channel, as the REP can then transmit the write PIN XORed with R. Techniques such as these can in principle prevent compromise of write PINs for tags via long-range eavesdropping, and thus reduce the overall threat of data corruption. They do not, however, address the problems of short-range eavesdropping and hijacking.

An entirely different and stronger approach to data integrity is possible using somewhat more heavyweight techniques. For example, the "minimalist cryptography" concept in [12] could be used to establish shared secrets between tags and the REP. On top of this might be layered a kind of lightweight message authentication code (MAC) as in [8]. Under the modeling assumptions of [12], this combination of techniques would permit the REP and tag to authenticate new pseudonyms.

3.3 Tag Simulation

Once the REP has acquired a tag, it can, of course, simulate it as desired in the presence of an RFID reader. As explained above, this has the benefit of making tag reading more reliable: The REP, as a higher-powered device can transmit information to a reader more reliably than a tag. The REP might essentially enforce the kind of data filtering envisioned in the "soft blocking" approach to tag privacy. "Soft blocking," however, relies upon a universal set of policy conventions. A REP, by contrast, can achieve a wholly personalized set of privacy policies. Additionally, a REP can enforce these policies in the presence of any reader – even a malicious one. We give two examples of REP capabilities unavailable in previously proposed approaches:

- *Geographical conditioning:* A REP may make decisions about whether to release information based on its geographical location. For example, a REP might release information about a pallet's RFID tags only when the pallet arrives at its destination. There is a variety of channels by which the REP might determine whether or not it is present at its destination, e.g.: (1) A built-in GPS unit; (2) Authenticated transmissions from readers; or (3) An authenticated notification from another protocol such as Bluetooth.

- *Object simulation:* To deceive attackers, a REP may simulate RFID tags associated with objects that the user does not possess. Here are two examples:
  1. A consumer can "carry" information about an object by simulating it. When the owner of a refrigerator wants to purchase a new handle of the correct type, or the owner of a stereo system wants to know which speakers are appropriate for her home theater system, she can simulate the associated RFID tags in order to acquire, carry, and convey this information conveniently.
  2. The owner of a Patek Philippe watch might program her REP to simulate the Patek Philippe RFID tag when she is present in upscale shops (so as to improve her level of customer service), but to mask her watch (or simulate a cheap one) when she is walking the streets.

Additionally, there are other scenarios in which a REP can enforce privacy policies. For example, jewelry retailers typically perform nightly inventories of their stock, given the high value of individual items. One can imagine that they would find RFID-tagging of their stock useful in this process. Such tagging, however, would make it possible for a competitor to scan a jewelry case quickly and in secrecy, and thereby learn the rate of stock turnover. A REP might simulate non-existent jewels to render this more difficult. This approach would, similarly, be very useful in military environments.

Finally, we note that a REP can transmit tag information to devices other than RFID readers. A REP might, for instance transmit tag data via WiFi, thereby serving as a bridge between RFID and other wireless systems.

3.4   Tag Release

When a REP is to release an RFID tag, it must restore the tag's original identity. This process is straightforward if the REP has unrestricted write access to the tag. The technique we introduce in section 3.2 for preventing swapping attacks introduces a problem here, however, as its aim is precisely to restrict the identifiers that may be written to a tag. We propose, therefore, that on release of a tag, the randomly assigned portion of its identifier be retained, and that the rest of its identifier be restored to its original state. For example, the identifier on an EPC tag has two segments, roughly speaking: (1) A (numerical) identifier segment that specifies the object the tag is attached to, e.g., says, "This is a 100g tablette of Valhrona chocolate" and (2) A unique numerical segment, effectively a serial number. During the period in which a tag is simulated by a REP, segment (1) can be effaced or overwritten by the REP, while segment (2) (or a portion thereof) is generated at random by the tag. When the tag is released, the randomness in (2) is retained, while (1) is restored. Effectively, then, a tag gets a new serial number at the time it is released.

This change in segment (2) could be problematic in some cases. For example, if a user has a warranty associated with an item that is referenced by its initial serial number, the user would like to retain that serial number. We note, however, that the REP can help provided serial-number translation as desired. For example, if a carton of milk has had its serial number changed through re-labelling, the REP can transfer the old serial number to a "smart" refrigerator when a consumer puts the milk away.

In the case where a tag has an associated PIN, of course, the PIN may be used to place the tag in a special state in which its serial number may be completely rewritten. Alternatively, physical mechanisms like reader proximity, as that described in [3], might trigger restoration of original tag state.

An important logistical question is how the REP is to determine *when* to release a tag. This process may in many cases be controlled by the user or performed automatically based on external environmental cues, e.g., when a user's home network informs the REP that the user has entered her home. Some experiments suggest that as tags enter the limit of range of a reading device, their response rate degrades [3]. Based on such information, a REP might be able to detect the removal of a tag from its vicinity and restore its initial state automatically. (To achieve early detection of impending tag departure from its read radius, a REP might periodically reduce its power level.) The opposite is alternatively possible: Release of a tag might be effected by bringing the REP into close proximity or actual physical contact with the tag. This latter case has a useful feature: Physical proximity is effectively a kind of authentication, and might serve as the basis for full restoration of a tag identifier, thereby bypassing the problem of serial-number-changes discussed above. For library books and similar items, this could be especially useful.

3.5 Putting Tags to Sleep

In principle, a REP can put tags to sleep while it is simulating them, and then wake them for identity re-implantation, thereby obviating the need for tag relabeling. ("Sleeping" is not supported by the EPC Class 1 Generation 2 standard, but could in principle be incorporated into inexpensive tags.) The process of waking, however, can be a problematic one. For logical access control, sleep/wake commands must be keyed with PINs so as to prevent malicious alteration of tag behavior. A problem then arises: Unless a tag identifies itself, a reader (or REP) cannot know which waking key to transmit; a sleeping tag cannot, of course, identify itself. Trial-and-error transmission of PINs to tags would be possible, but cumbersome. Alternatively, it is possible for a REP to broadcast a waking PIN to all tags in its vicinity, but given the likely movement of tags in and out of the field of control of the REP over the course of time, this approach seems impractical for consumer applications. This is particularly the case if a REP wishes to transfer control of a tag to a different device: the secondary device must be able to identify the tag of which it is taking control.

Putting tags to sleep *might* present a more feasible approach to access control if waking involves some form of physical access control. For example, it would be possible to touch an RFID device to a tag in order to wake it. We expect, however, that it would be cumbersome for consumers to have to engage in a fine-grained physical process to control the state of their tags.

In supply chains, where rigorous logistical controls are available, sleep/wake patterns may be more managable. In such settings it may make sense for a REP to put tags to sleep while simulating them. As maintenance of live tags is the technically more challenging option, it is the approach of having a REP relabel tags on a regular basis that we primarily explore in this paper. In supply chains, where rigorous logistical controls are available, sleep/wake patterns may be more managable. In such settings it may make sense for a REP to put tags to sleep while simulating them.

3.6   REPs and the EPCglobal Standard

We can make the basic REP approach work particularly effectively with Class 1 Generation 2 tags in commercial settings – if they have writeable IDs. (Many memory technologies such as EEPROM impose limitations on the number of times memory cells may be rewritten, but some thousands of rewrite operations should be supportable.) PIN management would also be essential to prevent swapping attacks, as EPC tags do not, of course, support our idea of tag-generated randomness in identifiers. Alternatively, the "block-and-simulate" approach would be workable here.

Unlike the application of REPs to provide personal privacy, REPs in commercial settings would manage a limited population of tags. The goal in this situation is to transport a container of items from one trusted environment such as a factory to another such as a distribution center. This transportation of goods has been a major source of loss for manufacturers and retailers alike.

Some have noted that the management of unique individual tag PINs would require a new data communications infrastructure to be built for this purpose among supply chain participants. By having the tags managed by a REP, one can reduce this key distribution problem to the authentication of a reader to the REP. REPs by their virtue of relaxed cost constraints could be Class 3 tags capable of public-key cryptography. Issuance of digital certificates to REPs and readers would eliminate the need for a new secret-key distribution infrastructure.

Upon arrival of a pallet at its destination, the reader and REP would perform public-key-based mutual authentication using their digital certificates. On completion of the protocol, the reader would issue a special command causing the REP to unconceal and relabel all the tags in the pallet with their true identities.

We feel REPs have much to offer in EPCglobal-enabled supply chains.

4   Conclusion

We have proposed the idea of a REP, a device that serves as proxy for basic RFID tags, such as those of the Class 1 Gen 2 variety. A REP renders RFID tags dormant and then simulates them to other devices, e.g., RFID readers. Thanks to its moderate-to-high computational ability, a REP can enforce sophisticated privacy and security policies, even taking factors like time and location into account. We have shown how REPs can protect the privacy of consumers and the sensitive information of industrial RFID systems, and can withstand attacks against the integrity of tag identifiers, e.g., swapping attacks.

As we have noted, in addition to restricting information access where appropriate, a REP can also facilitate communications in RFID systems. As RFID tags are passive devices and therefore not wholly reliable communicators, a REP can improve the reliability of communications with an RFID system by acting as a proxy for RFID tags. A REP can also communicate via protocols other than RFID, e.g., Bluetooth, thereby acting as a bridge between divergent communcation systems. We think that REPs are a powerful and practical notion and believe that Class 3 EPCglobal devices might serve as REPs in some degree, perhaps along some of the lines we have proposed here.

References

1. G. Danezis, 2003. Personal communications.
2. M. Feldhofer, S. Dominikus, and J. Wolkerstorfer. Strong authentication for RFID systems using the AES algorithm. In M. Joye and J.-J. Quisquater, editors, *Cryptographic Hardware and Embedded Systems (CHES)*, pages 357–370. Springer-Verlag, 2004. LNCS no. 3156.
3. K. P. Fishkin, S. Roy, and B. Jiang. Some methods for privacy in RFID communication. In *1st European Workshop on Security in Ad-Hoc and Sensor Networks (ESAS 2004)*, pages 42–53, 2004.
4. C. Floerkemeier, R. Schneider, and M. Langheinrich. Scanning with a purpose supporting the Fair Information Principles in RFID protocols. In *2nd International Symposium on Ubiquitous Computing Systems (UCS 2004)*, November 2004. Available at http://www.vs.inf.ethz.ch/publ/?author=floerkem.
5. S. Garfinkel. An RFID Bill of Rights. *Technology Review*, page 35, October 2002.
6. P. Golle, M. Jakobsson, A. Juels, and P. Syverson. Universal re-encryption for mixnets. In T. Okamoto, editor, *RSA Conference - Cryptographers' Track (CT-RSA)*, pages 163–178. Springer-Verlag, 2004.
7. A. Juels. Strengthening EPC tags against cloning, 2004. In submission. Referenced at rfid-security.com.
8. A. Juels. 'Yoking-proofs' for RFID tags. In *PerCom Workshops 2004*, pages 138–143. IEEE Computer Society, 2004.
9. A. Juels and J. Brainard. Soft blocking: Flexible blocker tags on the cheap. In S. De Capitani di Vimercatiand P. Syverson, editor, *Wireless Privacy in the Electronic Society (WPES 04)*, pages 1–8. ACM Press, 2004.
10. A. Juels and R. Pappu. Squealing Euros: Privacy protection in RFID-enabled banknotes. In R. Wright, editor, *Financial Cryptography '03*, pages 103–121. Springer-Verlag, 2003. LNCS no. 2742.
11. A. Juels, R.L. Rivest, and M. Szydlo. The blocker tag: Selective blocking of RFID tags for consumer privacy. In V. Atluri, editor, *8th ACM Conference on Computer and Communications Security*, pages 103–111. ACM Press, 2003.
12. Ari Juels. Minimalist Cryptography for RFID Tags. In C. Blundo and S. Cimato, editors, *Security in Communication Networks*, pages 149–164. Springer-Verlag, 2004.

13. AutoID Labs. 860 MHz-960 Mhz class 1 radio frequency identification tag radio frequency and logical communication interface specification recommended standard, version 1.0.0. Technical Report MIT-AUTOID-WH-007, Auto-ID Labs, 2002. Referenced in 2005 at http://www.autoidlabs.com.

14. D. McCullagh. RFID tags: Big Brother in small packages. *CNet*, 13 January 2003. Available at http://news.com.com/2010-1069-980325.html.

15. D. Molnar and D. Wagner. Privacy and security in library RFID : Issues, practices, and architectures. In B. Pfitzmann and P. McDaniel, editors, *ACM CCS*, pages 210 – 219, 2004.

16. Nokia unveils RFID phone reader. *RFID Journal*, 17 March 2004. Available at http://www.rfidjournal.com/article/view/834.

17. Michael G. Reed, Paul F. Syverson, and David M. Goldschlag. Protocols using anonymous connections: Mobile applicatons. In Bruce Christianson, Bruno Crispo, Mark Lomas, and Michael Roe, editors, *Security Protocols, 5th International Workshop*, pages 13–23. Springer-Verlag, LNCS 1361, April 1997. Available at http://chacs.nrl.navy.mil/publications/CHACS/1997/.

18. S. E. Sarma, S. A. Weis, and D.W. Engels. Radio-frequency identification systems. In Burton S. Kaliski Jr., Çetin Kaya Koç, and Christof Paar, editors, *CHES '02*, pages 454–469. Springer-Verlag, 2002. LNCS no. 2523.

19. S.E. Sarma. Towards the five-cent tag. Technical Report MIT-AUTOID-WH-006, MIT Auto ID Center, 2001. Available from http://www.epcglobalinc.org.

20. F. Stajano and R. Anderson. The resurrecting duckling: Security issues for ad-hoc wireless networks. In *7th International Workshop on Security Protocols*, pages 172–194. Springer-Verlag, 1999. LNCS no. 1796.

21. J. Stanley. Chip away at privacy: Library tracking system spawns Big Brother ire. *San Francisco Chronicle*, 2 July 2004.

22. R. Stapleton-Gray. Would Macy's scan Gimbels? competitive intelligence and RFID. Technical report, Stapleton-Gray & Associates, Inc., 2003. Available at http://www.stapleton-gray.com/papers/ci-20031027.PDF.

23. K. Takaragi, M. Usami, R. Imura, R. Itsuki, and T. Satoh. An ultra small individual recognition security chip. *IEEE Micro*, 21(6):43–49, 2001.

24. A. Tanenbaum, G. Gaydadjiev, B. Crispo, M. Rieback, D. Stafylarakis, and C. Zhang. The RFID Guardian project. URL: http://www.cs.vu.nl/ ∼melanie/rfid_guardian/people.html.

25. R. Tuchinda. Security and privacy in the intelligent room. Master's thesis, M.I.T., 15 May 2002.

26. S. A. Weis, S. Sarma, R. Rivest, and D. Engels. Security and privacy aspects of low-cost radio frequency identification systems. In Hutter et al., editor, *First International Conference on Security in Pervasive Computing (SPC)*, pages 201–212. Springer-Verlag, 2003. LNCS no. 2802.

Integrating Utility into Face De-identification

Ralph Gross, Edoardo Airoldi, Bradley Malin, and Latanya Sweeney

Data Privacy Laboratory, School of Computer Science,
Carnegie Mellon University, Pittsburgh, PA 15213
{rgross, eairoldi, malin, latanya}@cs.cmu.edu

Abstract. With the proliferation of inexpensive video surveillance and face recognition technologies, it is increasingly possible to track and match people as they move through public spaces. To protect the privacy of subjects visible in video sequences, prior research suggests using *ad hoc* obfuscation methods, such as blurring or pixelation of the face. However, there has been little investigation into how obfuscation influences the usability of images, such as for classification tasks. In this paper, we demonstrate that at high obfuscation levels, *ad hoc* methods fail to preserve utility for various tasks, whereas at low obfuscation levels, they fail to prevent recognition. To overcome the implied tradeoff between privacy and utility, we introduce a new algorithm, *k*-Same-Select, which is a formal privacy protection schema based on *k*-anonymity that provably protects privacy *and* preserves data utility. We empirically validate our findings through evaluations on the FERET database, a large real world dataset of facial images.

1   Introduction

Walk through the streets of any metropolitan area and your image is captured on an ever increasing number of closed-circuit television (CCTV) surveillance cameras and webcams accessible via the Internet. Consider some recent statistics. As of 2002, a survey of New York City's Times Square revealed there exist over 250 different CCTV's in operation [1]. In addition, researchers with the Camera Watch project of Carnegie Mellon University estimate that there are over 10,000 webcams focused on public spaces around the United States [2]. The dramatically decreasing costs of surveillance equipment and data storage technologies guarantees that these numbers will continue to increase.

Surveillance systems, including automated face recognition, must be held accountable to the social environments in which they are implemented [3]. Given the ubiquity with which surveillance systems are creeping into society, protection of images already captured and stored, must be developed. Currently, most attempts at enabling privacy in video surveillance and automated face recognition systems have been approached from an *ad hoc* perspective. For instance, researchers studying telecommuting have investigated the degree to which simple de-identification methods, such as "blurring" or "pixelating" an image, prevent

G. Danezis and D. Martin (Eds.): PET 2005, LNCS 3856, pp. 227–242, 2006.

the recipient of the image from determining the identity of the individual [4, 5]. In these studies, it has been repeatedly demonstrated that identity is sufficiently protected. As a result, the European Union's directive 95/46/EC of the Data Protection Act explicitly states that once an image is pixelated, it can be shared for research or law enforcement purposes. A simple Internet search produces several companies specializing in the development and commercialization of privacy protecting surveillance equipment - the justification being that their system can pixelate images.[1]

While simple filtering methods might prevent a human from recognizing subjects in an image, there is no guarantee that face recognition algorithms would be thwarted. In fact it has been shown before that *ad hoc* de-identification methods are unable to protect privacy if the methods are simply applied to gallery images as well [6]. In prior research, it was demonstrated that face recognition can be sufficiently thwarted using models built on formal privacy methods [6]. The k-Same algorithm provides the guarantee that a face recognition system can not do better than $1/k$ in recognizing who a particular image corresponds to. Moreover, this level of protection will hold up against any recognition system, human or computer, such that it is unnecessary to experimentally validate if images subject to the k-Same algorithm will be sufficiently protected. However, though privacy can be guaranteed, there is no accompanying guarantee on the utility of such data. In previous research, it was demonstrated that k-Samed images look like faces, but it is unknown if the image communicates information necessary for surveillance or classification purposes. The goal of this paper is two-fold:

– Provide experimental evidence regarding how *ad hoc* methods can not simultaneously protect privacy and provide data utility in face images, and
– Develop and demonstrate an algorithm which provides formal privacy protection that maintains data utility on classification challenges, such as gender and expression characterization.

The remainder of this paper is organized as follows. In Section 2 we survey related work. Section gives an overview of the face recognition algorithms used in the experiments. Section 4 defines face de-identification and introduces the k-Same-Select algorithm. In Section 5 we evaluate privacy protection and data utility for both *ad hoc* and formal protection algorithms. We conclude by discussing the findings of the paper in 6.

2   Related Work

In this paper we investigate technical issues regarding anonymity in face recognition systems. This issue is a specific topic within the more general area of how to protect privacy in communicated images. In this section, we briefly review

---

[1] For example see IES Digital's "SiteScape[2]" - http://www.iesdigital.com/pdfs/ssbrochure.pdf

several proposed methods and the difference between formal models of privacy and *ad hoc* strategies. [2]

There exist a number of methods by which an image can be obfuscated for privacy protection. In particular, proposed methods include pixelation and blur and various other distortion filters [7, 4, 8, 9, 5, 10, 11]. This set of obfuscating techniques prevent the rendering of the original image, but they do not provide intuition as to whether or not privacy is maintained. To test if these techniques do protect privacy, researchers investigate the degree to which these methods fool human observers of the obfuscated video [7, 10, 11]. Researchers ask individuals if they can determine the scene activities or identify the subjects. If the human can not answer such questions correctly, then it is claimed that privacy is being protected.

The previous is a feasible model of privacy, provided the entity receiving the video is a human without access to accompanying information, such as a database of images to compare the incoming video to. Senior et al. [12] note that if the human or computer on the receiving side of the obfuscated video has access to references images (e.g. non-obfuscated images of the video subjects), then care must be taken to ensure that transmitted images do not reveal information which can be used to match to a reference image (using techniques such as face, gait or scene recognition). Through a prototype called PrivacyCam, Senior et al. demonstrated how incoming video feeds can be segmented, stored in a database, and managed using multi-level security techniques.

Though Senior et al. present a privacy protection schema, there are no proofs or empirical analysis of whether or not their methods defeat recognition systems. Rather, this task was first addressed in 2003 by Alexander and Kenny, who investigated how individuals can fool automated face recognition systems [13]. In their study, they consider *ad hoc* methods (sunglasses, face paint, shinning laser pointer into camera). Their findings reported recognition rates at varying levels of such protection (e.g. the level of tint in the sunglasses) and provided levels at which the computer could not complete correct recognition. Yet, this evaluation of privacy is performed with the belief that the computer is not adaptive. For example, the authors submit an image of a subject wearing sunglasses and probe a database of faces in which no one is wearing sunglasses. This is a naïve strategy, since the computer (or the human provided with obfuscated image) can detect how an image has been augmented.

The issue of adaptive recognition is a serious and realistic concern, which is addressed in recent research by Newton et al. [6]. In their analysis, they assume a computer can mimic the obfuscation technique within the recognition system's gallery of images. They demonstrated that recognition rates of obfuscated images against non-obfuscated images are low as observed by Alexander and Kenny [13]. However, the recognition rates soar when the computer can augment the gallery of searched images. In certain cases it was discovered that obfuscation, such as

---

[2] This research does not consider issues regarding security or policy concerns, such as who is permitted to view the images, time limits on image storage, or encryption strategies for secure storage and communication.

pixelation, actually increases recognition rates above the baseline tests. Newton et al. [6] concluded that the main reason why *ad hoc* methods of privacy protection in video and face recognition systems are fallible is because there is no formal model of how privacy can be compromised or protected. To rectify this concern, Newton et al. [6] proposed a new obfuscating model called *k*-Same. The details of the *k*-Same method are discussed below, but from a model perspective, it is a formal protection strategy based on the *k*-anonymity framework of Sweeney [14]. In general, *k*-anonymity stipulates that for every piece of protected data, there must exist *k* pieces of data in the original dataset to which the piece of data could be representative of. Translated to the *k*-Same model, each face image presented to a face recognition system could be representative of *k* faces in the gallery.

The version of *k*-Same introduced in [6] protects privacy and preserve detail in facial structure, however, there are no guarantees of the utility of the data (e.g. "What is the gender of the face?" or "What is the facial expression?"). In this paper, we investigate how utility can be incorporated into the *k*-Same model of privacy protection.

3   Face Recognition Algorithms

Automatic recognition of human faces has been an active area of research in computer vision and related fields since the 1970s [15, 16]. In this section we describe in detail the two face recognition algorithms used in experiments (see Section 5): 1) Principal Component Analysis, a standard academic benchmark and 2) the commercial face recognizer FaceIt, which performed well in academic evaluations [17] and was among the best performing systems in the Face Recognition Vendor Test of 2000 [18] and 2002 [19].

3.1   Principal Component Analysis

Principal Component Analysis (PCA) is a method for the unsupervised reduction of dimensionality [20]. An image is represented as an n-dimensional vector (obtained by raster-scanning the original image), where each dimension corresponds to a pixel. Given a set of N sample images $\{x_1, x_2, \ldots, x_N\}$, we define the *total scatter* matrix $S_T = \sum_{k=1}^{N} (x_k - \mu)(x_k - \mu)^T$ where μ is the mean of the data. PCA determines the orthogonal projection Φ in

$$y_k = \Phi^T x_k, k = 1, \ldots, N$$

that maximizes the determinant of the total scatter matrix of the projected samples $y_1, \ldots, y_N$:

$$\Phi_{opt} = \arg\max_{\Phi} \mid \Phi^T S_T \Phi \mid = [\phi_1 \phi_2 \ldots \phi_m]$$

where $\{\phi_i | i = 1, 2, \ldots, m\}$ are the n-dimensional eigenvectors of S_T corresponding to the m largest eigenvalues (typically $m \ll n$). Two face images are compared by projecting them into the subspace using the projection Φ defined by the eigenvectors $\phi_1, \phi_2, \ldots, \phi_m$ and computing the Mahalanobis distance in the PCA subspace: $d_M(I, J) = (I - J)^T S_T^{-1}(I - J)$.

3.2 Commercial Face Recognizer: FaceIt by Identix

The recognition module of FaceIt is based on Local Feature Analysis (LFA) [21]. This technique attempts to overcome two major problems of PCA. First, the application of PCA to a set of images yields a global representation of the image features that is not robust to variability due to localized changes in the input [22]. Second, the PCA representation is non-topographic. In other words, nearby values in the feature representation do not necessarily correspond to nearby values in the input image. To address these problems, LFA uses localized image features. The feature images are then encoded using PCA to obtain a compact description. According to Identix, FaceIt is robust against variations in pose of up to 35° in all directions, gender, lighting, skin tone, eye glasses, facial expression, and hair style.

4   Face De-identification and Data Utility

In this section we define the algorithms used in the experiments of Section 5. We detail the naïve methods pixelation and blurring (Section 4.2) and the previously proposed k-same algorithm [6] (Section 4.3). Furthermore we introduce a new algorithm, k-same-select (Section 4.4).

4.1   Definitions

For the following we consider all face images i to be vectors of fixed size n with values between 0 and 255. We will use sets of face images, where we assume that no two images within the same set come from the same person. In particular we will refer to the *gallery* set of face images $\mathcal{G}$, which contains images of *known* individuals and the *probe* set of face images $\mathcal{P}$, which contains images of *unknown* subjects [23]. We can then define face recognition as follows:

Definition 1 (Face Recognition). *Given a set of probe images $\mathcal{P}$ and a set of gallery images $\mathcal{G}$, the face recognition function $f_R : \mathcal{P} \to \mathcal{G}$ associates every face in the probe set with exactly one face image of the gallery set.*

Let $\mathcal{F}_{\mathcal{P},\mathcal{G}} = \{f_R^1, f_R^2, \ldots, f_R^n | f_R^j : \mathcal{P} \to \mathcal{G}, j = 1, \ldots, n\}$ be a set of face recognition functions.

Definition 2 (Face Recognition Performance). *Let $Eval_f : [\mathcal{F}_{\mathcal{P},\mathcal{G}}, \mathcal{P}, \mathcal{G}] \to [0 \ldots 1]$ be an evaluation function which, for given probe and gallery sets $\mathcal{P}, \mathcal{G}$ associates a face recognition function $f_R \in \mathcal{F}_{\mathcal{P},\mathcal{G}}$ with the fraction of correctly recognized face images in $\mathcal{P}$.*

In this paper we will discuss different face de-identification methods.

Definition 3 (Face De-Identification). *Let* $\mathcal{M}_o = \{m_1, m_2, \ldots, m_i\}$ *and* $\mathcal{M}_d = \{\hat{m}_1, \hat{m}_2, \ldots, \hat{m}_i\}$ *be face images sets. We then define face de-identification as image transformation* $f_D : \mathcal{M}_o \to \mathcal{M}_d$ *such that* $f_D(m_j) = \hat{m}_j, m_j \neq \hat{m}_j, j = 1, \ldots, i.$

The implicit goal of a face de-identification method f_D is to remove identifying information from face images, so that $Eval_f(f_R, f_D(\mathcal{P}), \mathcal{G}) < Eval_f(f_R, \mathcal{P}, \mathcal{G})$. In Section 5 we will compare $Eval_f(f_R, f_D(\mathcal{P}), \mathcal{G})$ for different face recognition functions f_R and face de-identification functions f_D. k-anonymity provides a formal model of privacy protection [14]. Newton et al. extended k-anonymity to face image sets as follows [6]:

Definition 4 (k-Anonymized Face Set). *We call a probe set of face images* k*-anonymized, if for every probe image there exist at least k images in the gallery to which the probe image corresponds.*

Both, the k-anonymized probe set and the gallery set are assumed to be public.

The second focus of this paper is on data utility functions, which assign face images to one of multiple, mutually exclusive classes.

Definition 5 (Data Utility Function). *Let* $\mathcal{M}$ *be a set of face images. We then define* $u : \mathcal{M} \to \{c_1, c_2, \ldots, c_k\}$ *as data utility function, which associates each face image in* $\mathcal{M}$ *with exactly one class* $c_j, j = 1, \ldots, k.$

We assume that for each face image i the *correct* class c_j is known. Examples of image classes include facial expressions $\{neutral, smile\}$, gender $\{male, female\}$, and eye status $\{open, closed\}$.

Definition 6 (Data Utility Performance). *Let* $\mathcal{U} = \{u^1, u^2, \ldots, u^m\}$ *be a set of data utility functions. We define* $Eval_u : [\mathcal{U}, \mathcal{M}] \to [0 \ldots 1]$ *as evaluation function which computes the fraction of correct class associations for a given data utility function u and a face image set* $\mathcal{M}.$

In Section 5 we will compare $Eval_u(u^j, f_D(\mathcal{P}))$ for different data utility functions u^j and face de-identification functions f_D.

4.2   Naïve De-identification Methods

In this section we describe two *ad-hoc* de-identification methods typically used both in previous studies [4,5] and the popular press.

Pixelation. The process of pixelation reduces the information contained in an image through subsampling. For a given pixelation factor p, image sub-blocks of size $p \times p$ are extracted and replaced by the average pixel value over the sub-block. As the value of p increases more information is removed from the image. See Figure 1(a) for examples of applying pixelation with different factors p to face images. The subsampling effect of pixelation is further illustrated in Figure 1(b) where we plot the distribution of pixel intensity values across a face for original and pixelated images.

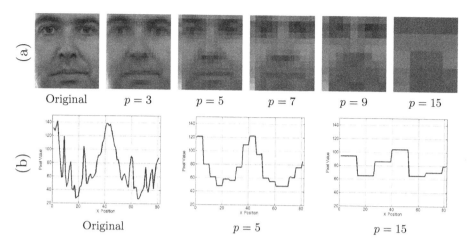

Fig. 1. Pixelation applied to face images. (a) shows example images of applying pixelation with different p factors. In (b) we plot pixel intensity value across the whole image at roughly eye height of the original image. The plots for $p = 3$ and $p = 7$ illustrate the subsampling effect of the pixelation operation.

Blurring. To blur an image, each pixel in the image is replaced by a weighted average of the pixel's neighborhood. A popular choice for the weighting function is a Gaussian kernel, which weights pixels near the center of the neighborhood more heavily. In two-dimensions, for coordinates x and y, the Gaussian blurring operator is defined as $G_\sigma(x, y) = \frac{1}{2\pi\sigma^2}e^{-\frac{x^2+y^2}{2\sigma^2}}$ [24]. The standard deviation σ controls the size of the neighborhood. The blurred image is then computed as

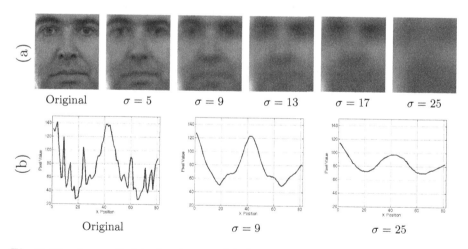

Fig. 2. Blurring applied to face images. (a) shows example images for multiple levels of blurring. Similar to Figure 1 we plot pixel intensity values across the face image in (b). The plot for $\sigma = 9$ and $\sigma = 25$ illustrates how blurring removes information from the image through averaging.

---

input : Face set $\mathcal{M}_o$, privacy constant k, with $|\mathcal{M}_o| \geq k$
output: De-identified face set $\mathcal{M}_d$

1 $\mathcal{M}_d \leftarrow \emptyset$
2 **for** $i \in \mathcal{M}_o$ **do**
3   **if** $|\mathcal{M}_o| < 2k$ **then**
4 | $k = |\mathcal{M}_o|$
5   **end**
6   Select the k images $\{j_1, \ldots, j_k\} \in \mathcal{M}_o$ that are closest to i according to L_2
     norm.
7     $avg \leftarrow \frac{1}{k} \sum_{m=1}^{k} j_m$
8   Add k copies of avg to $\mathcal{M}_d$
9   Remove $j_1, \ldots, j_k$ from $\mathcal{M}_o$
10 **end**

Algorithm 4.1: k-Same algorithm

---

input : Face set $\mathcal{M}_o$, privacy constant k, $|\mathcal{M}_o| \geq k$, data utility function u
output: De-identified face set $\mathcal{M}_d$

1 $\mathcal{M}_d \leftarrow \emptyset$
2 Let $\mathcal{M}_{o_1}, \ldots, \mathcal{M}_{o_l} \subset \mathcal{M}_o$ with $\mathcal{M}_{o_i} = \{x \in \mathcal{M}_o | u(x) = c_i\}$
3 $\mathcal{M}_{d_i} = ksame(\mathcal{M}_{o_i}, k), i = 1, \ldots, l$
4 $\mathcal{M}_d = \cup_{i=1}^{l} \mathcal{M}_{d_i}$

Algorithm 4.2: k-Same-Select Algorithm

---

convolution of the original image with the Gaussian blurring operator. Figure 2 shows example images of applying blurring with different σ values to a face image. The averaging effect of image blurring is illustrated in Figure 2(b) where we again plot the distribution of pixel intensity values across a face for both original and blurred images.

4.3 De-identification Using k-Same

The k-Same algorithm was first introduced by Newton et al. in [6]. Intuitively, k-Same works by taking the average of k face images in a face set and replacing these images with the average image. A version of the algorithm is described in Algorithm 4.1. Image sets de-identified using the k-Same algorithm are k-anonymized (see [6] for a proof). Figure 3(a) shows example images of a k-Samed face for different values of k. In Figure 3(b) we again show the distribution of pixel intensities across original and k-Samed face images. While the distributions change, overall characteristics such as the two local minima in the location of the pupils are maintained.

4.4 De-identification Using k-Same-Select

One of the shortcomings of the k-Same algorithm is the inability to integrate data utility functions. Notice that the k-Samed images in Figure 3 appear to change facialexpressions from neutral in the original image to smile in the image for

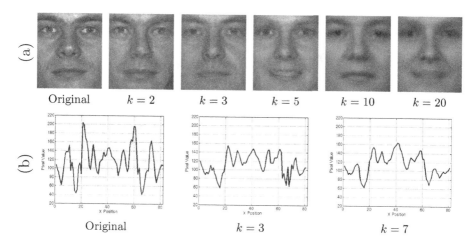

Fig. 3. Faces de-identified using the k-Same algorithm. (a) shows example images for different values of k. In contrast to pixelation and blurring the resulting image is still a face. This is also evident in the pixel distribution plots in (b). While the plots for $k = 3$ and $k = 7$ are different from the original plot they still show characteristics of the face (e.g. two local minima in the position where the pupils are). Note that the slight blurring visible at higher values of k are due to small misalignments between the images.

Fig. 4. Faces de-identified using the k-Same-Select algorithm with a facial expression data utility function. Note that expression stays constant across different levels of k-anonymization unlike in the examples shown in Figure 3.

$k = 5$. In order to address this problem we propose the k-Same-Select algorithm, summarized in Figure 4.2. Intuitively the algorithm partitions the input set of face images into mutually exclusive subsets using the data utility function and applies the k-Same algorithm independently to the different subsets. Due to the usage of the k-Same algorithm, k-Same-Select guarantees that the resulting face set is k-anonymized. Figure 4 shows examples of applying the k-Same-Select algorithm for different values of k using a facial expression utility function. Notice that the facial expression stays constant across all levels of k-anonymization.

5   Experiments

In this section we report results of face recognition and face classification experiments. We compare the performance of the naïve de-identification methods

Male Neutral   Male Smile   Female Neutral   Female Smile

Fig. 5. Examples from the FERET database [23] showing a male and a female subject displaying a neutral and a smile expression.

pixelation and blurring with the k-Same and k-Same-Select algorithms both in terms of privacy protection (Section 5.2) and preservation of data utility (Section 5.3).

5.1 Image Database: FERET

Our experiments are based on images from the recently released color version of the FERET database [23]. We use images of 833 subjects (474 male, 359 female), ranging in age from 20 to 70 years old. Experiments involving an expression data utility function report results on a subset of 584 subjects for which images showing both neutral and smile expressions are available. See Figure 5 for example images. For the PCA and the data utility experiments we use the manually determined locations of the eyes, the tip of the nose and the center of the mouth (which are distributed as part of the FERET database) to geometrically normalize the images for translation and rotation. We furthermore scale the images to a fixed size of 81x92 pixels. In experiments involving FaceIt the original images of size 512x768 are employed.

5.2 Evaluation of Privacy Protection

Evaluation Sets. Following Phillips et al. [23] we distinguish between *gallery* and *probe* images (see Section 4.1 for definitions). All results reported here are based on non-overlapping gallery and probe sets. We use the *closed universe* model for evaluating the performance, meaning that every individual in the probe set is also present in the gallery. For PCA recognition we randomly choose 20% of the subjects for computation of the eigenspace (see Section 3.1).

Results. Simulating a potential real world scenario, we evaluate both PCA and FaceIt using the original, unaltered images in the gallery set and images de-identified by blurring, pixelation, and application of k-Same and k-Same-Select

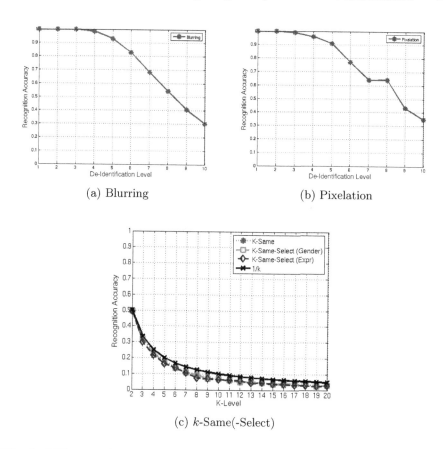

(a) Blurring

(b) Pixelation

(c) k-Same(-Select)

Fig. 6. PCA recognition rates for unaltered gallery images and de-identified probe images. Recognition accuracies stay above 90% for both blurring (shown in (a)) and pixelation (shown in (b)) for up to 5 levels of de-identification. In contrast, recognition accuracies for the k-Same, k-Same-Select gender and k-Same-Select expression are below the theoretical maximum of $\frac{1}{k}$ (shown in (c)).

in the probe set. In the experiments we vary the pixelation parameter p (sub-block size) between 1 and 21 and the blurring parameter σ (variance) between 1 and 37. Although the de-identification methods measure the amount of de-identification on different scales (e.g. level of blur vs. level of pixelation), for the purposes of this discussion, we normalize all methods to a common intensity scale which ranges from 0% to 100%.

PCA results are shown in Figure 6. In the case of both blurring and pixelation, recognition accuracies stay high ($> 90\%$) for up to 5 levels of de-identification (Figure 6(a) and (b)). In contrast, recognition accuracies for all variants of the k-Same and k-Same-Select algorithms are below the theoretical maximum of $\frac{1}{k}$ (Figure 6(c)).

Recognition accuracies for FaceIt are shown in Figure 7. Unlike PCA, FaceIt has not been trained on the evaluation image set. Recognition accuracies are

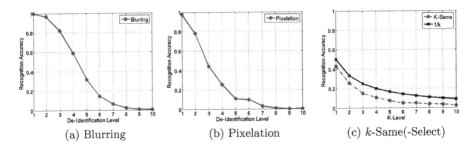

<table>
<tr><td>(a) Blurring</td><td>(b) Pixelation</td><td>(c) k-Same(-Select)</td></tr>
</table>

Fig. 7. FaceIt recognition rates for unaltered gallery images and de-identified probe images. Similar to the PCA case shown in Figure 6 higher levels of de-identification have to be choosen for blurring and pixelation in order to protect privacy. Accuracies on images de-identified using the k-Same algorithm again stay well below the theoretical maximum of $\frac{1}{k}$.

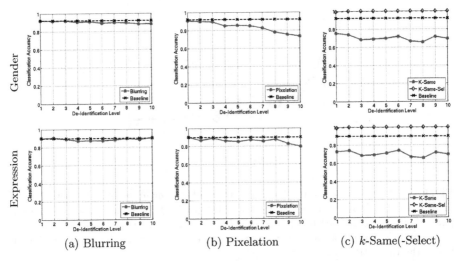

<table>
<tr><td>(a) Blurring</td><td>(b) Pixelation</td><td>(c) k-Same(-Select)</td></tr>
</table>

Fig. 8. Data utility evaluation. We show accuracies for the gender and expression classification tasks for images de-identified using blurring, pixelation, k-Same, and k-Same-Select. Data utility decreases for blurring, pixelation, and k-Same, and *increases* for k-Same-Select.

therefore generally lower for FaceIt than PCA. Nevertheless, the same observations hold. For both blurring and pixelation higher levels of de-identification have to be choosen in order to protect privacy.

Overall we can conclude that the k-Same and k-Same-Select algorithms are better in protecting privacy than the naïve approaches blurring and pixelation.

5.3   Evaluation of Data Utility

Experiment Setup. In order to evaluate data utility we set out to perform two classification tasks: gender and expression classification. For each task we use a Support Vector Machine classifier with a linear kernel [25]. We partition the dataset in 5 equally sized subsets, training in turn on four subsets and testing on the remaining fifth, reporting the average accuracy over the five experiments (5-fold cross-validation). This classification accuracy is our measure of data utility.

Results. We evaluate data utility for both gender and expression data on original, pixelated, blurred, k-Samed, and k-Same-Selected data, using the same levels of de-identification as described above. Figure 8 shows the results of the experiments, with the accuracy on original data plotted as "baseline". Data utility stays essentially constant for blurring (Figure 8(a)) and decreases for pixelation (Figure 8(b)) and k-Same (Figure 8(c)). Since the k-Same algorithm has no notion of data utility, images are potentially averaged across utility categories (as shown in Figure 3), effectively removing the relevant information. On the other hand, data utility *increases* for the k-Same-Select algorithm (Figure 8(c)), since information is not only preserved, but increased by averaging images of the same data utility class.

6 Discussion

In this section, we discuss several notable findings that emerged from our experiments, as well as some of the limitations and possible extensions to this research.

Note, in the experiments of the previous section, the notion of utility was quantified in terms of classification accuracy. Although the de-identification methods measure the intensity of the de-identification on different scales (e.g. level of blur vs. level of pixelation), for the purposes of this discussion, we normalize all methods to a common intensity scale which ranges from 0% to 100% de-identification.

6.1 Formal Methods are Better for Protecting Privacy

In previous studies, it has been claimed that *ad hoc* de-identification methods, such as pixelation and blurring prevent humans from reliably recognizing the identity of de-identified images [7, 4, 8, 9, 5, 11]. However, as our experiments demonstrate, these methods can not prevent a computer from reliably performing recognition; even at 40% de-identification the PCA algorithm achieves almost perfect recognition. In Figures 1 and 2, this roughly translates to pixelation level $p = 9$ and blur level $\sigma = 14$. Furthermore, at a de-identification level of 70% the computer recognition accuracy remains as high as 70%, or 7 correct recognitions out of every 10 probes! This corresponds to pixelation level $p = 15$ and blur level $\sigma = 25$. In contrast, the recognition rate for k-Same and k-Same-Select is controllable and inversely proportional to k, since both are derivative from the k-anonymity formal protection model. For example, when $k = 2$, a de-identification of 5%, recognition is approximately 50%. Moreover, it can be validated that both algorithms consistently permit lower recognition rates than the *ad hoc* methods (see Figure 6).

6.2   Flexibility of Formal Methods

As the level of de-identification increases, the *ad hoc* de-identification methods and k-Same incur a substantial loss in data utility in comparison to k-Same-Select. For the *ad hoc* methods, the main reason for this loss is that the specifications of pixelation and blur are inflexible. They can not be modified to explicitly account for a notion of data utility during the de-identification process. Similarly, while k-Same provides provable guarantees regarding privacy protection, for any protection level k, there is no criteria for utility preservation. However, the k-Same-Select algorithm provides an ability to preserve data utility. Unlike the previous de-identification methods, k-Same-Select is a *flexible* de-identification method; that is, it can translate any preconceived notion of data utility into de-identified images that encode that notion.

6.3   The Privacy/Utility Trade-Off

The pixelation, blur, and k-Same face de-identification methods exhibit a trade-off between privacy protection and data utility. This is because each of these algorithms de-identify images at the cost of loss of accuracy in classification tasks. k-Same-Select overcomes this trade-off by integrating prior knowledge of the notion of utility. In doing so, k-Same-Select allows for the preservation of discriminative features during the de-identification process and therefore provides an increase in classification accuracy over the prior methods.

The k-Same-Select algorithm basically functions as a mixture of a de-identification algorithm, k-Same, with a simple stratified learning techniques that dampens the sampling variability of the discriminating features. As a result, k-Same-Select provides an increased potential for data utility preservation in comparison to both k-Same and *ad hoc* methods. In a real-world implementation of k-Same-Select, we can make use of semi-supervised learning techniques [26] and of co-training [27], to learn gender and expression of probe images that are not excluded from the original probe image set. However, it is unclear whether k-Same-Select will increase or decrease the data utility in a real-world setting since stratified sampling techniques tend to help classification, whereas semi-supervised learning techniques tend to harm it. In future research, we expect to investigate the degree to which semi-supervised learning can facilitate the classification process.

We conclude that k-Same-Select is the only known algorithm that poses a challenge to the trade-off between privacy and utility. In our experiments, it was able to increase utility for any given level of privacy protection in a controlled setting. We believe it will be able to maintain the data utility for any given desired level of privacy protection in the real-world.

6.4   Conclusions

In this paper, we studied the degree to which *ad hoc* and formal face de-identification methods preserve data utility. Two distinct classification problems, expression and gender prediction, were specified and a machine learning method, in the form or support vector machines, was employed to measure the classification accuracy of de-identified images. Privacy protection was measured in the form of recognition accuracy against standard academic and state-of-the-art commercial face recognition systems. Our experiments demonstrate that formal face de-identification algorithms always dominate *ad hoc* methods in terms of providing privacy protection (i.e. incorrect face recognition). Furthermore, we demonstrated that formal de-identification methods can be extended to explicitly model criteria for utility preservation. As a result, we introduced a new formal face de-identification method, *k*-Same-Select, which is superior to prior de-identification methods in both privacy protection and utility preservation. The main drawback of our research is a need to specify criteria prior to de-identification occurs and, as a result, in future research we hope to determine a set of more generalized criteria.

References

1. Belsie, L.: The eyes have it - for now. Christian Science Monitor (November 7, 2002)
2. Sweeney, L.: Surveillance of surveillance camera watch project (2004)
3. Bowyer, K.: Face recognition technology and the security vs. privacy tradeoff. IEEE Technology and Society (2004) 9–20
4. Crowley, J., Coutaz, J., Berard, F.: Things that see. Communications of the ACM **43** (2000) 54–64
5. Neustaedter, C., Greenberg, S.: Balancing privacy and awareness in home media spaces. In: Workshop on Ubicomp Communities: Privacy as Boundary Negotiation, in conjunction with the 5th International Conference on Ubiquitous Computing (UBICOMP), Seattle, WA (2003)
6. Newton, E., Sweeney, L., Malin, B.: Preserving privacy by de-identifying facial images. IEEE Transactions on Knowledge and Data Engineering **17** (2005) 232–243
7. Boyle, M., Edwards, C., Greenberg, S.: The effects of filtered video on awareness and privacy. In: ACM Conference on Computer Supported Cooperative Work, Philadelphia, PA (2000) 1–10
8. Greenberg, S., Kuzuoka, H.: Using digital but physical surrogates to mediate awareness, communication, and privacy in media spaces. Personal Technologies **4** (2000)
9. Hudson, S., Smith, I.: Techniques for addressing fundamental privacy and disruption tradeoffs in awareness support systems. In: ACM Conference on Computer Supported Cooperative Work, Boston, MA (1996) 1–10
10. Neustaedter, C., Greenberg, S., Boyle, M.: Blur filtration fails to preserve privacy for home-based video conferencing. ACM Transactions on Computer Human Interactions (TOCHI) (2005) in press.
11. Zhao, Q., Stasko, J.: Evaluating image filtering based techniques in media space applications. In: ACM Conference on Computer Supported Cooperative Work, Seattle, WA (1998) 11–18
12. Senior, A., Pankati, S., Hampapur, A., Brown, L., Tian, Y.L., Ekin, A.: Blinkering surveillance: enabling video surveillance privacy through computer vision. IBM Research Report RC22886 (W0308-109), T. J. Watson Research Center, Yorktown Heights, NY (2003)

13. Alexander, J., Kenny, S.: Engineering privacy in public: confounding face recognition. In: 3rd International Workshop on Privacy Enhancing Technologies, Dresden, Germany (2003) 88–106

14. Sweeney, L.: k-anonymity: a model for protecting privacy. International Journal on Uncertainty, Fuzziness, and Knowledge-Based Systems **10** (2002) 557–570

15. Kanade, T.: Computer Recognition of Human Faces. Birkhauser (1977)

16. Zhao, W., Chellappa, R., Phillips, P., Rosenfeld, A.: Face recognition: a literature survey. ACM Computing Surveys **35** (2003) 399–458

17. Gross, R., Shi, J., Cohn, J.: Quo vadis face recognition? In: Third Workshop on Empirical Evaluation Methods in Computer Vision. (2001)

18. Blackburn, D., Bone, M., Philips, P.: Facial recognition vendor test 2000: evaluation report (2000)

19. Phillips, P.J., Grother, P., Ross, J.M., Blackburn, D., Tabassi, E., Bone, M.: Face recognition vendor test 2002: evaluation report (2003)

20. Belhumeur, P.N., Hespanha, J.P., Kriegman, D.J.: Eigenfaces vs. fisherfaces: Recognition using class specific linear projection. IEEE Transactions on Pattern Analysis and Machine Intelligence **19** (1997) 711–720

21. Penev, P., Atick, J.: Local feature analysis: A general statistical theory for object representati on (1996)

22. Gross, R., Yang, J., Waibel, A.: Face recognition in a meeting room. In: Proceedings of the Fourth IEEE International Conference on Automatic Face and Gesture Recognition, Grenoble, France (2000)

23. Phillips, P.J., Wechsler, H., Huang, J.S., Rauss, P.J.: The FERET database and evaluation procedure for face-recognition algorithms. Image and Vision Computing **16** (1998) 295–306

24. Sonka, M., Hlavac, V., Boyle, R.: Image processing, analysis, and machine vision. 2nd edn. Brooks/Cole (1999)

25. Cristianini, N., Shawe-Taylor, J.: An introduction to support vector machines. Cambridge University Press, Cambridge, UK (2000)

26. Seeger, M.: Learning with labeled and unlabeled data. Technical report, University of Edinburgh (2002)

27. Blum, A., Mitchell, T.: Combining labeled and unlabeled data with co-training. In: COLT: Proceedings of the Workshop on Computational Learning Theory, Morgan Kaufmann Publishers (1998)

Privacy in India: Attitudes and Awareness

Ponnurangam Kumaraguru and Lorrie Cranor

School of Computer Science, Carnegie Mellon University,
5000 Forbes Avenue,
Pittsburgh, PA, 15213, USA
{ponguru, lorrie}@cs.cmu.edu

Abstract. In recent years, numerous surveys have been conducted to assess attitudes about privacy in the United States, Australia, Canada, and the European Union. Very little information has been published about privacy attitudes in India. As India is becoming a leader in business process outsourcing, increasing amounts of personal information from other countries is flowing into India. Questions have been raised about the ability of Indian companies to adequately protect this information. We conducted an exploratory study to gain an initial understanding of attitudes about privacy among the Indian high tech workforce. We carried out a written survey and one-on-one interviews to assess the level of awareness about privacy-related issues and concern about privacy among a sample of educated people in India. Our results demonstrate an overall lack of awareness of privacy issues and less concern about privacy in India than has been found in similar studies conducted in the United States.

1 Introduction

As India is becoming a leader in business process outsourcing, increasing amounts of personal data from other countries are flowing into India. India's outsourcing business brought in $12 billion in 2003 and was expected to grow by 54 percent in 2004. The Indian outsourcing industry currently employs over 770,000 people and is expected to employ 2 million people by 2008 [16]. However, as the lack of privacy legislation in India may limit future growth, the industry is pushing for data protection laws [1], [7] [41]. Outsourced jobs often involve handling of personal information and sensitive data, including financial records and account information, and medical records [15]. While concerns have been raised about whether data privacy and confidentiality can be adequately maintained in a country that lacks privacy laws [1], [41], little is known about the privacy attitudes of the Indian workers who handle this data.

Many privacy surveys have been conducted in the United States, Europe, Australia, and Canada [22], [26], [27], [32], [45] but little information is available about privacy concerns in India. We conducted an exploratory study to gain an initial understanding of attitudes about privacy among the Indian high tech workforce. We carried out a written survey and one-on-one interviews to assess the level of awareness about privacy-related issues and concern about privacy among a sample of educated people in India. We also reviewed privacy policies at Indian web sites to understand the types of privacy protections being offered by Indian companies.

G. Danezis and D. Martin (Eds.): PET 2005, LNCS 3856, pp. 243–258, 2006.

The remainder of this paper is organized as follows: In the next section, we present a general overview of the status of privacy in India. In Section 3, we describe the methodology for our written survey, interviews, and web site survey. We present our results in Section 4 and discuss limitations and future work in Section 5.

2 India Today

India is the world's second most populous country, with about 1 billion inhabitants and a population growth rate of 1.44% annually as of July 2004. India is a country where 70% of the population lives in rural villages and 60% of the population is involved in farming and agriculture [30], [49]. The Gross Domestic Product (GDP) per capita purchasing power parity of India is about $2,900 [49]. New technologies that have brought with them increased privacy concerns in other parts of the world have been introduced more slowly in India than in Western countries.

As shown in Figure 1, Internet penetration in India has lagged significantly behind the US. While 55.13% of the US population were Internet users in 2003, only 1.74% of the Indian population were Internet users. The 2003 level of Internet penetration in India is similar to the level of Internet penetration in the US in 1993. In addition, there is a large difference between the US and India in deployment of both landline and mobile telephone lines. In 2003 there were 65 landline telephone lines and 47 mobile telephone lines for every 100 US inhabitants, while in India there were only 4 land line telephone lines and 1 mobile telephone line [33], [34].

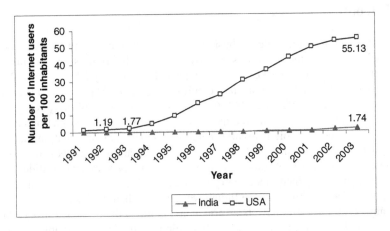

Fig. 1. Internet penetration in India and the US

2.1 Law

The Constitution of India, ratified in 1950, does not explicitly recognize the right to privacy [28]. However, the Supreme Court first recognized in 1964 that there is a right of privacy implicit in Article 21 of the Constitution, which states, "No person shall be deprived of his life or personal liberty except according to procedure established by law" [43]. Here there is no mention of the word 'privacy' instead the term 'personal liberty' has been used.

There is no general data protection law in India. In May 2000, the government passed the Information Technology Act (IT Act 2000), a set of laws intended to provide a comprehensive regulatory environment for electronic commerce. However the Act has no provision for protection of personal data [13]. It has been used to argue some privacy-related cases; however, its applicability is quite limited. For example, while the IT Act 2000 does not prohibit the use of hidden surveillance cameras, it does prohibit the electronic transmittal of obscene images, including those obtained through the use of hidden cameras. With the increasing use of cell phone cameras in Indian cities, the issue of video voyeurism has been gaining significant attention [14], [42].

In the last few years there have been discussions about creating privacy laws in India. As more and more companies from other countries are conducting business in India, there is an increase in concern about the lack of privacy laws in India [44]. Proposals are being considered for a law that would mandate privacy protections for data from other countries that is handled by India's outsourcing industry [41]. In the mean time, in response to recent incidents in which Indian outsourcing industry workers allegedly used personal information about customers of US companies to steal money from those customers, India's National Association of Software and Service Companies (NASSCOM) announced in April 2005, that it has begun creating a database of all employees working in the outsourcing industry. Called "Fortress India," this database will allow employers to screen out potential workers who have criminal records [8],[37].

2.2 Culture

Indian culture may play a significant role in shaping attitudes about privacy. Cultural values are known to affect a population's attitudes about privacy [3], [6], [17], [39], [40]. Hofstede developed a number of cultural values indices to measure cultural differences between societies. According to Hofstede, India is a *collectivist* society with lower Individualism Index (IDV) and higher Power Distance Index (PDI) compared to the US, which is an *individualist* society with higher IDV and lower PDI. Hofstede has shown that individuals in collectivist societies have more trust and faith in other people than individuals in individualist societies [19], [20].

Anecdotal evidence of Indians' tendency to trust that their personal information will not be misused can be found in recent Indian popular press reports that Indians are largely unaware of the extent to which databases of personal information are sold and traded among companies. When informed of this practice, the press reports that individuals are often shocked and outraged. Recently, news magazine *India Today*, featured a cover story titled "Privacy on Sale," illustrated with a cover photo of a man with a bar code stamped on his head [5]. *The Times of India* featured a special report on "The Death of Privacy" [47]. Similar stories have been showing up in the Western press for several years, but have only recently appeared in India.

The Indian joint family tradition [48], in which it is common for households to include multiple brothers, their wives, and their children (all living in a relatively small house by US standards), results in more routine sharing of personal information among a wider group of people than is typical in the US. Information that might typically be disclosed only to one's spouse or parents in the US is more frequently shared among uncles, aunts, and cousins in India. In addition, as it is common for Indian businesses to be owned and operated by large extended families, personal financial information is typically shared fairly widely among Indians.

3   Methodology

Our study included a survey, mental model interviews, and a review of web site privacy policies, all conducted during the summer of 2004. The methodology we used for each part of our study is explained below.

3.1 Survey

We developed a survey questionnaire to provide insights into attitudes about privacy of the Indian high tech workforce and technical students. We developed our survey instrument such that questions were comparable to questions on similar surveys administered in the US [10], [11], [18], [23], [24], 25], [26], [27], [36]. We developed our survey and pre-tested it on a sample of 30 students, professors and professionals. After refining our survey, we distributed 550 survey questionnaires at 12 companies and three universities in two Indian cities—Chennai and Hyderabad located in two different states (TamilNadu and Andhra Pradesh). Students were given about 20 minutes of class time to complete their surveys. Surveys were left with professors and professionals, and collected about a week later. We obtained 419 completed surveys (response rate of 76%). We eliminated surveys from 12 respondents who did not answer at least two of our six demographic questions, leaving us with 407 respondents in our sample.

Motivated by concerns about whether the Indian outsourcing industry can properly protect the personal data it handles, we decided to focus our survey on members of the Indian high tech workforce and students who might someday be employed by the outsourcing industry. Our sample included undergraduate students, graduate students, and professors from top Indian technical universities, as well as professionals. Although we did not restrict our sample to individuals currently employed by the outsourcing industry, we believe our survey respondents and interviewees have similar educational and socio-economic backgrounds as people employed by the outsourcing industry. In addition, students at the universities we surveyed are being recruited by the outsourcing industry. Ninety percent of our respondents were IT students or professionals.

Our sample is not statistically representative of any particular Indian community or of Indian Internet users. The average household income of our respondents was high by Indian standards, and our respondents were mostly well-educated and experienced Internet users. We believe that while not statistically representative, our sample is important for understanding workers in the outsourcing industry as well as the increasing more educated Indian high tech workforce. Table 1 summarizes the demographics of our sample.

Table 1. Characteristics of the sample (Annual Income calculated with $ 1 = Rs.45)

	N = 407
	Percentage
Age	
Less than 18 years	3.44
18 - 24 years	60.20
25 - 29 years	22.36
30 - 39 years	10.57
40 – 49 years	1.47
50 – 64 years	1.47
No answer	0.49
Sex	
Male	75.68
Female	24.32
No answer	0.00
Education	
Less than High school	0.25
Higher School	8.85
Some College	6.14
College Graduate	49.39
Post Graduation	33.42
Doctorate	1.23
No answer	0.74
Household annual income	
Less than $890	10.57
Between $891 and $1560	10.07
Between $1561 and $2220	9.83
Between $2221 and $3330	11.30
Between $3331 and $4440	10.57
Greater than $4441	26.54
No answer	21.13
Profession	
Computer related	45.45
Manufacturing	0.00
Teaching / Research	7.13
Student	44.72
Others	2.70

3.2 Interviews

We conducted one-on-one interviews to gain insights into the mental models people hold about privacy [35], [38]. We recorded interviews with 29 subjects and produced text transcripts. The interviews contained 17 open ended questions organized in several categories: *general understanding of privacy and security, security and privacy of computerized data, knowledge of risks and protection against privacy risks, knowledge of data sharing and selling in organizations and government, and demographics.* No personal information (name, email address, etc.) that would re-identify any individual was collected. We also used randomly generated numbers to identify the subjects in our notes so that the privacy of the subjects can be completely maintained.

Subjects were recruited who were at least 23 years old, with at least a Bachelor's degree, and at least 6 months work experience. The interviews were conduced in Chennai and Hyderabad, but many of the subjects were originally from other cities in India. Sixty-two percent of the subjects were male and 38% were female. The subjects ranged in age from 23 to 65 (75% were in the 23-35 category and 25% were in the

36-65 category). The average work experience was nine years. Thirty-one percent of subjects had only a bachelor's degree while others held graduate or professional degrees. Thirty-eight percent of subjects work in technical fields while 62% work in non-technical fields such as linguistics, accounting, and the arts. In this paper we refer only briefly to this interview study. A complete report of this study will be published elsewhere.

3.3 Website Privacy Policy Survey

We surveyed 89 web sites selected from the Google Indian shopping directory to determine whether they included privacy policies and what privacy protections were offered. At the time of our survey in the summer of 2004, 94 web sites were listed in this directory; however, five were unreachable [21]. For each privacy policy that we found, we recorded detailed information about the policy, (similar to the information gathered by Adkinson et al in their 2001 survey of American web sites [2]) including whether the site had a privacy seal, whether there was a corresponding P3P policy, whether the site collected personal information, whether the site shared personal information with third parties, and the choice options provided.

We selected the Google Indian shopping directory because it provides a list of e-commerce web sites that primarily serve the Indian market. Because most commercial Indian web sites have .com domains, they are difficult to identify, and whois information is not always a reliable indicator as to the market served. In future work it would be useful to survey the most popular web sites actually visited by people connecting to the Internet from India, although we expect that the most popular site list is dominated by non-Indian sites.

4 Analysis

In this section, we present our analysis of general privacy concerns, posting personal information, comfort level sharing different types of data, web privacy policies, trust in businesses and government, and web cookies.

We found no statistically significant differences between men and women, or between students and professionals, in the responses to the questions presented here. Therefore, we provide only the results for the complete set of 407 respondents. Throughout this paper we report our results as valid percentages.[1]

4.1 General Privacy Concerns

Alan Westin has used a number of standard survey questions about privacy concern to track changing attitudes about privacy in America since 1970 [51]. Similar questions have also been asked on other surveys [10].

We included a number of questions on our survey that had been included on Westin's surveys and other surveys of American Internet users. One question asked

---

[1] Valid percent is the percentage calculated after removing those surveys that had missing answers for the particular question. The complete questionnaire and the responses for each question can be obtained from the authors upon request.

subjects to report their level of concern about personal privacy, and another asked subjects to report their level of concern about personal privacy on the Internet. Seventy-six percent of Indian respondents were very or somewhat concerned about personal privacy and 80% were very or somewhat concerned about personal privacy on the Internet.

We compared our results with the results of a 1998 AT&T study of American Internet users drawn from a panel of readers of *FamilyPC* magazine, and found overall a lower level of concern among the Indian sample than among the American sample, as shown in Figure 2. Although we are comparing results of surveys administered over five years apart, we believe this comparison is still useful. The trend across several American surveys administered between 1994 and 2003 has been towards increasing levels of general privacy concern [25]. However, as individuals gain more Internet experience, their concerns about *online* privacy tend to decrease [3]. By comparing our sample with an earlier US sample, we are able to do a comparison between individuals with similar levels of Internet experience. In our sample, 27% of respondents had used the Internet for five years or more, and 16% had used it for two years or less. In the AT&T sample, 28% of respondents had used the Internet for five years or more and 23% had used it for two years or less. In addition, 67% of our respondents said they used the Internet several times a day and 13% said they used it once a day. In the AT&T sample, 65% said they used the Internet several times a day and 18% said they used it once a day.

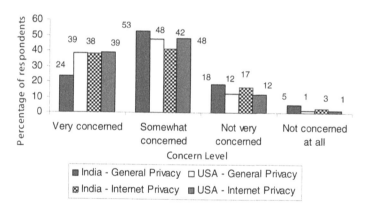

Fig. 2. General and Internet privacy concern in India, compared with 1998 survey of American Internet users [10]

4.2 Posting Personal Information

We asked several questions to gauge attitudes about common situations in India in which personal information is not well protected. Two of these situations involve the posting of personal information in public places.

One question asked students whether they were concerned about the posting of students' grades along with their full names on public notice boards on university campuses. This remains a common practice in India, although American universities now prohibit it (indeed, the practice is illegal for federally-funded institutions under the Family Educational Rights and Privacy Act). Some Indian universities even post grades on public web sites [29]. We found that 21% of the respondents we surveyed were very concerned and 32% were somewhat concerned about their university grades being posted, while 27% were not very concerned and 20% were not concerned at all. During discussions with Indian professors we found that many of them were aware that American universities do not publicly post student grades, and some had even unsuccessfully tried to convince their own universities to consider changing their policies on posting grades. While the survey and interviews indicate some level of awareness and concern about this practice, this was not a major concern of most of the people we surveyed.

We also asked respondents about the practice of publicly posting personal information about travelers at Indian railway stations and in train compartments, as shown in Figure 3. The posted information includes the last name, first name, age, gender, boarding station, destination, seat number, and passenger name record number for each passenger. We found even lower levels of concern about this practice than of the public posting of grades. The responses to our questions about public posting of personal information are summarized in Table 2.

Information in the chart: Age, Gender, Source station, Destination station, Seat number, First Name, Last Name, Passenger Name Record Number

Fig. 3. People checking the reservation charts at an Indian railway station [4]

Table 2. Level of concern about public posting of personal information

	Concern about public posting of grades	Concern about the railway posting personal information
Very concerned	21%	17%
Somewhat concerned	32%	23%
Not very concerned	27%	34%
Not concerned at all	20%	26%

4.3 Comfort Level Sharing Different Types of Data

We asked respondents how comfortable they were providing nine specific pieces of information to web sites. We found significant differences in comfort level across the nine types of information. Respondents were most comfortable sharing their age, email address, and health information with web sites. They were least comfortable sharing credit card number, passport number, email and ATM passwords, and annual income.

The 1998 AT&T survey asked a similar question about seven of the nine pieces of information we asked about [10]. Figure 4 compares our results with the AT&T survey results. Overall, our Indian respondents showed a greater level of comfort in sharing personal information with web sites than the American respondents. We expect that a 2004 survey of American Internet users would show increased comfort with sharing some types of information due to increased Internet experience, but lower comfort sharing email address as a result of concerns about spam, which was not nearly as big a problem in 1998. Only 38% of our Indian sample said they were somewhat or very concerned about spam, while 94% of American Internet users surveyed in 2001 said spam was a concern [26].

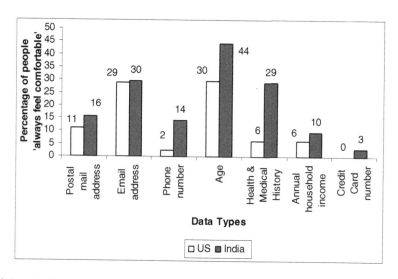

Fig. 4. Level of concern sharing different data with web sites, Indian survey compared with 1998 survey of American Internet users [10]

The most striking difference between the AT&T survey and our Indian survey is found in the level of comfort people have in sharing health and medical information with web sites. While 29% of our respondents always feel comfortable sharing health information with web sites, only 6% of respondents in the AT&T study said they always feel comfortable sharing this information. Likewise, 33% of respondents in the AT&T study and 21% of respondents in our study never feel comfortable sharing health information with web sites. More work is needed to understand why Indians are more comfortable sharing health information than Americans; however, we suspect it may have to do with Americans' concerns about job discrimination and health insurance. Few Indian workers currently have health insurance.

Similar to the AT&T study, we found significant differences in sensitivity to sharing three types of contact information: postal mail address, phone number, and email address. As shown in Table 3, our respondents were most comfortable sharing email address and least comfortable sharing phone number [10].

Table 3. Comfort level sharing contact information with web sites

	Postal mail address	Email address	Phone number
Always feel comfortable	16%	30%	14%
Usually feel comfortable	27%	30%	12%
Sometimes feel comfortable	29%	27%	26%
Rarely feel comfortable	16%	8%	20%
Never feel comfortable	12%	6%	29%

Our interviews provided further evidence of a relatively high level of comfort among Indians for sharing personal information. One subject said, "I am not concerned about others knowing about my physical mail address or email address but I am concerned if they get to know my credit card details." Another commented, "… my friends and family members know most of my information including financial and medical information." A third offered a comment that seemed to capture the views of many of our subjects, "As an Indian mentality we always like to share things."

4.4 Web Privacy Policies

In the US, there has been increasing pressure from the Federal Trade Commission for web sites to post privacy policies. In addition, companies in some regulated industries are required to post privacy notices. As of 2001, 83% of US commercial web sites had posted privacy policies [2], up from 66% in 1999 [12]. There are no requirements for Indian web sites to post privacy policies. However, as privacy policies are becoming increasingly expected on commercial web sites around the world, Indian web sites are beginning to post them. We examined 89 Indian e-commerce websites listed in the Google Indian shopping directory and found that only 29% had posted privacy policies. None of the Indian web sites were P3P (Platform for Privacy Preferences) enabled [9], while 5% of the American web sites that collected personally-identifiable information were P3P-enabled in 2001. Only one of the Indian web sites had a privacy seal, while 11% of American web sites had privacy seals in 2001, up from 8% in 2000 [2].

The Indian sites that posted privacy policies reported similar data practices as reported by American web sites in 2001. One of the most important differences was that Indian sites were much less likely than American sites to offer opt-out opportunities. A larger sample of Indian web sites is needed to do a meaningful comparison of more detailed online privacy practices.

Some of the privacy policies found on Indian web sites did not actually contain much information about the web site's privacy practices. For example, one privacy policy explained only the customers' responsibilities and not the company's responsibilities:

> The Customers shall not disclose to any other person, in any manner whatsoever, any information relating to [this website] ... or its affiliates of a confidential nature obtained in the course of availing the services through the website. Failure to comply with this obligation shall be deemed a serious breach of the terms ....

Given that privacy policies are uncommon on Indian web sites and rarely offer consumers any choices, we were not surprised to find that 35% of our respondents said they never read privacy policies and only 27% or our respondents said they sometimes or always read privacy policies. A 2001 US study found that 17% of American Internet users report never reading privacy policies and 36% report sometimes or always reading privacy policies [11]. It is unclear whether the apparently lower level of privacy concern in India is partially responsible for fewer Indian than American web sites posting privacy policies, or, whether the lack of Indian privacy policies is playing a role in limiting Indian awareness of privacy issues.

4.5 Trust in Businesses and Government

Other researchers have found that privacy concern levels tend to be correlated with distrust in companies and government [3], [36]. To understand the level of trust Indians have in companies and governments that collect personal information, our interviews included a number of questions about trust. We asked interview subjects to tell us their level of trust that both business and the government would not misuse their personal information. Subjects that gave a 0 to 30% chance of misuse of information were categorized as "highly trusting," subjects that gave a 31 to 70% chance of misuse of information were categorized as "somewhat trusting," and subjects that gave a 71 to 100% chance of misuse of information were categorized as "untrusting." Most of our subjects (86% for businesses, 81% for governments) were highly trusting, and very few were untrusting (7% for businesses, 4% for governments). Of the subjects who gave a numerical value in their responses, 13 out of 28 said there was a 0% chance that their data would be misused by businesses, and 11 out of 26 said there was a 0% chance that their data would be misused by the government. One subject said, "I believe in government, 100% they will not abuse it." These results suggest that the level of privacy concern among our interview subjects is fairly low.

These results are quite different from the results of an American study that asked about trust of business and government (although, it should be noted that there were significant differences in the way the questions were worded). A 2001 Harris Interactive study of American Internet users found that only 10% of people have high levels of trust for businesses and 15% have high levels of trust for the government [23], [24].

We also asked subjects about how much they trust businesses that buy personal information from the primary data collector to use for marketing. We found that respondents had less trust in these businesses, with only 65% trusting them not to misuse their personal information.

4.6 Web Cookies

Web cookies are used to identify repeat visitors to a web site and streamline online transaction processes. When asked about web cookies, 57% of our respondents and 52% of the AT&T respondents said they were concerned about web cookies, and 15% of our respondents and 12% of the AT&T respondents said they did not know what a web cookie is. Of those who knew what cookies were, 47% of our respondents and 23% of the AT&T respondents had never changed the cookie settings from the default setting. Figure 5 shows the browser cookies settings reported by respondents who knew about web cookies and compares our results with the AT&T study. The most significant difference between the two survey results is in the percentage of people who have never changed their cookie settings. Indian respondents were twice as likely to report never changing their cookie settings as the American respondents. We also saw a big difference in the percentage of respondents who configured their browser to warn about all cookies. This difference may be attributable to the increased use of cookies since 1998, making that setting quite disruptive to the browsing experience.

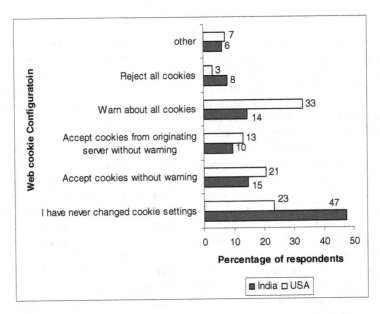

Fig. 5. Web cookie configuration reported by Indians compared with 1998 AT&T survey [10]

We presented two scenarios in which we described the use of persistent identification numbers stored in cookies that web sites could use to track their visitors; however, we did not use the word "cookie" in our descriptions. We found that 78% of our respondents would definitely or probably agree to the use of such identification numbers to receive customized service, while 58% of our respondents would agree to the use of such identification numbers to provide customized advertising. These results are quite similar to the findings of the AT&T study [10].

Overall, our Indian sample shows a moderate level of knowledge and concern about cookies that is not all that different from Americans in the 1998 AT&T sample. The biggest difference is that Indians were less likely to have changed their cookie settings than Americans. This may indicate less concern, less willingness to take steps to address the cookie concern, or less knowledge about browser cookie configuration.

5 Discussion

As specified earlier, this study was an exploratory study to understand the attitudes of Indians about privacy and see how they differ from Americans. We conducted a written survey and interviews, and analyzed privacy policies on Indian web sites. Overall, we found less concern and awareness about privacy among Indians than among Americans. There were large differences in attitudes about sharing medical information as well as in willingness to trust businesses and the government with personal information. Some of these differences may be attributable to cultural differences [3], or to the fact that Internet technology has been adopted earlier in the US than in India. More research is needed to better understand the reasons for these differences.

Concerns have been raised about whether the Indian outsourcing industry can properly protect personal data and new privacy laws are being proposed [15], [41], [44]. Our results suggest that the Indian high tech workforce may not be sufficiently aware of privacy issues, and that the outsourcing industry and international businesses may need to provide privacy training to their workers. This training could also be a part of Indian undergraduate education.

We were unable to do a direct comparison of our results with a more recent US study, due to the fact that more recent US studies did not ask the same questions that we asked. However, as more recent US studies have shown a trend towards increasing privacy concerns [25], we believe that a comparison of our data with data from a similar study conducted in the US during the same time period would likely show larger difference in the attitudes and awareness than shown in this paper.

We were also unable to do a direct comparison of our results with the results of studies conducted in Australia and Europe due to differences in the questions asked. In general we find that our Indian responsdents are less concerned about misuse of their personal information than Australian, German, and British survey respondents [31], [46]. One Australian study found that 41% of respondents reported setting their web browsers to reject cookies, while we found only 7% of our Indian respondents reported setting their browsers to reject cookies. Furthermore, the Australians surveyed were more than twice as likely to report reading privacy policies than the Indians we surveyed. Australians also reported lower levels of trust in government, and substantially lower levels of trust in retailers than we found in our Indian subjects. Finally, the Australians demonstrated a greater awareness of privacy issues than we found among our Indian subjects [46]. We expect our results to aid future researchers in studying privacy attitudes in India and cross-cultural attitudes about privacy.

Although we obtained some interesting results that are consistent with studies of Indian cultural values, it is important to recognize the limitations of our samples. The results we obtained cannot be generalized to the entire Indian population, or even to the entire Indian high tech workforce. We also understand that the level of privacy concern reported by respondents does not necessarily correspond to their actual behavior with respect to protecting their own privacy or maintaining the confidentiality of data they handle as part of their employment [50].

Future work might attempt to survey a random national sample, or to focus specifically on workers in the outsourcing industry. A study of outsourcing workers might include questions about how they handle customer data and evaluate their knowledge of relevant privacy policies. A common study conducted in both the US and India in the same timeframe would also be useful. As the penetration of the Internet and communication technologies is now increasing rapidly in India and westernization is having an increasing influence on Indian life, a longitudinal study involving annual surveys would be valuable.

Acknowledgements

The interview protocol used in this study was adapted from a protocol developed by Granger Morgan and Elaine Newton at Carnegie Mellon University. The authors would like to thank Raj Reddy for providing partial support for this study while the first author was a student at International Institute of Information Technology, Hyderabad, India. The authors would also like to thank Krishna Reddy T.S.V., who assisted with the website privacy policy analysis at IIIT Hyderabad. This research was partially funded by Carnegie Mellon CyLab and an IBM Faculty Award.

References

1. Achappa, Sigi. Outsourcing is a bubble in India. CIOL. October 2004. http://www.ciol.com/content/ news/ BPO/2004/104101402.asp.
2. Adkinson, F William, et al. Privacy Online: A Report on the Information Practices and Policies of Commercial Web sites. The Progress and Freedom. Special Report March 2002.
3. Bellman, Steven, Eric J. Johnson, Stephen J. Kobrin, and Gerald L. Lohse. "International Differences in Information privacy concerns: A global survey of consumers." The Information Society, 20, pp 313 – 324. 2004.
4. Beveridge, Colin. Photographs of India: Kolkota during 2001. http://www.colinbeveridge.com/travelarticle.asp?article=16. visited 16 Jan 2005.
5. Bhupta, Malini. Privacy on Sale. India Today International. Sep 27 2004.
6. Boni, De Marco, Martyn Prigmore. Cultural Aspects of Internet Privacy. Proceedings of the UKAIS 2002 Conference. Leeds. 2002.
7. Business Line. Tech job loss will be other industries' gain. October 2004. http://www.thehindubusinessline.com/2004/10/16/stories/2004101601900500.htm.
8. Business Standard. NASSCOM to set up employee database. April 2005. http://www.nasscom.org/artDisplay.asp?art_id=4247. visited 23 April 2005.
9. Cranor, Lorrie Faith. "Web Privacy with P3P." O'Reilly. 2002.
10. Cranor, Lorrie, Joseph Reagle, Mark S Ackerman. Beyond Concern: Understanding Net Users' Attitudes About Online Privacy. In Proceedings of the Telecommunications Policy Research Conference. Alexandria, VA. September 25-27, 1999. http://www.research.att.com/resources/trs/TRs/99/99.4/99.4.3/report.htm.

11. Culnan, Mary J, George R Milne. The Culnan-Milne Survey on Consumers & Online Privacy Notices. http://www.ftc.gov/bcp/workshops/glb/supporting/culnan-milne.pdf. Dec 2001.
12. Culnan, Mary J. Georgetown Internet Privacy Policy Survey:Report to the Federal Trade Commission. June 1999. http://www.msb.edu/faculty/culnanm/GIPPS/mmrpt.PDF.
13. Department of Information Technology. Information Technology Act 2000. http://www.mit.gov.in/it-bill.asp. visited 10 Nov 2004.
14. Duggal, Pavan. Licence to shoot. Yahoo! India News. December 24, 2004. http://in.news.yahoo.com/041224/48/2in9n.html.
15. Economist. Oursourcing to India: Safety Matters. 2 Sepetermber 2004. http://www.economist.com/finance/displayStory.cfm?story_id=3160118
16. Fannin, Rebecca. India's Outsourcing Boom. Chief Executive. http://www.chiefexecutive.net/depts/outsourcing/198.htm. March 2004 Vol. 198.
17. Fjetland, Michale. *"Global Commerce and The privacy clash."* The Information Management Journal. January/February 2002.
18. Fox Susannah. "Trust and privacy online: Why Americans want to rewrite the rules." The Pew Internet & American Life Project. 20 Aug 2000.
    http://www.pewinternet.org/pdfs/PIP_Trust_Privacy_Report.pdf. 2000. visited 22 Sep 04.
19. Geert, Hofstede. *"Cultural and Organizations - Software of the Mind - Intercultural Cooperation and its importance for survival."* McGraw-Hill. 1991.
20. Geert, Hofstede. Geert Hofstede Analysis. http://www.cyborlink.com/besite/hofstede.htm. 2003. visited 2 Oct 04.
21. Google directory.
    http://directory.google.com/Top/Regional/Asia/India/Business_and_Economy/Shopping/ visited on 10 June 2004.
22. Harris and Westin. The Equifax Canada Report on Consumers and Privacy in the Information Age. Equifax Canada. 1992.
23. Harris Interactive for The Privacy Leadership Initiative (PLI). "A survey of consumer privacy attitudes and behavior." 2001.
24. Harris Interactive for The Privacy Leadership Initiative (PLI). "Consumer Privacy Attitudes and Behaviors Survey - Wave II." July 2001.
25. Harris Interactive. Harris Interactive Poll on Surveillance Issues. 1,010 respondents. March 19 2003. http://www.harrisinteractive.com/harris_poll/index.asp?PID=365, visited on 18 Aug 2004.
26. Harris Interactive. Privacy On and Off the Internet: what consumers want. Privacy & American Business. 2001.
27. Harris, Louis and Associates and Alan F Westin. E-Commerce & Privacy: What Net users want. Sponsored by Privacy & American Business and Price Waterhouse, Inc. June 1998
28. Henry Michael. *"International Privacy, Publicity and Personality Laws."* Reed Elsevier. pp 233 - 250. 2001.
29. Higher Secondary (HSC) Merit List for 2004. Fergusson College. http://www.fergusson.edu/notices/2004/june/hscmeritlist.asp. visited 15 Nov 2004
30. Indian Child. Population of India http://www.indianchild.com/population_of_india.htm. visited 10 Nov 2004.
31. Information and Privacy Commisioner, Ontario. A Report to the 22nd International Conference of Data Protection Commissioners. September 2000.
    http://www.ipc.on.ca/scripts/index_.asp?action=31&P_ID=11425&N_ID=1&PT_ID=1135 1&U_ID=0. visited on 30 April 2005.

32. International Research Associates for the European Commission Directorate General Internal Market and Financial Services. Information Technology and Data Privacy. Eurobarometer 46.1. 1997.

33. International Telecommunication Union, "World Telecommunication Indicators 2003." * STARS Version 4.2. Washington DC. USA.

34. International Telecommunication Union. ICT Free Statistics. http://www.itu.int/ITU-D/ict/statistics/. visited 2 Oct 04

35. Johnson-Laird, P. "*Mental Models.*" Cambridge, MA: Harvard University Press. 1983.

36. Louis Harris & Associates and Dr. Alan F. Westin. Health Information Privacy Survey. for Equifax Inc. 1,000 adults of the national public. 1993.

37. Marcelo Ray and Khozem Merchant. Fortress India plan to combat online crime. The Financial Times. April 2005. http://news.ft.com/cms/s/ac5fb49a-abb9-11d9-893c-00000e2511c8.html. visited 23 April 2004.

38. Mead, H George. *"Mind, Self and Society."* University of Chicago Press, IL. 1962

39. Milberg, Sandra J, et al. "*Information privacy: Corporate management and national regulation.*" Organizational Science, 2000 INFORMS Vol. 11, No. 1, pp 35 - 57. January-February 2000.

40. Milberg, Sandra J, et al. Values, personal information privacy and regulatory approaches. Communications of the ACM. December 1995/Vol.38, No.12.

41. Overby, Stephanie. India to Adopt Data Privacy Rules. CIO Magazine (September 1, 2003). http://www.cio.com/archive/090103/tl_data.html

42. Pandit, Sharvani. The law isn't much help. The Times of India. 15 Jan 2005. http://timesofindia.indiatimes.com/articleshow/991390.cms

43. Privacy International. Country reports - Republic of India.http://www.privacyinternational.org/survey/phr2000/countrieshp.html#Heading3. visited 02 Oct 04.

44. Ribeiro John. Source code stolen from U.S. software company in India. Infoworld. Aug 05 2004. http://www.infoworld.com/article/04/08/05/HNcodestolen_1.html.

45. Roy Morgan Research. Privacy and the community. Office of the Federal Privacy Commissioner. July 2001. http://www.privacy.gov.au/publications/rcommunity.html.

46. Roy Morgan Research for The Office of the Federal Privacy Commissioner. Community Attitudes Towards Privacy 2004. http://www.privacy.gov.au/publications/rcommunity/index_print.html. visited 20 April 2004.

47. Suraiya, Jug and Vikas, Singh. The death of privacy. Times of India. 15 January 2005. http://timesofindia.indiatimes.com/articleshow/991395.cms.

48. The Joint Family, Encyclopedia Britannica Premium Service. http://www.britannica.com/eb/article?tocId=26070. visited 18 Oct 2004.

49. The World Fact Book. India. http://www.cia.gov/cia/publications/factbook/geos/in.html. visited on 25 Nov 2004.

50. Turner, Charles, and Elizabeth Martin, ed. "*Surveying Subjective Phenomena.*" New York: Russell Sage Foundation. 1984.

51. Westin Alan, Center for Social & Legal Research. Bibliography of surveys of the U.S. Public, 1970 – 2003. http://www.privacyexchange.org/iss/surveys/surveybibliography603.pdf. visited on 15 Aug 2004

Economics of Identity Management: A Supply-Side Perspective

Sven Koble and Rainer Böhme

Technische Universität Dresden
Institute for System Architecture
01062 Dresden, Germany
{sven.koble, rainer.boehme}@inf.tu-dresden.de

Abstract. In an online world, the temptation to exploit customer information for marketing purposes is a strong argument for customers to use a privacy enhancing identity management system. However, the success of this technology depends on the support from the vendors as well. Apart from practical aspects, such as usability, trustworthiness, and standardisation, economic aspects play a key role in this decision. This paper examines the cost-utility trade-off from a supply-side perspective with micro-economic models. Albeit still limited to the case of a monopolist supplier, we reflect the impact of different customer preferences towards privacy, and the possibility to implement price discrimination.

1 Introduction

The Internet enables companies to gather and analyse customer information on a much broader scale than conventional offline business did. This data is used for multiple purposes: On the one hand, it appears to customers that it is a requirement to deliver more tailored products and services. On the other hand, the data is privacy sensitive and it can be used for marketing purposes, eventually leading to price discrimination. Odlyzko [10] observes a tendency in private sector business to sacrifice customer privacy in order to charge customers differently for the same product. This is possible, because knowledge about customers implies knowledge about their willingness to pay.

Opinion polls indicate that the public is highly concerned about privacy [6]. Many respondents complain about a lack of privacy, and it is even considered as a main reason for individuals not to purchase online. For example, Gellman [7] shows that vendors may loose sales revenue if they do not care about privacy. As a result of the public concerns, *Privacy Enhancing Technologies* (PET) are on the agenda. As early as 1985, Chaum [4] predicted customer demand for a tool, which helps to enhance their privacy: An *Identity Management System* (IMS) supports its users to manage and protect their personal information [8]. To reach a high level of security and trust, sensitive data is ideally stored in each individual's computer instead of a central database.

It is evident that the acceptance by a large user-base is a prerequisite for the success of identity management and some effort is spent on researching user-friendly and thus compelling systems [5]. However, support from vendors and

G. Danezis and D. Martin (Eds.): PET 2005, LNCS 3856, pp. 259–272, 2006.

service providers is at least as crucial. This paper focuses on the supply-side perspective and tries to answer the question why—and under which conditions— companies have an incentive to introduce and support identity management systems (IMS).

This is the underlying economic trade-off: Offering interfaces to an IMS enables customers to prevent being tracked. Thus the interaction becomes less privacy invasive, and vendors could increase their customer base by attracting those subgroups, which would not have purchased before because of privacy concerns. We further refer to this group as persons with *privacy awareness*. On the downside, vendors loose the advantages from processing customer information. This can be quantified in the fact that it renders price discrimination useless.

The remainder of this paper is organised as follows: In Section 2 we present literature related to our research. Section 3 introduces a baseline model which assumes perfect price discrimination. More realistic price discrimination models with different price strategies are discussed in Section 4. For all models, the revenues are compared with the expected revenues after the introduction of an IMS. Finally, Section 5 concludes with a discussion of possible implications and directions for future research.

2   Related Work

The research in this paper has links to three areas of literature: general literature on privacy enhancing technologies, micro-economic textbooks, and specific economics of privacy.

Privacy Enhancing Technologies. In this paper we focus on identity management systems (IMS) as a privacy enhancing technology: Digital pseudonyms protect personal identifying information from the access of business counterparts. Thus the amount of sensitive data revealed can be reduced to a minimum [4, 5]. The EU funded project PRIME [12] actively researches and develops an operable IMS. For this paper it is only important to know that given an IMS, a vendor cannot price discriminate anymore due to the lack of information about the customer. Other useful properties of IMS, such as convenience and accountability, are left aside.

The pseudonym concept is related, but not similar, to Acquisti and Varian's notion of online and offline identities [2]. The distinction between *myopic* and *sophisticated* consumers—another concept from the same paper—is largely covered by the definition of privacy awareness in our work.

Micro-Economics. Fundamental micro-economic models, e.g., market structure or price discrimination, are discussed in [15, 9, 11]. Price strategies and different types of price discrimination especially for the online world are presented in [13]. Odlyzko [10] identifies a growing incentive for companies to price discriminate, hence diminishing privacy. In this paper, however, we analyse whether it might be profitable for the supplier to offer *more* privacy to its customers by supporting a privacy enhancing technology, precisely an interface to IMS. Note, that in this context "profitable" means increasing the vendor's revenue.

Economics of Privacy. Based on micro-economic models, there have been several attempts to include customer privacy into formal economic models (cf. [1] for an historic overview). Taylor [14] explains why the value of customer information largely depends on the ability to identify individual consumers and charge them personalized prices. Acquisti and Varian [2] analyse whether it is profitable for vendors to offer individual prices depending on the purchase history. They figure out that it is indeed profitable for the vendor if adapting privacy enhancing technologies (PET) is costly for his customers. Here, we analyse whether it is still profitable for the vendor to introduce a PET even if the adapting costs are zero (cf. A4 below).

3   The Baseline Model

In this section, a simple model of a single revenue-maximizing vendor (assumption A1) is presented, with a good that can be produced at zero marginal cost[1] (A2). This assumption is made to show that without marginal cost the vendor can sell to all customers and thus maximise his revenue. We also assume that there exist two groups of customers, one that is not privacy concerned (suffix $\overline{PA}$), and another with notable *privacy awareness* (suffix PA). This distinction can be justified against the backdrop of previous empirical findings [3]. The latter group will only purchase if an IMS is supported (A3). As already mentioned, the use of an IMS causes no cost for the customer[2] (A4). Since in the baseline model, preference and reservation price of the customer are the same, the demand function turns out to be linear. We further assume that the maximum price a on the demand curve, is constant for both groups (A5). The vendor can store and analyse all customer data if no IMS is in use (A6). In this case, the vendor will use the data to enforce price discrimination to gain extra revenue. In the baseline model, we assume perfect price discrimination (A7). This means that a vendor knows the individual willingness to pay of each customer[3], and there is no effective way for arbitrage (A8). Introducing an IMS will reduce this extra revenue from the earnings but, at the same time, extend the potential customer base to the group with privacy awareness.

The two cases, IMS or not, can be modelled in a demand curve diagram as shown in Figure 1. In the analysis we separate the total number of customers Q_T into two groups $Q_{\overline{PA}}$ and Q_{PA}.

---

[1] e.g., production cost of a ticket

[2] We assume that the software is installed and no additional cost from adapting the software appears. Further there is no rise in the product price.

[3] You could think of people who want to buy tickets for a concert. Every person would wear a cap with a sign: "I will pay v \$ maximum". Then the ticket vendor will sell a ticket to each customer for the price v on his or her individual cap.

1. **Revenue without IMS**
   - Customers without privacy awareness: We get the revenue by adding the areas A, B and C (see Fig. 1). The vendor sells at the consumer's reservation price. The demand curve $D(x) = a - b_{\overline{PA}} \cdot x$ (where a denotes the maximum price and x the quantity) under perfect price discrimination yields a revenue r of:

$$r = \frac{a^2}{2 \cdot b_{\overline{PA}}}$$

   - Customers with privacy awareness: No revenue, because of no demand.
2. **Revenue with IMS**
   - Customers without privacy awareness: As a result of the use of an IMS, no price discrimination is possible. We obtain the maximum revenue, if marginal revenue equals marginal cost—in this case zero. This is equivalent to maximise the area A (see Fig. 1). The demand curve $D(x) = a - b_{\overline{PA}} \cdot x$ yields a maximum revenue r of:

$$r = \frac{a^2}{4 \cdot b_{\overline{PA}}}$$

   - Customers with privacy awareness: Since IMS is supported, we have an extra demand from customers with privacy awareness. The demand curve $D2(x) = a - b_{PA} \cdot x$ gives the vendor's maximum revenue r:

$$r = \frac{a^2}{4 \cdot b_{PA}}$$

For the vendor, the use of an IMS pays off if he gains more revenue from customers with privacy awareness than loosing revenue due to turning away from price discrimination. The demand curves of the two customer groups just differ from the gradients $b_{\overline{PA}}$ and b_{PA}. So the only difference is the number of customers in each group. Therefore we define a factor f to model the proportions of customers with privacy awareness Q_{PA} and no privacy awareness $Q_{\overline{PA}}$:

$$f = \frac{Q_{PA}}{Q_{\overline{PA}}}, \text{ with } Q_T = Q_{PA} + Q_{\overline{PA}} \tag{1}$$

As shown in Fig. 1, area A will always be the same size as areas B + C. So with perfect price discrimination, the vendor doubles his revenue compared to the situation with a single flat price. By using an IMS the revenue from customers without privacy awareness will cut by 50 %. Therefore, to compensate, the number of customers with privacy awareness must be at least the number of customers without privacy awareness. Regarding factor f, we obtain two cases:

   - $f > 1$. The number of customers with privacy awareness is higher than the number customers without privacy concerns. A vendor could profit from supporting an IMS. The higher demand from customers with high privacy concerns outweighs the loss from not price discriminate the existing customers.

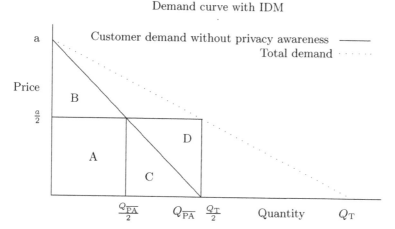

Fig. 1. The monopolist vendor gains extra revenue by supporting an IMS due to higher demand (C and D). At the same time, price discrimination becomes impossible (B and C). In this diagram, both demand curves ($D(x)$ and $D2(x)$) are equal, so the extra sales to customers with privacy awareness (C + D) balance the decrease in revenue due to missing price discrimination (B + C).

- $f \leq 1$. If the majority of customers is not privacy aware, it will not pay off for the vendor to introduce an IMS. The loss of revenue from missed price discrimination exceeds extra revenue from prospect customers with privacy awareness.

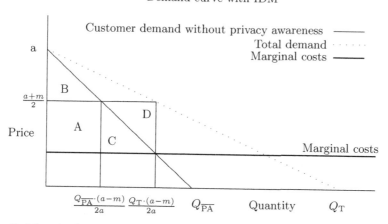

Fig. 2. Marginal costs $m > 0$: Higher demand due to the introduction of an IMS leads to increased revenue (C and D). At the same time, price discrimination is ruled out (B and C). Marginal costs reduce the revenue but leaving the ratio between A and (B + C) the same. In this diagram, both demand curves are equal, so the extra sales to customers with privacy awareness (C + D) balance the decrease in revenue due to missing price discrimination (B + C).

This relation is also true if real marginal costs exist (raise A2). As shown in Fig. 2, the marginal cost does not change the ratio between areas A and B + C. Here again, if a vendor supports IMS he looses half of his revenue from customers without privacy awareness.

The result is straightforward: Price discrimination doubles the revenue under the assumption that perfect price discrimination is possible (cf. A7). However, perfect price discrimination seems unrealistic because it is still very hard to know the willingness to pay of each individual customer. Therefore, in the following section, we contrast our first model with the simplest possible strategy for price discrimination, where only two groups of customers with different willingness to pay can be told apart. Then, a comparison of the results from perfect price discrimination with the results from higher degree price discrimination covers the entire range of realistic scenarios.

4   Models with Typical Price Strategies

In the baseline model, we considered perfect price discrimination. Since in many cases the vendor does not know the individual willingness to pay of each customer, an extension of the model is reasonable. As the simplest form of price discrimination we consider two disjoint groups with different willingness to pay:

- high v_h and low v_l willingness to pay

Again, we classify all customers Q_T depending on their attitudes towards privacy:

- number of customers with (Q_{PA}) and without privacy awareness $(Q_{\overline{PA}})$

Each of those two groups can have a different willingness to pay the high price. Therefore $\pi_{\overline{PA}}$ gives the percentage of customers *without* privacy awareness to pay the high price. And π_{PA} gives the percentage of customers *with* privacy concerns to pay the high price. In most cases, $\pi_{\overline{PA}} = \pi_{PA} \to \pi$, as there is no theoretical reason why the two groups should face different demand functions. However, according to an analysis of socio-economic variables of people who opted out from direct marketing calls in the U.S. [16], privacy seems to be a luxury good, which could be modelled as $\pi_{\overline{PA}} < \pi_{PA}$. In this paper, we draw all graphs with the assumption $\pi_{\overline{PA}} = \pi_{PA}$, although our formal analyses cover the general case.

4.1   One Purchase Period

First we consider one purchase period. This will help to understand the differences compared to the baseline model, i.e., the demand curve is discrete. In addition, we consider the price for which a vendor should offer his product if price discrimination is impossible.

If **IMS is not used**, price discrimination is possible and leads to a two-step demand curve with different willingness to pay (see Fig. 3). The maximum revenue r is the summation of the three areas A, B and C:

$$r = A + B + C \tag{2}$$

Customer demand depending on the willingness to pay

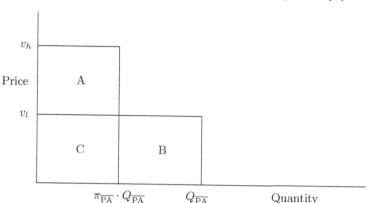

Fig. 3. Demand if IMS is not used: Revenue of area A and C if the vendor charges the high price v_h. Revenue of area B and C for the low price v_l.

If an **IMS is used**, then no price discrimination is possible. This results in higher demand, because customers with privacy awareness are purchasing as well. The three areas D, E and F (see Fig. 4) indicate the demand of those customers. Now the vendor has to decide, which price he is going to charge for his product. The price that maximises the vendors' revenue depends on the areas A and D as well as on the areas B and E. So we have to consider two cases:

– Case 1: $A + D > B + E$. The **high price** v_h will maximise the revenue. The overall revenue consists of the areas A and C from the customers without privacy awareness and the areas D and F of the customers with privacy awareness. The maximum revenue r is:

$$r = A + C + D + F \qquad (3)$$

For the vendor, the introduction of an IMS pays off if (3) > (2):

$$A + C + D + F > A + B + C$$

and holds the inequation

$$D + F > B$$

To calculate the areas, we insert the parameters v_h, v_l, $\pi_{\overline{PA}}$ und π_{PA} and get:

$$\pi_{PA} \cdot v_h \cdot Q_{PA} > (1 - \pi_{\overline{PA}}) \cdot v_l \cdot Q_{\overline{PA}}$$

we insert factor f (see Equation 1):

$$\pi_{PA} \cdot v_h \cdot f \cdot Q_{\overline{PA}} > (1 - \pi_{\overline{PA}}) \cdot v_l \cdot Q_{\overline{PA}}$$

Customer demand depending on the willingness to pay

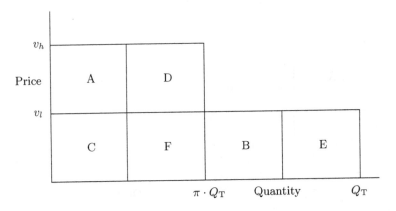

Fig. 4. Demand for IMS in use: If the vendor charges the high price v_h, revenue will be the area A and C plus the revenue from customers with privacy awareness (area D and F). Charging the low price v_l results in a revenue of the areas B and C plus the revenue from customers with privacy awareness (E and F).

and get:

$$f > \frac{(1 - \pi_{\overline{PA}}) \cdot v_l}{\pi_{PA} \cdot v_h} \tag{4}$$

- Case 2: A + D ≤ B + E. The **low price** v_l will maximise the revenue. The overall revenue consists of the areas B and C from the customers without privacy awareness and the areas E and F of the customers with privacy awareness. The maximum revenue r is:

$$r = B + C + E + F \tag{5}$$

For the vendor, the introduction of an IMS pays off if (5) > (2):

$$B + C + E + F > A + B + C$$

and holds the inequation:

$$E + F > A$$

To calculate the areas we insert the parameters v_h, v_l, $\pi_{\overline{PA}}$ und π_{PA}

$$v_l \cdot Q_{PA} > (v_h - v_l) \cdot \pi_{\overline{PA}} \cdot Q_{\overline{PA}}$$

Then we insert factor f (see Equation 1):

$$v_l \cdot f \cdot Q_{\overline{PA}} > (v_h - v_l) \cdot \pi_{\overline{PA}} \cdot Q_{\overline{PA}} \quad ,$$

and get:

$$f > \frac{(v_h - v_l) \cdot \pi_{\overline{PA}}}{v_l} \tag{6}$$

In both cases, we figured out a factor f (defined in (1)) indicating, when it is profitable for the vendor to support an IMS. As we set $\pi_{\overline{PA}} = \pi_{PA} \to \pi$, only the ratio α between the high v_h and low price v_l is variable: $v_h = \alpha \cdot v_t$ with $1 \leq \alpha < \infty$. The highest value of f and therefore the worst case, is at the *Intersection Point* IP (see Fig. 5). If $\pi > $ IP then $A + D > B + E$ which leads to Case 1. If $\pi > $ IP then $A + D < B + E$ which leads to Case 2.

To derive an upper bound for f, we solve (4) and (6) for π and get the equation:

$$\frac{1}{1 + f \cdot \alpha} = \frac{f}{\alpha - 1}$$

Solving for f leads to the quadratic equation where the root is given by

$$f = \frac{-1 \pm \sqrt{4\alpha^2 - 4\alpha + 1}}{2 \cdot \alpha}.$$

With $\lim_{\alpha \to \infty} f = 1$ we get the worst case for factor f. $\lim_{\alpha \to 1}$ defines the best case $f = 0$.

One period: Introduction of IDM pays off, if demand increases by factor f

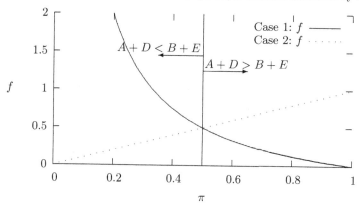

Fig. 5. One purchase period: The diagram shows the minimum fraction of new demand f_{crit}, which is necessary to make the introduction of an IMS profitable. Case 1 shows the curve for charging the high price, Case 2 for the low price. Factor f depends on the fraction π of customers willing to pay the high price. The ratio, high price to low price, was set to $v_h = 2 \cdot v_l$, yielding to an intersection point IP at $\pi = 0.5$.

4.2   Two Purchase Periods

If it is not possible for the vendor to decide, whether a customer has a high or low willingness to pay, he can at least learn from observing multiple purchase periods. Therefore we model two purchase periods (t_1 and t_2) to increase the revenue by enforcing price discrimination in the second period t_2. Assuming that customers without privacy awareness base their purchase decision on the price they currently face (A9) and considering the concept in [2, p. 11], a price strategy pays off for the vendor. This price strategy offers a high price v_h and records whether or not the customers purchase in the first period t_1. The vendor offers a person who has not purchased in the first period a low price v_l in the second period t_2. This strategy yields revenue of two purchased quantities from persons with high willingness to pay and one purchased quantity from persons with low willingness to pay. This results in a maximised revenue r:

$$r = (2\pi_{\overline{PA}} \cdot v_h + (1 - \pi_{\overline{PA}}) \cdot v_l) \cdot Q_{\overline{PA}} \tag{7}$$

If **IMS is not supported**, this price strategy is possible. With the demand shown in Fig. 3 we obtain a total revenue r:

$$r = 2 \cdot (A + C) + B \tag{8}$$

If an **IMS is supported**, price discrimination is impossible. Therefore we get a higher demand, because customers with privacy awareness are purchasing as well. The increased demand of those customers is shown in Fig. 4 with the areas D, E and F. As in Section 4.1, the vendor has to decide which price to charge to maximise his revenue. He has the possibility to charge the high price v_h where only customers with high willingness to pay are going to purchase, thus $r = 2 \cdot (A + C + D + F)$. By charging the low price v_l all customers are going to purchase the good, $r = 2 \cdot (B + C + E + F)$. This leads to two cases:

– Case 1: A + D > B + E. The **high price** v_h will maximise the total revenue across both periods. The overall revenue consists of the areas A and C from the customers without privacy awareness and the areas D and F of the customers with privacy awareness. The maximum revenue r is given by

$$r = 2 \cdot (A + D + C + F) \tag{9}$$

For the vendor, the introduction of an IMS pays off if (9) > (8), thus:

$$2 \cdot (A + D + C + F) > 2 \cdot (A + C) + B$$

$$2 \cdot (D + F) > B$$

To calculate the areas, we insert the parameters v_h, v_l, $\pi_{\overline{PA}}$ and π_{PA}

$$2\pi_{PA} \cdot v_h \cdot Q_{PA} > (1 - \pi_{\overline{PA}}) \cdot v_l \cdot Q_{\overline{PA}},$$

than we insert factor f (see Equation 1):

$$2\pi_{PA} \cdot v_h \cdot f \cdot Q_{\overline{PA}} > (1 - \pi_{\overline{PA}}) \cdot v_l \cdot Q_{\overline{PA}}$$

and get

$$f > \frac{(1 - \pi_{\overline{PA}}) \cdot v_l}{2 \cdot \pi_{PA} \cdot v_h}. \tag{10}$$

– Case 2: A + D ≤ B + E. The **low price** v_l will maximise the total revenue across both periods. The overall revenue consists of the areas B and C from the customers without privacy awareness and the areas E and F of the customers with privacy awareness. The maximum revenue r is:

$$r = 2 \cdot (B + E + C + F) \tag{11}$$

For the vendor, the introduction of an IMS pays off if (11) > (8):

$$2 \cdot (B + E + C + F) > 2 \cdot (A + C) + B$$

$$2 \cdot (E + F) > 2 \cdot A - B$$

with the parameters v_h, v_l, $\pi_{\overline{PA}}$ und π_{PA}:

$$2 v_l \cdot Q_{PA} > 2\pi_{\overline{PA}} \cdot (v_h - v_l) \cdot Q_{\overline{PA}} - (1 - \pi_{\overline{PA}}) \cdot v_l \cdot Q_{\overline{PA}}$$

we insert factor f (see Equation 1):

$$2 v_l \cdot f \cdot Q_{\overline{PA}} > (2\pi_{\overline{PA}} \cdot v_h - (1 + \pi_{\overline{PA}}) \cdot v_l) \cdot Q_{\overline{PA}}$$

$$f > \frac{2\pi_{\overline{PA}} \cdot v_h - (1 + \pi_{\overline{PA}}) \cdot v_l}{2 \cdot v_l}. \tag{12}$$

In both cases, we figured out a factor f (defined in (1)) which tells us, when it is profitable for the vendor to support an IMS. As we set $\pi_{\overline{PA}} = \pi_{PA} \to \pi$, only the ratio α between the high v_h and low price v_l is variable: $v_h = \alpha \cdot v_t$ with $1 \leq \alpha < \infty$. The highest value of f and therefore the worst case, is at the *Intersection Point* IP (see Fig. 6). If $\pi >$ IP then $A + D > B + E$ which leads to Case 1. If $\pi >$ IP then $A + D < B + E$ which leads to Case 2.

To derive an upper bound for f, we solve (10) and (12) as shown in Section 4.1. We obtain $\lim_{\alpha \to \infty} f = \frac{1}{2}$ as an upper bound for the minimum required increase in demand (worst case for factor f). Again, $\lim_{\alpha \to 1}$ leads to the best case $f = 0$. Note that the upper bound is only half as much as in Section 4.1, where the assignment to the high and the low groups was directly observable to the vendor.

5   Conclusions and Future Work

The question why companies have an incentive to introduce and support identity management systems is answered by a measure of increased demand. The higher demand is caused by customers with privacy concerns, which compensates for the disadvantage if the vendor refrains from processing customer data. First we analysed a baseline model where perfect price discrimination can be applied. The result is that the introduction of an identity management system (IMS) pays off for the vendor if the demand has at least doubled. Then, we presented a

Two periods: Introduction of IDM pays off, if demand increases by factor f

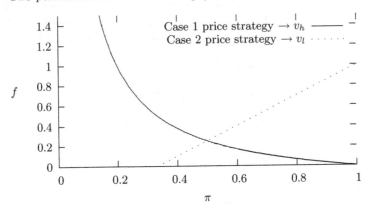

Fig. 6. Two purchase periods: The diagram shows the minimum fraction of new demand f_{crit}, which is necessary to make an introduction of an IMS profitable. Switching from price strategy to high price v_h is shown in Case 1. Case 2 shows switching from price strategy to low price. Factor f depends on the fraction π of customers willing to pay the high price. The ratio, high price to low price, was set to $v_h = 2 \cdot v_l$, yielding to an intersection point IP at $\pi = 0.5$.

more realistic model with one or two purchase periods. Separating two disjoint groups, high and low willingness to pay, we regard the simplest form of price discrimination. For one purchase period, we showed an upper bound of at most doubled demand. Regarding two purchase periods, where price strategies come into account for price discrimination, this upper bound diminished to maximum 50 % higher demand. Hence, we learn that even details of the way vendors process customer data before supporting IMS, substantially affect the decision criterion. In all cases, the increase in demand depends on the ratio of the high and low price as well as on the willingness to pay the high price. As companies may also profit from switching to IMS, this is another strong argument for supporting the development of identity management systems.

Especially for companies with a high percentage of patron customers (willing to pay the high price) the required new demand is small. This means that only a tiny group of persons with privacy awareness, compared to the customers who are not privacy concerned, have to become new customers so that an introduction of an IMS pays off. Combining this with evidence about a positive correlation between privacy awareness and willingness to pay (c.f. [16] for a study on U.S. data) gives valuable information to developers of IMS about potential early-adaptors of the new technology. Future work remains to be done in gauging sources and extent of privacy awareness in the population, for instance by means of survey research. Incorporating the so quantified measures may refine the proposed models and thus increase the quality of the forecasts.

The proposed model is likely to be too pessimistic, because real world price discrimination always goes along with arbitrage. Since we neglected possible arbitrage (cf. A8), the gains from price discrimination tend to be over-estimated. So, raising A8 is up to future work. Also, this paper solely analyses a monopolist structure and further work should be done in competitive markets, where the gains from price discrimination are more limited, and pricing strategies have implications on market share. In turn, the assumption that IMS cause price discrimination to vanish completely needs to be questioned, too. As the systems give users the possibility to decide themselves, which data they want to reveal, incomplete price discrimination might still be possible if customers voluntarily opt for sharing information [3]. When rewarded with rebates and other incentives, it is likely that even the strongest IMS might be bypassed by a large share of customers (presumably those without privacy awareness). Accordingly, an (experimental) economic study of the *demand-side* economics of identity management with respect to price discrimination could help to answer these questions. Finally, the models used in this study reduce the effects of IMS to its function to prevent price discrimination. Apart from this, an IMS offers a couple of other desirable properties, such as increased accountability (hence, fewer defaults of payment), higher data quality, and process simplification. Future models should also consider a quantification of these factors, optimally with facts based on empirical data.

To draw a conclusion, it is evident that the success of IMS is not only a technical but also an economic issue. The challenge is in combining both fields and to come up with the appropriate models reflecting the technical conditions, thus requiring more interdisciplinary research. This paper is just a modest step towards this direction.

Acknowledgments

This work was supported in part by the EU Network of Excellence "Future of Identity in the Information Society" (FIDIS, http://www.fidis.net) and by a stipend from the PET Workshop 2005. The views and conclusions contained herein are those of the authors and should not be interpreted as necessarily representing the official policies.

References

1. Acquisti, A.: Security of Personal Information and Privacy: Technological Solutions and Economic Incentives. In J. Camp and R. Lewis (eds), The Economics of Information Security, Kluwer (2004)
2. Acquisti, A., Varian, H.: Conditioning Prices on Purchase History. http://www.heinz.cmu.edu/~acquisti/papers/privacy.pdf (2001)
3. Berendt, B., Günther, O., Spiekermann, S.: Privacy in E-Commerce: Stated Preferences vs. Actual Behavior. *Communications of the ACM* **48**:4 (2005), 101–106
4. Chaum, D.: Security Without Identification: Transaction Systems to Make Big Brother Obsolete. *Communications of the ACM* **28** (1985) 1030–1044
5. Clauß, S., Köhntopp, M.: Identity Management and Its Support of Multilateral Security. *Computer Networks* **37** (2001) 205–219

6. Electronic Privacy Information Center (EPIC): Public Opinion on Privacy.
   `http://www.epic.org/privacy/survey/`
7. Gellman, R.: Privacy, Consumers, and Costs
   `http://www.epic.org/reports/dmfprivacy.html` (2002)
8. Hansen, M., Berlich, P., Camenisch, J., Clauß, S., Pfitzmann, A.: Privacy-Enhancing Identity Management. *Information Security Technical Report* **9** (2004) 35–44
9. Mankiw, N. G.: Principles of Economics. South-Western, Mason, OH (2004)
10. Odlyzko, A.: Privacy, Economics, and Price Discrimination on the Internet. In: Fifth International Conference on Electronic Commerce, ACM (2003) 355–366
11. Pindyck, R., Rubinfeld, D.: Microeconomics. Prentice Hall, London (1998)
12. Privacy and Identity Management for Europe (PRIME)
    `http://www.prime-project.eu.org/`
13. Shapiro, C. and Varian, H.: Information Rules: A Strategic Guide to the Network Economy. Harvard Business School Press (1998)
14. Taylor, C. R.: Private Demands and Demands for Privacy: Dynamic Pricing and the Market for Customer Information. Department of Economics, Duke University, Duke Economics Working Paper 02-02 (2002)
15. Varian, H.: Intermediate Microeconomics. W.W. Norton & Company, New York (2003)
16. Varian, H., Wallenberg, F., Woroch, G.: Who Signed Up for the Do-Not-Call List? Paper presented at the *Third Workshop on Economics and Information Security*, University of Minnesota (2004) `http://www.dtc.umn.edu/weis2004/varian.pdf`

Author Index

Lecture Notes in Computer Science

For information about Vols. 1–3918

please contact your bookseller or Springer